The Politics of Time

Critical South

The publication of this series is supported by the International Consortium of Critical Theory Programs funded by the Andrew W. Mellon Foundation.

Series editors: Natalia Brizuela, Victoria Collis-Buthelezi, and Leticia Sabsay

Leonor Arfuch, *Memory and Autobiography*
Paula Biglieri and Luciana Cadahia, *Seven Essays on Populism*
Aimé Césaire, *Resolutely Black*
Bolívar Echeverría, *Modernity and "Whiteness"*
Diego Falconí Trávez, *From Ashes to Text*
Celso Furtado, *The Myth of Economic Development*
Eduardo Grüner, *The Haitian Revolution*
Premesh Lalu, *Undoing Apartheid*
Karima Lazali, *Colonial Trauma*
María Pia López, *Not One Less*
Achille Mbembe and Felwine Sarr, *The Politics of Time*
Achille Mbembe and Felwine Sarr, *To Write the Africa World*
Valentin Y. Mudimbe, *The Scent of the Father*
Pablo Oyarzun, *Doing Justice*
Néstor Perlongher, *Plebeian Prose*
Bento Prado Jr., *Error, Illusion, Madness*
Nelly Richard, *Eruptions of Memory*
Silvia Rivera Cusicanqui, *Ch'ixinakax utxiwa*
Tendayi Sithole, *The Black Register*
Maboula Soumahoro, *Black is the Journey, Africana the Name*
Dénètem Touam Bona, *Fugitive, Where Are You Running?*

The Politics of Time
Imagining African Becomings

Edited by
Achille Mbembe and Felwine Sarr

Translated by Philip Gerard

polity

Originally published in French as *Politique des temps* © 2019 Editions Jimsaan, Dakar, Sénégal

This English edition © Polity Press, 2023

Excerpt from 'The Refugee Crisis Isn't about Refugees. It's about Us' by Ai Weiwei, 2 February 2018. Copyright © Guardian News & Media Ltd. 2022

Polity Press
65 Bridge Street
Cambridge CB2 1UR, UK

Polity Press
111 River Street
Hoboken, NJ 07030, USA

All rights reserved. Except for the quotation of short passages for the purpose of criticism and review, no part of this publication may be reproduced, stored in a retrieval system, or transmitted, in any form or by any means, electronic, mechanical, photocopying, recording, or otherwise, without the prior permission of the publisher.

ISBN-13: 978-1-5095-5109-5 – hardback
ISBN-13: 978-1-5095-5110-1 – paperback

A catalog record for this book is available from the British Library.

Library of Congress Control Number: 2022936447

Typeset in 10.5 on 12pt Sabon
by Fakenham Prepress Solutions, Fakenham, Norfolk NR21 8NL
Printed and bound in Great Britain by TJ Books Ltd, Padstow, Cornwall

The publisher has used its best endeavors to ensure that the URLs for external websites referred to in this book are correct and active at the time of going to press. However, the publisher has no responsibility for the websites and can make no guarantee that a site will remain live or that the content is or will remain appropriate.

Every effort has been made to trace all copyright holders, but if any have been overlooked the publisher will be pleased to include any necessary credits in any subsequent reprint or edition.

For further information on Polity, visit our website:
politybooks.com

Contents

Preface — viii
Achille Mbembe and Felwine Sarr

I

From Thinking Identity to Thinking African Becomings — 3
Souleymane Bachir Diagne

Notes for a Maroon Feminism — 19
From the "Body Double" to the Body as Such
Hourya Bentouhami

Weaving, a Craft for Thought — 41
Writing and Thinking in Africa, or the Knot of the World's
 Great Narrative
Jean-Luc Raharimanana

II

Africa and the New Western Figures of Personal Status Law — 55
Abdoul Aziz Diouf

Rethinking Islam — 65
Or, the Oxymoron of "Secular Theocracy"
Rachid Id Yassine

The Impossible Meeting   73
A Free Interpretation of J. M. Coetzee's *Disgrace*
Hemley Boum

III

Circulations   85
Achille Mbembe

On the Return   96
The Political Practices of the African Diaspora
Nadia Yala Kisukidi

Reopening Futures   117
Felwine Sarr

IV

Un/learning   129
Rethinking Teaching in Africa
Françoise Vergès

The Bewitchment of History   145
Mohammed Dib's *Who Remembers the Sea*
Soraya Tlatli

Currency, Sovereignty, Development   158
Revisiting the Question of the CFA Franc
Ndongo Samba Sylla

V

Memories of the World, Memory-World   179
Séverine Kodjo-Grandvaux

Cum patior Africa   194
The Political Production of Regimes of "the Nigh"
Nadine Machikou

The Sahara: A Space of Connection within an Emergent Africa,   221
from the Anthropocene to the Spring of Geo-Cultural Life
Benaouda Lebdai

Migrations, Narrations, the Refugee Condition   235
Dominic Thomas

VI

Humanity and Animality   245
(Re)thinking Anthropocentrism
Bado Ndoye

The Tree Frogs' Distress   253
Lionel Manga

To Speak and Betray Nothing?   263
Rodney Saint-Éloi

The Paths of the Voice   268
Ibrahima Wane

Notes   273
Index   316

Preface

Achille Mbembe and Felwine Sarr

This book represents a sequel to and continuation of its preceding volume, *To Write the Africa World*. Authored by many, it is the product of The Ateliers of Thought in Dakar, an autonomous, collaborative platform for intellectual and artistic work that was established in 2016 for the purpose of investigating the present and future of our world from the vantage point of Africa, and of contributing through these efforts to the renovation of critical thought in the contemporary context.

New voyages of thought are being charted across the globe. The routes they take today are not necessarily those of yesterday, when everything routinely passed through Europe. In the Global South, new and original voices are rising up and, with boldly new terms and categories, taking on the challenge of thinking our shared earth. Moreover, although its indicators may have yet to adequately distinguish themselves from the daily noise, a new certainty is slowly but surely imposing itself. Africa is not merely the place where part of the planet's future is currently playing itself out. Africa is one of the great laboratories from which unprecedented forms of today's social, economic, political, cultural, and artistic life are emerging.

Often, these new forms of life, thought, and the social come to light in unexpected places. Brought forward by actors who are neither highly visible nor very well known, these forms become concrete in assemblages that draw deeply from the long memory of societies even as they assume strikingly contemporary, indeed futuristic, guises. This polymorphic creativity and the velocity that comes with it cast serious doubt upon bodies of knowledge passed down from the distant and not-so-distant past, at times cruelly exposing their limits. The new forms call for an unprecedented renovation of paradigms and methods, of analytical tools, vocabulary, and discourses – in short, they call for the creation of new languages and bodies of knowledge with the power to mobilize the archives of the Whole-World [*Tout-Monde*] to provide new intelligibility for the various upheavals in process.

In this book, the authors weigh in on one of the upheavals in process, the upheaval of time [*temps*] in the plural – which is to say, that of multiple times [*des temps*] and their entanglement. For it is not only a question of acceleration and runaway systems, but also of times moving at multiple speeds, of times composed of different momentums, continuities, ruptures, to say nothing of different regressions, dispersions, and bifurcations. In short, at least when one looks from Africa, all one sees are *times in migration* [*temps en migrance*].

To describe this *concatenation of times*, the contributors to the present volume have practiced a kind of writing that is itself in movement – even in transit – and that mixes a diverse set of vocabularies. They draw eclectically from works of literature, philosophy, history, geography, art, economics, sociology, pedagogy, and poetry to weave together their problematics, to stretch them further, to translate them and to transpose them. The book has been deliberately composed in several genres, and the reader is invited to move freely between them. Taken together, the different contributions not only express a form of reasoning at once malleable and metamorphic; they trace the lineaments of a common concern – namely, how to envision a *politics of time* in contemporary conditions.

But what do we mean by "politics of time"? On a planetary scale, we are witnessing the emergence and crystallization of a new cycle in the redistribution of power, resources, and value. Another partition of the world is being charted at the same time as other *geo-graphies* [*géo-graphies*] of the Earth are being traced. If this cycle awakens hope in expanded possibilities of life and action for many human groups, it is no less the case that, more or less everywhere, it produces collisions, promotes an unequal redistribution of vulnerability, and provokes new and ruinous compromises with forms of violence belonging at once to the future and to the archaic past.

More than ever, the world is dominated by the specter of its own end and by the fear of obliteration and extinction. With the collapse of grand hopes for transformation, the idea of a happy ending was thrown out, opening the door to a proliferation of cynical fictions, beliefs, and multiple forms of bewitchment. Two forms of disenchanted thinking dominate our era. The first – apocalyptic thinking – invites us to contemplate the coming collapse and to plan for the end. It is concerned with how we will finally come down to earth. The other applies itself to the task of rethinking utopia and the future in the language of technological messianism. Human redemption, so goes the claim, will paradoxically be achieved through technological escalation.

The contributions assembled in this volume distance themselves from these thematics of closure and vertigo. They ask whether one can, by taking Africa as a point of departure, seize hold of any options on the future. In other words, is it possible to politicize time beyond the alternatives of apocalypse and technolatry [*technolâtrie*]? If so, then how, in what terms, and to what end? Are there different possibilities for inhabiting Africa – and, beyond Africa, the world?

This is no simple task, since in one kind of narrative Africa has long been expelled from the time of history. This is certainly the reason why the greatest part of African thought has devoted so much energy to repoliticizing time. In this context, repoliticizing time has consisted in recovering the traces and reconstructing the memory of the past, not only as proof of historicity but also as a labor on oneself, with the hope that this work of rehabilitation would in the end permit the formation of other ties with oneself and with the world. Repoliticizing time has long consisted in the attempt to seize the past as a transformative force. Creatively reinterpreted and retranslated, such a force was thought capable of opening up new spaces of possibility. It could spark a movement that would carry Africa out of the waiting room of history where the continent's external masters thought they had confined it. Under such conditions, time would no longer be experienced as an uninterrupted succession of ruptures, constraints, and impossibilities. By reconnecting with the transformative kernel of its past, Africa could at last return to being a power – which is to say, something that contains its own capacity within itself.

The contemporaneity of multiple worlds and of different historical depths has always been a feature of African societies. This volume is no longer concerned with refuting the theses, now old and anachronistic, that history is immobile, or stalled, or waiting to begin.

How might one transform the present and the past into a future? How might one produce a bifurcation in the real? Imagine other African possibilities? Invent ways for passing from the potential to its multiple actualizations? These, we suspect, have been the questions at the heart of the modern study of Africa and its diasporas. How, therefore, can one envision a politics of the future, if not, as a number of contributions to this volume suggest, by reopening a space for the unpredictable and the possibility of an infinity of becomings? It is most certainly not a question of liquidating the past, but rather of attaining that juncture where different times meet, the precise point of their entanglement, of seeking out new ways to inhabit the world and new chains of relations. The time for refutation is over. It is now time for conditional affirmation – that is, for the exploration of other possibilities for a future yet to be written, a future with neither promise nor guarantee, an emergent future rich in possibilities and charged with life.

It is this emergence that the present volume heralds.

Part I

From Thinking Identity to Thinking African Becomings

Souleymane Bachir Diagne

Souleymane Bachir Diagne is Professor of Philosophy and of Francophone Studies at Columbia University in New York. His recent works include: Bergson postcolonial: l'élan vital dans la pensée de Léopold Sédar Senghor et Mohamed Iqbal *(Paris: CNRS Éditions, 2011);* L'encre des savants: réflexions sur la philosophie en Afrique *(Paris: Présence africaine & CODESRIA, 2013);* Comment philosopher en islam *(Paris: Philippe Rey / Jimsaan, 2014);* Philosopher en islam et en christianisme *(with Philippe Capelle-Dumont) (Paris: Cerf, 2016);* En quête d'Afrique(s): universalisme et pensée décoloniale *(with Jean-Loup Amselle) (Paris: Albin Michel, 2018); and* La controverse *(with Rémi Braque) (Paris: Stock, 2019).*

> [W]hat matters is not philosophy as such but critical thought. It is such thinking that we must develop today ..., to imagine the possible beyond the real, to make sure that the platitudes of the present do not become the measure of all things but are themselves measured, relativized, put in their proper place, ranked in order and made subordinate to other demands, that they are weighed against norms that push us forward and that free us from conformism and resignation.
>
> Paulin Hountondji[1]

Africa is, like all the other continents, multiple, diverse; there one thinks a thousand different things in more than a thousand different languages. Were one, nonetheless, to attempt to sum up in a single word (an impossible task, to be sure) contemporary African thought

– as it is presented in the works of authors as different from one another as Paulin Hountondji of Benin; Felwine Sarr, Animata Diaw-Cissé, or Ramatoulaye Diagne of Senegal; Achille Mbembe of Cameroon; Tanella Boni of the Ivory Coast; Kwasi Wiredu or Kwame Appiah of Ghana; Charles Bowao or Abel Kouvouama of the Congo; Abdou Filali-Ansary of Morocco … – one could argue that African thought has passed from yesterday's thinking of identity, which was part of the struggle against colonialism, to today's thinking of becomings. What will happen to African existence in its various iterations, and to its weight in a world grown finite, confined by financial, economic, human, electronic, and cultural flows – that is, by the different facets of globalization? What is happening and what will happen to the weight – or, rather, to the value – of what we are, to our ways of being in the world, to these African faces bearing witness to the human adventure? Such questions were already part of the response to colonial negation. At the time, the answers provided were, among others, negritude, the African personality, the Arab renaissance – in other words, incarnations of political and cultural nationalism, expressions of identity that we had hoped would all one day converge upon the realization of a Pan-African ideal. *Today*, where do these responses and that ideal stand? Put differently – what are the responses *today*? What are they in a world no longer structured by an opposition to Africa's negation – even though that negation sometimes re-emerges in comments, seemingly of another time, by politicians from former colonial powers who come out saying that Africans have yet to fully enter history, or that colonization represented nothing but the desire to share the metropole's culture. I will consider here the movement whereby the meaning of African existence and "presence" ceases to denote the resistance, defense, and illustration of an identity and turns into a question of pluralism and becomings. It will be argued that we have moved from the reactive, mass Africanity [*africanité*] that was the appropriate response to colonial negation toward a system of thought adapted to a situation that obliges Africanity to understand itself as open and diverse and to attend to the problem of cultural and religious pluralism – a problem whose urgency is indicated by the tragedies that Africa is once more experiencing today, at the very moment that it plainly represents the continent of the future.

For this reason, I trust one will excuse me for occasionally speaking in the first person plural (for saying "we") and for at times being prescriptive (for saying "we must"): I do so because, when it comes to this movement of thinking becomings, I am one of the interested parties.

Against Negation: Saying Who and What We Are

Who and what are we?
Admirable question.

Aimé Césaire[2]

In the immediate postwar period, in 1947, Alioune Diop, a Senegalese intellectual, founded a journal with the title *Présence africaine* in Paris, at the heart of the Latin Quarter. "Présence africaine" was also the name of the publishing house that followed shortly after the creation of the journal. The very site that became – and today still is – the location of Présence africaine, 25 bis rue des Écoles, was a symbol in and of itself. A presence of Africa had affirmed itself alongside the temples that one of its colonizers had dedicated to Knowledge: next to the Sorbonne, a stone's throw away from the École polytechnique on the rue de la Montagne-Sainte-Geneviève, not far from the École normal supérieure on the rue d'Ulm. A little farther away, at Les Deux Magots and the Café de Flore by Saint-Germain-des-Prés, the intellectual history of the postwar period was also being written. In this environment, Présence became a meeting place for intellectuals, writers, and students coming from Africa or living in diaspora, as well as for progressive French intellectuals. The mission that Présence had given itself was the production of knowledge: knowledge of Africa, knowledge of oneself through Africa, knowledge for Africans …

Independence was in the air. The year 1947 was when India and Pakistan acquired sovereignty. The 1948 publication of the *Anthologie de la nouvelle poésie nègre et malgache de langue française* by Senghor, with Jean-Paul Sartre's preface, *Black Orpheus* [*Orphée noir*], an existentialist celebration of the power of human emancipation wielded by Africa, was one of Présence's two major achievements at the hour of its birth. The other was the publication of *Bantu Philosophy* [*La philosophie bantou*] by the Franciscan friar Placide Tempels. For the first time, Tempels's book associated African culture with what was taken to be the quintessence and very spirit of European civilization – that which set it apart from the rest of humanity: philosophy. Indeed, as Husserl had declared not too long before, in 1933,[3] it was on account of this spirit that

India would do well to Europeanize as much as possible; whereas a Europe that had attained full self-consciousness and a perfect understanding of its own *telos* would know that it had no reason to Indianize itself [*s'indianiser*] in any way whatsoever.

Ten years later, in 1957, Présence published *Nations nègres et cultures* [translated in abridged form as *The African Origin of Civilization: Myth or Reality*], the work in which Cheikh Anta Diop made the case for an African presence at the origins of human civilizations. In the field of history, the publication of Diop's book marked a crucial date and an essential contribution to the project of deconstructing the Hegelian pretense that the History of Spirit was a *telos* which belonged to a particular form of humanity. In the same year, 1957, Ghana acquired independence, an independence that its first president, Kwame Nkrumah, understood as a simple step in the greater march toward the organic unity of a free Africa, the *sine qua non* for the affirmation of an African presence in the world. Behind this march, behind the self-affirmation that was both its condition and its objective, Nkrumah discerned a philosophy based on the consciousness of a unity that waited to be forged, of a reconstructed identity to be realized as a "new harmony" – one which would see Africanity integrate Christian and Islamic interpretations into itself not as disruptions but as contributions: consciencism [*consciencisme*] was thus expected to illuminate the forward march of the continent.

Africa is not only the Sub-Saharan region of the continent – what Hegel thought he could call "Africa proper." In its northern regions, the discourse had also been – in a manner analogous to what we have just seen – one of the *nahda*, the *re-birth* (in Arabic) that was meant to answer the colonial negation and whose claims were an essential component of the identitarian discourse of African Arabness. In one guise or another, the external shock of Europe's colonization of the Arab world had prompted a question that one could formulate in the following way: what has happened to our identity so that now, in our current condition under European domination, we observe our former greatness reduced to nothing? Posed in this manner, the question implied a return to what had constituted that greatness: Islam. As a consequence, being reborn to oneself, to one's own identity, meant returning to the fundamental principles of a golden age. It follows that every rebirth, in this sense, is a fundamentalism. This return to the foundation, this re-founding of the self, however, still needed to be defined. It could mean for Islam to once again take up the spirit of movement that coincides with its very culture, which has always been anxious to break with the servile imitation of tradition (*taqlîd*) and which is based on the right – in truth, the obligation – not to blindly "do what our fathers did": the right not to reproduce the tradition that, as Samir Amin correctly maintains, might itself constitute a definition of modernity. But "going back" could also mean putting forward what was, or what is thought to be, the "original purity" of a foundation that has been recast as the objective. In this case, the insistence is placed on the reconstitution of a model – human history being nothing more than an effort to hold on to the sacred model, to what Henry Corbin calls a hiero-history [*hiéro-histoire*] forever closed on itself. In this instance, the refoundation would be *Salafism* – which is to say, a return to the ways of acting and perceiving that were practiced by the "pious ancestors" (*salâf as sâlihîn*).

The discourse of identity always oscillates between these two ways of understanding what it means to re-found the self – the two interpretations, incidentally, not being necessarily antithetical. Those who think that fidelity consists not in the imitation of a fossilized model but rather in the continual movement of self-invention and of one's own modernity may well call themselves the true heirs of the *Salâf* (after all, if the Salafist reading of Islam took aim at the Sufism that was so important to Islam in Africa, the Sufis, for their part, regard themselves as the genuine continuation of what was once the first community of believers). It was thus in the name of the genuine spirit of Islam that, long ago, Al-Afghani admonished Muslim scholars for ignoring the demands of modernity, and that, in the same terms, his Egyptian disciple Mohammad Abduh, who powerfully influenced Arab nationalism and reformism in the twentieth century, recalled the importance of history as progress and not as the waning of identity away from a perfect model. For that is the crux of the question: how is one to think identity in time? Is it necessary to consider time as the enemy of being? Or should one heed the fact that time constitutes the very texture of identity in the prophetic saying "do not vilify time, for time is God"?

The Question of Becomings: Thinking and Living Pluralism

Where do we stand today with the infinite task of affirming the presence of Africa in the world? What is to be done in today's conditions?

A genuinely multicultural world that would counter Eurocentrism and its new avatars still awaits construction. Today, the principal form of Eurocentrism is not one culture's assertion that its values can dictate the norms that all others must follow. It is, rather, the form that grants the West the exorbitant privilege of being the only culture capable of reflecting critically on itself. In other words, today's Eurocentrism is no longer one of values but of the question – recognizably Nietzschean – of the value of values: a question, it is said, that in its true, authentic sense can only be posed in "the West." Thus, where other civilizations are by nature condemned to cling to their visions of the world to the point of fanaticism – *adhering* like "oysters," to use Valéry's expression[4] – Western civilization is taken to be the only civilization capable of maintaining a critical distance with respect to what is held to be the norm. In response to this form of Eurocentrism, let it be said that, when it comes to genuine culture – that is, culture expressing the humanity of man [*de l'homme*] – there is no such thing as zero aptitude for self-criticism. To claim otherwise would mean relinquishing all hope in the possibility of an encounter between cultures.[5]

Now, the African situation today calls for critical thought more than it ever has before. This is the meaning of the call Paulin Hountondji issues in his response to the philosophical questionnaire created by the philosopher Lansana Keïta, and which I chose as the epigraph for the present reflection:

> It is such [critical] thinking that we must develop today …, to imagine the possible beyond the real, to make sure that the platitudes of the present do not become the measure of all things but are themselves measured, relativized, put in their proper place, ranked in order and made subordinate to other demands, that they are weighed against norms that push us forward and that free us from conformism and resignation.[6]

Making sure that the possible marches in advance of the real, illuminates it, and draws it forward, is the task that awaits us today. The project we have called "Présence africaine" must now confront the crisis of meaning [*une crise du sens*] produced by three decades of exponentially growing poverty on the continent. Even if it is undeniable today that the seeds of change are real, and there are reasons for thinking that Africa is a continent with which one will have to reckon now and in the future, the rates of growth that indicate progress have been slow to translate into jobs. This manifests itself in the distress of African youth who, more anxious about what will happen than about identity, picture their future in an elsewhere of emigration. The daily drama of the waves closing over young Africans who have drowned in the Straits of Gibraltar is a constant reminder of how imperative it now is to subordinate identity to becoming, to think of meaning in the present as a projection coming from the future and not from the past.[7] For the fate of African identity in the world depends above all on Africa's disoriented youth, who rock back and forth between two aspects of a single anxiety: demobilizing skepticism and a range of fanaticisms.

In confronting the danger of deadly fanaticisms represented today by Boko Haram in the north of Nigeria or by the groups ravaging northern Mali, it is important to affirm pluralism, its virtues and its necessity, as a response to the challenges of the present and the future. Two urgent tasks stand before contemporary African thought: the reinvention of an African sense of religious pluralism, and the reinvention of an African sense of cultural pluralism.

Religious Pluralism

In the acceptance speech he gave in Stockholm for the 1986 Nobel Prize in Literature, Wole Soyinka took advantage of the spotlight and the attention the whole world directed upon him to recall an important and magnificent lesson that our continent has for humanity. This lesson provided a response to the philosopher Hegel, who, as part of a larger effort to cast African humanity out of the theatre of universal history, had written that, in this land cloaked "in the dark mantle of the night," monotheism's concept of a unique, transcendent God never came close to being formulated. The truth, Soyinka essentially argued in his Stockholm speech, was that Africa was not mired in the ignorance of monotheism, but that it was instead the land of pluralism. If the veneration of a supreme divinity existing beyond all intermediary, ancestral spirits constituted the religious identity of a given people, then it made no sense for this people to seek to convert another people to itself. Thus, if it was natural for the monotheism that Hegel had in mind to invent, in the name of the uniqueness of the True God, the oxymoron of the "holy war," Soyinka observed that such a notion was entirely foreign to African religious identity.

From a historical perspective, Soyinka may have been largely correct. But, if one considers the situation today and makes projections for tomorrow, it is clear that the reality of religious identities on the continent is that of Abrahamic monotheisms. The Christian and Muslim religions are spreading at greater speed in Africa than anywhere else, in a race that occasionally resembles a competition. As deplorable as it may be, the gods of the traditional religions have withdrawn from our world, and there is no use holding on to the romantic vision of an essentially, and therefore naturally, tolerant Africanity. One can only wish that the inter-religious violence which we see – all too often, alas – take place, in Nigeria for example, would succeed in convincing us of one thing: for the twenty-first century that we are embarked upon, we must here and now reinvent an African sense of the multicultural, of ethnic and religious pluralism. Perhaps we will be able – as the filmmaker Sembène Ousmane was in film after film (for example, in his magnificent *Guelwaar*) – to go on thinking that a traditional, African spirit of tolerance has outlived the old, local religions, and that this spirit can assist in such a reinvention. Nonetheless, whatever the case may be, it is a fact that the reinvention will first take place in the dialogue between the multiple identities which today constitute – and tomorrow will continue to constitute – the religious and cultural landscape of our continent. The attention that a Pan-Africanist organization like CODESRIA devotes to these questions shows that the intellectuals of today's Africa have made the urgent need to reinvent an African sense of religious pluralism part of their thinking.

Interfaith dialogue is the concern of the world as a whole, confronted with the cacophony of religious identities. Today, any worthwhile, future-oriented thinking about what societies and cultures faced with globalization are becoming must assign a central place to the renewed role of the religious as a force of identification – a force which, as such, should be able to contribute to stability and security, but which has also proven itself capable of engendering violence: religious identity, as one can confirm on our continent and elsewhere, is of all identities the easiest to mobilize and the readiest to plunge into deadly madness. Because it is particularly exposed, Africa has an essential role to play in the promotion of a discourse of mutual religious understanding, of a spirit of tolerance that is not simply a resigned acceptance of difference but an active welcoming of it. And African intellectuals first and foremost have the responsibility to respond to the demands our times make upon us in this regard, which include, among others: the promotion and diffusion of information about religious fact and interpretation; the explication of what should be the real signification of secularism; the insistence on the meaning and virtues of pluralism – put simply, reflection on the production of an African modernity.

Until now, the task of reflecting upon religious fact and interpretation has not been among the issues around which African intellectuals have rallied *en masse* – at least not those whom one routinely thinks of when one uses that word, that is, those who were trained in modern universities and that certain people baptize as "europhone" to distinguish them from intellectuals trained after the fashion of African "traditions" or in the madrasa. Precisely here lies one of the sources of our problems: the opposing of two cultures and the fact that, as a rule, African social sciences, those of the so-called europhone intellectuals, have until now neglected the role of the religious. More precisely, they have left the work of reflecting (though most of the time this can scarcely be called "reflection," given what that word implies about critical spirit) on the future of religious interpretation to those who proclaim themselves its professionals and conservers. For that matter, one must relativize the difference between "europhones" and "non-europhones." What constitutes the identity of intellectuals beyond the language in which they formulate their thought – be it English, Mandinka, Portuguese, Hausa, French, Arabic, or another language – is that thought is never a peremptory dogmatism, but instead an anxious concern for the many ways in which the True can be said, a critical line of argument that integrates the possibility, legitimacy, and necessity of a pluralism of interpretations. The global phenomenon of religious fervor, which Gilles Kepel has called the "revenge of God" and which is particularly apparent and influential in Africa, obliges those who by profession think with critical distance to contribute to clarifying the meaning, for today's world, of the permanent dialogue of texts and contexts which produces the dynamism of religions. Moreover, whether intellectuals take up the reflection on religions or not, the latter are nonetheless present today in what is commonly considered the intellectuals' privileged domain: university campuses. That religious affiliations – evangelicals, born-again Christians, or Islamic associations – should today be so present in spaces that in the past were more likely to be identified with political ideologies says much about the current situation in Africa. There is another extreme case where religion has a direct impact on the African intellectual: this happens when – as was, in the darkest extremities of horror, recently the case in Algeria – the journalist or the university professor becomes the target of killers who, acting in the name of

God, judge their victim, in his very being, to be an incarnation of what must be eliminated.

One might think that the issue of religious identities, and the need to develop pluralist politics and attitudes with reference to them, is a question that has only been posed today, at a time when such identities have taken center stage. Nonetheless, one will note that a text disseminated "in the newspapers" calling for cooperation between the two most important religions of the Book on our continent was written by Léopold Sédar Senghor in 1960, the year that saw the majority of African countries become independent. One will also note that this text seems to address itself to our time of religious fervor in which, as in the Ivory Coast, political problems end up becoming confrontations of identity and assume the appearance of a religious war.[8] In 1960, an era marked by the nationalist project and the will to modernization, Senghor – following in the footsteps of Gaston Berger, the inventor of the term "prospective" – was already anxious to see Christianity and Islam, which shared a claim on the hearts of Africans ("because," he wrote, "black African animism is in the process of disappearing"), play their rightful part in this project and advance together, in mutual respect, toward their modernity. In the language of Senghor's spiritualist socialism, that sounded like this:

> The aim of Islamism and of Christianity ... is *to fulfill the will of God*. In order to fulfill this will, which is to gain heaven, we must achieve brotherhood among men, through justice for all men here on earth. Indeed, what is such justice if not equality of opportunity given from the beginning to all men regardless of race or condition; and, along with work, the equitable distribution of national revenue among citizens, of world revenue among nations and finally, the equitable distribution of knowledge among all men and all nations?[9]

Pursuing justice through work, with an attention to equity, and in brotherhood is the principle of movement – a motion driven by a permanent tension toward the future and not the servile imitation of "tradition" – as it is inscribed in the heart of the Christian and Muslim religions. Senghor reads this principle of movement in the following words, taken from the Gospels: "But strive first for the kingdom of God and his righteousness, and all these things will be given to you as well" (Matt. 6:33 [New Revised Standard Version]); and from the Qur'an: "God does not change the condition of a people unless they change what is in themselves" (Qur'an 13:11 [M. A. S. Abdel Haleem]).[10]

It is in our power to recapture for today, and for this twenty-first century that we have embarked on, the spirit in which these passages were written nearly a half-century ago. The task was then – but is even more so today – to proclaim how crucial it is for Africa that its religious identities, and the Christian and Muslim identities in particular, fully realize that there can exist nothing but "respect" between them. Such respect is warranted for a host of reasons, each one of which should be recalled and made comprehensible to the public. There are the theological reasons that are explored in interfaith dialogues; there is also the very special history of the two Abrahamic religions first meeting on the African continent. In the din of today's fanaticisms, one cannot overemphasize the fact that the first time Islam appeared on African soil was when, fleeing persecution in the Arabian Peninsula, Muslim emigrants were welcomed and protected by the Christian community of Abyssinia. Moreover, to this history it would be necessary to add that the presence of Judaism – the oldest of the Abrahamic traditions – in the Maghreb bears witness to the fact that both Muslims and Jews were victims of the *Reconquista* and the destruction of an Andalusian civilization whose history – in its essential traits, if not in every instance – had been characterized by tolerance and pluralism.

As important as respect between religious identities is for our continent, it is equally crucial that today these identities contribute to an unfurling of the modernity that they carry in themselves. Moreover, there is no doubt that the two – mutual respect (tolerance in its most elevated sense) on the one hand, and the movement toward modernity on the other – are connected. We must insist that it is a question of the modernities (in the plural) that the different religious traditions carry in themselves and not a question of imitating an external model – not a "westernization" premised on the assumption that *modernity = the West*. Neither will we consider the West (although here too one must beware essentialisms) as a foil – that would be absurd. We will be more inclined to consider the West as a mirror that permits each interpretation to examine how it has made use of its own principle of movement toward increased freedom, greater justice, and more equality in order to become the equal of what it sees.

And, in this movement, we will lay particular stress on freedom for women, justice for women, equality for women, and we will do so with the help of education. It has often been said that women once occupied the place of honor in African societies and that outside influences progressively reduced their role. There is no doubt that historical reality is more complicated and more differentiated than this caricatural image of a matriarchy taken to be representative of African identity everywhere before being overturned by a patriarchy from the outside. And yet, it is no less the case that the old gods could bequeath us no better legacy before dissipating in the sunlight of the monotheisms than this spirit of matriarchy, which would permit us to better read – so as to better promote – the emancipatory intention of the religions of the Book with respect to women.

Cultural Pluralism

Léopold Sédar Senghor can also be helpfully reread in light of today's efforts to think and live the plurality of ethnic identities. We would do well to return to his texts, where he conceives of Africanity as an assemblage of Arabness and negritude.[11] To better grasp the implications of what he writes and its signification for us today, let us recall once more Hegel, who, when he grounded the historical development of spirit in geography, hoped to read Africanity directly from the map of the continent.[12] This resulted in him isolating and separating from one another an Egyptian identity, an identity of Mediterranean North Africa, and an Africanity "in the proper sense" (those are Hegel's words) – defined as the very spirit of non-separation from the natural element, the spirit of a dark earth, closed on itself and thus passed over by progress. Egypt he attached to Asia. As for North Africa, he incorporated it into a larger whole in which the Mediterranean was an inland sea: he thus made the initial stages of France's colonization of Algeria in 1830, which he applauded, into a normal gesture of appropriation in conformity with the movement of Spirit.

Hegel's dismemberment of Africanity has elicited responses from some of the greatest thinkers of our continent. The entirety of Cheikh Anta Diop's considerable body of work can be read as *another* philosophy of history, in reaction to the Hegelian negation. His œuvre reinscribed ancient Egypt back into the continent and restored a historical depth to African intellectual history that remains to be explored. At the same time, Diop's work traced a continuity between African history and the history of the Muslim world in general – in North Africa, in Egypt, in Islam's holy sites. No longer will one be able to make the Sahara into the wall that it never was in the first place, and, once the precious manuscripts of Timbuktu and elsewhere have finished supplying the sciences and humanities of Africa with the literary tradition that is their own, then, to the general benefit, we will have refuted the prejudice that claims that African identity, by its nature, has always expressed itself in oral culture.[13]

But to what degree have we, in our efforts to think African identity, adopted a Hegelian point of view on ourselves, making the Sahara into a wall dividing distinct identities? Léopold Sédar Senghor's objective in his writings on Arabness, negritude, and their convergence in Africanity was less to describe essences and their composition than to dispel the threat of violence posed by overly reductive identities ignorant of pluralism. This task continues to confront us today. In a public conference attended by the intellectuals of North Africa, the poet Senghor insisted on the importance of flows, on reciprocal information, on hyphenation, and not on essences: on the topic of African Arabness, which naturally exists in a continuity with the Middle East, he remarked how it had been determined by a situation that linked it internally, indissociably, to Berber, Mediterranean, and Black African identities; how, long before it became fashionable to say so, African Arabness bore witness to what we call "hybridity." That said, the desire to reduce hybridity, to flatten the multiplicity of identities into a single dimension, is a form of violence that can generate conflicts that go on to assume cultural, linguistic, or, at times, also military forms.

Across the Maghreb today, an energetic cultural, linguistic, and sometimes political Berber movement – a genuine 'return of the repressed' following upon a reductive Arabization – has come to demand that multiculturalism in the Maghreb become an attitude and a politics where Berber and Black African identities[14] – the *Gnawa* cultures, as they are called, after a corrupt form of the word "Guinea" – occupy their rightful place. In a general sense that extends beyond this region, it will be by embracing multiculturalism as a principle everywhere on our continent that we will build a genuine African union.

Having spoken of reductive identifications, we must now return to the deadly identities evoked in the introduction. Not everything is solely a conflict of identities. To those who have understood what one has taken to calling the "humanitarian catastrophe," rather than the "ethnic cleansing" or the "genocide," in Darfur as evidence of Arabization's assault on the Black African identity of Sudan (what irony that "Darfur," a name that used to designate the whole of Sub-Saharan Africa, in Arabic means "the country of the Blacks"[15]), the officials of the country respond that one must consider the economic reality behind the strife: the conflict's true foundation is not a question of ethnicity, it is rather the eternal, quasi-cosmic clash between nomadic economies and sedentary economies of all times and places.[16] Even if this were the case, the question nonetheless remains: why is it so tempting to express this clash in terms of identities? What makes it so easy to turn tribes who have created an Arab identity for themselves against populations that they perceive as other, if it is not in fact the evocation of such an identity and such an alterity? – if it is not the mobilization of the one against the other?

It is necessary to develop multicultural attitudes and political programs everywhere, but it is especially urgent to do so on a continent where one of the numerous forms that insecurity takes is what we might call "existential" insecurity: insecurity linked to identity itself. In addition to other calamities, Africa is the continent of identitarian catastrophes: to witness the theft of one's identity is one of several possible dangers on a continent where at times the hunt for "those not from here" has been pursued to the point of producing "non-natives" [*allogènes*], of turning non-foreigners into foreigners. It thus happened that from one day to the next Ugandans saw themselves reduced to their Indian origin, transformed into foreigners and soon after into refugees, before finally acquiring the condition of exiles.[17] The worst incarnation of identitarian catastrophe is, of course, civil war: the moment in which citizenship vanishes and cedes the whole field to ethnicity; where, in consequence, institutions cease to serve a national identity, and armies, which are that identity's ultimate guardians, splinter into militias.

Nothing, in my opinion, better expresses the identitarian catastrophe and the fragmentation it produces than the manner in which a Congolese scholar experienced the battle of Brazzaville during the civil war. He told me that, little by little, as the deadly confrontations between militias multiplied, he realized that, with respect to his own safety, he did not live in the "good" neighborhood – the neighborhood where those from his "region" lived. With a heavy heart, this universalist had at last to confront the fact that his life and the lives of his family depended on his identification with an ethnic group and this identification's translation into geography: he moved into "his" neighborhood.

Not just the lives we live together in the state forms that we inherited from colonization, but, in the final analysis, our African identity itself must be constructed on the basis of a pluralism that seeks a dialectical equilibrium between citizenship and ethnicity: a pluralism that resists both the temptation to separatism, which would have each identity be a nation of its own, and the temptation of cultural and political domination by a single group, which could be translated into ethnic cleansing. Proponents of what one would call a democratic/liberal point of view would say that citizenship is the only important consideration: the citizenship of individuals who have bracketed all their other forms of belonging to participate collectively in the public sphere, where no *politics of recognition* is necessary. Opposed to this point of view is what we could call the democratic/communitarian perspective, which claims to have reality on its side: to bracket what one is is quite frankly impossible, and to say otherwise is often a way of depriving minorities of their right to recognition. But let us move beyond this theoretical impasse by considering the example of the conflicts in the Niger River Delta during the 1990s. It is common knowledge that in this region of Nigeria the control of oil revenue has mobilized populations on the basis of identifications that are, at one and the same time, ethnocultural and civic.[18] That ethnicity can also be a form of citizenship (one thinks here, beyond Africa, of Quebec in Canada) and not simply its contrary is doubtless something we are asked to think about today if we are to bring about a pluralism capable of combining the entire range of cultural dynamics with what the philosopher Jürgen Habermas has called a "constitutional patriotism."

Conclusion: Affirming an African Presence in a World of Cultural Diversity

Having become "postcolonial," our world is, ideally, in the process of attaining the *sine qua non* of a genuine and complete humanism: the recognition by every culture of the singular contribution of each culture. In reality, we are far from such a goal. To be sure, the imperialist apologetics for legitimate cultural domination are no longer propounded and we have learned to start "paying attention" (in both senses: to be "politically correct," and to show authentic concern for the other) to different ways of seeing and acting. But recognition is not everything; recognition presumes a *subject* whereas, in today's world, we are primarily confronted with *mechanisms*. We are no longer in a situation where colonized subjects strive to have their identities recognized, where Orpheus tries to make himself understood by singing in an unheard-of language that expresses his unique point of view on Being. We are confronted with a process of commodification that only recognizes what has already been formatted to accord with its norms.

A world where cultural works are not abandoned to the blind mechanisms of commodification is a world which we Africans have an interest in contributing to. The project of an "African presence" is also one of the stakes in this struggle. Within institutions like the World Trade Organization, the fight for this other world was waged in the name of the "cultural exception" [*l'exception culturelle*]. Fortunately, this *unfortunate* expression has been supplanted by a genuine reflection today taking place within UNESCO – the more appropriate forum – on the meaning of *cultural diversity* and the best way to affirm it as a fundamental human value.

To affirm cultural diversity as a value is also to make it one of the ends of education. Therefore, the university is once again the principal site for responding to the challenge of a multicultural world. It is important that, no matter where they are located, universities committed to liberal education with the aim of producing citizens of today's world consider it necessary to host, alongside other disciplines, centers or programs for African studies. In addition, it is often the case that the presence of African studies in such universities also implies the presence of African scholars, who are said to represent Africa's new intellectual diaspora. If it is possible to see this diaspora as a resource siphoned off the continent by *brain drain*, one must also regard it as one of the conditions for an "African presence" in the world of scholarship. To be sure, universities in Africa must not be left out. It is especially important that the teaching of diversity be considered essential and that we put an end to the interminable *tête-à-tête* with the "West." We need to understand our African presence in the world in relation with what is happening in India, China, and Malaysia, which all carry significant weight in today's world and will only become more important. If the cultural nationalism of the independence period raised the question of Africanity as part of a face-off with the "West," reorientation of our "concern" [*souci*] toward horizons other than the West is just as essential to the question today.[19]

Notes for a Maroon Feminism
From the "Body Double" to the Body as Such

Hourya Bentouhami

Hourya Bentouhami is Associate Professor of Political Philosophy at the University of Toulouse-Jean Jaurès. Her work examines the influence of postcolonial theories on political theory (especially on notions of identity, culture, and recognition, on the memory of slavery, and on reparative justice), as well as their contribution to a re-elaboration of feminism. Among other publications, she is author of Le dépôt des armes: non-violence et désobéissance civile *(Paris: Presses universitaires de France, 2015);* Race, cultures, identités: une approche féministe et postcoloniale *(Paris: Presses universitaires de France, 2015); and, with Mathias Moschel, of* Critical Race Theory: introduction aux textes fondamentaux *(Paris: Dalloz: 2017).*

> My womb was sealed
> with molten wax
> of killer bees
> for nothing should enter
> nothing should leave
> the state of perpetual siege
> the condition of the warrior.
>
> Lorna Goodison, "Nanny,"
> *I Am Becoming My Mother*

Marronage, the escape of slaves from plantations in pursuit of their freedom,[1] has demonstrated that slavery, the plantation economy, and slave societies organized around an "economy of death" did not represent an ineluctable fate.[2] Still, it is only between the lines, by scrutinizing the records of courtroom testimonies, fugitive slave ads in the local press, or complaints filed by planters and colonizers (and, to a lesser degree, through the stories of the slaves themselves) that one can grasp, through the mediating voices, the voice of the fugitive slaves attesting to their desire for freedom and to its actualization.[3] The war waged against the Maroons was all the more brutal for the fact that their very existence was experienced as a direct threat to the plantations, owing in part to their frequent raids, but above all to the fact that their escape and their presence as fugitive slaves – without masters – invalidated those theories and practices that cast the "negro" as a being unworthy and incapable of freedom. Fugitive slaves made a possible abolitionism visible, and they made it sensible: their existence bolstered the desire for freedom among other slaves and even among certain "engaged" whites. The Maroons' strategies of war, which were *ruses de guerre*, gave life to revolutionary resistance struggles, like that of Toussaint Louverture and his comrades, from which women were hardly absent. Such was the case with the use of camouflage, and with surprise tactics involving ambushes conducted in geographical and climatic conditions of which the attackers were sole masters, making them invisible fighters. Archival documents indicate that women played a significant role in the resistance's tactic of camouflage: whether by hiding fugitive slaves (when they were not fugitives themselves) or arms, or by their concoction of lethal tinctures, but also by their enthusiasm in battle and their participation in raids on the plantations.[4] As a result, the attested fact that marronage *existed* and that societies of Maroons *were founded*,[5] in every social world where slavery was practiced,[6] brings to light a different practice and a different thinking of emancipation, which, in the absence of weapons like those of the enemy, were organized chiefly around resisting capture and defying pursuit through the perfect mastery of one's territory.[7] Marronage has allowed us to go beyond reductive typology and comprehend the figure of the slave as something other than a being resigned to servitude; and it has allowed us to trace a continuity between slaves' acts of resistance on the plantation – in the form of the refusal to work, for example – and the "grand marronage": *the decision to escape*. This image of indomitable resistance to one's own destruction has attracted certain feminists, starting with Monique Wittig, for whom the lesbian is like a Maroon slave who has to flee hetero-patriarchal society to escape its mode of appropriation (one of whose pillars is the exchange of sexual and affective services for food and shelter).[8] That said, to draw this analogy between feminist emancipation and emancipation from slavery renders the voice of Maroon women inaudible. Women who marooned were anything but secondary figures whose experiences disappeared behind the experience of Maroon men. Despite the fact that they seem to have represented only a minority of most Maroon communities, the size and significance of their role are indisputable and, in my estimation, indicative of the emancipatory potential of marronage, understood as more than just the escape from the plantation.

The utopian vision that marronage holds for feminism is as yet wholly unexplored. Elucidating it requires the restitution of the history of Maroon women and of their deep belief in a form of liberation that demands more than just emancipation from slavery [*affranchissement*]. Admittedly, the modesty of the archive means that the presence of women in these stateless territories and the role women played in developing their rules of survival are often reconstituted in the form of myth. However, it is on the basis of mythical accounts – preserved in, among other places, the memory of descendants of Africans and Maroons and in the topographical imaginary[9] – that we know about the importance of Maroon women's role. Thus, when one focuses on the history of Maroon women, one learns that it is often in the form of a mythical account that their proper names are invoked: Grand-Mère Kalle on Reunion Island, Queen Nanny in Jamaica, or Solitude in Guadeloupe. Of course, it is also possible, using an approach that comprehends experiences of slavery via reference to available historiographies, rather than mythical or literary constructions,[10] to study marronage through the voices of women and through the gender relations that marronage brings to light.[11]

Nonetheless, there are several questions that must be settled: given that numerous sources agree on the dominance of patriarchal filiation in marronage, what does it mean to take an interest in Maroon women from a feminist point of view? In the former interpretation, marronage represents the restoration of a masculine dignity that had been undermined by slavery's regime of matriarchal filiation – the woman's womb being the literal matrix of slavery. The hypothesis that marronage redeems virile dignity from the emasculation of plantocratic society [*la société plantocratique*] has a tendency to unduly distort and misrepresent the social antagonism present at the heart of the slave family by opposing slave women and slave men. The error lies in minimizing the fact that, for slave women, maternity was by no means free: as Françoise Vergès has demonstrated, maternity was the mine from which slavery extracted its profits and formed the basis of large-scale capitalist accumulation.[12] The fact that their wombs were coveted certainly did not give slave women power over their own bodies, nor over those of their children, and even less over the other slave bodies on the plantation – the absence of this power renders the argument that marronage represented a reversal of power dynamics untenable. In addition, there were also Maroon women leaders, a fact which qualifies the idea that Maroon leadership answered the need for a reconstruction of male virility.[13]

A study of marronage that focuses on women in order to reconceive the Maroon tradition as a paradigm of feminist utopia is entirely justified. That men made up the majority in Maroon communities hardly invalidates this focus on women, since Maroon societies were far from the only communities that were male by majority. Depending on the period under consideration – but particularly in the early days of slavery and, in certain regions, nearly until its end – male majorities existed in both slave "societies" and colonizer societies.[14] Our task here is to consider what becomes of the women. If we agree that one is born a slave via the womb of one's mother, we can reinterpret Maroon communities in light of a set of impossibilities within the slave system that makes the plantation a site not only for the exploitation of labor, but also of an "expropriation of identity" [*expropriation identitaire*] and a *conjugal, familial, and genealogical dystopia*. That is to say, slaves had no possibility of familial autonomy (their marriages fell under the master's control), or of sexual, maternal, or paternal autonomy, or of free circulation, or of cultural expression (owing to the dissolution of ethnic groups). Furthermore, it was extremely rare to obtain freedom through manumission, since this would have implied that the manumitted women had been the master's "concubines."[15] Interracial marriage being forbidden by law, slave women thus provided ancillary, affective, and sexual services for free – the latter, in particular, exposed them to the vengeful violence of white mistresses when they did not consider the rape of Black women an "opportune relief" from conjugal promiscuity. It was certainly possible for a slave woman who had had children with her owner to be freed along with her children upon the death of the owner, but such manumissions were not practiced systematically and could always be revoked by heirs.[16] The latter occurred often enough – nor was it rare for heirs to sell emancipated slaves to pay off debts, or to assuage their own jealousy.

Maroon communities – not least because of their diverse forms of existence – may be interpreted as an expansion beyond the plantation of the "slave garden" and all the affective ties reconstituted in the slaves' domestic sphere, both of which were formidable sites of resistance to slavery's machinery of destruction.[17] For Angela Davis, the slave garden symbolizes the realization of a form of negative equality between slave men and women in domestic labor.[18] Maroon territories constitute a new kind of community of care that, on the plantation, was confined to certain, restricted limits of time and space. Off the plantation, Maroon men and women took charge of the common good represented by their territory–refuge and performed labor that was not directly appropriable by whites.[19] In fact, just as women transformed the domestic space of the plantation into a common space, they also managed to take advantage of the *necessary* hostility of nature in Maroon territories to bring about communities of care, communities where one gives oneself a new name and resituates oneself within a creolized, rather than originary, culture.

The culture of Maroon communities is Afrocentric: if a Maroon woman is not necessarily a Black and/or African woman, in the majority of cases she is.[20] This is important to note, since, considerable regional differences notwithstanding, the role of women in parts of West Africa at the time of the transatlantic slave trade was more advantageous than it was in the West. This is borne out by the figure of the priestess – and, in a more ordinary way, of the caregiver[21] – who comes to occupy the center of the symbolism that developed around Maroon women leaders such as Romaine the Prophetess, Marie-Jeanne, and Henriette Saint-Marc in Haiti. More concretely, beyond their association with these protective figures, women were sometimes seen as possessing a traditional right to sever their conjugal ties, with the possibility of a divorce brought about on the woman's initiative.[22] Importantly, the essentials of agricultural labor in Africa fell to women, which meant that they could use food strikes to secure respect for their rights.[23] Arlette Gautier suggests that what one observes here are the outlines of a different history of modernity: "the opposition between inside and outside does not hold for these women," who may, for example, participate in the market, as is the case for Hausa women.[24] Without idealizing the situations that African women found themselves in at the beginning of the modern era, one could even conclude that, owing to the real possibility for certain of them to interrupt and contest aspects of their condition, the schema of appropriation for subaltern women was vulnerable to being disrupted by their efforts.[25] And the system of matrimonial alliances was indeed transformed in Afrocentric Maroon societies. Women were no longer the only thing that circulated from one family to another (or from one ethnic group to another); everything circulated, but not by means of the capitalist circuit (the exchange of muscles, genitals, and wombs between plantocratic merchants, notaries, and owners), or according to the patrimonial economy (daughters, sisters, and nieces as use values and exchange values), but after the manner of the "filibuster" [*flibusterie*][26] – which is to say, as war spoils and fake names (in the sense that the latter no longer correspond to those on the owner's registry). Marronage may thus be understood as a rupture in the matrix of the race.[27] The territory produced by marronage gives form to an "erratic" circulation of bodies and signs;[28] it not founded on the circulation of capital but on the reparation of the community and resistance to the world of slavery.

Marronage is not only the reconstitution of a site of domestic survival – a place where maternity particularly, and affective ties more generally, might be reclaimed. It is also the possibility of taking part in decisions affecting the community, according to a conception of freedom that we see as indicative of a *struggle against recognition* – in the attempt, that is, to escape what has long been taken as the archetypical metanarrative of human liberation, namely, Hegel's dialectic of the master and the slave. Our goal is to show how Maroon women at once participate in the schema "either liberty or death" that characterizes Hegel's dialectic of recognition, and, at the same time, how they escape it – not, as Simone de Beauvoir would have it, because every woman is partially complicit in her own domination, but rather because the desire for recognition is prisoner to the colonial model of appropriating bodies. By affirming their desire for liberty at the expense of their lives, Maroon women show how marronage – both with respect to its relative institutionalization in "society" and with regard to its cosmological significance as the vagabondage of souls[29] – constitutes a new way of governing oneself articulated around a powerful impulse to conserve one's being and freedom by means of the community. In this sense, a Maroon feminism is, properly speaking, a movement for the *liberation* of women that cannot be reduced to the desire for their mere emancipation [*affranchissement*]. Feminism is thus rethought from the principle of community – unlike individualist feminism which, with its skewed interpretation of the slogan "my body, my property," found a frame for its historical discourse in the scheme of property ownership. Indeed, resistance to the *collective* appropriation of women tends to assume the form of a claim to individual liberty understood as *private* property. A certain form of legal feminism – which in part promotes women's victimhood – has fallen into the trap of setting emancipation against collective appropriation, having done nothing more than renegotiate the terms of appropriation from a collective modality to a private one. Today, this clouded perspective on emancipation still generates the obligation to frame the legitimacy of feminist demands in legal rhetoric, where the meaning of "my body, my property" is perverted into a possessive individualism. However, the slogans "my body, my property" or "our bodies, ourselves" can also be considered in light of the meaning that the marronage of slave women gives them – namely, a collective emancipation that does not claim the status of a victim waiting to be "saved" or "protected." In short, Maroon feminism is not a metaphor. Drawing from slave women's historical experiences of marronage, it instead designates the possibility of interrupting the production of what I call *body doubles* [*corps-doublures*]. A body double, in my sense, is a body whose existence is legitimated through the obligation to clothe itself, like a *double*, in the body of another, considered of greater worth and for whose wellbeing the double is then responsible. Were it necessary to glean a single, powerful idea from Maroon feminism, it would be the idea, anchored in its historical context, of putting an end to the deadly doubling of bodies, with the goal of reclaiming for oneself a body of one's own [*un corps propre*] as a member of a community.

Liberation: A Struggle against Recognition

A certain form of freedom *stricto sensu* may be abstracted from the world of plantocratic slavery. Indeed, the freedoms authorized by the system that organized "social death" had been introduced into the slave system and lent it ideological force,[30] since these freedoms depended on the power of masters who were often, if not exclusively, whites.[31] Slavery was thus a matrix for the construction of the color line, of the racial categorization of society and power, and for the *whitewashing* [*le blanchiment*] *of the very idea of freedom*: having been constituted as a homogeneous group distinct from whites, Blacks could be granted certain "exceptions" without thereby calling into question the legitimacy of the racial and sexual order of plantation societies. On the contrary, exceptions reinforced this ideological and material order: manumissions [*affranchissements*], the possibility for certain people of color to become slaveowners, or to serve in armed "Black militias," actually *contributed* to the durability of the slave system. Nonetheless, these "exceptions" to the rule do not minimize the importance of the economy of death in plantocratic societies. Slaves – men and women – could enjoy a form of freedom under control; they could circulate "freely" with a note from their master. But it is one and the same ideology that reigns in the monitored circulation of slaves, in the carefully supervised arming of Blacks in slave-hunting militias, in the possibilities for persons of color – including for free Black women of color[32] – to open businesses or even to become owners of slaves, and in the various modalities by which one might purchase one's freedom or acquire it in recognition of services rendered (sexual services included): a desire to maintain the slave or the Black in a situation of subjection *including when he or she is free*.[33] In fact, emancipation [*l'affranchissement*] through marriage – extremely rare given the laws against interracial unions – establishes a continuum between the condition of servitude and freedom, because the woman continues to provide the affective and sexual services that were previously extorted from her.[34] To restate the matter from the perspective of social psychology, the point is to cultivate the belief that *the only freedom possible is the freedom mediated by the recognition by the master* – which is to say, by the white master – a fact which explains why manumissions [*les affranchissements*] were relatively rare occurrences.[35] If the freedom of whites was taken as "a natural condition of their whiteness, Blacks, by contrast, had to justify their claims to freedom, to show themselves deserving of it."[36] Freedom for Blacks was seen as compensation for good conduct:

> Ultimately, in slave society, Black freedom was viewed, from a legal standpoint, not as a gift from God but as a result of the largesse of the White community. Blacks had to find favor in the eyes of Whites through various behaviors, including fidelity to their masters, willingness to betray servile revolts, and – in the case of women – willingness to have sexual relations with their overlords. Even so, freedom granted could be revoked anytime the White authorities felt that the freed persons constituted a burden on White society, failed to live up to specific social, moral and other obligations that the society imposed on them, or engaged in activities that the authoritarian state considered inimical to its interests. In 1731 the Jamaican legislature passed a law imposing loss of freedom on any free Black or free Coloured person who refused to serve in the militia against runaways.[37]

The legislative conditions that made possible the idea of a *revocable freedom* for Blacks and former slaves also encourage what Frantz Fanon describes in *Black Skin, White Masks* as the complex of the "searcher" [*quêteur*]: Blacks who look to whites for approval of their being and their acts.[38] For Simone de Beauvoir, the infantilism that patriarchy forces upon women produces a similar effect – it is an infantilism that consists in the *parade* [*parade*], in the ostentatious search for the approval of others and especially of one's parents.[39] From this perspective, one could say that slavery infantilizes Black men by teaching them to become women in the Beauvoirian sense of "becoming-woman" – which is to say, it teaches Black men to see themselves perpetually through the eyes of whites (men and *white women*) so as to benefit from the latter's approbation and favor. And yet such approval is only obtainable in a context of enduring white privilege, just as, according to Beauvoir, it is only obtainable for white women in the context of enduring male privilege.

This "captive" liberty consisting in the adoption – even by force[40] – of a logic of maintaining the slavery of other slaves – the enslavement, in a sense, of one's *alter egos*, of one's other selves – belongs to what Roger Caillois and Homi Bhabha have called *mimicry* or "mimetic freedom" [*liberté mimétique*]. For Caillois, *mimicry* consists in "becoming an illusory character oneself, and of so behaving" – it means playing a role.[41] My point is that, for slaves, such mimicry results from the incorporation of the institution of slavery to the point of assuming the freedom of a fake [*d'un faux*], of a double [*d'une doublure*]. By this, we mean that the double is encouraged to imitate the master: they are caught in this imitation, without ever being allowed to confuse themselves with the person they double. The body double [*le corps-doublure*] is precisely the subject born of slavery's essential injunction: "be my body," the master says, and thereby enjoins the enslaved to become other, to alienate themselves in the master's desire. As a result, in the case of emancipation or *de facto freedom* [*liberté de fait*] – also known as "savanna freedom" [*liberté de savane*], freedom without a certificate of manumission's official guarantee – what we are really dealing with is a mummified form of freedom that is still obliged to coax the master's love. In my estimation, such *mimicry* corresponds to the material dimension of appropriation that seizes the entire being of the slave destined to be a body-for-another [*un corps-pour-autrui*] and, a fortiori, what Fanon calls a "negro-toward-death" [*un nègre-pour-la-mort*]. This is corroborated, for example, by the existence of the "replacement negro" [*nègre de remplacement*] in court cases where slaveowners found themselves accused of murder: in such cases, the slave – in their capacity as "substitute for the guilty" – could be accused in the master's stead.[42] *Mimicry* is thus the result of a deadly doubling born of the master's desire: the master who tells the slave "be my body," assume for me all the burdens of my body, be my body double in all menial and thankless tasks, but know that this borrowed body you assume does not give you the right to be the master in the place of the master.

Hence the very strong historical resonance that exists between the psychoanalytic idea that "the Ego is not master of its own house" and the condition of the slave. Although Freud intended his statement as a general description, it tragically captures the specific psychic dislocation of slaves as subjects institutionally forbidden to be themselves and condemned instead to play a role. Not only is the Ego an illusion, but, in cases where the man or the woman has been constituted as a "negro"/"negress," the Ego is also another's: double alienation, double illusion. As body doubles, slaves find themselves obliged to put on costumes that distance them ever further from themselves. As Homi Bhabha writes, in the colonial context, "the question of identification is never the affirmation of a pre-given identity ... it is always the production of an image of identity and the transformation of the subject in assuming that image. The demand of identification – that is, to be *for* an Other – entails the representation of the subject in the differentiating order of otherness."[43] Put differently: the slave sees him- or herself seen though an other; the slave becomes this other, the master's double, which is what one expects of him or her. It is impossible to say "I" without identifying with the master. And this impossibly derives from the negation of the slave's own body through the obligation to put on the body of the master. Thus, in his analysis of the figure of the "house Negro," which he invokes to underline the psychological damage of racism, Malcolm X testifies to the personality disorders inherent to slavery as an institution: "If the master got sick, the house Negro would say, 'What's the matter, boss, *we* sick?' We sick! He identified himself with his master, more than his master identified with himself."[44] This impossibility of saying "I" without assuming the body of the master bears witness to the colonization of the desire for recognition – to its conversion into a sign of allegiance.

The very construction of the legal category "free persons of color" [*Libres de couleur*] testifies to the color freedom acquires in this context.[45] As Françoise Vergès reminds us, there was no need for the precision of "free whites," since being recognized as white naturally signified being free.[46] In a certain sense, this shackled and revocable liberty is founded on what in psychoanalysis one might call a delusional constellation. It establishes the conditions for both a Black paranoia (the fear of being recognized as Black or as a fugitive slave, grounded in the real fear of being denounced or captured) and for a white paranoia: the paranoia that Fanon attributes to whites who, sick with power, are continually on the lookout for the smallest sign of irreverence from a Black. This interpretation of freedom as something that can be revoked induces a delusional and neurotic split, which is directly translated into a legal text like the 1857 Tennessee legislation that gave a free or emancipated Black man the right to become a slave of his own free will! As Thompson documents, Texas, Louisiana, and Maryland all promulgated similar laws, in 1858, 1859, and 1860 respectively.[47] Even more explicitly, an 1859 Arkansas law granted a form of exception to the expulsion of all free Blacks and free persons of color from its territory: those who had been authorized to remain in the state for longer than one year were required to choose a master (for themselves). Put differently, freedom implied recognizing a master in every white person – including every white woman.

But the central tenet of this production of body doubles was that no one confuse the doubled bodies (the masters) with the body doubles (the slaves).[48] In practice, the bodies of free Blacks and free persons of color were also marked to make them readily recognizable: through prohibitions against wearing distinctive signs of wealth or ceremony, which were held to be the very sign of whiteness.[49] Indeed, the fragile and revocable character of this freedom – always conditional and marked by neurosis – has prompted certain historians to caution against the urge to translate the term "fugitive Blacks" [*Noirs fugitifs*] by "fugitive slaves" [*esclaves fugitifs*].[50]

Marronage's refusal of the captive freedom to be won in the struggle for recognition guided Toussaint Louverture when, against Napoleon Bonaparte, he laid claim to "the more expansive liberty." Bonaparte wanted to become the guarantor of the freedom and equality of Saint-Domingue's slaves and persons of color out of consideration for the colony's special situation with respect to other colonies – which had not succeeded in establishing the same balance of power with France. Anxious to reinstitute slavery in all the colonies, Bonaparte would not suffer obstinate Saint-Domingue to be an exception of liberty [*exception de liberté*], save to the degree that *such liberty were exceptional* [*exceptionnelle*], the fruit of the Republic's largesse. Hence his proclamation: "Good Blacks, remember that the French people recognizes your freedom and the equality of your rights, that they will be written in gold letters on the flags of all National Guard battalions stationed in the colony of Saint-Domingue."[51] To this, Toussaint Louverture responded: "It is not a circumstantial liberty, a freedom conceded to us alone, that we desire; we desire the unqualified adoption of the principle that no man, whether born red, black, or white, may be the property of his fellow."[52] What Toussaint was refusing in this offer of "negro freedom" [*liberté des nègres*] under Napoleonic patronage was precisely a freedom soiled by a relation of master and slave – as if freedom needed a master to serve as guarantor. Toussaint fought neither for manumission [*affranchissement*] nor to be constituted as the exception to the rule, but rather for a universal, unalienable freedom. In this respect, the revolutionary leader *marooned* [*fit marronner*] the very concept of freedom by refusing the idea of a unilateral recognition granted as if it were a favor.

This refusal to become what sociology calls a *token* (an alibi or a symbolic quota) is particularly evident in the case of Maroon women, and for the reasons we have already indicated: for women in a world of slavery, the only possibility of living in relative freedom was manumission, which is one reason why the sense of absolute freedom in marronage found vigorous expression among women.

"Liberty Is More Valuable than Life" (Harriet Jacobs)

If there is one thing in women's experiences of marronage that might fall under the paradigm of the Hegelian dialectic of master and slave, it is most certainly the stubbornness for freedom [*entêtement pour la liberté*] that a number of Maroon women embodied. Whereas Hegel considers this stubbornness (*Eigensinn*, literally "self-will") a subaltern form of resistance dependent upon the conditions of slavery,[53] Orlando Patterson regards it as indissociable from the risk of death that the philosopher holds to be freedom's ultimate test.[54] In effect, for Patterson, this freedom is first exercised in the condition of servitude, through the "petit marronage" of resisting work, whether by the occasional escape or by resorting to poison or even suicide. In this respect, the death risked in the "grand marronage" is of a piece with these acts of internal resistance on the plantation. And, as a matter of fact, historiography reports the voices of numerous Maroon women who had a higher regard for freedom than for life. Such was the case for Harriet Jacobs, for whom "liberty is more valuable than life."[55]

Such stubbornness in the cause of freedom was a sentiment shared by many Maroon women, and expresses itself in four forms: first, as *a stubborn commitment to escape* – cruel repressions and punishments notwithstanding. Given such cruelty, this stubbornness testifies indirectly to the abuses to which women were subjected on the plantation. Such was the case of Coobah, purchased in 1761 at the age of 15 by Thomas Thistlewood, who assaulted and raped her. She contracted a venereal disease over the course of the four subsequent years and suffered from yaws. Beginning in 1769, she repeatedly escaped: eight times in 1770 and five times in 1771, despite the severe punishments that awaited her – pillorying, whipping, branding of the forehead, an iron collar for her neck, months in chains.[56] Rape being a weapon for demoralizing slave women and not, as is often claimed,[57] a technique for preserving the sexual decency of white women, the marronage of women who had been raped defied the regime of terror by their act. A second affirmation of this stubbornness was the acceptance of death as punishment for resistance, and particularly for escape. In C. L. R. James's words: "When Chevalier, a black chief, hesitated at the sight of the scaffold, his wife shamed him. 'You do not know how sweet it is to die for liberty!' And refusing to allow herself to be hanged by the executioner, she took the rope and hanged herself."[58] On similar occasion, a mother comforted her daughters who wept as they walked to the gallows: "Rejoice! Your wombs will not beget slaves."[59] As a third form of stubbornness, suicide could constitute deliverance as well as an affirmation of one's own value, since, in contrast to the slow or violent deaths chosen by the oppressor, suicide on several levels represented the possibility of deciding for oneself the meaning of one's own death.[60] A final form of affirming one's own freedom entailed killing the master or destroying his property (farm animals, fields, harvests, but also women and slaves as other properties owned by the master), or else killing one's own children, since the latter too were the master's property and destined to become slaves in their own right. From this perspective, one understands why the ethics of death that informed the action of Maroon women, and by which death itself broke free of the slave system, compelled the authorities to make the executions of female resistors public: Solitude was executed publicly after having given birth; Marthe-Rose, suspected of having induced Delgrès to resist and of having incited slave soldiers to kill white prisoners, was hanged publicly. The cruelty of the repression also showed the whites' fear of being poisoned by slave women: "After the failure of the 1802 slave revolt in Guadeloupe, all black nurses at the military hospital in Pointe-à-Pitre, where rising mortality among General Richepance's troops was attributed to poison, were rounded up and shot."[61]

Use of poison was one strategy by which slave women often attained justice. "In the decades leading up to emancipation in 1848, trials of slave women for poisoning and requests by slaveowners to deport suspects from French colonies were quite common."[62] Deemed a "malevolent scourge" when not employed by owners to capture fugitive slaves,[63] the use of plants rendered efficacious by the preparation of the *pharmaka* allowed slave women either to ease their own suffering or to take life without immediately running the risk of being punished by death.[64] In this respect, the fact of possessing a poison (or, rather, knowing how to dose the *pharmaka*) allowed women to exercise an invisible power – a power which fed white paranoia, since Black women had access to their masters' kitchens. Fright at the prospect of powerful plants in the hands of women reached its peak in marronage, as indicated by the myth of the "bubbling cauldron of Queen Nanny," the Maroon woman leader whom the British took for a witch.[65]

In each of these cases, death intervenes to break the cycle of "death in life." For us, this "death in life" belongs to the double, to the borrowed body in an economy that makes the body of the slave into a body by default. To kill (oneself) is thus a way of escaping the deadly cycle of doubling that institutes the "negro" as a being-for-another [*un être-pour-autrui*], a negro-toward-death [*un nègre-pour-la-mort*], who must assume the risks connected to work, to reproduction, and even to civil responsibility, as shown in the example of the "replacement negro" in court trials. At stake, therefore, is putting an end to this production of a body whose existence is restricted precisely to the restoration and redemption of other beings, pursued to the detriment of its own conservation, and carried to the point that its own existence becomes superfluous, inscribed within a "necropolitics."[66] According to Achille Mbembe, the plantocratic system represents a government of the living [*du vivant*] (a biopower) on an even larger scale than what Foucault analyzes to describe the stage of European modernity summed up by the formula "to make live and to let die." In practice, slave plantations take up this maxim of government, since the owners' goal is to maximize the exhaustion and destruction of ignoble bodies so that other, more worthy lives may be repaired and made to live. There is thus a doubling in operation at the heart of biopower: for certain subjects (whites) to be "made-to-live" [*faire-vivre*], it is necessary that others (non-whites) be "made-to-work" [*faire-travailler*] to the point of being "made-to-die" [*faire-mourir*]. It follows that the system of the double is guided by two logics of substitution: the negro-double substitutes for the master in all servile tasks (including thankless domestic work for the benefit of white women), and this substitution sustains and confirms a strict hierarchy between the body of the master and the body of the slave. However, substituting for the master's body is only possible to the degree that slaves are substitutable for each other – this time according to a principle of equivalence that holds between "negros" and that denies them any form of singularity. More specifically, female "negresses" were considered substitutes for male "negros" in a capitalist, plantocratic economy that needed to postulate a perfect equivalence of all muscular force, a situation which contributed to the masculinization of Black women.[67] With this in mind, one would be obliged to look at those aspects of slave women's becoming-Maroon that participate in the critique of the specific gender assignments derived from the capitalist model of accumulation characteristic of the plantation: Black women were not constructed as a weak sex [*un sexe faible*] but as a sex so supposedly hardened for labor (agricultural, ancillary, and reproductive) as to be, in the eyes of whites, disqualified from any pretention of being recognized as women. In the elaboration of the racialized gender norms specific to this context, marronage was also a way for Black women to contest the denial of their femininity and their maternity. In their combat for and defense of Maroon communities, however, marronage also gave women an occasion to redefine a new virility that had not been prescribed by the capitalist exploitation of female muscle. In fact, Maroon women who became warriors contributed to the recoding of non-masculine forms of virility as well as masculine forms of femininity. These can be understood as figures of lesbianism, as one can hear in the contemporary Jamaican expression "man-royal," with which the eighteenth-century Maroon Queen Nanny was associated and which today refers – albeit pejoratively – to the lesbian as the pageantry of a man [*un homme d'apparat*], a sexual substitute for men.[68] Thus, resounding in the marronage of women – the use of poison included – one must hear the stubborn will to put an end to the doubling of one's own life in slavery. Beyond the desire to break with the *mimicry* discussed above – and which amounted to making one's life into a pale image of a white person's life – it was a question of putting a stop to the pageantry of masculinity [*masculinité d'apparat*] that in practice did not confer rights to the same treatment as the masculinity of men. For example, even though women performed the same agricultural labor as men, it was impossible for them to become supervisors. Marronage meant putting an end to this existence as a double, *as a negro* who, in the shadows, works, writes, and thinks for another, and it meant restoring a vision of the non-alienated double, as it appeared in Afrocentric cultures.

In these cultures, the double possesses a significant metaphysical and anthropological connotation. In addition to the symbolic importance of twinness, in many cultures persons are themselves considered to be their own doubles.[69] The double is the object of a specific kind of care that, quite precisely, abolishes the idea of hierarchy as framed by a dialectic of the original and the copy (which, for its part, corresponds to the Western metaphysics of the double as framed by slavery, the latter being the production par excellence of the body double). In fact, at the moment of death, the double remains at a person's side, and the purpose of the funeral rite is precisely to make the double take leave of the body so that it may rejoin the body's breath. Even when one performs therapeutic dances, one attends to the needs of the double so that the physical body may heal.[70] By contrast, mourning becomes impossible when the double remains attached to the dead person and to the living ones whom it will haunt – just like the tragic death [*la malemort*] of the child Beloved in Toni Morrison's novel of the same name. In light of these beliefs, one comes to understand how the system of doubling attempted to destroy the very notion of person, to efface the traditional meaning that it could have in certain Afrocentric cultures, where doubles are embedded in persons, providing access to ancestors and to a rich, animist universe in which everyone is more than him- or herself. For those on the Middle Passage, mass suicide was a possibility, since it was thought that one's soul would thereby return to Africa, the place of the ancestors.[71] This capacious sense of the double and of the vagabondage of souls was replaced by a culture of the double subjected to the One of the plantocratic economy, where the very figure of the "negro" was of a double condemned to become a war machine directed against itself.

Conclusion: Maroon Revolution and the Experiment of "Equaliberty"

Which revolution are we talking about? The call of the forest, of the mornes and other alpine cirques energized, as by the beat of a drum, women and men who stubbornly insisted on returning freedom to the wild. Today these voices are whispers, fleeting lines difficult to recall. And yet their power resonates and their presence is real, even in the form of an allusion. Marronage was indeed revolutionary in that it created the possibility of a community of dignity based upon self-defense, upon penetrating and even disappearing into a nature become camouflage:

> Maroon negros do not flee, they ditch. Masters of subterfuge, they slip off, steal away, vanish in a cloud of guiles: red-herrings, deceits, stratagems, ruses of all kinds. As runaways, Maroon warriors only persist in their being by disappearing; out of their disappearance they forge a many-sided weapon. In their perpetual movement of attack and retreat they find themselves accompanied, supported, joined in battle by women, children, seniors, and spirits: an entire diaspora in motion from which will surge new forms of life.[72]

Maronnage is, at one and the same time, about ensuring that one is forgotten and about remembering oneself to white and Black slave hunters and slaveowners. The very exigency of these acts of disappearance and dazzling reappearance as strategies for survival is why, from today's perspective, this world seems not only to have disappeared, but to have never existed in the first place. To explain such evasion as a strategy of combat and a possibility of freedom is the reason for thematizing a feminism that "maroons" [*un féminisme marronnant*] – that slips from the paths of recognition. That is how Maroon women appear to us in the archives: as fugitives, lines of flight, withdrawn into a clandestinity whose phantom trace seems at once unlocatable and yet very real.

Much is at stake in the memory of these lines of escape. A strong belief in an "equaliberty" animates Maroon women who refuse the idea of revocable liberty in the form of de facto, circumstantial, or manumitted freedom: all these freedoms carry within them an inequality that ends up justifying the racial and sexual order. With the concept of "equaliberty," Étienne Balibar refers to the truly revolutionary idea that holds liberty to be indissociable from equality and, more than that, maintains that equality is ultimately identical to liberty: both are mutually implicated as demands of humanity.[73] If, for Balibar, the imbrication of liberty and equality can be found in the Declaration of the Rights of Man of 1789, it is also present, as Aimé Césaire argues, in the interpretation that Toussaint Louverture offers of the Declaration by calling for the universality of liberty: what is recognized as true for the "negros" of Saint-Domingue must also be true for all "negros," even when they are not Blacks. To be sure, Louverture is neither a Maroon nor a woman. Still, marronage and Maroon women above all provided a model for thinking abolitionism as a "liberation of liberty" – that is, as the refusal to see liberty converted into its opposite, namely into a simple privilege, as in the paradigmatic example of a slave attaining freedom by marrying her master.

The very existence of a marronage, and particularly of a marronage of slave women, bore witness to the desire *to stop this engendering of the double* (including through the refusal to give birth)[74] by putting an end to the masquerade of freedom and equality offered by a unilateral form of recognition. To be sure, neither flight nor death represents Maroon feminism's last word, but they manifest the force behind the intention to give one's death a meaning that neither the master nor the slave system can appropriate. It is about giving oneself a body of one's own that would find the meaning of its existence in the fact of belonging to a community of care. In this sense, Maroon feminism is also to be understood as a *redefinition of "care" in light of these reparative practices addressed to one's own body inside the community*, and not in the sense of individual women taking charge of the group's young and infirm. Indeed, the point is to understand how this Maroon feminism is a feminism of survival, invested, for example, in knowing how to prepare food that will not be poison to one's children – hence the effort of Maroon women to learn about plants and their active powers.

One must also see in the marronage of women the creation of communities of women, in a solidarity that expresses their stubborn pursuit of liberation and refusal of appropriation.[75] Such solidarity is captured by Bernard Moitt's account of the following incident: "On August 17, 1769, a group of slave women abandoned a Saint-Domingue plantation, but not before attempting to persuade another group of women, whose function was the pounding of millet and other domestic labors, to join them."[76] In such solidarities, Maroon women are no longer "Black" or "of color" – not even "creole." For, as a practice, "Maroon" is precisely what designates the flight beyond the color line, while, as a *name*, "Maroon" is what *designates the interruption of color.*[77] Spanish colonizers designated fugitive slaves as "marrons" to associate them with animals who had reverted to a wild state, but, despite all the hunts and all the violence to which they were subjected, what Maroon women managed to achieve was precisely the de-ethnicization of their skin, their sex, and their wombs. Their refusal to submit to the colorization of dignity and respect is what makes fugitive women Maroons. Such is the irony of a word that, while literally designating a color, comes to figure, metaphorically, the resistance to color. If the question is to know how we might call ourselves heiresses [*heritières*] to women suicides, poisoners, infanticides, warriors, soldiers – to women so stubborn and frenzied in the cause of freedom that they were able to confront and accept death – the reason is because such engagement on behalf of one's own liberation, such refusal to serve as an alibi in the game of recognition or to accept the circumstantial freedom of manumission, such stubbornness in believing oneself worthy of life and of liberty – all of these legacies have made the marronage of women into a living utopia.

Bibliography

Balibar, Étienne. *Equaliberty: Political Essays*, trans. James Ingram (Durham: Duke University Press, 2014).

Bastide, Roger, and Germaine Dieterlen, eds. *La notion de personne en Afrique noire* (Paris: L'Harmattan, 1993).

Beauvoir, Simone de. *The Second Sex*, trans. Constance Borde and Sheila Malovany-Chevallier (New York: Vintage, 2011).

Bentouhami, Hourya, and Nacira Guénif-Souilamas. "Avec Colette Guillaumin: penser les rapports de sex, race, classe. Les paradoxes de l'analogie." *Cahiers du genre* 63, no. 2 (2017): pp. 205–19.

Bhabha, Homi K. *The Location of Culture* (New York: Routledge, 1994).

Bland, Sterling Lecater, ed. *African American Slave Narratives: An Anthology* (Westport: Greenwood Press, 2001).

Bonniol, Jean-Luc. *La couleur comme maléfice: une illustration créole de la généalogie des Blancs et des Noirs* (Paris: Albin Michel, 1992).

Boumediene, Samir. *La colonisation du savoir: une histoire des plantes médicinales du "Nouveau Monde" (1492–1750)* (Vaulx-en-Velin: Les Éditions des Mondes à Faire, 2016).

Caillois, Roger. *Man, Play and Games*, trans. Meyer Barash (Chicago: University of Illinois Press, 2001).
Camp, Stephanie M. H. *Closer to Freedom: Enslaved Women and Everyday Resistance in the Plantation South* (Chapel Hill: University of North Carolina Press, 2004).
Carby, Hazel V. "'Hear My Voice, Ye Careless Daughters': Narratives of Slave and Free Women before Emancipation." In *African American Autobiography: A Collection of Critical Essays*, ed. William L. Andrews (Englewood Cliffs, NJ: Prentice Hall, 1993).
Carlès, James. "Décoloniser la danse contemporaine." Presented at "Penser les décolonisations" conference at the University of Toulouse-Jean Jaurès, Toulouse, France, June 2, 2017.
Césaire, Aimé. *Toussaint Louverture: la Révolution française et le problème colonial* (Paris: Présence africaine, 1981).
Cravens, Mary Caroline. "Manumission and the Life Cycle of a Contained Population: The VOC Lodge Slaves at the Cape of Good Hope, 1680–1730," in *Paths to Freedom: Manumission and the Atlantic World*, ed. Rosemary Brana-Shute and Randy J. Sparks (Columbia: University of South Carolina Press, 2009) pp. 97–120.
Cummings, Ronald. "Jamaican Female Masculinities: Nanny of the Maroons and the Genealogy of the Man-Royal." *Journal of West Indian Literature* 21, no. 1/2 (2012): pp. 129–54.
Davis, Angela. *Women, Race & Class* (New York: Random House, 1981).
Davis, Charles T., and Henry Louis Gates, Jr. *The Slave's Narrative* (New York: Oxford University Press, 1985).
Dorlin, Elsa. "Les espaces-temps des résistances esclaves: des suicidés de Saint-Jean aux marrons de Nanny Town (XVIIe–XVIIIe siècles)." *Tumultes* 27, no. 2 (2006): pp. 37–51.
———. *Se défendre: une philosophie de la violence* (Paris: La Découverte, 2017).
Falquet, Jules. "La combinatoire *straight*: race, classe, sexe, et économie politique – analyses matérialistes et décoloniales." *Cahiers du genre* 4, no. 3 (2016): pp. 73–96.
Fanon, Frantz. *Black Skin, White Masks*, trans. Richard Philcox (New York: Grove Press, 2008).
Fouchard, Jean. *Les marrons de la liberté* (Paris: Édition de l'École, 1972).
Garcia, Jesus. *Africanas, esclavas y cimarronas* (Caracas: Fundación Afroamérica, 1996).
Gautier, Arlette. *Les sœurs de Solitude: femmes et esclavages aux*

Antilles du XVIIe au XIXe siècle (Presses universitaires de Rennes, 2010).

Genovese, Eugene. *Roll, Jordan, Roll: The World the Slaves Made* (New York: Vintage, 1976).

Giacomini, Sonia Maria. *Femmes et esclaves: l'expérience brésilienne, 1850–1888* (Paris: iXe, 2016).

Goodison, Lorna. *I Am Becoming My Mother* (London: New Beacon Books, 1986).

Gottlieb, Karla. *The Mother of Us All: A History of Queen Nanny, Leader of the Windward Jamaican Maroons* (Trenton: Africa World Press, 2000).

Hegel, Georg Wilhelm Friedrich. *Phenomenology of Spirit*, trans. A. V. Miller (New York: Oxford University Press, 1977).

hooks, bell. *Ain't I a Woman: Black Women and Feminism*, 2nd edn. (New York: Routledge, 2014).

Jacobs, Harriet. *Incidents in the Life of a Slave Girl: Written by Herself* (New York: Oxford University Press, 1988). First published 1861 by L. Maria Child (Boston).

James, C. L. R. *The Black Jacobins: Toussaint L'Ouverture and the San Domingo Revolution*, 2nd revised edn. (New York: Vintage, 1989).

Linebaugh, Peter, and Marcus Rediker. *The Many-Headed Hydra: The Hidden History of the Revolutionary Atlantic* (London: Verso, 2000).

Mbembe, Achille. "Nécropolitique." *Raison politique* 21, no. 1 (2006): pp. 29–60.

Moitt, Bernard. *Women and Slavery in the French Antilles, 1635–1848* (Bloomington: Indiana University Press, 2001).

Moore, Brian L., B. W. Highman, Carl Campbell, and Patrick Bryan. *Slavery, Freedom and Gender: The Dynamics of Caribbean Society* (Kingston: University of the West Indies Press, 2003).

Morenas, Joseph Elzéar. *Précis historique de la traite des Noirs et de l'esclavage colonial* ([1828] Geneva: Slatkine, 1978).

Morgan, Philip D. "Colonial South Carolina Runaways: Their Significance in Slave Culture," in *Out of the House of Bondage: Runaways, Resistance and Marronage in Africa and the New World*, ed. Heuman Gad (New York: Routledge, 2016). First published 1986 by Frank Cass (London).

Oudin-Bastide, Caroline. *L'effroi et la terreur: esclavage, poison et sorcellerie aux Antilles* (Paris: La Découverte, 2013).

———. *Travail, capitalisme et société esclavagiste: Guadeloupe, Martinique (XVIIe–XIXe siècles)* (Paris: La Découverte, 2005).

Patterson, Orlando. *Freedom in the Making of Western Culture*, Vol. I of *Freedom* (New York: Basic Books, 1991).

———. *Slavery and Social Death: A Comparative Study* (Cambridge, MA: Harvard University Press, 1982).

Payet, Marie-Ange. *Les femmes dans le marronnage à l'île de la Réunion de 1662 à 1848* (Paris: L'Harmattan, 2013).

Price, Richard, ed. *Maroon Societies: Rebel Slave Communities in the Americas* (Baltimore: Johns Hopkins University Press, 1979).

Rediker, Marcus. *À bord du négrier: une histoire atlantique de la traite* (Paris: Seuil, 2013).

Rochmann, Marie-Christine. *L'esclave fugitif dans la littérature antillaise: sur la déclive du morne* (Paris: Karthala, 2000).

Snyder, Terri L. *The Power to Die: Slavery and Suicide in British North America* (University of Chicago Press, 2015).

Tabet, Paola. *La grande arnaque: sexualité des femmes et échange économico-sexuel* ([1987] Paris: L'Harmattan, 2005).

Thompson, Alvin O. *Flight to Freedom: African Runaways and Maroons in the Americas* (Kingston: University of the West Indies Press, 2006).

Touam Bona, Dénètem. *Fugitif, où cours-tu?* (Paris: Presses universitaires de France, 2016).

Vergès, Françoise. "'Le Nègre n'est pas. Pas plus que le Blanc': Frantz Fanon, esclavage, race et racisme." *Actuel Marx* 38, no. 2 (2005): pp. 45–63.

———. *Le ventre des femmes: capitalisme, racialisation, féminisme* (Paris: Albin Michel, 2017).

Wittig, Monique. *The Straight Mind, and Other Essays* (Boston: Beacon Press, 1992).

X, Malcolm. "Message to the Grass Roots: November 10, 1963, Detroit," in *Malcom X Speaks*, ed. George Breitman (New York: Grove Press, 1965) pp. 3–17.

Weaving, a Craft for Thought
Writing and Thinking in Africa, or the Knot of the World's Great Narrative

Jean-Luc Raharimanana

Jean-Luc Raharimanana is a writer, poet, playwright, and director. Initially a journalist for Radio France Internationale, he first turned to teaching before committing himself fully to writing. A politically engaged artist, he is the author of over 20 works, including Revenir *(Paris: Payot/Rivages, 2018) and* Empreintes *(La Roque d'Anthéron: Vents d'ailleurs, 2015).*

Dakar, December 2017

Do we write for our contemporaries? Do we think for our contemporaries? For me – but not only for me – the answer is clearly no. The time of a book, just like the time of a thought, surpasses the life of an author and surpasses the life of a reader. To write is to stretch the past – toward the future. Unless one seeks to start a relationship with a particular readership, a seduction where finding recognition is the final aim, writing and thinking in Africa, or from an African perspective, leads into a minefield where the contemporary is the tension that could cause us to step in the wrong place. For far too long, African thought has been phagocytized, swallowed, and digested – centuries of successive Arab and Western domination have prevented a free narration of our relationship to the world.

It is time to pick up the narrative thread, from the beginning – accounting, of course, for the contingency and violence of history, but also lucidly identifying the occurrences of our alienation:

in what ways did we once find meaning in this world? In this humanity? How did we preserve our skins, our memories, from our nudity of being [*notre nudité d'être*]? How did we extend the territory of the possible of our futures?

To weave words is to find oneself at the site of both art and reconciliation: the art of painting what comes to our lips, reconciliation of our thoughts with what we feel, with what others make us feel. One can weave out of pleasure or to clothe oneself. One can clothe history, pick different colors, present oneself as one wishes; but one can also receive clothing – clothing that suits us and clothing that doesn't ...

To weave is to think of the future.

So, begin with a myth, without really telling the story, follow the thread of the narrative to reach what interests us: our nudity. By nudity, I mean the initial, fragile state in which we find ourselves facing the vastness, and even monstrousness, of the world; I mean the natural state into which we are inducted, on the same terms as all beings of the world; I mean the acknowledgment of our smallness, and of the challenge that awaits those of us who continue in our existence.

At the start of starts, who knows when, in the era of *fahizay* – in those times – human beings are naked and in great want: no sooner are newborns born than they die. Man and woman get together and ask themselves why Zanahary made them so, made them fragile and at the mercy of everything: at the mercy of the seasons, of the animals, of that internal weakness that exposes them to sickness before it begins the irremediable work of digging the chasm of death. The two decide to pose the question to the Sky; the man leaves, the woman stays behind to take care of the children – almost all of them dying.

The man will meet not with trials that require heroism (I told you that we would cut straight to the point, examining the nudity of man [*l'homme*]), not with trials that oblige him to perform this or that physical feat, but with Zanahary's strange ways. Exposed to the sun on a scorching, barren earth, zebus without hides suffer in a cloud of mosquitos and endure being bitten thousands of times. They have been there, these humped cattle without hides, since the birth of the world; there the mosquitos are, on the skinless flesh. The man attempts to help the zebus – wasted effort. The zebus tell him to continue his journey but to remember them when he meets Zanahary's daughter, since only the latter can deliver them from their misfortune.

The man will meet a butterfly caught in a spider's web and will be surprised to learn that beauty is susceptible of being taken captive – that such beautiful wings, colorful and so admirably designed, might be prisoners.

He negotiates with the spider for the liberation of the butterfly in exchange for several mosquitos. The spider accepts but does not break with its nature: "Whoever enters its home stays there." Grateful, the butterfly tells the man to remember it when he meets Zanahary's daughter.

The man will finally meet a blind woman guarding a well. Her empty eyes stare at the bottom of the well, as if fixed there eternally. She does not seem to notice the man's presence. No sooner does he approach her than she throws him into the hole. The man then finds himself on the other side: a fertile land, a mild land, a land where rice fields stretch as far as the eye can see.

The man arrives before Zanahary (I'm also skipping the story of the trials he underwent before getting there, in the presence of the creator god of feet and hands, of the North and the South, of the East and West, of the High and the Low, of the Seas and the Skies, of the Day and the Night, save to say that these are neither physical tests nor riddles to solve, but rather choices that essentially appeal to his humility – all of us have at some point in our lives faced such choices: the versions of the trials this man endures can thus be infinite). He does not sit on Zanahary's mat when the latter invites him to, since never in his life has he seen fabric, or such beautiful fabric. Neither does he eat from the god's plate of gold or silver; he does not eat the rice, even when it is served in a bowl made of coconut. He simply states the reason for his visit. Zanahary avers that it is indeed his daughter, the youngest, who has the solution to his problem, for she is the goddess of life and fertility: he need only recognize her and bring her back to earth ...

Zanahary presents his wife and his three daughters. They resemble one another like four peas in a pod. *Be careful not to make a mistake*, Zanahary says, *only one can follow you, otherwise you will be choosing misfortune, a misfortune even greater than the one you know now*. The man is at a loss for what to do when he notices a butterfly fluttering above one of the daughters' heads; he points to her; she is the youngest daughter. Zanahary tells them that they may go now and offers a bottle full of life as well as an ear of rice. They leave the Sky, followed by the butterfly.

The trip back proves uneventful, except for when they find themselves again before the spider, its web barring the entire passage. With a simple movement of his hand the man can push aside the web, but he is fascinated by the sight of the spider in the process of weaving its house. He asks it for permission to pass, the spider opens a path – and, from that day on, it sometimes happens that the spider visits the house of the humans, as an expression of hospitality and passage; from that day on, it aids us in keeping the mosquitos at bay and shows us the patience and ingenuity needed to take care of a house.

They arrive before the herd of zebus without hides. The man cannot hold back a pang of emotion; he gives several animals a little out of his bottle: they suddenly find themselves with new hides and tremendous vigor – so tremendous that, even though the mosquitos remain on their backs, this time they have no effect. Other animals approach: some without bones, some without this, some without that (this is the storyteller's chance to embellish the narrative a little and to say things that make the crowd laugh or participate in the telling – for example, how, owing to its incongruous requests, the chameleon ended up with such bulging eyes, such unstable colors, such a long tongue, etc.). In the end, a trickle of life is all that remains in the bottle. The man and Zanahary's daughter climb up on one of the zebus – storytellers bicker over the question of whether it is a male or a female zebu. We won't settle the matter here!

They arrive before the blind, old woman who asks them to use a needle to remove the purulent scabs that seal her eyelids. This they manage to do – thanks to Zanahary's daughter, especially. In a moment of unobstructed vision, the old woman opens the wells, the wells transform into a powerful river, the old woman's eyelids immediately shut again, the man and Zanahary's daughter (who had kept the needle) are carried off by the river – still on the zebu's back, but the strong surge of a wave knocks the animal over: Zanahary's daughter is dragged along the bottom while the man breaks the bottle against a protruding rock, the last trickle of life escapes, its tiny filament caught by the butterfly.

While the man manages to climb back onto the zebu's back, Zanahary's daughter does not rise back to the surface. She tells the man that she will stay there, at the bottom of the water. She tells him that he can come to see her any time, through songs, through prayers, through other means (I admit that it would take the whole night to name all the possibilities for reaching this deity who becomes the daughter of the water, in the river henceforth sacred and full with life).

On the back of his zebu, the man returns to his wife alone, with the ear of rice as his only trophy. (We did not forget this detail, did we? You will ask me how, after so many misadventures, the man was able to hang on to the rice.) He is still naked. His children are still not doing well. His wife has grown extremely thin. With the help of the zebu and the water which has risen to the edge of the village, the man cultivates the rice – storytellers also bicker over the origin of rice; we will tell them that this is the right version!

Having only a tiny filament [*filet*] of life, the butterfly soon dies. But it leaves a cocoon from which the man will recuperate thread for lambas – fabrics – so that he can dress his family: thread of fabric, continuation of the thread of life; the chrysalis metamorphoses into a butterfly; life goes on.

But, in order to weave, it is of course necessary to retrieve the needle that sank to the bottom of the river with Zanahary's daughter; the man will dive to the bottom so that he may negotiate with Zanahary's daughter and retrieve the needle for his wife's benefit. This is why in certain tribes the husband's dowry for his wife is a needle retrieved from the bottom of the water – a custom practiced above all in tribes of weavers.

The thread left by the butterfly is the last filament of life: it is fragile, rare, non-eternal. It is for this reason that humans die, not having been able to take advantage of the entire bottle offered by Zanahary, owing to the generosity man showed for the zebus and the other animals (terrible storyteller that I am, I forgot to tell you that, on the way back, the man and Zanahary's daughter also encountered moribund plants; the man did not fail to give them a little life).

And when they die, humans too entrust their last filaments of life to the butterfly; at that point, the particular life, the particular soul, goes back down, to be with Zanahary. When it comes to Zanahary's daughter, she is still around, in the water, making the earth fertile, caring for children, granting the prayers of Living Beings [*des Vivants*], but heaven help those who make the wrong wish!

The time of the tale having finished, now is our chance to talk! Let's avoid false modesty and not shrink from adopting the posture of the master – that is, of someone who dispenses knowledge to those eager to receive it – for who besides us can transmit our own stores of knowledge, our own cultures, free from the eye of the specialist, of the ethnologist, or of any other scholar? Emancipation also comes through the act of taking up and bearing a vision of ourselves, for such thinking has been denied our continent, Africa, for too long. It has been denied the Africa one calls "underdeveloped," the Africa one calls "developing," the Africa one calls "emergent" ... as if one were talking about a child who had not yet reached maturity. Never mind the contradiction that arises when people simultaneously affirm that Africa is the cradle of humanity, the land of the ancestors and of ancient wisdom.

I wanted to begin with this tale because it communicates a certain vision of life in Madagascar: this vision is *Ay*, a vision dear to my friend J. A. Ravelona, a painter of the soul and of the invisible ties that connect living Beings. I expressly said living Beings and not just human beings. "Living Beings" includes the animal, the plant.

Ay is life, in the form of a thread that circulates in being, through blood, sap, flesh, and bones. It is a fragile thread, subject to events, diseases, emotions, to ill will – and, happily, to goodwill too, to care.

Tradition has it that the thread that forms a cocoon is carried by the silkworm – such is life: one must pull the cocoon's thread without breaking it, delicately, with care. One unwinds the thread, one unwinds life. And, the entanglement of such threads, the entanglement of such lives, is what makes up society. Similarly, to produce a fabric, we start with a delicate thread. Each thread requires special care but, once knotted, woven together with another or others, it grows stronger: the one reinforces the other; no one can live alone. Narratives, in the form of motifs, come into being, are visible on the shared fabric. Such is the case for History and Destiny. Starting from a thread of no apparent importance – unique, individual, thin – we converge upon a universal scene.

One wears the fabric, one removes the fabric, one changes the fabric, one exchanges, discards, forgets, likes, dislikes, repairs, accepts, sews, resews, tears, dyes, puts away, gives, purchases, keeps. One may replace the word "fabric" with "culture," "history," "philosophy," "thought," "religion," etc. As the thread of centuries unspools, a nation, a country, changes fabrics, changes dress and appearance, but such dress and such appearances always issue from the contributions of others, from the entanglement – desired or not – of multiple destinies.

Africa was stripped bare, literally. It was presented as the land of savages walking naked in the savanna. The question was not even whether Africa had or soul or not – it was forced into slavery, colonized, evangelized, all for a good cause. Such nudity is always present in the collective unconscious when one talks about Africa.

Heat, idleness, lack of punctuality, contemplation of Nature, wild animals ...

Lack of fabric, lack of history, was that not what a president of the French Republic dared to state during a famous speech in Dakar? Moreover, whenever Africa is shown wearing clothes, it is dressed in feathers, or in leaves, or in natural materials – without ingenuity, outside of civilization.

In our tale, nudity is not connected to the absence of such civilization, nor to indecency, nor to a lack of culture; it raises the question of the human being's fragility, from the moment of its arrival in the world: having nothing, prey to everything. The nude man had to act and solve the question of survival.

Putting on or changing clothes – even if the act is governed by a collective code – partakes in individual liberty. Under slavery and colonization, however, this individual liberty would disappear, just as the liberty of the whole continent would simultaneously slip away.

The Church decides to dress Africa: pants, shirt, robe. Traditional clothing is strongly disadvised when not prohibited. This is another step in the negation of identity, since, as everyone knows, the cowl makes the monk [*l'habit fait le moine*]! Africa abandoned its fabrics, its materials, and the activities that go with them; dressing in a Western fashion was soon considered – what am I saying? was soon imposed – as "modern," "advanced," "in style." Why else don one's own alienation over one's skin? It wasn't for nothing that on the Asian subcontinent Gandhi took up the spinning wheel for the purpose of making his own clothes and incited his people to do likewise: to retain its dignity, its independence, its identity, but also to find an economic response to the colonizer's industrial textile monopoly. The spinning wheel is now a symbol of liberty on the Indian flag, and traditional clothing, or clothing inspired by it, is now worn habitually and on a daily basis. Other African nationalists have learned the lesson: Jomo Kenyatta, Mobutu ... Instead of the uniform and uniformity of the colonizer, the local costume and the defiant diversity of the resistor. Slaves were clothed in rags and the bare necessities to conceal their genitals, spruced up when they waited on the more highly "evolved." Uncle Tom has never changed his clothes. The colonized go to church in a suit and tie – women wear dresses, their bodies covered from head to toe. Before embarking on the conquest of its liberty, Africa had to literally confront both the nudity and the costume that had been forced upon it.

Stepping back is necessary in weaving to obtain a more global sense of the work, just as it is with details and fine embroidery [*les petites mains*]: the threads may grow so tangled that one doesn't know how to continue, the stiches are not sufficiently regular, etc. Africa needs observers, thinkers, and individuals earnestly working on the question of reconstruction: people capable of escaping the present emergency, the permanent emotion that the continent's situation produces in us, for its fabric, in shreds since the dark days of the slave trade, continues to unravel. The dictators did not help the situation, nor the carelessness of governments, nor the wars, nor the corruption, nor the endless exploitation of natural resources ... How are we to untangle the threads? Where is the alienation to be found? Where are the victories to be found? Which are the traumas? Which constitute the new ways of relating to society, to politics, to history, to the economy, etc.? How are we to pick the work back up and not forget a single element?

A particularly important tendency in colonization insists on forming ties [*tisser des liens*], establishing relations [*nouer des relations*] – one need only listen to the speeches of diplomats and politicians to notice the prefabricated formulas: our two countries shall band together, shall strengthen ties ... Of necessity, ties have indeed been formed – the Living develop fondness for and attachments to one another in every context, including violence – but such weaving began with a great tear, the ripping to shreds of the African fabric. Every thread of this fabric was affected; no part of its surface was spared.

Before continuing, I would like to share an anecdote – no one knows whether it was a historic reality or mere myth experienced as if it was real, but that's beside the point ...

At the time of his campaign for hegemony on the island, the great King Andrianampoinimerina faced another powerful king. They challenged one another through the medium of *kabary* – the grand oration. Andrianampoinimerina showed his laba – his toga – in the middle of which he had earlier pierced a hole – in the place where the kingdom of Antananarivo was located. He told his rival: "We come from the same country; if I begin to rip my lamba from the middle, everything will quickly be reduced to shreds. You are on the edge; you can rip the fabric from where you are, but the tear you make will be easily mended. Join me! Be my ally! Be my kinsman!" The other powerful king recognized the wisdom of Andrianampoinimerina and banded together with him.

The question to ask is the following: In what part of our fabric did the tear begin? At our centers, in our profoundest depths? In this case, should the fabric perhaps be discarded? At our edges or peripheries? With the possibility of repair? How are we to gauge the loss? How do we choose what to keep and what to discard? Must one always go through the effort of restitching, of repairing, at the risk of being poorly dressed? Is it necessary to keep the patchwork? Out of past miseries, inherited rags, can we produce something original, invent a style? Is the trace left by the tear always necessary? Must memory always be worn and seen? Is it possible to continue today with the same tears? Is it necessary to start over entirely? Invent something completely new – but, I wonder, can that really exist – something that arises from the earth with no reference to what was already done ...?

Recognizing the tear begins by first identifying it: the loom will not work if there is a rip, one must figure out what's stuck before one can go forward. Since independence, the African continent has experienced one hitch after another, without taking time to step back, to analyze the situation, to make a choice. Wanting to heal means examining the wound, producing a diagnosis, providing care, observing the scar, and starting afresh from new flesh, from new skin. Confronting history is a question neither of victimization nor of masochism. Recognizing that Africa has suffered is well and good; seeing where it continues to suffer is better. As in a trial, the victim needs to be officially recognized for living to be possible again. To say that Africa was a victim does not indulge the pain – it seeks justice and starts the healing process. It is about finding the tear and stitching the time of life together again – a present, a future. To soothe. To heal. And then to find pleasure in oneself and in life. To invigorate *Ay* and every fiber of which we are made.

We said at the beginning of this text that, for too long, African thought has been phagocytized, swallowed, digested. African thought is not dead. It is in languages, proverbs, tales, myths, literature, music, painting, in the arts, in the artisanate, in initiatory rites, in the philosophies and worldviews that nourish ceremonies, folklore, family bonds, social ties, etc. Successive centuries of domination block the free narration of our relations with the world, but, in the end, those times were unable to efface us from the society of the Living [*des Vivants*]. Africa is here; Africa is in us. It is also in others, in jazz and modern music, in painting, in food, in the imaginary, in the very blood of humanity. We have to celebrate this resilience, to understand how, in order to survive, our ancestors were obliged to invest the other and persevere intact in its clothes. Oppressors may harm their victims, but they do not escape untouched; the dye does not always pick what to color when multiple fabrics intertwine and tangle.

So we need to continue the narrative, spin our own writings again. Such spinning is both a conquest of freedom and a free painting of the course of our history. The spinning cannot content itself with the contemporary moment. It should be the mat on which one day – quite far off, as far off as possible – our children, and the children of our children, will take their seats, sitting so that they may fully live the narrative that we have freely chosen in order to participate in the World's Great Narrative.

We need not fear the future, be afraid of what's to come. Our children will know how to meet it so long as the transmission is not broken, so long as the loom continues to work. The apparatus shows its utility; one must service it and be careful not to break it. This transmission is not destined exclusively for our children, but for the children of all the Living [*les Vivants*]. The victim knows pain and, under no circumstances, wishes to relive or reproduce it. In one of my plays, *Rano, rano* – created at the Théâtre les Bambous on Reunion Island – I went so far as to say that *the victims must educate those who debased them, the victims must bring clarity to the torment of days*. It is for this reason that there exist museums about repression: museums about the Shoah, about slavery, about colonization – too few in France, alas, and still so few in Africa, to transmit the monstrosity of these acts to everyone. The experience of pain is a form of knowledge. Future oppressions will traffic in the same evils; we are already familiar with the harm they inflict – who, indeed, would say otherwise? Even a small child feels the negativity of domination; it is a matter of explaining these often insidious processes.

One must depoliticize the debate, decolonize the arguments and the approaches, demystify, flip perspectives, shake up received ideas, biases, etc., confront our own ghosts – our ghosts of today, the persistently high levels of violence, massacres, genocide (Rwanda, Burundi, Congo …), land grabs, deforestation … and one must change clothes if necessary, when it is definitely not working, when it itches, when it is too tight, when we find out that it does not look good …

The thread is infinite. The butterfly lives for a day, but what a day it is! A day of light, a day of colors, a day of levity and liberty, a day of beauty! The butterfly is a generation: generations die and make way for others. The thread is always there, in the cocoon that the chrysalis leaves behind century after century, for as long as there is *Ay*, for as long as there is the breath of life, for as long as there is energy circulating within us ...

Part II

Africa and the New Western Figures of Personal Status Law

Abdoul Aziz Diouf

Abdoul Aziz Diouf is a lecturer in the Faculty of Law at the University Cheikh Anta Diop of Dakar in Senegal. His field of research includes private international law, family law, the law of civil liability, the philosophy of law, and legal theory.

Introduction

As the person's first place of abode, the body is a site of diverging representations issuing from different civilizations. Owing to their anthropological structure, discourses about the body separate legal cultures from each other. By virtue of its multiple articulations and attributes – sex, sexuality, marital status, filiation, etc. – the body raises questions of identity that legal science [*la science juridique*] treats under a special category: *le statut personnel* or "personal status."[1]

What does personal status include? Its ideological nature implies its relativity in terms of comparative law. Its principal function being to define "Man" [*l'Homme*] in his axiological and social expression, personal status takes on a heterogeneity of meanings depending on whether it is understood on the basis of Western legal models (*civil law* and *common law*) or contemporary African forms. Nonetheless, this hermeneutic gap, which distinguishes the normative arrangements [*montages normatifs*] of Africa and the West with respect to the construction of personal status, is not ontological. Western positivism, whose pre-Cartesian roots can be observed in the twelfth-century "medieval revolution of the interpreter" that accompanied Early Scholasticism,[2] marks a point where the Romano-canonical legal tradition diverges from other legal civilizations in how it conceptualizes the law and, by extension, man's legal status. After having subjected nature to its unlimited power, postmodern Western legalism subsequently accorded itself a new object: the human.[3] Infinitude – technoscience's principal characteristic when it is put forward as the central method for defining personal status – constitutes a negation of an entire legal tradition based upon the alterity of the human species. The history of Western law is unique by virtue of its having renounced its dogmatic nature. In accordance with the priority granted sociological explanations and "efficiency," it is now scientific "reason," and not the law, that founds the domain of the *words* and *things* in social space. From such a perspective, personal status, which owes much to the West's current scientistic paradigm, emerges out of a biologistic worldview supplemented by modern psychoanalysis. That Western legal systems keep their distance from metaphysical pretensions makes the genealogical problematic a feature of our Brave New World. Novel legal institutions, unprecedented in the history of law, have started to take account of the reification of the body observable in the new dynamics of Euro-American societies:[4] same-sex marriage, transgender identities, surrogate motherhood, post-mortem insemination, the freezing of oocytes, etc. All fantasies aside, the explosive transformation that biomedicine has sparked in how personal status is understood in the West lends legitimacy to the fears surrounding transhumanism[5] and posthumanism.[6]

The new Western epistemology, characterized by the Subject's appropriation of the body, has not emerged without repercussions for non-Western legal systems.[7] Africa is an example. The circulation of legal subjects beyond the borders of their states of origin further extends the analysis of the impact of these new Western figures of personal status in international private law. In other words: can Africa still be impacted by a Western scientism that its legal systems do not acknowledge? Legal fiction [*la fiction du droit*], and more specifically the fiction of international private law, would answer this question in the affirmative. It is because the geographic frontiers that states set down in the abstract are not systematically convertible into barriers that readily block the penetration of institutions belonging to foreign civilizations that a serious reflection on the conditions of their reception becomes a legal necessity. The inscription of others into an intimacy that is foreign [*une intimité étrangère*] – an occurrence consubstantial with human history itself – occupies a special place on the legal agenda. The use of methodologies developed by scholars of comparative law who specialize in conflicts between legal systems makes it possible to take up the problem of civilizational difference [*l'altérité civilisationnelle*] in a manner appropriate to its truly multilateral, relational dimension. What should we make of this legacy of dialogue in the legal present? Today, a survey of how Western and African legal systems coordinate with one another about the power that subjects have over their bodies reveals an aporia. Nonetheless, this impasse is not grounded in a radical difference between Western and African representations of personal status, although such a difference does constitute a conflict of civilizations,[8] whose historiography predates Samuel Huntington.[9] The introduction of a neo-functionalism into Western methods of resolving conflicts over personal status heralds a coming crisis that will shake international private law concerning the human body. The change in paradigm directly reconfigures the contours of the body's identity for African subjects in the West, but it also calls into question the status of the Western subject in Africa.

The Body of the African Subject in the West

The legal identity of the African subject's body (B), far from depending on its political space of origin, currently finds itself subjected to the new metamorphoses that affect personal status in Western legal systems (A).

The current state of personal status in the West

In the West, the subject's identity in social space was traditionally based upon a principle of distancing [*distanciation*]. Politics was something that interfered in the relation between subjects and their integration in society. In how it was staged, the totemic quality of personal status rested upon a *taboo* or a *prohibition*: personal status was the other face of *Oedipus*, of *Narcissus* ... The ritualized association of legal personality with a subject understood as distinct from its body would find a corollary in the unavailability and immutability of the legal subject.[10]

The rudiments of personal status in the West could not have developed without an understanding of the world as an object of experience possessing a metaphysical structure. With the Enlightenment, the narrative of "Man" as a rite, as a totem, became a requiem. In legal science, one of the principal consequences of Western legalism was the mutation of the (objective) *law* into subjective *laws*. The hypertrophy of the individual thus marked the arrival of a new paradigm in the conceptualization of personal status. Western "reason's" break with all axiology obliged the state – the classic guarantor of personal status's theatricality – to share its monopoly over the writing of the social *text* with the Subject. The subject's appropriation of its identity heralded a pluralism of personal status. This phenomenon of identity "à la carte," a striking feature of contemporary personal status in the West, opens a veritable Pandora's box with respect to the genealogical constitution of the human person. The disappearance of taboo from the sphere of personal status encourages a "butcher's conception of filial bonds" [*une conception "bouchère de la filiation"*] in Euro-American legal systems.[11] The economism that currently permeates Western legal systems has created a market of filiation in which merchants in lab coats supervise the new industry of manufacturing the human. Surrogate motherhood,[12] post-mortem insemination,[13] the freezing of oocytes,[14] medically assisted procreation for same-sex couples,[15] etc.: by treating the human as a mere physical–chemical object, the advances of personal status in the West reduce genealogy to a simple question of biology.

Today, it is within the confines of this liberalism, marked by the reification of the person, that the body of the African subject in the West must seek out its territory of expression.

The territory of expression of the African body in the West

The unshakable nature of the subject's legal identity imposes itself upon the fiction of spatial divisions.[16] Sex, name, filiation, conjugal status, religion, etc. – in principle, attributes understood to be consubstantial with the person who possesses them can be exported, irrespective of the state in question. By definition, personal status is tied to nationality and not to the specific territory that happens to host the person. With the exception of certain common law countries and particularly the United States,[17] this Savignian tradition holds in all legal civilizations.[18] According to this line of thought, the presence of African subjects in the West does not, in theory, amount to a negation of their initial corporeality [*corporéité initiale*]. Two Malians who get married in France will find the validity of their union subject to the conditions of Malian and not French law; an unmarried Nigerian woman who gives birth in Spain will find the status of her child (legitimate, natural, adulterine, etc.) determined by Nigerian and not Spanish law; a Senegalese man who passes away in Germany can be subject to either Senegalese or to German laws of succession ... When African identitarian patrimonies are exported to the West for the purpose of supporting Africans living abroad, this transfer is accompanied by a technique of distanciation that, in each instance, denies African subjects the possibility of renouncing the application of the legal rules of their states of origin. The inaccessibility of Western law for African subjects, far from being identifiable with a *control* of their bodies, is motivated by a concern for otherness [*un souci d'altérité*]. As a consequence, the indivisibility of legal identity of the person allows international private law to ensure the primacy of cultural relativism in the international sphere. The fact that personal status is linked to national law and not to the subject's domicile (dwelling place) thus assures the cultural unity of all the nationals of a given state, regardless of where they might be located geographically. Mancini grasped this political dimension of personal status earlier than most.[19] Owing to its economic precariousness and the instability of some of its governments, Africa is a continent of emigration. Despite the fact that many of its citizens live in the West, Africa can nonetheless use the conception of personal status advanced by international private law to restore cultural ties between its local subjects and those living in diaspora.

Alas, the tradition of placing otherness at the foundation of international private law is progressively fading away.[20] The westernization of the world (i.e., globalization) in the legal sphere leads to a negation of civilizational relativism. The integralism [*l'integrisme*] of (Western) human rights has in recent years modified the classical trajectory of international private law. The current dominance of sociologism results in the disconnection of personal status from nationality and its association instead with the foreign subject's dwelling place.[21] In this respect, the identity of the African body is rewritten by the Western *text*. The shift of personal status from nationalism to territorialism [*territorialisme*][22] within Western international private law restricts the field in which African identity can express itself in the West.[23] In terms of methodology, functionalism serves the narcissism of Western legal systems. The African body's specific range of possibilities is denied in two ways: on the one hand, African subjects have gained access to Western legal identities from which they were traditionally barred; on the other hand, these same subjects have lost their ability to access their own, African personal status when they are in the West.

Motivated by the goal of assimilation, granting Africans access to Western personal status marks the lapsing of the principle of distancing as a driving force of international private law. The African subject comes to enjoy Western identity through legal voluntarism[24] and through a multiplication of rules of conflict said to be "of material coloration" [*à coloration matérielle*].[25] Under the auspices of "human rights," Western legal institutions such as transgender identity, same-sex marriage,[26] surrogate motherhood,[27] the freezing of oocytes,[28] etc., are within reach of African populations living in certain Western countries today. In other words, African corporeality is currently in a position to reinvent itself in the West. The mutation of the African body induced by Western legal models produces a fragmentation of African personal status in the international domain. Depending on whether they are in Africa or the West, African subjects are divided in their identitarian construction. In this respect, space performs the task of breaking apart the political unity of African corporeality.

On the margins of the opening up of Western personal status to Africans, *control* over the African body in the West is also achieved by barring that body's access to the identity conferred by its state of origin. Police statutes, public policy, the principle of proximity, and the instrumentalization of the notion of "evading the law" [*fraude à la loi*] are a few of the many techniques that have all but prohibited the circulation of certain African legal institutions in the West. Regardless of whether such legal institutions merit re-evaluation in the contemporary context,[29] it remains the case that African cultural objects such as polygamy, masculine privilege in Muslim succession, the determination of the married couple's domicile by the husband, hierarchies in filiation (e.g., legitimate child, natural child, adulterine child), etc., recoil before the current expansion of Western public policy.

Now that we have reviewed the African body's negation in the West, it is only natural that we turn to the various ways in which African legal systems have responded to the expression of the Western body in its current scientistic articulations.

The Body of the Western Subject in Africa

The de-ideologization [*désidéologisation*] of African legal systems presupposes that these spaces accept the Western body, unless more thought is given to the possibility of a future Black African *ordre public*.

The presupposed acceptance of the Western body in Africa

A quick digression on the legal instruments that regulate the diversity of identities present in Africa suffices to illustrate their tropism toward European models. The bilateral method, a characteristic feature of Romano-Germanic law, has migrated into nearly all African legal systems. Grounded in a materialist understanding, bilateralism presupposes a world structured according to the binary of *being* and *having*. Viewing the world through this lens, legal science divides what it sees into three categories: personal status (the identitarian problematic), things (the universe of goods), and obligations (contract, liability, etc.). Borrowed from the West, such Savignian materialism (the bilateral method) breaks with the Black African legal tradition whose categories are essentially grounded in a perception of the universe as a metaphysical order, contrary to the simplistic Western dichotomy of *being* and *having*. The bilateral method was conceptualized in the nineteenth century on the basis of a postulated unity of European culture, the product of a Judeo-Christian heritage with an added touch of Enlightenment reason. The presupposition of a common Western identity necessitated a neutral method (bilateralism) of resolving conflicts over personal status between Western subjects of different states.[30]

The structuring of private international law in Africa according to an exogenous Western epistemology implies the disarticulation of Africa's identitarian space.[31] The a priori application of the bilateral method in the category of personal status allows for the Western body's installation in Africa, except in cases where its real incompatibility with African *ordre public* is confirmed.

Prolegomena to an African ordre public *that would limit the range of possibilities of the Western body*

In principle, the inclusion of transgender identity, same-sex marriage, scientific methods of procreation, etc., in the category of personal status encourages their reception within African legal systems. Let the following three cases illustrate how the bilateral method's neutrality is currently realized on the African content.

First case: two Dutch men, officially married in Holland, chose afterward to change their domicile to Congo-Brazzaville. Their matrimonial status produces a conflict with respect to the ownership of a piece of property. In principle, the referral of the Congolese judge should grant jurisdiction to Dutch law, which is the national law of the same-sex partners (and, in principle, thereby validate the expression of same-sex marriage in Congo-Brazzaville).

Second case: a Swedish man officially becomes a Swedish woman in the eyes of Swedish law. She (or is it he?) marries a Spanish man in Finland. After the marriage, the Spanish husband passes away in Togo, leaving behind a considerable estate in that country. Can the surviving transgender spouse obtain from the Togolese judge recognition of her title to inheritance? In principle, yes! The bilateral structure of Togolese law grants jurisdiction to Spanish law (the national law of the deceased husband) and Spanish law recognizes transgender identity and, by extension, the Swedish woman's status as an heir.

Third case: a biological mother from California, in agreement with her gestational surrogate and by means of a surrogacy agreement, becomes a legal parent under California law. Afterward, she marries a Senegalese man and acquires Senegalese nationality. By this process, she hopes that her child by surrogacy can also profit from Senegalese nationality. Taken in the abstract, Senegalese laws concerning nationality do not, in principle, bar the acquisition of Senegalese nationality by a child whose mother became Senegalese by naturalization.

In each of these three working hypotheses, the new Western figures of personal status use the bilateralism of the Savignian method like a Trojan horse, allowing the Euro-American body to penetrate African space. Nonetheless, the so-called reception of such new Western identities within African legal systems is nothing more than a presumption. African magistrates, once they judge that, despite their apparent applicability, such new Western identities are in fact contrary to *ordre public*, have the power to forbid their application. Basing themselves on the *ordre public*, the Congolese judge will be able to apply the local law that negates the conjugal status of the Dutch same-sex couple, the Togolese judge will be able to deny the transgender Swedish woman's title to inheritance, and the Senegalese magistrate will be able to refuse Senegalese nationality to the child born of a surrogacy agreement. But what does *ordre public* mean?

In private international law, *ordre public* – literally, 'public order' – incarnates the limit to otherness; it is the frontier of tolerance that a legal system can accept. In its definition, *ordre public* refers to the values that a human society deems fundamental for its longevity – those without which its legal system would lack coherence. In this respect, *ordre public* attempts to prevent the anthropological structure of international private law from becoming hostage to an exaggerated cultural relativism.[32]

While *ordre public* is easy to define, specifying the term's content is a very complex issue in Africa. African legal systems are palimpsests. In international private law, *ordre public* is principally concerned with identitarian coherence, and yet the sedimentation of earlier Arab and Western invasions (the continent's Muslim civilization and its European colonization, respectively) in contemporary Africa have made identifying such a coherence very tenuous. Africa is the most syncretic, the most culturally mixed place in the world. Churches, mosques, synagogues, sacred woods, agnostic faiths, etc.: all these sites vie with each other in the production of the African subject's identity. Black African, Arab Muslim, and Western civilizations – with the possibility of soon being joined by Chinese civilization – babble on, each producing different echoes within African legal systems. The hybridity of African legal systems makes grasping their internal coherence challenging. In contrast to Western judges who are conscious of the civilizational unity of their legal system, African magistrates, in their pursuit of the *ordre public*, have to confront a whole range of identities [*un camaïeu identitaire*]. Faced with the impasse provoked by the positivity of Africa's identitarian texts, African magistrates will have to establish the intelligibility of the *ordre public* on the basis of social normativity. The future of the new figures of Western personal status in Africa should be approached in light of the dogmas that lie at the origin of the continent's normative arrangements [*montages normatifs*]. When constructed upon a meta-positive basis,[33] the Black African imaginary pictures human beings as finite and, in so doing, sets a limit to identitarian constructions. Picturing man exclusively through an insupportable, positivist lens, Western scientism radically distances itself from the frames that produce *Homo africanus*. The aporetic views that these two civilizations hold about Man [*l'Homme*] justify African magistrates' use of *ordre public* to avoid a piercing amplification of the asynchrony of their legal systems.

Rethinking Islam

Or, the Oxymoron of "Secular Theocracy"

Rachid Id Yassine

Rachid Id Yassine *holds a doctorate in sociology from the School of Advanced Studies in Social Sciences (EHSS) in Paris, and is a lecturer in the Center for the Study of Religions at Gaston Berger University in Saint-Louis, Senegal, where he also coordinates the African Observatory of the Religious. Trained in sociology, anthropology, and religious studies, his work focuses principally on Islam and regionalism. He is the author of several articles and books, including* Rethinking Identity: Essay of Critical Sociology on the Identity of Fact, *translated by Caroline Cadiet (Perpignan: Halfa, 2015).*

I must begin by making several disclaimers that the complexity of my subject matter, on the one hand, and the formal constraints of this brief text, on the other, oblige me to make. Given the discursive order in which it is articulated, there is no doubt that my argument will strike some as somewhat provocative or even subversive. Today, the words we use to talk about the religious in general, and about Islam in particular, are highly charged, drawing on a range of different registers in which affect typically holds the upper hand. With my contribution, I thus run the risk of disturbing the relatively fixed and reassuring points of reference with which public debate habitually treats Islam.

To be sure, public discourse exhibits a far greater diversity than it might seem. And yet, despite its plurality, such speech is organized to form a discursive order. To be brief, it is possible to clearly distinguish at least three types of discourse that, complementing one another in their complex, technical interrelations, together form a whole. To illustrate them, I will make use of the different discursive registers foregrounded by Gilles Deleuze and Félix Guattari, and follow Dominique Wolton's practice of distinguishing social spaces on a functional basis.[1]

Very summarily put, first there is *media discourse*, which participates in the register of *affect* whenever its principal role amounts to reassuring and assuring the *flow* of information and the *expression* of society's concerns in the *common space* [*l'espace commun*]. In this respect, media discourses work together to retroactively maintain the society's *cultural order* and its *aesthetic* norms. In practice, media and conventional literature gather together and offer up both the things which *affect* society and the things for which society shows *affection*.

Then there is *political discourse*: that which has or aims to have the force of law. Its register is that of the *percept* to the degree that, in *political space* [*l'espace politique*], one is concerned with making *decisions* and thereby with stating the appropriate course of action to take with respect to the outside world and alterity, according to the perception that one (passively) has of them or that one (actively) makes of them.

Finally, *ideological discourse* applies itself to supplying the motives, principles, and logics of justification and legitimation for what society feels (*affect*) and perceives (*percept*). Ideological discourse thus falls under the register of the *concept* whenever it presides over a discussion that, taking place in *public space* [*l'espace public*], promises to provide a coherent understanding of the world – that is, it sees to the construction of a society's *symbolic order* and of the *ethical* norms on which social action can be based.

Naturally, contemporary public discourse about the religious varies according to the contexts and circumstances in which it is articulated. As internally diverse as it may be, public discourse always ends up being translated and expressed in the form of one of the discursive orders. When it comes to the case of contemporary public discourse about Islam, it is clear to everyone that the discursive apparatuses involved offer different, conflicting affections, perceptions, and conceptions of Islam. Chronic polemics and controversies being the privileged mode of public debate on these issues, the discussion of Islam in public space predictably finds itself at an impasse.

It is important to note that one of the reasons for this situation is related to the ethnocentrism of the scholarly discourses with which one has struggled to explain or understand what Islam is. These discourses employ languages and imaginaries that have been strongly marked – even traumatized – by a conflictual relationship to the religious [*au religieux*]. For the scholar whose thought aims at the real [*le réel*], there exists a gulf between the discourse of actors and their practices, between social representations of reality and social reality itself. The idea of secularism [*laïcité*] illustrates this situation perfectly.

And I willingly accept a certain risk of being misunderstood, or only understood with resistance, by minds for whom bringing together the secular idea [*l'idée laïque*] and Islamic fact [*le fait islamique*] is – really, and not ideally – an unthinkable proposition. It is interesting to note, for example, that when Hesna Cailliau turns to Islam in her study of religions she stresses that "the Hanafi school [historically, the first school of Islamic jurisprudence] developed a *secular* jurisprudence *avant la lettre*."[2] But the most eloquent example is certainly the oxymoron that Louis Gardet took from Louis Massignon:[3] after a lifetime devoted to the study of Islam, Massignon came to the conclusion that "Islam is a *secular* and egalitarian theocracy"![4]

There is something about this seeming oxymoron that invites us to leave behind binary thinking and to revise our categories of analysis, in order that we might grasp the reality of Islamic secularism or secular Islam that other observers find so enigmatic.[5] It is a welcome pretext for refreshing critical reflection in light of a new set of stakes independent of the various figures of political Islam and the plurality of secular models. By no means are we merely playing with words, distorting the relevant imaginaries so as to Islamize secularism or secularize Islam. This need not be the case, since the better approach is to base oneself in the empirical reality of the social facts [*faits sociaux*] and apply oneself to making them intelligible with the help of thought, tools, and scientific methods.

Moreover, from the perspective of what Jean-Paul Charnay has called "deep Islam" [*l'islam profond*], Islam's empirical diversity appears as an argument for the singularity of its unique, cosmological architecture, which connects religion with politics without ever confounding them. From Salafism to Sufism, and exempting neither its most doctrinaire nor its most liberal versions, one could indeed claim that Islam is religiously secular or secularly religious, though only on the condition that one specify that secularism does not imply a necessary rejection of transcendence. Without such a condition, it is worth noting, secularism itself becomes religious and capable of being institutionalized in the form of what Raymond Aron has called a "secular religion" [*religion séculière*], or in the Rousseauist notion of a "civil religion," revived by Jean Baubérot and seemingly corroborated by references to a "secular spirituality" and a "secular morality" in public debates.[6]

In practice, some maintain that secularism is a value (ideological) that one upholds, rather than being solely – and already – a principle (political) that one respects. This debate is not audible in countries with Muslim majorities; in these countries, secularism is generally perceived as univocal. The ambivalence that Muslim countries show toward Freemasons is symptomatic of social imaginaries that are circumspect with respect to the secularism associated with the group. The latter is understood by opposition to Islam and presented, in one way or another, as adjunct to democracy. To cite only the most recent example: various pressures have led to the postponement of the 26th "African and Malagasy Humanist and Fraternal Meeting" that was supposed to take place in Dakar in early February 2018.

Nonetheless, one must insist on the heterogeneity of the Muslim world's experiences of democracy. For example, if Islam in the Maghreb and Islam in Sub-Saharan Africa have much in common, they also exhibit differences that are just as important. While it is true that these African societies have, at least in part, been forged by the same religion, it is no less the case that, owing to the different social and political forces animating their respective public spaces, the nation-states of North Africa express their relation to the secular idea [*l'idée laïque*] differently than those of West Africa.

Moreover, if secularism and democracy are often presented as interdependent, we have also learned – from the experiences of Turkey, Iraq, and Tunisia, if nowhere else – that this is not always the case. Dictatorships have been able to establish (or to establish themselves upon) secularism as an ideological tool for the political regulation of the religious. Whereas Western experiences of secularism have generally buttressed themselves on democracy, it is no accident that authoritarian versions of secularism have emerged in countries with Muslim majorities where Islam represented (and still seems to represent) a social and political force whose popularity the ruling police or military regime has sought to neutralize.

Rethinking Islam requires taking note of the effectiveness of secularization in contemporary Muslim societies, on the basis of a critical reading of conventional discourses on the relationship between religion and politics in Islam. From Albania to Senegal, from Turkey to Ethiopia, and not exempting Syria and Tunisia, a number of countries with Muslim majorities invoke secularism in order to fix the limits of public order. Today, Muslim countries as a group are again interrogating, more or less directly and more or less violently, the relationships that exist between democracy and secularism. The recent military coups against the democratically elected presidential regimes of Egypt and Turkey – the first successful, the second not – as well as the Muslim Brotherhood's political activism in Senegal all bear witness to the ambivalent role that secularism plays. If such facts oblige us to question the viability of secular democracy in countries with Muslim majorities, they do so on the basis of politics and not the religious. Nonetheless, it would appear that at least three conditions are prerequisite to this possibility.

To be specific, it is important that one first break with the Christian-centered model of secularization [*sécularisation*], according to which secularism [*laïcité*] is unthinkable in Islamic contexts. This evolutionary narrative figures secularization as a singular process grounded in the religious experience of societies that historically have been shaped by Christianity, societies which continue to put their own experience forward as both universal and necessary. Now, this is simply not the case. Other societies have their own experiences of modernity, which is necessarily multiple.[7] And, if religion is a political institution in "Christian societies," politics is a religious institution in "Muslim societies." In the first case, the social order is conditioned by religious faith; in the second, it is governed by political reasoning [*la raison politique*]. As Réda Benkirane astutely points out, one would have to be wholly uninformed, or else very dim-witted, to preach the primacy of reason over faith to societies whose own political experiments with rationalism predate modern Europe's by several centuries. Designating less the ebbing of religion's influence on society than the ebbing of its visibility in society, secularization can hardly be understood as a singular process.

Next, one should take note of the consensual separation between political and religious orders in contemporary Muslim societies, irrespective of whether this separation is achieved through what one calls official Islam, political Islam, liberal Islam, or Islamic brotherhood. Ultimately, it is permissible to regard Islam as a potential contributor to the secularization of society from the moment it advances a vision of the world in which the religious and the political are incessantly being negotiated according to local democratic conditions.

From here, one would certainly want to re-examine the contemporary state of Islamism [*islamisme*]. But such an inquiry would profit from being pursued with reference to the development of *laicism* [*laïcisme*] as a different model for regulating the religious. *Laicism* represents an ideological exacerbation of the secular principle [*de la laïcité*], and of secularism [*sécularisme*] more generally. It is secularism in the service of cultural fundamentalism – which, for its part, I call "Occidentalism." This fundamentalism encompasses a set of aesthetic, mythical, and ideological attitudes that together help to prop up the dominance of an imaginary, instrumentalized West. Occidentalism is not to be understood as the flip side of Edward Said's Orientalism; it is not the ambivalent offshoot of a fantasized West that one dreams of dominating. Although some commentators press for its adoption, this definition contradicts the Occidentalism incarnated by the nineteenth-century Russian reformists who pushed for the adoption of Western cultural values. Occidentalism is thus better understood as a cultural fundamentalism that vindicates the supremacy of a mythical West that one wishes to see dominant. Here too it is no accident that in the media Islam took center stage as "belligerent" resistor to the West's "well-meaning" hegemony only after the Cold War.

In societies with Muslim majorities, public space is the stage for a more or less violent rivalry between partisans of these two ideological options – Islamism and Occidentalism – which nonetheless agree that secularism and Islam are mutually exclusive. If, for both of these options, to be, and especially to behave, entirely Muslim or, conversely, faithfully secular remains an impossibility, it is because each one understands itself as a cosmopolitanism contesting, from its point of view, the "globality" [*mondialité*] of the other.

Rereading the religious experiences of political power in traditionally Christian and Muslim countries allows those who cannot do without such binaries to conceive the possibility of secularism in Islam and Islam in secularism without falling into reductive comparisons or mobilizing partisan logics and simplifying divisions. If the categories used to apprehend and evaluate the religious and the political are different, it should also be remembered that, by and large, the terminology of social sciences comes from Western societies. For his part, Henri Sanson already noted this problem at the beginning of his article on secularism in Algeria. He wrote that it can indeed "seem paradoxical to talk about secularism in a Muslim country! After all, doesn't Western terminology [*le langage occidental*] train us to think that secularism exists only where there is a distinction between faith and reason, or else between the spiritual and the temporal, and, finally, where there is an institutional separation between church and state?"[8] Even when one employs such *Western terminology*,[9] one realizes that religion and politics – if not theoretically, then certainly empirically – have never really been confused in Islam. This is no anachronism. And it is just as secularism demands.

If Islamism confuses them and Occidentalism isolates them, contemporary Africa finds itself at the confluence where religion and politics meet. Africa offers a promising stage for the joining of secularism and democracy in societies with Muslim majorities, upon the condition that one avoid the Islamist amalgam of religious and political orders and refuse the Occidentalist insistence on their illusory separation. Otherwise, one is driven into paradoxes and oxymorons by which one comes to see Massignon's definition of Islam as "secular theocracy" as nothing but what Simon Njami would call "gros-mot-logie" – that is, a pedantic science of obscenities.

Bibliography

Aron, Raymond. "L'avenir des religions séculières." *La France libre* 8, no. 45 (1944): pp. 210–17.

Baubérot, Jean. "Existe-t-il une religion civile républicaine?" *French Politics, Culture & Society* 25, no. 2 (2007): pp. 3–18.

Cailliau, Hesna. *L'esprit des religions: connaître les religions pour mieux comprendre les hommes* (Toulouse: Éditions Milan, 2003).

Carré, Olivier. *L'Islam laïque ou le retour à la Grande Tradition* (Paris: Armand Colin, 1993).

Charnay, Jean-Paul. *Islam profond: vision du monde* (Éditions de Paris, 2009).

Deleuze, Gilles, and Félix Guattari. *What Is Philosophy?*, trans. Graham Burchell and Hugh Tomlinson (New York: Verso, 1994).

Gardet, Louis. *La cité musulmane: vie sociale et politique* (Paris: Vrin, 1954).

——. *Les hommes de l'islam: approche des mentalités* ([1984] repr., Brussels: Éditions Complexe, 1999).

Göle, Nilüfer. "Snapshots of Islamic Modernities." *Daedalus* 129, no. 1 (2000): pp. 91–117.
Luizard, Pierre-Jean. *Laïcités autoritaires en terres d'islam* (Paris: Fayard, 2008).
Massignon, Louis. *La passion de Hallâj, martyr mystique de l'islam*, Vol. III ([1975] repr., Paris: Gallimard, 1990).
Sanson, Henri. "Laïcité islamique en Algérie." *Revue des mondes musulmanes et de la Méditerranée* 29 (1983): pp. 55–68.
Wolton, Dominique. "Les contradictions de l'espace public médiatisé," in *L'espace public*, ed. Éric Dacheux (Paris: CNRS Éditions, 2008).

The Impossible Meeting
A Free Interpretation of J. M. Coetzee's *Disgrace*

Hemley Boum

Hemley Boum was born in Cameroon, where she studied anthropology before taking a degree in international trade in Lille. She is the author of three novels in which she explores the themes of city life, tradition, and History as they manifest in day-to-day relations with friends and family and through which she invites her readers to reflect on humanity beyond the platitudes, from the inside. Her works include Le Clan des femmes *(Paris: L'Harmattan, 2010);* Si d'aimer ... *(Dakar: La Cheminante, 2013), recipient of the Ivory Award for francophone writers;* Les Maquisards *(Dakar: La Cheminante, 2015), recipient of the Grand Prix Littéraire de l'Afrique Noire and La Cene Littéraire's "Les Afriques" Prize for Engaged Literature; and* Les jours viennent et passent *(Paris: Gallimard, 2019).*

David Lurie is a 52-year-old university professor, but he could just as easily have been eighty-two. David experiences himself as an old man, thinks like an old man, observes and endures social changes like an old man watching his world and his certainties crumble as his body breaks down. He is passionate about the Romantic poets and would like to devote himself to research in that vein; circumstances being what they are, he is obliged to instruct uncultured students in the nuances of a poem by Wordsworth, or the melancholic metaphors of a poet like Byron. Far from gratifying to begin with, David's situation grows worse on account of the changes introduced by the streamlining of the university system. Once a professor of modern literature, David finds himself adjunct professor of communications: "Because he has no respect for the material he teaches, he makes no impression on his students."[1] David adapts to his social and intellectual demotion in his own way: he resists, he learns to settle for less.

The book opens with the private life of its protagonist. Twice divorced, he cultivates what he considers a hygienic and entirely satisfying relationship with a prostitute, Soraya. He sees her once a week, for two hours, and that suffices for his happiness: "He is in good health, his mind is clear. By profession he is, or has been a scholar, and scholarship still engages, intermittently, the core of him. He lives within his income, within his temperament, within his emotional means. Is he happy? By most measurements, yes, he believes he is."[2]

But David Lurie wants more; no matter how hard he tries to convince himself of the contrary, he has not renounced passion's torments. His relationship with Soraya ends when he transgresses its understood, pre-negotiated boundaries by mistaking her professionalism for affection.

That's when he meets Melanie: one of his students, and 30 years his junior. He begins an affair with her, igniting at last the fire that he seeks and that will end up consuming him. Melanie does not give her consent – not really, not explicitly.

> "Stay. Spend the night with me."
> ...
> "Why ought I to?"
> "Why? Because a woman's beauty does not belong to her alone. It is part of the bounty she brings to the world. She has a duty to share it." ...
> "And what if I already share it?"
> ...
> "Then you should share it more widely."[3]

David Lurie believes what he says: in the game of seduction, when Eros takes control, the woman's beauty becomes the property of the man. It is her duty to offer it to him. He adds Shakespeare to the mix, intellectualizes his drives.

Melanie puts up a timid resistance to which David's sovereign desire accords no place. She lets it happen to her, rather than participating; she endures his frenzy, the agitation that she has provoked in him – for which she is in part responsible, as he tells her, and which he cannot contain. His pleasure is total, irresistible. Even when the situation gets out of control, when Melanie's boyfriend threatens him, when he is obliged to compromise himself by giving her a good grade for an exam she did not take, David cannot will himself to renounce her little body – young, faultless, and tantalizingly submissive.

The situation grows increasingly toxic, as one would expect – as he indeed expects, without however suspecting that disaster would arrive so quickly and with such force: "If only he had known the time would be so short!"[4]

Melanie and her family file a complaint for harassment; he is asked to appear before a university commission charged with making an inquiry into his case.

At the hearing, David Lurie is grand, handsome; he appears here as he never ceased to appear to himself in his mind's eye. He acknowledges his wrongs, pleads guilty to all charges, but refuses to humble himself to the point of asking forgiveness or even justifying his actions. He wants the law and only the law; he has committed a reprehensible act and accepts the prescribed punishment. He will not, however, submit to public humiliation; he refuses the castration that society wishes to subject him to for having followed the deepest part of his own nature – indeed, for having obeyed the most "natural" part thereof. He is dragged in the dirt by the media, ostracized by his fellow teachers. Neither can his friends come to his defense, since he revolts against the public repentance that their support would require. David will be judged by all before his trial and then condemned in the eyes of the law. He suffers being blacklisted with the stoicism of someone who knows they are being judged by philistines. He is forced to resign and decides to leave Cape Town for a time, taking refuge with his daughter, who owns a farm inland.

This, one might think, is where the novel begins. Nonetheless, the prologue is necessary for understanding who David Lurie is. A white man, entering old age in a South Africa where, in order to construct a new nation [*une nation nouvelle*], Mandela and De Klerk are proposing a *tabula rasa* of the past. Written in the rainbow ink of resilience, forgiveness, and mutual affection, and featuring the nation's heroes and architects as protagonists, a new novel [*un nouveau roman*] is being presented to the world.

The reality is far less exalted, far closer to Amos Oz's dictum "make peace not love." Peace "is not a burst of love or mystical communion between enemies but precisely a fair and sensible compromise between opposites."[5] If the violent and degrading ties that bind the races of South Africa cannot be undone by noble sentiments, the fact remains that they continue to be harmful and deadly for the social body as a whole. The old habits – the anger and the resentment – will not vanish, but radical political change, a more equitable negotiation of the spaces of freedom, remains necessary all the same.

David Lurie is a "good white man" [*un bon Blanc*]: educated, cultured, he likes poetry and opera, has traveled the world, seems open-minded. While he refuses the obligation to love someone he doesn't (if one thing is clear, it is that his loves are his affair), one can imagine that he would willingly support a negotiated peace founded on a thorough understanding of the interests of each party. Still, the new society rattles him, knocks him off balance. He knows its codes but will not stoop to make them his own; at bottom, he does not accept their legitimacy [*bien-fondé*]. He makes no attempt to impose his convictions (which are quite meager in themselves) but, deep down, he knows he is right. He has always been right, never having had to confront his own position in the world with the needs of others more than was absolutely necessary. When he collides violently with these other legitimacies, he stonewalls: he will not negotiate the limits of his liberty, will not tolerate any intrusion into that inviolable sphere. David takes up too much space and will not cede an inch – or, rather, he will not cede what is required for a more equitable distribution of the political and philosophical space created with the end of apartheid. He still believes he can face down what's coming, that he can maintain a semblance of reserve [*de quant à soi*]: he is mistaken.

Up to this point, the characters are not described by the color of their skin. At one moment in the story, David transforms Melanie into meláni (Gk. "the dark one"), alluding to a reality that the narrator does not explore. In Steve Jacobs's 2008 film adaptation of the book, Melanie and the prostitute Soraya are played by two mixed-race actresses: Nathalie Becker and Antoinette Engel. David has two ex-wives, both white, and a history of short-lived relationships with other white women. But his fall will be precipitated by Melanie and Soraya, the two women with whom he enjoys a position of domination. They are young, fragile women of color: one makes a living as an escort while concealing her existence as a spouse and a mother; the other is David's student, a slightly lost young woman looking for her place in the world. And, if David is far from being a brute, he makes extensive use of what he is, and of the power that he represents, so that he may possess much more of them than they are ready to offer.

The racial question, which one suspects will be central and which until this point has only been hinted at here and there, comes center stage with David's trip to Salem, the little town in the country's interior where his daughter lives, and with the entrance of Petrus as a character.

In Salem, in the Eastern Cape, the racial question can neither be poeticized – Melanie, meláni – nor alluded to or described metaphorically. It is a palpable, incontrovertible reality of daily life.

Lucy, David's daughter, is a lesbian. She has just broken up with her partner and lives alone on a farm where she grows flowers and vegetables that she sells at the market. She also runs a kennel; people trust her to look after their dogs while they are away. She first hired Petrus as a handyman, but a government grant has since allowed him to purchase some of Lucy's land and move there with his family.

David does not understand his daughter's choices. He is critical of how she looks, of her lack of coquetry. Nor is he happy to see Petrus so close, and Lucy's neighbors fare no better in his estimation. But, lest we forget, our protagonist is a "good white man," urban and cosmopolitan by inclination, with a weakness for young, fashionable women, and accustomed to mixing with people of culture. He does not approve of his daughter's choices but he manages to summon a well-meaning condescension. She deserves better; she has sufficient means to acquire "better." But he is a man – a modern, loving father capable of accepting his child's choices without necessarily approving of them.

Their life is overturned the day they are assaulted in Lucy's house by three individuals. The author does not need to specify that the assailants are Black:

> Three men are coming toward them on the path, or two men and a boy. They are walking fast, with countrymen's long strides. The dog at Lucy's side slows down, bristles.
> "Should we be nervous?" he murmurs.
> "I don't know."
> She shortens the Dobermanns' leashes. The men are upon them. A nod, a greeting, and they have passed.[6]

The words, the construction of the sentences, spell out the danger that these individuals represent well before the crime is committed.

They lock David in the bathroom while they violate his daughter. After, they take the valuables, kill the dogs, and splash David with ethanol, igniting the fuel before escaping with the car. Everything is contained in this scene. The thing he had been waiting for, the threat which he had felt obscurely since the beginning, and against which he had tried to defend himself without daring to name it: "So it has come, the day of testing. Without warning, without fanfare, it is here, and he is in the middle of it."[7] The Black men penetrate his private space by force, partition him off in the WC like excrement, sully his daughter with their seed, attempt to reduce him to ashes, kill the dogs who were supposed to assure his protection, and make off with the valuables. He is reduced to the most total, the most abject condition of powerlessness. The man who feared being castrated by the civilized part of society, the part he no longer understood, nor even attempted to understand, finds himself submerged and dislocated at the hands of its savage and barbarous part. It imposes itself upon him; it rapes him too; brutally, it forces him into submission. It strips him of everything that makes him a complete, intact being. It breaks him.

There are few metaphors in this book. The style is direct to the point of dryness: there is no touch of humor, no breath of poetry. Coetzee drops us deep into David's body, into his mind, his guts. We know all about the sexual obsessions that never entirely abandon him. When he decides to visit Melanie's family to offer them an apology, he meets her younger sister, a pre-teen beauty. Even as he feels the pangs of contrition, our hero cannot help himself from fantasizing about the possibility of having both sisters in his bed ("an experience fit for a king"),[8] about his feelings of superiority, about his own complacency. The incursion is not made by an "I" acting in solidarity and unspoken agreement, but with the reserve of the third person. We follow each private step of David's fall as strangers, as non-authorized spectators, as voyeurs: "The events of yesterday have shocked him to the depths. The trembling, the weakness are only the first and most superficial signs of that shock. He has a sense that, inside him, a vital organ has been bruised, abused – perhaps even his heart."[9]

Lucy turns away from her father. He would like her to press charges for rape; she limits herself to reporting the assault and the theft. He holds Petrus, who happened to be absent just at the time of the events, responsible, or at least complicit. She refuses to incriminate him even when, during a party at Petrus's house, she recognizes his brother-in-law as one of her aggressors. She isolates herself, withdraws into the house, lets herself go, and refuses any help from her father. He would like her to leave the farm where no one, not even he, can promise her even a modicum of security. For David, the question is economic: Petrus wants Lucy's farm; he organized the attack to frighten her. For there to be justice and reparation, she has no choice but to file a complaint, identify those responsible, and seek protection in the law. For Lucy, that would mean alienating Petrus and putting an end to any hope of keeping her farm, her life here. Only, Lucy does not want to leave. For all her father's urgings, threats, and entreaties, she refuses to let herself be chased out.

The men's desire had been inspired by hatred and contempt. More than to possess Lucy, they wanted to debase her, humiliate her. Lucy speaks of an old claim, an ancient debt that people like her have to pay to people like them: a tax collected by force as payment for her ancestors' seizure of a land that did not belong to them and for the harms that resulted from that usurpation. Today, the place she occupies as owner of this land is no longer secure. Here, in Salem, the balance of power is skewed; a reparation commensurate with the crime is unimaginable. They leave her with no other choice – either run or pursue legal action. She invents a third way, improbable and mad: she negotiates a peace. Against implacable barbarity, she pits her indomitable vulnerability. She does not weigh in on the reimbursement of a centuries-old debt, since no one asks her opinion – neither the assailants, convinced of their rightful claim, nor David, issuing his patriarchal injunctions. She pictures the solutions available to her if she hopes to preserve the integrity of her body and guard her mind from madness, and she chooses to give up part of her freedom and part of her dignity so that she may retain the right to live on her land.

Out of all these outrages, a child is conceived. Lucy chooses to keep it and to accept Petrus's proposition of marriage. There is no question of sentimentality; it is a rational alliance, as marriage has long been in most places. The man promises shelter and protection for her and her unborn child; she gives him her land. She does not like men; he is not attracted to her. He may lay claim to his rights once, as when one shakes hands to seal a contract, but no more than that. It is not about that. We are in a primitive society where bonds of blood and inheritance are the only thing that matters. Petrus and Lucy understand one another implicitly. David cannot bring himself to accept this world, for which he feels profound contempt and which causes him pain, but he has nowhere to go. The prospect of his blood mixing with the Other's makes him imagine the impending disappearance of everything that he is, of everything that he believes. He watches with fright the approach of the vilified Great Replacement [*Grand Remplacement*].

Many readers have interpreted *Disgrace* as an acerbic critique of the myth of post-apartheid South Africa as a successful multiracial, pluricultural nation, or else as a portrait of the anxiety Western society experiences when faced with what I would call "the new legitimacies" [*les nouvelles légitimités*].

David Lurie is narcissistic to the point of absurdity, and his perspective on others is a ragbag of prejudices:

Women of color: irresistibly sensual and nothing else. "He has always been drawn to women of wit. Wit and beauty. With the best will in the world he could not find wit in Meláni. But plenty of beauty."[10]

Lesbians: "Sapphic love: an excuse for putting on weight."[11]

Blacks: professional rapists, inveterate fornicators (Petrus is polygamous, Lucy will be his third wife), conniving, lethally dangerous, irremediably foreign.

The young, single women, believers ... in his eyes, no one is spared.

Still, to fully understand the character, it helps to study his connection to Bev Adams's dogs.

David works as a volunteer for Bev, who is Lucy's neighbor and who owns a sort of pound where she performs euthanasia on animals, especially dogs. Whereas Lucy looks after the spoiled, purebred dogs of white families, the dogs that live out their last days at Bev's are abused, sick. They have reached the end of the line and, for the most part, they come from the Black community. In both cases, the Black community's deadly violence touches even them, confirming, in our hero's view, that coming together is impossible [*l'impossibilité d'une rencontre*].

David is fond of these animals. When they are put down, he assists with tenderness and compassion, and he insists on bringing their dead bodies to the incinerator himself. Sometimes he sheds tears of pity for the poor creatures. The less control he has over his own life, the more invested he becomes in offering the dogs a dignified death. Victims of the ambient madness that surrounds them, these suffering animals invest Coetzee's work with an unexpected force. They testify to life's dark side, the forces that we carry inside ourselves: the secret, animal self, at once wild and defenseless, and which no one wants to expose to the eyes of others. The self that suffers twice over and dies in silence when the world falls to pieces.

David's despair cannot be brushed aside; his distress is real, abysmal. His reading of what happens to Lucy and him, and of the choices that Lucy goes on to make, is clear, perceptive, and bleak. Lucy cuts her filial tie to him and allies herself with someone she sees as more powerful. Her father knows that in this situation the balance of power is unstable and alliances ephemeral; all that is certain is his daughter's vulnerability and his powerlessness to protect her. In a situation where one does not know what it is that has inspired the predators' covetousness, nor whether that thing is something one is prepared to part with without a fight, no possible negotiation is imaginable. The innocence that one lost, that one fantasized, is not coming back. Even the dogs, which were once trained to growl at the sight of a Black person, are not innocent. No form of repentance will attenuate the cruelty of fate. He counsels flight, she refuses. From here, there is no exit, since, although she begs him to go, he cannot bring himself to abandon her.

The rainbow nation's finest hour was when young people of all colors danced in the streets to celebrate Nelson Mandela's rise to power. Then, when hopes evaporated the morning after the revolution, the life-and-death struggle for land and the subjugation of defenseless bodies set in once again, exacerbated this time by the fact that the boundaries between oppressors and oppressed had become porous.

David Lurie is not one of those Afrikaners animated by a visceral hatred of Blacks. Nonetheless, he has until now been a member of the ruling class, one of the lords who today are expected to relinquish part of their privileges. The new arrangement shakes his comfortable universe to its very foundation, for he knows now that the loss of privileges will bring on vicious struggle for which he is not prepared. In his nightmares, he tries to escape a man with a "face like a hawk, like a Benin mask, like Thoth": the Black man as a cruel and vengeful god; the former prey has become the predator, determined to obtain his fresh pound of flesh.[12]

As Elsa Dorlin writes,

> The apparatus of power that distinguishes those who hunt and are hunted does not seek to impose a general hunt of everyone by everyone, but rather the reduction of everyone to the condition of prey, diluting and rendering invisible the relations of domination in a world that everyone experiences as "unlivable" but where only certain people are killable and may in practice be pursued.[13]

And David Lurie falls into the universe of potential prey.

The character is like John Maxwell Coetzee, a professor of literature born in Cape Town. David incarnates a familiar figure of the author. They are contemporaries – involuntary heir in David's case, active participant in Coetzee's – of the end of a world (apartheid) and the beginning of another, a new era which is recomposing South Africa's social landscape without being able to stem its congenital violence. The end of the political effort that kept the Black community under the thumb of whites represents the bursting of a valve, since, alongside the new liberties, South Africa's wounds reach deep into a constellation of racial and ethnic conflicts, of which apartheid had been only the most fully realized form. The end of the regime will not exhaust the well.

Coetzee cannot be ignorant of the fact that the difficult social mix [*la difficile mixité*] of today's South Africa continues to produce a violence which falls disproportionately on the Black community, and which, all too often, is inflicted by other Black South Africans. In South Africa, many more Black women are raped than women like Lucy Lurie, and there are few occasions for the cupidity of a man like Petrus to succeed at the expense of a man like David Lurie.

The question is, why did the author reverse the paradigm? What does the disgrace of his protagonist show us if not the secret, unspoken fear of the oppressor, the fear that makes any negotiation impossible?

I am reminded of a phrase of Mahmoud Darwish:

No, no victim asks his torturer:
Are you me? If my sword were bigger
than my rose, would you wonder
whether I would act similarly?[14]

There is in Coetzee a calm impertinence, an absolute freedom of thought: it irradiates his body of work. As a reader, one asks oneself: who else but him could have written something like this? And immediately afterward adds: there was no way to say it differently.

Part III

Circulations

Achille Mbembe

Achille Mbembe is Professor of History and Political Science at the University of the Witwatersrand in Johannesburg, South Africa, as well as a researcher at the Wits Institute for Social and Economic Research. He is the author of many works in French and in translation, including La naissance du maquis dans le Sud-Cameroun *(Paris: Karthala, 1996);* De la postcolonie: essai sur l'imagination politique dans l'Afrique contemporaine *(Paris: Karthala, 2000) [*On the Postcolony, *trans. A. M. Berrett, Janet Roitman, Murray Last, and Steven Rendall (Berkeley: University of California Press, 2001)], and* Politiques de l'inimitié *(Paris: La Découverte, 2016).*

Of all the challenges that Africa faces in this new century, none is more urgent and full of consequences than the mobility of its population. To a large degree, the continent's immediate future will depend on its capacity to free up forces of circulation, to set up spaces and territories through which one can move as frequently as possible, over the widest possible distances, at the greatest possible speeds, and, ideally, without meeting any barrier whatsoever. Whether it take the form of a generalized defection or a preconceived plan, it is inevitable that populations will enter into circulation, if only because of the combined – and still unpredictable – effects of demographic growth, the intensification of predatory economic behavior, and the dynamics of climate change.

Moreover, the great social struggles taking place in Africa this century will not only be about the transformation of political systems, the redistribution of resources, and the reallocation of wealth. They will also be about the right to mobility. Nor will digital creation fail to participate in such circulatory processes. The demand for mobility will give rise to profound tensions and upset the future equilibrium not just of the continent but of other regions of the world, as the so-called migration crisis has already made clear. It is for the purpose of reflecting on such upheavals that we have come together.

Situations of Enclavement

To truly grasp such upheavals, we must turn our backs on the neo-Malthusian discourses which, frequently nourished by racist phantasmagorias, continue to proliferate. The "scramble for Europe" is, in this respect, a big myth. That one out of four of the planet's inhabitants happens to be African does not, a priori, constitute a threat to anyone. After all, of Western Europe's 420 million current inhabitants, hardly 1 percent are Sub-Saharan Africans. Of the 1,277,292,130 inhabitants attributed to the African continent, only 29.3 million live abroad. Of these 29.3 million, 70 percent have not left for Europe, or for any other part of the world. They have resettled in other African countries.[1] The reality is that, in addition to having a relatively small population for its size (30 million square kilometers), Africa hardly emigrates. Compared with other continents, the circulation of goods and persons in Africa is impeded by numerous barriers. Our historical moment tells us: the time has come to dismantle these obstacles. Many regions scarcely admit movement. They have very few avenues of communication. In many cases, transportation takes place with the help of draft animals or, when possible, in a saddle – if not on a woman's back. Where they do exist, roads are subject to all the contingencies of the terrain: exceedingly dense forests and flooded rivers and streams constituting so many internal borders.

But natural obstacles are not the only challenges. In a study of the political economy of road traffic in North and South Kivu (Democratic Republic of the Congo), Peer Schouten, Janvier Murairi, and Said Kubya reveal the extraordinary extent to which the Congolese road system is militarized. They identify five types of roadblocks. Some have the function of taxing the right to pass, whether of road users or their cargo. Others are linked to the exploitation of natural resources. They allow one to tax [*ponctionner*] miners as well as their products. As for markets, roadblocks are set up at the entrance and/ or exit of localities on market days. On top of that, add the posts that various armed actors place at the outer limits of their areas of influence. Individuals are allowed to cross over simply in exchange for a passage fee [*frais de passage*]. Finally, as the last additions to this panoply, come the roadblocks placed at the administrative limits between two decentralized entities [*entités décentralisées*].[2]

Institutions born of colonization, roadblocks were used by the colonial state as a method of restricting mobility and filtering the movements of subjected populations for the purpose of encouraging sedentarization. They also represented an essential feature of the fiscal apparatus [*dispositif*] – controlling transit hubs being a great help to authorities eager to levy taxes effectively. Moreover, under the colonial state, mobility and circulation obeyed a logic of corridors and tunnels. Where it existed, infrastructure (railroads, roads – rarely with asphalt) connected centers of extraction to ports of exportation by the quickest route possible.[3] The effects they had on the immediate environment they passed through were virtually null. Priority was given to the most profitable form of circulation, most colonial spaces being essentially characterized by enclavement. This tension between the fixed and the mobile would characterize the construction of territorial sovereignty during colonization. At times, it would manifest itself in the form of excessive restrictions on mobility, and on border crossing in particular – at others, in the form of fluid and detached relations between the center of the state and its margins.[4]

The isolation that such enclaves produce on the continent remains a pervasive reality; setting up roadblocks has outlived colonization.[5] One way or another, their placement refers back to distinct forms of the circulation of value. They are compulsory crossings following the movement of the goods and people to be taxed; they are embedded in economic circuits which are themselves in constant motion and for which distance and modulations of speed count as added value. In these instances, what matters is not liberating the mobile elements of the society, nor investing in infrastructures that can generate flows and circulations, but creating focal points and other bottlenecks for the purpose of siphoning off wealth and preying on travelers.

The intensification of extractive logics has done little to loosen Africa's extensive enclave situation, and the introduction of the neoliberal schemas that now determine the actions of African states has helped even less. On the one hand, as Hélène Blaszkiewicz explains, the extroverted transportation plans put in place during the colonial period are in fashion once again. But the creation of new infrastructures has not followed a logic of disenclavement with respect to remote or marginal regions. It proceeds in accordance with "a logic of speed and of profitability of movement." Of course, this logic "privileges the flows from mining operations, which are the most profitable and the most globalized of the commercial flows, together with the infrastructures that make them possible": the continual acceleration of these flows is given highest priority.[6] As in the colonial period, the system of circulations remains characterized by fragmentation and the creation of "tunnels." Infrastructures were built to link sites of extraction to seaports for exportation. The proportion of tarred roads has increased only minimally with time, and railway lines are making little progress. The costs of circulating remain prohibitively high and, with them, the costs of migration as well.

On the other hand, the economy of extraction draws together enclaves that are sometimes situated offshore. The latter are characterized by the greatest possible freedom from their surrounding conditions.[7] As Nicolas Donner explains, in these cases it is a question of immunizing oneself against the potential dangers of the host environment, which is the condition for the circulation of the resource. It is as though these enclaves were located in an empty, hostile environment. Almost entirely artificial, these space capsules function like watertight zones, cut off from their immediate surroundings by all kinds of protective coats, walls, and restricted access areas. And yet they are connected to the rest of the wide world. Just like neoliberal logics, extractive systems do not, strictly speaking, constitute bottlenecks. Nonetheless, they do participate in the ever-increasing concentration of activities at certain critical points of the territory. If they are doubtless contributing to the spatial reorganization of contemporary Africa, it is not by encouraging the mobility of people. On the contrary, they aggravate situations of enclavement within African countries. In such a context, it may be possible to imagine a different life elsewhere. But to actually plan a departure and then hit the road is another matter entirely. Leaving is not within everyone's reach.

Innumerable physical and ecological constraints further limit the possibilities of circulation, to striking effect. As we mentioned, this is particularly the case in forested countries. Such constraints notwithstanding, historically African societies have never been isolates. In fact, these societies can only be understood by means of the reality to which circulations give rise. *Circulations* is indeed the right word – were it not for them, human groups and social units would not have held together. In the past, circulations not only referred to movement, displacement, and mobility; they also referred to practices of extension [*pratiques d'extension*] and to practices of complementarity [*pratiques de complémentarité*]. Over such wide, arid spaces, spatial relations were composed of *comings and goings*, of *crossings* and *traversings* [*traversées*] – structured as they were by complex polarities. All things considered, the great African desert was never an empty space – neither with respect to human habitations, nor with respect to resources.

Contrary to a tenacious myth, migration has never dominated life in the desert to the exclusion of all else. In the desert, one always found both nomads and sedentary populations. As Denis Retaille rightly notes, the Sahara was always populated in "distinct centers" based upon "oasal and urban establishments": "In the desert, centers of population are linked by axes running from north of the great desert to the south (and partially from the east to the west), trans-Saharan routes being grouped in zones corresponding to specific ethnic groups: Moors in the west, Tuareg in the center, Toubou in the east."[8]

It is therefore important to keep in mind the *distinction between migrations (whether legal or illegal) and circulations*. By "circulations," one should understand a series of complex operations by means of which a society invents, through movement and exchange, a vital equilibrium with its environments, or is able to give form to such environments and to link them to one another. Circulations should thus be apprehended both in terms of social plasticity and in terms of rhythm. Most of the time, what matters is forging networks of alliance. Such networks need not be territorialized. This is not to say that inequalities do not exist; nor that they escape institutionalization. In fact, they are insistent – as can be seen in the more or less permanent presence in Saharan societies of a servile population, or in the pre-eminence of warrior factions within such societies over the course of history. Ultimately, most wars are waged over control of transportation routes and, with them, over circuits of exchange. They culminate in the accumulation of captives and in the constitution of a servile population, or else a protectorate subjected to a tribute system. But, even for slaves, it is impossible to suppose any purity with respect to descendance. Cultural assimilation is a reality. As Retaille observes, there is a place not only for captives, but also for clients, and even for forms of so-called contractual kinship.

Furthermore, one must envision circulations in their structural tie to sedentary logics. Truth be told, one never finds one without the other. It is rare when mastery over a territory does not involve controlling a population center. Even predatory behavior depends upon an ability to follow tracks, observe comings and goings, control crossings and junctions – in short, the organization of exchanges. Nor is it the case that circulation and nomadism eliminate the need for attachments and residences, as many geographers have shown. Such residences may take the form of houses "where the elderly, a portion of the women, and the children remain." There, too, one can find "the descendants of slaves who have become sharecroppers of oasal farms producing wheat and dates."[9]

The Contraction of the World and the Violence of Borders

Meanwhile, the human costs of European border control policies continue to grow, increasing the risks faced by potential migrants. One no longer keeps track of the number of people who have died trying to cross.[10] Each week brings its share of stories, each just as scabrous as the last. Often they are stories of men, women, and children who have drowned, succumbed to dehydration, been poisoned by toxic chemicals, or died by asphyxiation on the coasts of the Mediterranean, the Aegean, the Atlantic, or, with increasing regularity, in the Sahara Desert.[11]

The violence taking place along borders and the violence exerted by borders have become a striking feature of the contemporary condition. Little by little, the struggle against so-called illegal migration is assuming the form of a social war conducted at a planetary scale. Waged more against classes of population than against particular individuals, it now combines techniques borrowed from the military, police, and security services, as well as from the bureaucratic-administrative sphere, unleashing, in the process, outbursts of a cold – though, at times, no less bloody – form of violence.

In this regard, it is enough to observe the huge administrative machine that allows thousands of legally established people to be cast into illegality every year; to note the sequence of expulsions and deportations conducted under the most appalling conditions;

to take stock of the progressive abolition of the right of asylum and the criminalization of hospitality.[12] What can one say, after all, about the use of colonial technologies for regulating migration in the digital era, with the cortège of daily violence that such technologies imply: from the interminable profiling, the incessant hunt for undocumented people, the numerous humiliations suffered in detention centers, the haggard eyes and handcuffed bodies of young Blacks dragged down the corridors of police stations, this one leaving with a black eye, that one with a broken tooth, a cracked jaw, a disfigured face – what can one say about the crowds of migrants who are stripped of their last pieces of clothing and their only blankets in the dead of winter, who are not allowed to sit on public benches, who arrive to find the faucets providing potable water shut off?

Nevertheless, this century will not only be a century of obstacles to mobility set against a backdrop of the ecological crisis and the increase in speed. It will also be characterized by a planetary reconfiguration of space, a constant acceleration of time, and a profound demographic fracture. Indeed, by 2050, roughly two thirds of humanity will be gathered on two continents. Sub-Saharan Africa will have 2.2 billion inhabitants, or 22 percent of the world population. By 2060, it will be among the most populated regions in the world. Humanity's demographic shift toward the Afro-Asian world will be a fait accompli. The planet will be divided between a world of old people (Europe, the United States, Japan, and parts of Latin America) and an emerging world, home to the youngest and largest populations on the planet. Europe and America's demographic decline will continue inexorably. Migrations will not stop. On the contrary, Earth is at the cusp of new exoduses.

The accelerated aging of the rich nations of the world is an event with considerable implications. It is the opposite of the massive upheavals unleashed by the demographic excesses of the nineteenth century, which culminated in Europe's colonization of vast stretches of the Earth. More than before, governing human mobilities will be the means by which a new partition of the globe will come into being. A new kind of planetary fracture will divide humanity. It will pit those who enjoy the unconditional right of circulation – and its corollary, the right to speed – against those who, essentially on racist grounds, will be excluded from the enjoyment of such privileges. Those who will have seized hold of the means of production of speed [*moyens de production de la vitesse*] and of technologies of circulation will become the new masters of the world. They alone will be in a position to decide who can circulate, who need not be condemned to immobility, and who will be obliged to travel under more and more draconian conditions.

In this new global order of mobility, if Africa does not take up the reconfiguration of its spatial economy, it will find itself doubly penalized, from the inside and from the outside. This is because Europe has decided not only to militarize its borders, but to extend them to greater distances. These borders no longer stop at the Mediterranean – they are now situated along the fugitive routes and sinuous paths used by potential migrants. The borders move in step with the trajectories the would-be migrants follow. In reality, it is the body of the African, of every African taken individually and of all Africans as a racial class, that now constitutes Europe's border.

This new type of human body is not just the body-skin [*le corps-peau*] and the abject body of epidermic racism, of segregation. It is also the body-prison [*le corps-prison*], double of the body-border [*le corps-frontière*]: the body whose mere appearance in the phenomenal field at once inspires distrust, hostility, and aggression. The geo-racial and geo-carceral imaginary that, not too long ago, apartheid South Africa had brought to such refinement has not ceased to universalize itself.

Moreover, Europe would like to arrogate to itself the unilateral right to determine which Africans are allowed to circulate and under what conditions they may do so, even within the confines of the continent. Having dismembered Africa in 1884–5, 21st-century Europe is now attempting to turn the continent into an enormous Bantustan and to aggravate its differential inclusion within circuits of war and capital while simultaneously intensifying its vulnerability to predatory behavior. What Europe's policies of combatting immigration really seek is thus the advent of an unprecedented regime of planetary segregation. The latter is, in several respects, the equivalent of the "racial policy" [*politique des races*] that Joseph Gallieni instituted in the French colonies. Africa is the principal target.

Governing forms of mobility at a global scale represents, alongside the ecological crisis, one of the major challenges of the twenty-first century. The reactivation of borders is one of several short-term responses to the long-term process of populating the planet. Borders, however, are no solution. They only aggravate the contradictions produced by the contraction of the planet. In practice, our world has become very small indeed. In this regard, it is different from the world of the "Age of Discovery," the world at the time of colonial exploration, conquest, and settlement. It no longer stretches out to infinity. Today, the world is finite, traversed every which way by all sorts of uncontrolled and uncontrollable flows, by movements of migration, and by movements of capital – linked to the extreme financialization of our economies and the forces of extraction that dominate most of them, particularly in the Global South. To all this, we must add the immaterial flows introduced by the advent of electrical and digital reason, the increase in speed, and the overturning of regimes of time.

Let No African Be Treated as a Stranger on the Continent

In such a context, how should we think of the Africa to come? If, in fleeing their countries of origin, many Africans rush off to places where no one waits for them and no one wants them, the same can be said for people from other regions of the world who, strange as it may seem, come to Africa hoping to start a new life. Although it may not seem so, the continent too is on the verge of becoming the center of gravity for a new cycle of planetary migrations. Chinese are settling not only in the hearts of the continent's great metropolises, but even in its remotest villages, while colonies of African merchants are establishing themselves in several Asian megalopolises.[13]

Dubai, Hong Kong, Istanbul, Guangdong, and Shanghai have taken the torch from the great destinations of Europe and America. China draws tens of thousands of foreign students, while emerging powers like Brazil, India, and Turkey are not far behind. An extraordinary vernacularization of forms and styles is under way, transforming Africa's large cities into global capitals along baroque, creole, and mestizo lines. But, so that Africans do not see themselves transformed into the rejects of a planet dotted by towering miradors, Africa must become its own center, its own force, a vast space of circulation, a continent-world [*continent-monde*]. It must complete the project of decolonization by forging, for itself, a new African politics of mobility.

The realization of such a project will not be possible without cultural decolonialization. In order to settle their scores with their own history and give their imaginations urgently needed stimulation, Africans must purge themselves of the desire for Europe and learn to keep the best of themselves and their people in Africa.

Indeed, the desire for Europe can be neither their existential horizon nor the last word about their condition.

Territorial decolonization imposes itself as a next step. Historically, nothing justifies splitting the continent between the north and south of the Sahara Desert. Furthermore, no African, or person of African origin, should be treated as a stranger anywhere on the African continent. Increasingly, the debalkanization of the continent seems to be one of the conditions for protecting African lives menaced all across the world.

To achieve this goal, it is urgent that we entirely rethink the principle of freezing colonial borders that the Organisation of African Unity adopted in 1963. Since African states enshrined their intangibility, the borders inherited from colonization have become a legal cornerstone that Europe exploits to accelerate the "bantustanization" of the continent. Decolonization will not be truly achieved until each African enjoys the right to circulate freely across the entirety of the continent. A first step in this direction would consist in generalizing the granting of visas, upon arrival, to all travelers holding an African passport. In the long run, the liberalization of the right of residence should complement each person's right to free circulation.

The greatest challenge that Africa faces is not demographic. It is not, as it was during the colonial period, the challenge of fixing borders, restricting passage, intensifying local ties, and forcing populations to adopt immobility and sedentariness. On the contrary, it is managing circulations so that they can grow more intense on the continent. It will be by intensifying mobilities, and developing interconnections between places, that the old spatial and infrastructural schemes inherited from colonization will be dismantled. State sovereignty was constructed through the delimitation of borders, by means of their neat distinction between the inside and the outside. It was also the result of practices of enclavement and of breaking up territories. All that mattered was access to ports and, with them, the multiplication of avenues for exportation.

Today, the challenge is removing the obstacles to mobility by abolishing the multitude of border posts, by erasing the physical as well as political barriers to the flow of traffic, and by debureaucratizing movement. Large-scale infrastructure projects (regional highways, regional trains, international seaports and airports, navigable waterways) will be needed to create networks of communication that transcend national frontiers. One will need to facilitate the circulation of merchandise and brainpower, to encourage the creation of an Afropolitan public space. This is how Africa will speed up, and how Africans will be able to move cheaply throughout the interior of their continent. Going forward, such a long-term historical and cultural perspective should inform how we conceive the terms of transregional development and how we move toward a greater transnationalization of African society and the intellectual, artistic, and cultural life of the continent.

No State without a Population Abroad

Now that the ground has been cleared and the polemic is over, it is time to pose some fundamental questions. We have long lived in a world where every state was assumed to have a corresponding population, and each population had to reside in its state. This postulate of residing in a given territory (the principle of sedentariness) was seen as one of the conditions for the creation of a habitable world.

Yet the massive crises that we have experienced since the beginning of the century have not only exposed the limits of this principle of sedentariness – the latter is now giving way to the principle of intermixing [*principe d'entremêlement*]. Many places are indeed suffering increasing devastation; whole regions are emptied of their inhabitants, and a number of now unlivable spaces have been abandoned. Nowadays, very few people feel sure about their home. As Isabelle Delpla astutely points out, "faced with parts of the country nearly deserted by their inhabitants, or with whole countries being depopulated," many individuals "no longer know whether they find themselves inside or outside their borders."[14] At the same time, between humans and non-humans, division, parcelization, and entanglement increasingly go hand in hand. From now on, living and becoming imply all sorts of ties and connections.

Migrants and refugees are thus only symptoms. If it is true that there is no state in the world without a population abroad, then the true question concerns the conditions under which the Earth, in its planetary dimensions, might effectively transform itself into a true cradle for all humans and into a shared horizon for all living beings.[15] Now is the time to invent new ways to inhabit the planet. And how are we to do so, if not by imagining political and state forms and ways of belonging that are ever more flexible, pliable, and mobile?

On the Return
The Political Practices of the African Diaspora

Nadia Yala Kisukidi

Nadia Yala Kisukidi *is a lecturer in philosophy at the University of Paris 8 Vincennes-Saint-Denis, where she is a member of the research center Laboratoire d'études et de recherches sur les logiques contemporaines de la philosophie (LLCP). She was Vice President of the Collège International de Philosophie (2014–16) and currently serves as its Program Director. She has published several articles on twentieth-century French philosophy, on the philosophy of religion, and on African intellectual traditions.*

(O my language, calm and lull the child who does not know that the map of spring must forever be redrawn)
     Aimé Césaire, *Notebook of a Return to My Native Land*[1]

How might "Africans, by exercise of their powers of vision and by virtue of the uniqueness of their concrete experiences within their societies, work to reconcile the use of the understanding and revolutionary praxis"?[2]

We might revisit the question that Valentin-Yves Mudimbe raised for the final decades of the twentieth century – revisit it, while at the same time revising its terms. Let us no longer talk about "Africans," but about "African diasporas" – those that today crisscross European societies, speaking their multiple languages: English, French, Spanish, German, etc. These diasporas bear the histories of numerous migrations – some of them tragic, some of them happy. They carry stories attached to the memory of a land, of a soil, stories that remember exile, deracination, and, sometimes, happy departures, elective wanderings.

Such *African* diasporas, no matter where they occur, also carry dreams along with them: dreams that revisit the past, that invent different futures, that imagine ways to inhabit the present and settle down. Still, of these many dreams, one in particular persists with a special tenacity. Unshakable, it is fixed firmly in the mind: the desire to return.

To return – that is, to go back to the place one came from. Africa.

When it issues from diasporic imaginaries, such a desire sounds like a paradox. The difficult term "diaspora" – which appears in the third century BCE in the Septuagint[3] – describes the history of human groups (peoples, communities, etc.) who live dispersed across the map and who develop a transnational mode of existence. One is obliged to picture diaspora as a unity that "diffracts" (Édouard Glissant) and multiplies itself. And, in each of these multiplications, each of these reflections, the origin is no longer substantially present. A simple trace that recalls a birthplace, now far away, and that justifies, with greater or lesser coherence, the processes of recognition through which diasporas conceive of and fantasize their unity.

From this perspective, one comes to understand the various names diasporas have been given or have chosen for themselves. Often designation proceeds by means of a reterritorialization of identity: one appropriates the names of continents, the names of countries, the names of cultures/peoples, as well as racial signifiers (*African diasporas, Congolese diasporas, Kongo diasporas, Black diasporas*, etc.).

The history of displacements and mobility to which the idea of diaspora refers is always bound – in discourse, if nowhere else – to the idea of an anchorage point [*un ancrage*]; dispersion is not necessarily the renunciation of the desire for the natal [*le désir du natal*]. Living in diaspora reclaims the substance of such desire by affirming the possibility of being close to the origin. The desire to return expresses nothing else: for every diasporic existence, the good life, authentic and unspoiled, is the one that remains attached to its roots.

Nonetheless, one can imagine another way of understanding this desire to return, "to return to Africa" – an interpretation that has nothing to do with the rhetoric employed by majorities or with the discourse of identity, be it single or multiple. Consciously or stutteringly, it expresses itself through various Afro-diasporic experiences and practices in Europe. I would like to show how, within the desire to return as it is articulated in Europe, one can trace the outlines of a creative, subversive politics that reconciles understanding and praxis.

Desire to Return and Suspicion

The idea of a return to Africa has a long history that has structured Pan-Africanist thought as well as different expressions of Black nationalism. In the first instance, its geography is determined by the "Atlantic triangle" (Europe, Africa, the Americas), around which one traces several "classical routes of return."[4]

The idea is nourished by the dreams of slaves, who, deported to the Americas, would fantasize their escape, their liberation. It acquires substance in "projects for the mass relocation of Blacks to Africa" conceived by slave societies, and that eventually gave birth to Sierra Leone.[5] It draws together the various maritime, political, and commercial undertakings of Marcus Garvey's Black Star Line and, among the members of the Rastafari movement in Jamaica, it fed desires for a promised land.[6] The history of returns to Africa, which begins with the deportations across the Atlantic, follows multiple paths: hopes of escape, orders of expulsion, politics of separation, etc.

The desire of a "return" to a continent, Africa, understood to be the exclusive reference point uniting those who, by violence and coercion, were obliged to disperse – this desire is not dead. It persists in contemporary societies, and, specifically, it persists in "afrodiasporic" European societies.

Initially, one might harbor suspicions about the persistence of such desires to "return" and about the kind of rhetoric that comes with them. One has reason to be suspicious, given where they are articulated: Europe. All the more so, given that such desires seem to point immediately to a failure: the creolizations that shape the globalized world have not destroyed the will to identify subjectively with the land, with the permanence of roots, with what is fixed, and even with the idea of the nation.[7]

The idea of returning taps into the deadly virtualities of what Édouard Glissant calls "atavistic cultures" – that is, forms of cultural identification that are centered around the idea of a "single root" and that proceed "from the principle of a Genesis and the principle of a filiation with the aim of seeking legitimacy on a land which, from that moment onwards, becomes a territory."[8]

Neither creative nor subversive, in these instances the desire to return merely repeats the familiar refrains that identify cultural authenticity with the exclusivity of territorial or national rootedness [*enracinement*]. One could hardly attribute any emancipatory political potential to such a desire. It ends up falling into three different traps: the postulate of privilege, the obsession with identity, and the fascination with the rhetorical strategies of the majority.

Diasporic privilege

In the contemporary European context, the desire to return to Africa crashes headlong into the reality of the migrations to Europe from Africa: to be specific, it collides with the problem of the right to asylum and the reception of refugees. The aim of pointing this out is not to contrast a desire to return to Africa with another desire, deemed more powerful: the desire for Europe. Europe is not the first destination of African migrations – not even in cases where violence and oppression force people to seek refuge elsewhere.[9]

In all their diversity, African migrations to Europe exhibit the specifically police-like form [*la forme policière*] that politics has assumed in the West: define zones of relegation, construct walls, repel at the border, identify the undesirables. Such anti-migration policing, which impacts both economic migrants and political refugees indiscriminately, sketches the contours of what Patrick Chamoiseau calls a "new barbarism."[10]

When politics assumes such a police form, desires to "return" betray what otherwise goes unsaid: to be able to articulate them presupposes a situation of privilege. A privilege is a right, an exclusive advantage that a group or individual possesses in contravention of the common rules. Viewed from this angle, the desire to "return" expresses a "diasporic privilege" that rests, in practice, upon a right of residence or a right of birth. Not a "right of the blood" (*jus sanguinis*), but rather a right tied to legal status and to the attractiveness of the territory: to be born within a powerful nation, administered in such a way that its nationals do not find their ability to circulate obstructed by the politics of security and migration that, at the global scale, circumscribes zones which certain populations have no possibility of leaving. Diasporic privilege, in this sense, is the privilege of members of diasporic communities who have been able to establish themselves, and/or who have grown up, in wealthy nation-states – their prerogative consists in never being the objects that borders are built to keep out.

For people of African descent either born or living in Europe, one could say that the desire to return to Africa is, before anything else, the sublimated expression of a legal and administrative reality: in effect, some territories grant an unlimited right to circulate and full enjoyment of the benefits tied to nationality. From this perspective, "returning" to the place where one never lived or else lived only briefly, "returning" to the place where one was not born, represents the contradictory, nostalgic desire of those with the possibility of *not* going back. The right to stay where one is without being coerced to leave is what the desire to return looks like in its negative modality. In this regard, the desire to return authorizes every folklore, every idealization, every projection: it invents an idyllic Africa capable of healing the world, and Europe, of its deadly vices, and it does so without having to leave its place ... in the West.

Their diverse itineraries notwithstanding, Afro-European diasporas are perhaps first of all European. Examined with suspicion, the desires to return that they nourish can seem like the dreams of the privileged: the sublimations of intimate ruptures, linked to the wish to know the country of a relative or a friend – utterly remote from every geopolitical and material concern and thus blind to what police checkpoints along the border and the movement of migrations bear witness to.

Identitarian obsession

If it is not the expression of diasporic privilege, the desire to return can appear as a dream saturated with identitarian obsessions, which endlessly repeat the motifs of nationalist rhetoric that have structured European political discourse and practice since the nineteenth century.

In *The Black Atlantic*, Paul Gilroy encourages us to be suspicious of diasporic discourses that reterritorialize themselves around a unifying reference to a soil or a continent.[11] Framed that way, the idea of return remains bound to poetic and political imaginations associated with Romantic/modern approaches to culture, where forming popular solidarity necessarily implies defending the life of an authentic national culture.

For Gilroy, on the contrary, the political and poetic force of diasporic reality consists precisely in the radical manner with which it breaks the connection between the idea of a "people" or a "community," on the one hand, and the idea of "cultural authenticity" or "rootedness," on the other. The exiles, displacements, and relocations that the Black and African diasporas have experienced yield a critical framework that can be deployed to disqualify any recourse to a homogeneous and reified conception of identity in the domain of Euro-American and Afro-diasporic politics. *The Black Atlantic* describes this transnational, transcultural form of politics, whose existence amounts to a critique of ethnic and cultural absolutism. Rather than the continent, preference goes to islands, archipelagoes, waves. Instead of sedentary statism, one elects nomadic variations. Against the rhetoric of roots, one champions identity as a relation, the identity-rhizome [*l'identité-rhizome*]. In the place occupied by the idea of the nation-state, one substitutes a transnational political utopia. And, accordingly, against the idea of the "return," one pits heterological processes of self-construction, integrating the other – every other, every other possible place – into the definition of what persons, peoples, and communities are.

By rights, the political imaginary tied to the idea of diaspora should free us from the ideas of nation, of land, of soil, of continent. The insistence on returning weighs down the emancipatory virtualities legitimately acquired by the fact of living in dispersion.

Rhetorics of the majority

In this light, the insistence on returning to the continent amounts to a new mirage. Despite their direct experiences of movement, multiplicity, and disaffiliation, Afro-diasporic communities allow themselves to be subjugated by discourses of territory and identity. *Afro*-French. *Afro*-American. *Afro*-British. Preceding the national affiliation is the atonic, monotonous repetition of the prefix "Afro-," displayed like a sign of the origin.

This repetition, when it is not enjoined from the outside but claimed in the first person, is somewhat misleading. It undermines all the political and creative potential of the idea of "diaspora": to disaffiliate oneself from the national, to break the logic of borders and administrations, to create new forms of plurality indifferent to the question of the origin.

It pays to reread the work of Richard Marienstras.[12] At the heart of his analyses lies the following question, which he raised in relation to the diasporas of French Jews during the 1970s: does the identity and longevity of the Jewish diaspora rest on the centrality of Israel as a nation-state? More generally, belief in the nation-state is held to be the exclusive form of normality; it removes all doubts about the future of the identity under construction. By this means, the idea of the nation-state supplies diasporic becomings [*les devenirs diasporiques*] with the illusion of their ontological coherence.

This belief encompasses all of identity politics within two schemas: assimilation/integration, or else separation. Assimilation implies the dissolution of the Other into the Same. Integration sets out the mechanics of the injunction whereby the Other is obliged to respond to the expectations of the Same or risk sanction. Separation describes the radical disjunction of the Other and the Same: it opens the possibility of dividing territory – or it doesn't.

And yet, no matter how they come about, diasporas, if they are to exist *as such*, must not adopt the logic of existing nationalities. They would be better off, instead, assuming a form of life *sui generis* by deciding to constitute themselves as transnational, transcultural "minorities." Here, minorities are not understood in the sense of being less numerous in comparison with the general population of a state. Diasporas are not minorities because they are necessarily "minorized" [*minorisées*] – which is to say, despised and relegated to peripheral zones. Diasporas are minorities in the sense that, by their very existence, they undermine a majoritarian system [*système majoritaire*][13] – that is, a system of hegemonic norms determining a set of codes and dominant social practices within a nation-state.

Freed from the historical context in which he produced it, Marienstras's work suggests that, in diasporic imaginaries and practices, recourse to the logic of the nation-state – or, to use Glissant's terms, to the logic of the "territory" – legitimates the rhetorical strategies of the majority in which forms of cultural and political life are arbitrated by the state.[14] The desire to return can be interpreted as a validation of such majoritarian rhetoric by diasporic populations which are not only smaller, but, as it happens, often "minorized" in the West.

Hiding behind the prefix "Afro-," the signifier "Africa" has the value of a synecdoche in which "Africa" as a Whole stands in for one of its parts, for the nation-state ("Senegal," "Democratic Republic of the Congo," "Algeria" …). Alternatively, the signifier "Africa" could allude to a political utopia, thoroughly theorized or vaguely idealized: a state-continent ontologically structuring the identity of the diasporas that claim it as their own. In both cases, the desire to return allows groups who refuse either to be thought of or to think of themselves as minorities to reactivate rhetorics of the majority – which, in the end, amounts to the validation of the idea of the national.

Nonetheless, another understanding of the desire to "return" might be ventured, which arouses none of these forms of suspicion. This understanding insists on doing justice to a unique experience: that of the absent community [*la communauté absente*].

Thinking the Absent Community

The experience of the absent community

Return – since it is impossible to belong. Impossible to belong to communities that, in Europe, have resurrected the deadly practice of glorifying land and ethnicity – that, nostalgic for their former imperial greatness,[15] construct unity, as Cheikh Anta Diop says, "on the basis of bitterness."[16] And sometimes it is impossible to belong to the African societies themselves – since one has never lived there, since no family, no friends await one there. For the continent produces its own castaways, its own lines of racial exclusion, its own forms of xenophobia – be they inherited from the history of colonialism or not.

Such instances of impossible belonging derive from asymmetries. Nonetheless, they bring to light what the sociologist Abdelmalek Sayad, in a completely different context, calls the "double absence": in Africa as in Europe, the members of African diasporas appear as exogenous elements and are summoned to identify themselves.[17] Such "double absence" describes diasporic subjects' exposure to racist, chauvinist, and xenophobic violence. The proliferation of such imperial summonses lies at the heart of the experience of the absent community.

Betraying a nostalgia for fusion and transparency, the idea of community can seem to be a vague notion that conveys an idealized, ancestral vision of the social fact [*du fait social*]. Political modernity bears witness to the definitive forfeit of this idea as a means for thinking the totality of the social. For, as Maurice Blanchot reminds us in *The Unavowable Community*, the term "community" is commonly used to designate two types of social groupings, which in practice are difficult to distinguish from one another. On the one hand, there is the "traditional community": the de facto sociality that "is imposed on us without our having the liberty of choice in the matter."[18] The "elective community," on the other hand, is a social form existing "through a decision that gathers its members around a choice without which it could not have taken place."[19] Strictly speaking, these two forms of community are not irreducible. (Is the choice in so-called elective communities really free? Do traditional communities not structure themselves around the free will of those who want to forge a common destiny?) Nevertheless, the two forms seem to be traversed by different conceptions of the nature of the social tie. The first rests on the principle of dissolution, fusing "the elements only to give rise to a unity (a supra-individuality)"[20] – biological (blood, "race"), religious (mystic body, God), etc. The second rests on the principle of "putting in common" [*mettre en commun*], understood as "a shared will to be several."[21]

Both of these conceptions of community are traversed by processes of identification; they imply strategies of recognition and logics of assignment that distribute bodies inside and outside the limits that the community gives itself.[22] All communities put a condition on acceptance: the necessary identification of those who, for various reasons, ask to enter, to establish themselves therein. The identification procedures are not simply descriptive (compilations of characteristics defining an individual); they are also normative and prescriptive: they bring with them a certain number of expectations. They indicate what one must be in order to be part of the community and what one must do in order to satisfy communitarian requirements [*l'exigence communautaire*]. To be truly French or Congolese, an authentic European or African, for example.

The experience of the absent community is the experience of being constantly ordered to identify oneself, an identification on which one's acceptance or rejection then hangs. The experience of the absent community is not the experience of the absence of community. The absence of community can be supplemented, filled. It refers to a situation of privation, of lack that can be compensated: what's missing, since it can always be specified (we know what we don't have), determines the form of what is sought. To experience the absent community, on the contrary, is to be confronted with the fact that no one will make an effort to support the possibilities of an existence [*les possibles d'une existence*] without first insisting that one identify what that existence is. This request for identification is paradoxical: it demands the identification of someone who has already been categorized (*Black, Arab, Muslim, veiled, African* ...) and designated as unassimilable. Its object consists in repeating the gesture of exclusion around which the borders of the communitarian [*les frontières du communautaire*] reaffirm themselves.

The criteria of identification – racial, national, cultural – are fixed a priori. The experience of the absent community is one of naked, systematic exposure to the gaze that scrutinizes, checks, judges, and evaluates. The gaze might belong to an instituted order (army, police, administration, school, party, etc.) or it might issue from one's immediate circle (family, work colleagues ...). The eye that surveils individuals without their knowledge and unmasks them guarantees the integrity of the community.

The experience of the absent community cannot be compensated. It describes the systematic nature of an experience of relegation that produces the unassimilable, the inauthentic, the unintegratable. The subjects who go through it carry with them a lasting awareness of their constitutive inadequacy to form community – the impossibility of *being with* – no matter where they might find themselves.

"Home ... is many things": Afro-cosmopolitanism and multiple identities

Ultimately, however, isn't this experience of the absent community just a reinterpretation, in a melancholic key, of a diasporic situation that, otherwise, is both desirable and valorized – namely, the possibility of possessing multiple identities? To circulate inside multiple identities sketches another modality of communitarian life, which articulates itself in a contradictory manner: a community formed by those who live at the frontier of every community. The production of the common exceeds the territories of the national, the racial, the culturally authentic.

Early in the twenty-first century, the term "Afropolitanism" emerged within literary and theoretical circles as a way of characterizing fluid, hybrid approaches to identity in the context of Afro-diasporic experience.[23] Afropolitanism describes an African form of cosmopolitanism. Such "Afro-cosmopolitanism" has a political virtue: it unambiguously refutes all forms of ethnic chauvinism and racial differentialism that impose strict definitions of African *being*.

In a famous account, the writer Taiye Selasi sketched the characteristics of this "newest generation of African emigrants":[24]

Afropolitans are a "funny blend." They check multiple ethnic boxes or are simply "cultural mutts." Polyglots. Subjectively, they are attached to Africa (nation-state, city, family), while at the same time evolving, in all naturalness, in the cities of the G8. They are recognized all over the world for their creative and innovative powers. They are not "citizens of the world" but, rather, "Africans of the world." The idea of Afropolitanism celebrates the multiple identities that traverse Afro-diasporic groups, while simultaneously laying claim to an attachment to Africa.

The idea has nonetheless been criticized for depoliticizing Afro-diasporic experiences. The Afropolitan that Taiye Selasi describes realizes a subjective economy characteristic of neoliberal capitalism at the end of the twentieth century:[25] the model of the individual as an entrepreneur of the self. The Afropolitan: merely a figure of end-of-the-century capitalism, adapted to the Afro-diasporic context and countering the Afropessimist clichés of "an Africa that loses" with the symbolic and economic attractiveness of "an Africa that wins."

The "Africa that wins" is dispersed, multiple; it circulates between all cultures, and its adaptation is the sign of its success. Surreptitiously, the rhetoric of multiple identities transforms itself into a euphemistic promotion of flexibility – that is, of a certain ability to respond or effectively react to the fluctuating demands of the global marketplace.

For this reason, one might question the actual fecundity that the rhetoric of multiple identities possesses for politics. As necessary as its critique of identitarian barriers and reifying approaches to the national is, such rhetoric has little to say about the relations of power that materially structure and direct the social field.

Nonetheless, at one moment in particular, Taiye Selasi's text manages to strike a chord: with the paradox presented in its conclusion. After the paean to motion, to Afropolitan hybridity, comes the question of "return." Even Afropolitans not born in Africa, even those who have never been there, who no longer have family there, ask themselves whether they should "return." Pressing political questions (inequalities, the power relations between North and South) emerge as the text's end point, albeit in the mode of the guilty conscience. As if, in the end, feelings of loss and debt remained constitutive of these Afropolitan subjectivities, who had left to conquer the world. This would make Afropolitan consciousness into a form of unhappy consciousness, bearing the diffuse sentiment of culpability that torments the souls of Africa's prodigal sons and daughters.

Return and double presence

The experience of the absent community presupposes the existence of a subject who navigates between several different places. Its purpose is not to affirm, in a melancholic mode, a multiple, exploded identity – sapping the imaginaries of the hearthstone, of the brick foundation, of home. It does not assuage the guilty conscience of those who should have been in one place but chose to settle someplace else, and who experience remorse or indifference with respect to the fates of those they left behind. The rhetoric of non-correspondence [*la rhetorique de l'inadéquation*] between subject and community does not conceal a paean to hyper-adaptability, to the fluctuations of the market, to the succession of trends, to the spirit of the times.

Neither tragic, nor guilty, nor bitter, in practice the experience of the absent community pulls away from the question of cultural and national identities. It opens possibilities for political practice, where, beneath the abandoned dreams of community, the question of the return poses itself anew.

But where does one return to when one is absent from every community? What return is adequate to the one who remains inadequate? Why persist in "returning" if the very question of provenance and origin no longer makes sense to those who live in dispersion?

To be absent from Africa, to be absent from Europe. To be absent from the place where one was born or from where one's family and friends come from; to be absent from the place where one grew up and where one actually lives. Such a "double absence" is the unique biographic signature of inadequate lives [*des vies inadéquates*]. To be sure, it tells of suffering and of the inner conflicts belonging to what W. E. B. Du Bois calls "double consciousness."[26] But it also contains a practical question addressed to all those who are doubly absent: how can one think/re-invent one's presences – one's double, one's multiple presences in this world?

Double absence is resignified as a kind of imperative: how to invent one's double presence in Africa and in Europe? How might one create the conditions of possibility for double habitability [*habitabilité*]? Not merely with respect to the administrative and juridical form of bi-nationality, but in a concrete and political form: creating effective possibilities for inhabiting two or more places – *at the same time*. To inhabit means to live in a territory where all the possibilities of human existence are not violently stifled – where the material means of subsistence that assure the conditions of a decent life are guaranteed.

Here, the question of the return – or rather of a continual back-and-forth between Africa and Europe – surfaces under new premises as a political demand. The utopian virtualities borne by the idea of diaspora derive not from the fact that individuals assume "multiple identities," but rather from the fact that they take responsibility for the political contradictions that come with choosing to be present in several places.

These political contradictions assume a specific form when they traverse the Afro-diasporic existences that have settled in Europe. These lives often unfold in large European metropolises (Paris, Brussels, London, Lisbon, Berlin) where the tragic continuities binding the colonial past to the neocolonial present are visible and, at times, multiplying. Relations between European/Western societies and African societies are asymmetrical, based on predatory economic relationships: the conditions of growth and abundance that certain lifestyles demand rest on the exploitation and proletarianization of other societies, and of their populations.[27]

Coming from Europe, the demand to return to Africa implies a politics. It does not consist exclusively in questioning identities, be they joyful or wounded, but rather in taking responsibility for the contradictions that emerge from the desire to live in two places whose relations with one another are structured by relationships of inequality and domination. A decent, serene life in these locations requires reversing a geopolitics of inequality that targets excess existences and useless, discardable [*jetable*] populations.[28] Neither an identitarian nor a moral gesture, laying claim to a double presence, to a multiplied presence in the world, reconnects with "revolutionary praxis" (Mudimbe).

In Europe, the demand to return – to move back and forth – that Afro-diasporic dreams keep alive is repoliticized outside identitarian and cultural frames, which afterward become of only secondary importance. Returning does not mean going back home but creating conditions of habitability in places that are singularly familiar [*singulièrement familiers*] – places in which, for different reasons, it is impossible to settle or remain.

At its core, life in diaspora harbors real virtualities of utopian politics – those of a situated rather than an abstract internationalism. This internationalism does not assume responsibility for the world's becomings [*des devenirs du monde*] in an *idealized* manner, basing itself on the theoretical postulate of a shared humanity. On the contrary, it is concerned with the concrete steps taken by subjects called to action by the future of the places that have forged – and that continue to forge – their attachments, their biographies.

Round Trip and Geopolitics of Hope

Afro-diasporic Renaissances: two brief accounts

I would like here to propose two examples and break with the analytical dimension of this text by beginning a story. It is neither a sociological study nor a personal history, but the account of two collective experiences that each follow routes of return.

In July, 2017, I was invited to participate in the fifth meeting of the African Summer School in Verona, Italy.[29] The first meeting was sponsored by the former Italian Minister for Integration in the Letta Cabinet, Cécile Kyenge.[30] The African Summer School is a summer university, open to all African, Afro-diasporic, and European youth. It supports the development of entrepreneurial projects that return to Africa and offers various forms of instruction to this end (courses on African philosophy, African culture, personal development, "business," etc.)

Open to multiple ideological approaches, the School nonetheless conceives of its methods as part of a project of "African Renaissance." The idea, expressed for the first time in the texts of Cheikh Anta Diop, can be subjected to multiple interpretations, some of which are mutually exclusive.[31] Nonetheless, the African Renaissance, understood in light of Diop's thought, describes "a project by which African peoples reclaim historical initiative."[32] Such a reclamation can be more precisely described as follows: "By reclaiming of historical initiative, one should understand the reclaiming of capacit[ies] for conceiving, anticipating, undertaking, creating, and innovating."[33] Diop's œuvre invites us to think of the African Renaissance as a process for Africa's *total* emancipation, with no separation of economic, cultural, scientific, and political questions.[34]

The questions raised by the School's students (Afro-Italians for the most part) concerned the economic models most conducive to a renaissance. They were accompanied by identitarian and cultural anxieties that had been exacerbated by acts of racism in Italy.[35] The desire to return cannot dispense with a sustained reflection on the need for refuge: a safe place, where one can gather one's forces and fully unfold the creative virtualities of one's existence without being constantly subjected to racial injunctions ("Look! A negro!"[36]) that constrict the possibilities of a life.

The second story recounts a journey of integration for African and Afro-diasporic youth, organized in Accra in August, 2017, on the occasion of the sixtieth anniversary of Ghana's independence.[37] West African youth met with young Afro-Europeans from Belgium and France, asked them about their relationship to the continent, inquired about their desire to return and the possibility of settling in Africa. This trip resulted in an act: the realization of a transcultural, transnational political solidarity, celebrating Kwame Nkrumah's legacy and the renewal of the Pan-African ideal. Solidarity was realized in spite of separation, differentiated histories, and the plurality of identities. The organizers' opening remarks drew explicitly on Glissant and on his critique of rooted identities [*identités racines*]. What unifies those who are separate is a *project* and not a *given fact* (a culture, a biology, an identity): defending the lives of Africans, and descendants of Africans, in Africa and everywhere else in the world.

These two experiences instantiate one sense of the reconciliation of understanding and praxis that Mudimbe called for. The brief presentation that I have been able to provide is clearly subjective. Those who also shared in these experiences will not necessarily recognize themselves in my account. My own experiences of them were shaped by what I wanted to see, what I hoped to find: the possibility of politically assuming my double presence, without being subjected to the identitarian injunction. To be doubly present while remaining defiantly unassimilable and inauthentic. As the poet Léopold Sédar Senghor might say: "to assimilate, not to be assimilated."[38]

Round trip and solidarities

The desire to return, when conceived independently of identitarian frames and thoughts of authenticity, defines a politics of multiple solidarities, implying reciprocal attachments and engagements for the sake of the welfare of populations of African descent throughout the world. No community *fixed in advance* predates the formations created through solidarity: although solidarities can result from experiences shared beforehand, they only produce the common [*du commun*] after the fact. An identity is not a solidarity. More or less the fruit of fantasy, identity has the appearance of a *given* [*un donné*], despite the fact that it is constructed, piece by piece. Solidarity, by contrast, is a political construction for which nothing must be given in advance; it rallies behind a project of emancipation on whose basis new bonds are formed.

The "return to Africa" and the round trips that it implies can be understood as projects of political solidarity. These projects do not propose an ethics that demands assistance be given to subjects who are judged to be weak or vulnerable (as in humanitarian reason) or else backward (the principle of co-development). Taking a stance against the proliferation of "out-worlds" [*hors-mondes*], where routines of violence are normalized, they support the co-creation of egalitarian spaces.[39]

Contrary to what it seems to evoke, as a qualifier, the expression "of African descent" [*afrodescendant*] makes no claim to a continuity of blood or lineage. True, it alludes to forms of what Aimé Césaire calls "solidarity in time":[40] multiple, differentiated memories of removal that recall brutal separations from Africa. But, above all, the term implies another solidarity, horizontal this time. According to Césaire, in addition to grasping the "same harsh reality" of their colonial and para-colonial conditions, the solidarities in formation choose to fight back, to activate a political dynamic of hope.[41]

There is no doubt that the "return" of Afro-European diasporas to Africa in the twenty-first century represents a cultural process: a return to the "initial unity."[42] But one must bear in mind that this process entails no re-education of the individual: the point is not to drive subjects to confession, to subject them to procedures of truth [*procédures de vérité*] so that they might prove that they have not been contaminated by the frills of whiteness and the West! "Solidarities in time" describe the *possible* unity of what remains heterogeneous; neither normative nor prescriptive, such solidarities are completely content with the unassimilable and the inauthentic. Such solidarities are not punitive: guilt is not the condition of possibility for the bond they form.

But Césaire's distinction also allows us to reflect on the dynamics of return outside a strictly cultural frame. Additionally, and above all, what emerges from the movement of diasporas back and forth between Europe and Africa is a geopolitics of hope: a geopolitics of minoritarian dynamics, rather than a simple analytics of territorial conflicts and power relations between states at the global level.

A geopolitics of hope describes the various modalities for politically reinvesting space from a minoritarian perspective. The global scene is structured by the borders drawn by states; these borders block the movement of human lives while simultaneously ensuring, through a system of rules, the free circulation of capital and commodities. The world's asymmetrical logics of "borderization" structure the multiplicity of power relationships at work in contemporary neoliberalism.[43] They explain social and political inequalities, as well as the power asymmetry between North and South. Moving back and forth from Europe to Africa, diasporas are animated by the hope to undermine these relations of power – to undermine them both where they are produced and where they cause harm; so that, no matter where one lives, no force threatens to asphyxiate or destroy what is possible for one's life.

Practices

The demand to return can be grasped in a strictly political sense linked to the material critique of inequalities. This political demand emerges outside the rhetorics of identity and of the majority, free of any suspicion of neocolonialism tied to diasporic privilege. By leaving behind the impossible dream of belonging to the community (the experience of the absent community), it defines the contours of a *situated* political practice of solidarity, obliging us to rethink the concepts of nation-state, sovereignty, territory, and contemporary reconfigurations of imperialism – all from the ground up.

Returns can assume three concrete forms:

(1) resettling without going back: to forget Europe and return to a continent where, sometimes, one has never been and where no family awaits;
(2) moving back and forth: to live in two places, without privileging either of them;
(3) remaining so that one can leave: remaining in Europe to prepare the material conditions for return.

In the three cases, the juxtaposed spaces are invested in a singular way, both affectively and politically. Forgetting Europe, living in between [*la vie-entre-deux*], and deferring return represent just as many stories of humiliation and failure as narratives of strength. They imply several kinds of practices that affect both places of departure and places of arrival.

Three examples. In Europe, the act of claiming "African descent" and projects for returning open up a vast space for creation within legal and political domains, setting the stage for actions aimed at disrupting narratives of the nation and obstructing the reproduction of inequalities that encumbers the functioning of institutions. The task is to complicate the history of European nation-states, to join in the dismantling of national narratives built on hierarchies of rejection, to oppose conservative political forms that feed logics of exclusion grounded in the intersection of categories of gender, race, and class. It is time to take action simultaneously in the arenas of representation and of reparations, on behalf of freedom of movement and the politics of reception – to work toward the habitability of a Europe presently undone by postcolonial melancholia and the hysterical "fortress" fantasy.

In Africa, the practices born of the return encourage the criticism of legal codes regulating nationality, and gesture toward a continental unity beyond the violence of its various chauvinisms, walls, and borders – all of which are, to varying degrees, contested, protected, or effaced by flows of sand, traffic, and weapons. It is a matter of questioning the relationships between Africans in Africa, by means of a sustained struggle against the multiple reconfigurations of racism and xenophobia that traverse the whole of the continent. But it is also a matter of rethinking the relationships of the continent with its diasporas, which, at the very minimum, means challenging the legal principle of exclusive nationality in the countries that apply it.[44] Broadly speaking: what place might the diasporas occupy in the political futures elaborated for the continent?

In Europe and Africa, a sustained hope – inspired by the long history of solidarities among Blacks and people of African descent – works toward undoing the unequal relationships that structure the relations between the two continents. The contestation of the CFA franc and the denunciation of the old imperial practices that at times still govern the relationships of Western powers to their former colonies (military interventions, applications of soft power, etc.) are examples of diasporas politically reinventing their double presence in Europe and Africa.

Reflections on "return" examine circulations, movements, and migrations, but they also invite us to think about what it really means to become sedentary [*se sédentariser*]. Not all sedentarizations are "mothers of conquest," products of an inextinguishable thirst for rootedness.[45] To move in, to fix one's abode, is also to create the conditions of possibility for a stable life, where one can stand on one's feet. To have a roof over one's head, a shelter for protection; to watch one's family and friends stay put, grow, and sometimes grow apart; to come and go, to forge lasting bonds: to inhabit places where existence is not in danger.

In situations where military, racial, economic, and imperial violence are threaded together, the desire to return opposes paeans to migration as exemplifying ideal cosmocitizenship [*cosmocitoyenneté*]. Politically, it promotes the disassembling of predatory logics so that it may participate in the consolidation of habitable places.

The desire to return seems to be a singular expression of the fact of living in dispersion. It nonetheless participates in a political choice for which nothing is prescribed in advance. Life in diaspora may very well manifest indifference with respect to the cultural and political imaginaries that traverse it.

For this reason, the desire to return does not always fall back upon traditions of reactionary thought. The attachment to the places that forge a biography need not feed a fetishism of the origin. There is an experience of return that is not satisfied with the melancholy of loss. It charts a political course outside the tracks of assimilation and separation that affirms the double presence of subjects at once indefatigable and inauthentic.

Bibliography

Blanchot, Maurice. *The Unavowable Community*, trans. Pierre Joris (Barrytown, NY: Station Hill, 1988).
Bonacci, Giulia. *Exodus! Heirs and Pioneers, Rastafari Return to Ethiopia*, foreword by Elikia M'Bokolo, trans. Antoinette Tidjani Alou (Kingston: University of the West Indies Press, 2015).
Césaire, Aimé. "Culture and Colonization." *Social Text* 28, no. 2 (103) (Summer 2010): pp. 127–44.
——. *Notebook of a Return to My Native Land*, trans. Mireille Rosello and Annie Pritchard (Tarset: Bloodaxe Books, 1995).
Chamoiseau, Patrick. *Migrant Brothers: A Poet's Declaration of Human Dignity*, trans. Matthew Amos and Fredrik Rönnbäck (New Haven: Yale University Press, 2018).
Chivallon, Christine. *La diaspora noire des Amériques: expériences et théories à partir de la Caraïbe* (Paris: CNRS Éditions, 2004).
Deleuze, Gilles, and Félix Guattari. *A Thousand Plateaus: Capitalism*

and Schizophrenia, trans. Brian Massumi (Minneapolis: University of Minnesota Press, 1987).
Diop, Cheikh Anta. *Black Africa: The Economic and Cultural Basis for a Federated State*, trans. Harold J. Salemson, expanded edn. (Chicago: Lawrence Hill, 1987).
Du Bois, William Edward Burghardt. *The Souls of Black Folk*, ed. Henry Louis Gates, Jr. and Terri Hume Oliver, Norton Critical Editions (New York: W. W. Norton, 1999).
Dufoix, Stéphane. *La dispersion: une histoire des usages du mot diaspora* (Paris: Éditions Amsterdam, 2011).
Ewondo, Patrick. "L'afropolitanisme en débat," in "Blackness," ed. Rémy Banzenguissa-Ganga and Thomas Fouquet, special issue, *Politique africaine* 136 (December 2014): pp. 105–19.
Fanon, Frantz. *Black Skin, White Masks*, trans. Richard Philcox (New York: Grove Press, 2008).
Gilroy, Paul. *Postcolonial Melancholia* (New York: Columbia University Press, 2004).
Glissant, Édouard. *Introduction to a Poetics of Diversity*, trans. Celia Britton (Liverpool University Press, 2020).
Glissant, Édouard, and Alexandre Leupin. *The Baton Rouge Interviews with Édouard Glissant and Alexandre Leupin*, trans. Kate M. Cooper (Liverpool University Press, 2020).
Lazzarato, Maurizio. *The Making of Indebted Man: An Essay on the Neoliberal Condition*, trans. Joshua David Jordan (Amsterdam: Semiotext(e), 2012).
Marienstras, Richard. *Être un peuple en diaspora* (Paris: Les Prairies ordinaires, 2014).
Mbembe, Achille. *Critique of Black Reason*, trans. Laurent Dubois (Durham, NC: Duke University Press, 2017).
——. "Le grand débarras." *AOC*, May 2018, http://aoc.media/opinion/2018/05/02/le-grand-debarras.
——. *Out of the Dark Night: Essays on Decolonization*, trans. Daniela Ginsburg (New York: Columbia University Press, 2021).
Mudimbe, Valentin-Yves. *L'autre face du Royaume* (Geneva: L'Âge d'homme, 1973).
Nascimento, José Do. *Les chemins de la modernité en Afrique: pour changer l'Afrique, changeons de paradigme* (Paris: L'Harmattan, 2017).
Ogilvie, Bertrand. *L'homme jetable* (Paris: Éditions Amsterdam, 2012).
Sayad, Abdelmayek. *The Suffering of the Immigrant*, trans. David Macey (Cambridge: Polity, 2004).

Selasi, Taiye. "Bye-Bye Babar." *The LIP Magazine*, March 3, 2005, http://thelip.robertsharp.co.uk/2005/03/03/bye-bye-barbar.

Senghor, Léopold Sédar. "Vues sur l'Afrique noire, ou assimiler, non être assimilés," in *Liberté 1: Négritude et humanisme* (Paris: Le Seuil, 1964).

Reopening Futures

Felwine Sarr

Felwine Sarr is a Senegalese professor and writer. He teaches at Gaston Berger University in Saint-Louis, Senegal. His academic work focuses on economic policy, development economics, epistemology, and the history of religious ideas. To date, he has published Dahij *(Paris: Gallimard, 2009)*, 105 rue Carnot *(Montreal: Mémoire d'encrier, 2011)*, Méditations africaines *(Montreal: Mémoire d'encrier, 2012)*, Afrotopia *(Paris: Philippe Rey, 2016, translated into English by Drew Burk in 2019 for University of Minnesota Press)*, and, with Bénédicte Savoy, Restituer le patrimoine africain *(Paris: Philippe Rey/Seuil, 2018, translated into English by Drew Burk as* The Restitution of African Cultural Heritage: Toward a New Relational Ethics *in 2018). He is co-founder of the publishing house Jimsaan, and the Editor of the* Journal of African Transformation *(CODESRIA-Uneca).*

The emergence of Western modernity had for a principal characteristic the promise of a future marked by progress in all spheres of social life. In this regime of historicity, the days to come were marked by the promise of greater wellbeing. Despite its undeniable advances with respect to public freedom, technological improvement, and the modernization of social life, Western modernity has witnessed the faith in a progress driven by the ascending march of human history first flag and then collapse. After the Great Depression, Auschwitz, Hiroshima, and the Gulag, the metanarrative of

Humanity's progress carried forward by Reason has broken down. The crises and various dystopias that have accompanied the reign of instrumental reason have succeeded in undermining the belief in a better tomorrow. In the West, they have also led to a relationship to time characterized by a hypertrophy of the present – what the historian François Hartog calls "presentism." Characterized by its excessive presentism, postmodernity has become a time in which the future holds no promise – or little save the hope of escaping the multiple disasters (ecological crisis, societal dissolution, public health catastrophes, mounting insecurity) that tomorrow holds in store. The end of utopias, decreed after the collapse of the grand narratives that promised the coming of a new time (communisms, socialisms …), seems to characterize our era. The only expectations that still seem viable are those that project a technological future or a posthumanism.

For societies thought to have fallen behind in the normal march of the world (Africa, Latin America …), this question of the future is posed a little differently. To them, one continues to hold out the promise of economic development, of democracy and societal modernity on the horizon, waiting to be seized. Such retroactive teleologies induct them into a relationship of societal mimetism, and maintain them in the myth of a linear course of history and progress. These societies are called on to complete the steps and attain the societal conditions which other societies have already reached, as if the only destiny imaginable were the reproduction of the singular, Western societal model offered as an example. Their differences, their sociohistorical particularities, their temporalities, their relationship to the past, present, and future are in this way negated and read exclusively as manifestations of backwardness [*du retard*]. It is in this context that I would like to reflect not only on what it would mean for such countries to reopen their futures [*de rouvrir leurs futurs*], but also on what it would mean for the postmodern societies of Europe and America to do so.

For African nations, how to think their destiny (their present and their future) is a crucial question – how to think it while mobilizing their mythological universes, their history, their cultural references, their symbolic capital. In this endeavor, it is less a question of distinguishing oneself by falling back upon identitarian bases, or of vaunting an imaginary purity, than it is of grounding oneself in existing cultural resources for the purpose of extracting vital elements. A hydroponic future is unimaginable: the future depends on the secretions and alluvions of one's soils and suns. Every society, culture, or civilization transmits a heritage. Each perpetuates a cultural matrix that conserves the dynamism of its identity across time by transforming it in step with the evolution of the world.

It is also a question of allowing for the plurality of histories. It is impossible to conceive of a single history for all human societies. It is about leaving behind the Eurocentrism tied to linear, progressive schemas of History, and of dropping Europe's master-narrative, whose model the world's other peoples are condemned to adopt or unhappily repeat. It is about accepting the plurality of collective ways of being, the multitudinous forms of societal life, the diverse modalities for producing being that we call cultures – and it is about accepting *the possibility of there being many worlds within the world.*[1]

Moreover, to be complete, the analysis of the history of societies must bring together different scales (global, transnational, regional, local) which penetrate one another, and allow researchers to account for the phenomena under investigation.[2] History shows that all societies have trajectories, perspectives, dynamics, and temporalities of their own, which can be connected to others.

Before we turn to questions tied to multiple futures, let us stop for a moment in the present and address the way in which the contemporaneity of African societies is depicted. The present of the African continent is frequently represented in the modality of the dystopia. Its social wellbeing is judged according to categories of evaluation derived from economism, which has monopolized the language for assessing social wellbeing since the eighteenth century. Dimensions of the social that pertain to culture, to psychology, to relationality, to the quality of the bonds forged with the living are generally absent from the lexicon used to evaluate the wellbeing of societies. What's more, our era is characterized by an obsession with evaluation, with the statistical abstraction of the real, with quantification as a major part of signification – all of which derives from the now predominant use of the managerial lexicon for the purpose of qualifying social life.

Why must futures be reopened? To exit a time without promise. The construction of meaning [*sens*] or teleonomy is fundamental for societies. All societies have a need to appropriate their own present and future, and to invest the latter with meaning [*sens*]. Can this be done without reactivating the myth of progress? The times to come will always be times of emergent possibilities. But these possibilities are often the bearers of contradictory dynamics; one notes the coincidence of advances (in techniques, in society ...)

and retreats (ecological crisis, genocides, forms of domination and destruction ...).

The difficulty lies in giving form to futures, since they are often unprecedented and need not arrive in recognizable guises. Still, they may nonetheless bring with them a desire for greater collective wellbeing, an intentionality, and a potential energy (for example, attending to [*soigner*] the quality of the relation to the living by reinvesting that relationship with value serves to open futures).

How can we invent a regime of historicity that breaks with teleological visions of history, on the one hand, and, on the other, casts off presentism as an atrophy of the past and a negation of the future?[3] Presentism – when it decrees the end of history (Fukuyama), for example – not only has the effect of annihilating the future, rendering vain any possibility for action; it also results in the perpetuation of the current state of things (current inequalities and contemporary systems of domination).

One possible path lies in historicizing events by showing that what seems "natural," fixed, or self-evident is the product of a complex process, of a history, of movements, of dynamics resulting from a social construction, and is, for this reason, susceptible to being deconstructed.

A Reconsidered Relationship to One's Cultural Resources

For the African continent, reopening the future begins with a reinvented relationship with its traditions and its cultural resources, avoiding the pitfalls of fetishization and self-hatred. Such reinvention makes possible the remobilization of symbolic capital with the power of germinating and reactivating one's cultural and social resources.

Over the long course of their history, African societies have been able to weave and reweave the social tie and "form society" [*faire société*]. They have produced rich and significant societal innovations that have allowed them to confront the challenges of their long and complex history. This is not the place to list them all and so enter into a regime of proof. But it is worth underlining that, whether in the domain of justice (public mediation known as "palabre," reparative justice), or in the domain of conflict resolution, or in the creation of communities and the moral philosophies that sustain them (Ubuntu ...), or the integration of the other and of difference (the notion of kinship, of the extended family), these societies possess a large repertory of resources which not only offer possibilities for responding to current challenges, but could also inspire others elsewhere in their attempts to restore social ties and reconstruct politics.

Nevertheless, reopening futures also means reinventing the current forms of politics and economics on the continent. Most African nations gained independence in the late 1950s or early 1960s. As regards political organization, most of these states adopted the system of representative democracy, with its various modalities for choosing representatives and leaders. The efficacity of this model is questionable. The recurrence of political crises in the aftermath of elections leads us to wonder whether the model can be definitively established on the African continent. In addition, the basic ingredients of meaningful democracy, beyond the mere formal organization of elections, are cruelly lacking. These consist in a functioning system of checks and balances, the existence of deliberative spaces that allow the greatest number of people to participate in political decisions, and the existence of a social contract grounded in an equitable distribution of wellbeing.

It should be noted that so-called representative democracy is in crisis everywhere. In Europe, as in the United States, it has been taken hostage by various oligarchies (economic and financial blocs, intellectual and media elites). One has cause to wonder whether it has not been evacuated of its true content, particularly when it reaches the point of promoting xenophobia, sexism, and vulgarity (USA/Trump) and when it ceases to tolerate a plurality of politico-economic options or to allow citizens to genuinely participate in the decisions that concern them. In today's Burkina Faso and Tunisia, where a civil society and democratic culture are in emergence, the desire for democracy issues from popular revolutions that put an end to dictatorial regimes. The forms of political organization emerging in these spaces are constructing and consolidating themselves within the *non-linearity* of their social and political history. The political forms produced endogenously in such places merit close examination, as do the promises of reinvention that such forms carry inside them.

On the Need to Reinvent Political Forms

African societies must reinvent their modes of political organization and anchor their institutions within their history and their cultural dynamics. For them, it is a question of producing their own forms of representation, deliberation, and participation. Precolonial Africa knew various schemas of political participation based on socio-professional category, age, class, etc. On the collective level, how does one produce efficacious speech [*une parole qui opère*]? What forms allow the greatest number of people to participate in political choices and decision-making processes? The plurality of historical experiences that the world bears within it could provide a source of inspiration.

The idea is to construct human collectivities that control their own destiny and give it form. For these African countries, it is a matter of rethinking the model of the nation-state. This model emerged in Europe after the Treaty of Westphalia (1648), which was brokered to put an end to the Wars of Religion. European nations of that period were rather homogeneous from an ethnic and confessional point of view, and it was relatively easy to superimpose a nation over a territory. In the African context, where rich ethnic diversity is the rule and where territories move and fluctuate, one can question the pertinence of the nation-state as a form. In short, it is absolutely necessary for the African continent to reflect on the forms of political organization that emerged out of its long and complex social history (processes of legitimating representatives, organization of checks and balances). But the continent must also reflect on forms of governance that are not necessarily linked to the state. Various forms of self-management [*autogestion*] already exist on the continent, and are anchored in forms of politics and the social produced by several social groups.

On the Need to Reinvent the Economic

It is a question of starting from the observation that the dominant economy is in crisis, and moving on to think of the economy as a cultural process and to recognize the necessity of reinventing its relationship to the social field.

The context we are in is thus that of a neoliberal economy in crisis. The symptoms of this crisis are persistent inequality and the incapacity of the greater part of the world to satisfy its basic needs with dignity within the system. This is why the situation is less linked to episodes of financial crisis (like in 2008) than to the fact that the dominant economy is failing in its fundamental mission: to help to improve the wellbeing of the greatest number. Its principal features are the globalization of trade – in reality, the privatization of commercial profits – and the mutualization of the associated risks and negative effects (Anthropocene, climate change, ecological crisis). The crisis of the neoliberal economy is fundamentally a crisis of meaning, and its ends: it is rooted in a mechanist cosmology and a utilitarian vision, the product of the nineteenth-century European episteme (order, progress, rationality). Since that time, economic discourse has functioned as an *eco-myth* [*un écomythe*] within modern (industrial) societies – its function being the ordering of the real according to the narrative that the discourse makes of it.

Africa can and should be a privileged testing ground for the reinvention of the economic. The African continent is not deeply implicated in the industrial adventure of the twentieth century; for a very long time, its societies have employed economical practices [*formes d'économicité*] based upon circularity and relational economics; the challenges that the continent faces oblige it to rethink the categories of work, of commercial trade, of production, and the objectives of the economy – not just for the present, but also for the century to come. The question is: how?

- It is a matter of examining the economical practices employed in African countries and identifying in what ways they are creative, innovative, and could offer avenues for rethinking the economic in a more global sense. To commence serious reflection on postcapitalism is of the utmost necessity.
- The economic behavior of African societies is embedded within their respective socio-cultures. The economic is not a separate order. It is characterized by circularity, as well as reciprocity. In traditional African societies, the economic formed part of a larger social system. To be sure, it performed its classical functions (subsistence, resource allocation ...) but, importantly, it was subordinate to social, cultural, and civilizational ends.
- All economic institutions are historical inventions (savings, credit); there is nothing universal about them, nor are they pure products of reason. It is necessary to historicize their genesis and combat the impression that the die has been cast once and for all. Capitalism in its neoliberal version is not ineluctable. But it will not be a comprehensive, global solution that brings down the system; it will be singularities. Through its long labor of standardization, globalization has produced a sort of undifferentiated, universal economic culture. Everything that retains an irreducible alterity will rise to meet it, pitching a culture of high definition against a culture of low frequency and poor resolution.

Uchronias and Counterfactuals

I would like to finish by underscoring the importance of the imaginary in the process of creating the real. Cornelius Castoriadis has shown that societies first institute themselves in the possibilities for thinking and imagining that they open up. The latter play a fundamental role in giving form to conceivable futures. Counterfactual reasoning – that is, the act of imagining what would have taken place "if" things had happened differently – opens the possibility of other presents and other futures. Alternative history – "uchronia" – consists in changing part of the past and imagining what could have happened, and then, within that optic, imagining what would be possible. Counterfactual reasoning tests the relation between what is and what could have been. Taking an interest in possible futures that did not materialize, in aborted projects, in unattained ideals allows one to question the idea of history's linearity and contest the notion of a time that flows toward a precise meaning, goal, or end. This reinforces the idea that the facts (events) could have been different; what took place, this present that we are living, is only one of a plurality of possibilities – and the future before us is therefore not predetermined. Uchronian fictions help to bring to light the past's different potentialities and permit the creation of alternative temporal paths. The gaze they direct into history discloses its possibilities, but they also allow unfinished processes of emancipation to be taken up anew.

The history that failed haunts what can be born. "L'inaccompli bourdonne d'essential" – *the unfinished buzzes with the essential*, René Char asserts. Unrealized futures, utopias/dreams, have been reactivated at different moments in history. Many successful struggles for liberation are the repetition [*reprise*] of earlier attempts that failed and from which later generations learned (Rwandan Patriotic Front, Rwanda 1973, 1990, 1990, 1994). Because it allows one to reactivate the power of utopias, alternative history is a forceful driver of change.

Conclusion

Over the last decades, the futures of African countries have been captured through the inscription of their teleologies into the Global North's game of catch-up [*rattrapage*], according to the rules of a societal mimetism. To reopen futures for African countries is a task first achieved in the space of thought and the imaginary. To give birth to an imagined community, the reconstruction of narratives about Africa (the appraisal of its present and the metaphors of its futures), along with the production of the bodies of knowledge necessary for the types of societies Africans want to establish (the epistemological question), are of fundamental importance. The point is to cast off progress, development, and modernity as civilizational imperatives and allow for the arrival of uncharted futures belonging to another regime of historicity, but bearing within them the basic aspirations of African populations.

A profound cultural mutation is under way on the African continent. Africa can become a laboratory-continent and use its spaces to reinvent the economic, the political, and the cultural. It has all the attributes necessary for such reinvention: youth, space, resources – the fact that it was not fully implicated in the industrial adventure of the twentieth century. It is for this reason that Africa can forge a different path and propose a different equilibrium between economic, ecological, political, and cultural orders. By freeing up new horizons of expectation, it could open out its spaces of possibility upon infinite universes.

Part IV

Un/learning

Rethinking Teaching in Africa

Françoise Vergès

Françoise Vergès holds the Global South(s) Chair at the Collège d'études mondiales at the Fondation Maison des sciences de l'homme in Paris. A filmmaker and independent curator, she has published in both English and French on topics including republican coloniality, memories of slavery and colonialism, circulations of ideas and objects across the Global South, decolonial feminism, and the writings of Aimé Césaire and Frantz Fanon. Her most recent work, A Decolonial Feminism *(trans. Ashley J. Bohrer, New York: Pluto Press, 2021) explores the representation of decolonialism as a debasement, and reconnects with feminism's utopian force.*

It seems that the only way to communicate with the white world is through the dead, dry leaves of a book.
Russell Means[1]

The path of the new school leads through the transformation of our minds and our behavior.
Thomas Sankara[2]

How should we teach? How should we learn? What should we be taught and why? What is the aim of education and teaching: is it to learn to think critically? To adapt oneself to changing conditions? Is one to learn obedience? Or a sense of dignity? These questions – which have been, and still are, at the core of philosophical reflection (and whose archive is not confined to the West) – have also been, and still are, inseparable from the theories elaborated by social movements, revolutionary struggles, and projects for national liberation. In Africa, such movements participated in this reflection, particularly during the time of independence. Since then, however, education and teaching on the continent have become a matter of numbers and a question of "lagging behind," a situation regularly deplored by international institutions, the African Union, and European governments alike. Progress, where it has occurred, has yet to meet the need, and the narrative remains framed by numbers. Hence, a 2015 UNESCO report notes that "sixteen of the twenty worst performing countries over the last fifteen years are African," going on to explain that "even with respect to the most closely examined of such objectives – namely, universal access to primary education – only seven countries have met the target." Moreover, "25% of the world's illiterate adults are today living in Sub-Saharan Africa, whereas fifteen years ago Africa's share was 20%."[3] In 2018, the Global Partnership for Education (GPE) – a longstanding partner of the World Bank – stated that "the most striking challenges with respect to education are in Africa"; that "Sub-Saharan Africa remains the region with the lowest rates of school enrollment"; and that "half of Africa's youth is not enrolled in school."[4] This is the vocabulary of "development," of catching up, of the education needed to combat obscurantism: a discourse in which the situation of young girls (which is indeed deplorable) is presented as the symptom of backwardness.[5] Stress is placed on the future, and education is looked at as a "strategic lever."[6] We are far – very far – from Frantz Fanon, for whom education rests on a theory of the body and the mind, both of which need to free themselves from a form of education that is but an apprenticeship in submission and an internationalization of self-loathing. We are equally far from W. E. B. Du Bois. Indeed, we are far from an entire body of thought. In light of these remarks, does it not once again become urgent to take an active interest in the content of education, and in its possibilities on the African continent in the twenty-first century? Such questions might seem secondary given the staggering scale of the problems: the need, across the continent, to build thousands of schools each day, to publish textbooks, to train teachers, to found universities. Conversely, could we not also decide that there is an opportunity here for us to seize: to build the edifice *and* the curriculum, the architecture of the place of learning *and* the architecture of the content, the training of teachers *and* the invention of a methodology suited to young Africans in the twenty-first century? The *theoretical* question must not vanish behind the logic of pragmatism or of "reality," the latter serving as a mask for logics of production. At a moment when the university confronts privatization at a global scale and the humanities find themselves under attack, but also when, everywhere, students are calling on their institutions to become more open, less based on hierarchies of class and gender, a decolonization of knowledge – a theoretical reflection on teaching in Africa, on its contents, its methods, its goals, its architectures – seems urgently necessary.

Pedagogy of the Oppressed, Pedagogy of Emancipation

By analyzing the educational system as colonial and therefore mutilating, alienating, incomplete, and contributing to the reproduction of inequalities of class, race, and gender, social movements and liberation struggles have all placed education at the center of their construction of the imagined community to come. The educational system (including school and university levels) is never neutral: it manufactures a way of being, of thinking, of reflecting, and of analyzing, and, by these means, seeks to discipline, to pacify, and to propose narratives – privileging, for the most part, reductive accounts over complex ones. Transformation is therefore inevitable. Transformation takes place through the revision of the curriculum, through an attention to forgotten narratives, to methods and knowledge that encourage the transformation of the self. Transformation means taking an interest in the way in which the humanities were written, in how they have excluded certain groups and peoples from their understanding of the human. One need only think of the Maroon schools that slaves set up to learn to read and write; or of the institutions that African Americans opened to circumvent their exclusion from white universities; or of the courses offered by unions, nationalist movements, and women's movements; or of the circulation of texts, brochures, and images disseminating an anticolonial vocabulary. The theoreticians of emancipatory pedagogy have proposed a new humanism, a new feminism, as the basis for a method and a curriculum that encourage the transformation of the oppressed subject into an autonomous person. They have proposed a *pedagogy of emancipation* – what Paulo Freire calls a *pedagogy of the oppressed*. As Freire explains, this pedagogy:

> must be worked out *with* the oppressed and not *for* the oppressed, whether they be an individual or a people, in the tireless struggle to recuperate their humanity.... The big question is to know how the oppressed can participate in elaborating the pedagogy of their liberation, given that they "carry" the oppressor within themselves and are therefore doubles and inauthentic.... Indeed, they cannot contribute to the emergence of their liberatory pedagogy until they realize that they "house" the oppressor within themselves.[7]

In this historical movement of a vast and global scale, African contexts have generated propositions that, for the most part, continue to be neglected by theories of education. In the twentieth century, these reflections intensified with the struggle for decolonization. Those who fought colonialism asserted that liberation was not confined to the acquisition of rights, the reclamation of sovereignty, or the creation of a state. For them, education was the site that ought to favor the kind of self-reflection that was indispensable if former colonial subjects were to unlearn the colonial ideas and representations that they had absorbed about their world and about the world in general, ideas and representations which made them consent to their own oppression. Having insinuated themselves into the minds of the colonized, racism and colonialism modeled the images the colonized could have of their egos, their bodies, and their world: there could be no emancipation without undertaking the process of decolonizing the ego. Amílcar Cabral, Kwame Nkrumah, Frantz Fanon, Thomas Sankara, Albert Memmi, and Nelson Mandela all insist on the importance of this path, over whose course something is loosened – where that which posed an obstacle falls aside and the world becomes meaningful again. The long path toward freedom includes this moment of education that must stay open, for each moment presents a new opportunity to learn. Literature, poetry, cinema, and art accompany these theories of dispossession [*dépossession*], in the sense that they set the self free from morbid and lethal images, practices, and representations. In other words, to learn, first one must *un-learn* [*dés-apprendre*]: not so one can turn the past into a clean slate, but so one can untie the binds that imprison and impede. And, to unlearn, one must imagine new methodologies, new narratives, curricula, syllabi, and, above all, allow oneself to question what has become natural – the spatial arrangement which, from the moment one enters the classroom, announces the gender hierarchy, the hegemony of the text over all other forms of expression, the unshakable authority of pedants, the position of power that authorizes them to abuse it, the course of study that blindly imitates that of the West. The construction of the first postcolonial institutions in Africa brings with it the creation of academic publishing houses and research centers. And the contribution of African researchers to literature, poetry, the arts, philosophy, economics, feminism, to all the social and human sciences as well as to the other sciences, contributes to the expansion of critical theory. All of this is irrefutable, but the Africa of research [*l'Afrique de la recherche*] must also join the intellectual movement that confronts, head on, the attack on the humanities, the privatization of institutions, as well as the additional problems raised by the multiple and massive entanglements of living beings [*du vivant*] in the age of neoliberal capitalism's acceleration.

In the twenty-first century, what form should Africa's institution of education and teaching take? It cannot remain the domain of international "experts" alone – they produce studies that are certainly very instructive, but generally quite removed from the objective of decolonizing knowledge and institutions (we will explore what this objective entails at greater length below). Transformed into subchapters of "educational theory" [*science de l'éducation*], education and teaching have been progressively recolonized by economic and accounting vocabulary. The experts have two responses: the first is to adopt the model proposed by the economist Milton Friedman, whose entire theory aims to limit the power of the state; the second is to increase the responsibility of the state. In neither case is there much attention to content or method. The model of educational vouchers that Friedman defends is grounded in a recognition of the necessity of public education, but it hopes to guarantee the freedom of parents by encouraging homeschooling and the private financing of part of the education system. The model is entirely confident in the individual's ability to make a choice. Freedom is its most important principle. The other response – that of forcing the state to assume greater responsibility for education – calls attention to the dangers of privatizing teaching, but it does not reflect on how educational institutions are structured. At best, it favors a logic of addition (at the university level, this means creating new departments to respond to different demands). Neither of these logics addresses the frustration, demands, and curiosity that have emerged in recent years around the subject of the decolonization of knowledge – one of these being the massive protests that shook higher education in South Africa in 2016.[8] Nonetheless, the demand for a *decolonization* of knowledge and institutions that was voiced on that occasion did not result in a real critical, theoretical reflection. Today, too, the complexity of the process of decolonization is all too often reduced to magical incantations in which the return to the "knowledge of the ancestors," the "Africanization of knowledge," or the teaching of indigenous bodies of knowledge in African languages suffices to guarantee the pertinence of one's answers to theoretical and practical problems – problems which require a true labor of thought. On the practical side: to finally overcome the demographic deficit imposed by the politics of the Trade and empire, Africa will need to build schools and universities quickly. But in order to teach what? And how? Which humanities? Which history of art, of cinema, of theatre? Which social sciences? How does one expand the canon? How does one reconcile democratization and massification – a recurring conundrum for schools and universities? How does one revalorize the learning of so-called manual skills? And what should be the architecture of these schools and universities? What kind of campus would be most appropriate, given demographic, environmental, and climatic demands? How does one reconcile the so-called natural and life sciences with human and social sciences, which are also interested in nature and life? Africa can escape neither the mounting tide of educational proposals put forward by large communication multinationals with budgets greater than those of most African states, nor the conditions these organizations exact for the construction of their campuses. It cannot escape the problem of "logically" connecting the content and method of instruction with market demands, the consequences of concentrating schools and universities in urban centers, the implications of increasing costs of instruction (the costs of research, libraries, technology ...).

Imagining the African Campus

Nevertheless, one could say that Africa is fortunate to find itself obliged to address these questions (and on a massive scale) *today*. The opportunity has come: the stakes are clear; the incredible archive opened up by postcolonial, decolonial, environmental, queer, feminist, and indigenous studies has recently become available; and the large number of African youth eager to acquire knowledge, to contribute their energy and creative abilities (already visible in the numerous apps proposed by African start-ups, by their responses to the absence of the state) is an advantage. This is not to underestimate the indifference that African governments exhibit toward education – building schools and fighting illiteracy are not new problems. It is a matter of taking what's missing as a point of departure and, paradoxically, refusing the logic of "catching up." Nor is it a question of training engineers, doctors, sociologists, philosophers, the future employees of call centers or of the caretaking industry according to the dominant model, but of confronting challenges from a perspective that, by affirming the freedom to imagine alternatives, is in a position to propose new ways of teaching and learning. Africa has at its fingertips an incredible heritage – the archives of its past and those of the world – but it can also avail itself of new technological instruments, the incredible burgeoning of scientific research in Africa and about Africa, the rediscovery of ties to other continents that are not limited to bonds of domination and oppression, the explosion of the arts.

Now that the aura of the West as the "world's horizon" is fading, and the idea of education as the diffusion of enlightenment from high to low, illuminating those peoples "enveloped in night,"[9] is losing ground, the time has come for us to seize the opportunity for ourselves. We have not moved beyond an ideology that divides the world between peoples thought to "naturally" possess the qualities required for creating "the best of civilizations" and the peoples seen as lacking, which prevents them from being "complete" (this lack is also attributed to women, to so-called deviants, to minorities …). With its long history, this ideological pillar serves as a point of convergence between patriarchy, colonialism, capitalism, and the ideology of infinite technological progress, which feeds Promethean thinking. This ideology possesses a strong power of attraction: each human being who perceives themselves as incomplete wants to believe in the promise of completeness, and if you are defined as bearing the shameful mark of lack, you will do everything you can to escape such infamy and attain wholeness. Everything converges to reinforce this economy of lack [*économie du manque*] – school, advertising, the vocabulary of the liberal economy – which masks structural inequalities. *Devitalizing* this ideology, robbing it of its force, is one of the steps in the process of renewing pedagogical thought. This ideology of lack is racist and sexist because it implies that people of color, women, and sexual and religious minorities are originally inferior and places the burden of catching up on their shoulders. The notion of "success" – as it is defined by neoliberalism or by the economy of social networks (i.e. the number of friends and *likes* that is connected with your "profile" and that becomes an exchange *value*) – needs to be reconsidered so that we may better illustrate the criteria for success in education. What the African American feminist Barbara Christian in 1987 called "the race for theory" – playing on the two senses of "race" – remains meaningful: Christian related the hegemony in the academic world, and its gender, class, and racial hierarchy, to the perpetuation of racism.[10] The logic of this "race" transforms teaching and education into a field for promoting the ego and feeding narcissism. Against such a logic, Christian proposed a method in situ where the unexpected has its place: "I, therefore, have no set method, another prerequisite of the new theory, since for me every work suggests a new approach. As risky as that might seem, it is, I believe, what intelligence means – a tuned sensitivity to that which is alive and therefore cannot be known until it is known."[11]

For several years now, the anthropologist Aarti Kawlra and I have been using a similar method during workshops in Asia and Africa, and in what I called "The Atelier," which each year brings artists, activists, and researchers together in Paris. This method of collaborative, *situational* pedagogy accepts the unexpected and remains open to ideas that emerge on the spot – to learn by learning [*apprendre en apprenant*]. Insisting on the collaborative dimension, this method also includes an attention to the body, to the way in which the space either blocks or facilitates collaboration. It insists on the acknowledgment of the material and perceptible environment, on a reflection on the way hierarchies install themselves, "naturally."

If, as Rabindranath Tagore writes, school "is a manufactory specially designed for grinding out uniform results," how does one make room for the unexpected?[12] In a lecture on his childhood at school, Tagore offers a telling anecdote on the disconnect imposed by school (but also by the university), where bodies are obliged to remain silent and immobile. As a child, Tagore witnessed a teacher express surprise and annoyance at the sight of a young student climbing a tree in order to sit on a branch and study. He immediately demanded that the child get down; the next period, however, he encouraged the same student to go to the botany lesson. Tagore concluded that the school had fostered in him the sense of having been born "in a world where there are no trees."[13] For the teacher, the abstract knowledge of the tree replaced the personal experience of it. Put differently, education is a gradual apprenticeship in establishing a distance between knowledge and the living [*le vivant*], between what I learn at school and what I observe in life. Not even reading, which lies at the core of education, is allowed to be a source of sensual pleasure. And yet reading a text can produce physical pleasure and a feeling of happiness. The disjunction between school and life is a regular feature of school memories. In our own lives, however, we know that we also learn outside of books – that the senses have an important place in the acquisition of knowledge. Many careers are based on the use of senses, as in hearing, touching, smelling. Learning to cook, for example, is more than reading a recipe; it means *watching, smelling, tasting*. Nor is the mechanic's job an exclusively manual activity that requires no thought. Indeed, as the philosopher Matthew Crawford puts it in *Shop Class as Soul Craft*, "the disappearance of tools from our common education is the first step toward a wider ignorance of the world of artifacts we inhabit."[14] Having become a mechanic, Crawford warns his reader that he wants "to avoid the kind of mysticism that gets attached to 'craftsmanship'" and searches, instead, to rehabilitate "the ethics of maintenance and repair." Now, if there is one continent where such an ethic can be found, it is certainly Africa! However, such an ability to maintain and repair is not deemed an ethic – at best, it is considered a sign of resourcefulness, and its objects, sewn, stitched, and patched together, end up in galleries where their life drains out from them.

"The Master's Tools Will Never Dismantle the Master's House"

This sentence by the Black queer feminist poet Audre Lorde was delivered during a 1979 conference on Simone de Beauvoir's *The Second Sex* in New York; then, as now, it moves one to think. Placing herself within the long tradition of Black radicalism in the United States, Lorde echoed contemporary remarks by James Baldwin or the Black Panthers, for whom the reconquest of cultural autonomy, as an instrument for the genuine decolonization of the mind, was the precondition for the recovery of African Americans' pride and freedom. For Lorde, who drew on her experience as a Black, lesbian woman and mother, using the master's tools to demolish the master's house meant that the possibility of change would be limited to very narrow bounds. Using the master's tools might allow one to temporarily defeat him at his own game, but it would not lead to real change. In making this point, Lorde did not rule out every possibility for emancipation. White guilt, she assured us, was useless; one had to risk venturing onward "without guarantees," as Stuart Hall would say. Like Fanon, she encouraged us to think ahead and dare to imagine a form of freedom. Decolonization was not the arrival of a world one had dreamt of – nor was it revenge. The following statements by Fanon could constitute, with Lorde's remarks, the intellectual point of departure for imagining a methodology for Africa.

> I have not the right as a man of color to research why my race is superior or inferior to another.
> I have not the right as a man of color to wish for a guilt complex to crystallize in the white man regarding the past of my race.
> I have not the right as a man of color to be preoccupied with ways of trampling on the arrogance of my former master.
> I have neither the right nor the duty to demand reparations for my subjugated ancestors.
> There is no black mission; there is no white burden.[15]

One must move beyond the West's patriarchal, universalist vision of teaching as a "civilizing mission." This educational ideal contributed to colonial and imperialist ideology, but also to the project of the postcolonial state. Nor is the debate over. What should we do with the immense library at our disposal – the colonial library that Valentin-Yves Mudimbe describes so well in *The Invention of Africa* – and with all the other libraries? For African researchers such as Oyeronke Oyewumi, Ifi Amadiume, or Jimi O. Adésinà, the "intellectual dependence" upon concepts coming from the West compromises all attempts to understand and learn from African societies. In this sense, "gender" [*genre*] is not admissible, since "authentic African societies" cannot be studied with "foreign" conceptual tools.[16] In this debate, the philosopher Fabien Eboussi Boulaga's contribution remains both inestimable and inescapable. He uncovered the alienating fetishism of the two hegemonic positions: the search for a largely fantasized past glory on the one hand, and the servile mimicry of a triumphant West on the other. This lesson should be our point of departure. In addition, the admission that certain concepts are inadequate for analyzing how life and death, war and peace, or sexuality were conceptualized in Africa should not shut down all debate over forms of circulation and borrowing.

In practice, new experiments are taking place all across the world, adding to a significant library of decolonial methods and curricula. I am thinking of the Black Lives Matter Syllabus;[17] of "Māori Movement," a physical education program targeting young Māoris, adapted for contemporary needs but based on so-called traditional methods of apprenticeship;[18] or The Ateliers of Thought which began two years ago in Dakar.[19] It remains urgent, however, that we think about what will constitute the methods and contents of education and teaching in Africa, and that we conceive these possibilities as a *theoretical* and philosophical question, and not a strictly economic or sociological one.

In conclusion, I would like to revisit a method based on *un-learning* [*dés-apprendre*]: that of The Atelier which I have organized since 2015. The goal is simple: are we capable of creating together, collaboratively, leaving aside all constructions of the all-powerful master? Artists – practicing graphic arts, photography, dance, theatre, film – poets, philosophers, sociologists, writers, and activists are invited. The objective of 2016's Atelier II was to create in the span of two days an exposition that would evoke the proliferation of non-hegemonic narratives and representations in the postcolonial French republican context, while avoiding the model of the colonial exposition – the juxtaposition of images. It was a question of denationalizing the map, of provincializing France, of illuminating circulations, itineraries, and unexpected or unpredictable elements that characterize the space where the history of subaltern peoples is written. Participants were invited to bring images, books, objects, sounds, cooking recipes, songs, flags, geological maps, imaginary maps, travel narratives, the front-pages of newspapers, photographs, films, musical instruments, more books – all for the purpose of ephemerally realizing a cartography, which, though inevitably incomplete, would introduce multiple approaches and interpretations. The organizing principle was the following: we would start with what we have – our experiences, practices, knowledges, languages, memories – and with what we had brought, rejecting in the process the hegemonic logic of the economy of lack. Absence and lack had been central notions in colonial discourse and are central notions for imperialism and neoliberal capitalism. Atelier II took place in the empty space of a gallery, in whose center we placed objects, books, photos … On the first morning, we met in four groups (North, South, East, West) to discuss a series of themes – borders, camps, citizens, migrants, memory, culture. In the beginning of the afternoon, we began to trace the itinerary of our exposition by arranging, either together or in groups, the various objects. As one of the joint actions [*geste en commun*], I prepared a *massalé* of potatoes and green beans, and we cooked some rice during the Tuesday morning session. We finished the exposition in the early afternoon and did a tour. We discovered performances and readings of poems and texts, films about voguing, mock-ups [*maquettes*], an altar to the ancestors, photos. At 5 o'clock, the exposition was opened to the public; it finished the same evening that it opened. Indeed, we wanted to abide by two principles: nothing new would be brought after the first morning, and the exposition would be ephemeral. In June 2017, the fourth edition of The Atelier had as its theme *DYSTOPIAS/UTOPIAS/ HETEROTOPIAS*. This is how I summarized the idea prior to the event: the European literary genre utopia stages a world of happiness and peace; dystopia, a society whose errors produce an apocalyptic world. In the Global South, however, dystopia has become part of social life – genocides, the Trade, slavery, colonialism, massacres, forced labor, economic dependence, imperialism, wars. Given the progress of environmental destruction, systematic precarization, the difficult if not impossible access to resources Westerners take for granted (potable water, electricity, public health, legal defense …), dystopia seems to have become global. Starting from an acknowledgment of such historically situated dystopias, The Atelier imagines a utopia open to heterotopias. Here, utopia is understood as the force and energy of revolt, as an invitation extended to dreams of emancipation, and as an act of rupture: the courage to think beyond the bounds of what appears "natural," "pragmatic," "reasonable." In other words, this means that, although everything tells us that the hegemonic system is as natural as night and day, that time itself belongs to the powerful master, we overturn the order, we tear down the curtain that masks what is possible, we mark a break that sends the unjust order reeling – literally reeling in its composition, its certitudes, its symbolic organization. When we take such a step, then we are in utopia. Utopia – an expectation; a vision for the future; the prefiguration of *what is not yet the case*; an open, terrestrial, tangible, and immaterial space; a time that darts forward. Whereas the European narrative chooses the city as the site of revolutions and uprisings, we will start from the *forest*: place of spirits, witches, rebel bandits, resistance fighters, and Maroons [*marrons*]. The choice of the forest inscribes The Atelier into a memory and a history by taking a historically situated utopia and the symbolic act that instituted it – *the Bois Caïman oath*. On August 14, 1791, in a clearing in the middle of the forest, on a stormy night, amidst thunder and lightning and torrential rain, the Maroon leader Boukman says a prayer in creole: "Our God, so good for us, orders us to seek revenge for the wrongs we have suffered; he will guide our weapons and assist us ... Listen to the voice of freedom, speaking in our common heart." The ceremony concludes with an oath in which everyone present swears before Boukman and a priestess that they will join the fight for freedom set to begin on August 22, 1791. With this revolution, the slaves of Saint-Domingue shattered the logic of the world that had normalized slavery – which had already existed for three centuries – and subsequently led to the creation of the Haitian republic. Atelier IV would build on this counter-narrative and on those of the Maroons, witches, and rebels who were able to produce a regime of historicity free of lethal melancholy, carrying within themselves a *historical becoming* [*un devenir historique*].

When The Atelier took place in June 2017, one day consisted of a long walk in a forest close to Paris. This was an attempt to break away from the academic architecture that frames discussion, where one is seated around a table or before a podium – as if only these arrangements made thinking possible. We were not idealizing the walk, for often walking is also an occasion of suffering and anxiety, associated with survival, exile, and escape. Our walk had the objective of disturbing the space of academic architecture, a disciplinary structure which imposes its own law: to conduct the conversation seated, in a subtle (or not so subtle) hierarchy. Walking imposes a rhythm, and walking in nature transforms the act of talking and thinking as a group. One is forced to harmonize the movement of one's body and one's breath. The next day, we went to the Seine, to the river, passing thereby from the forest to the pavement and on to the water – that Seine in whose waters rest bodies of the Algerians drowned in 1961. We made our way next to the art venue La Colonie, where we held a constituent assembly. This assembly resulted in the drafting of a manifesto for restoring to utopia the radical power of the instant-break [*moment-rupture*]. The point was not to suggest that this method should become the *sole* method; it merely indicates the possibility of a *theory in practice* [*une théorie en pratique*]. As a form of teaching, it encourages sharing and exchange, the peaceful handling of dissensus, of friction, an attention to the body posing questions (echoing Fanon), respect, silence. The manifesto (text below) was not read but performed and danced.

A tremendous opportunity lies open to the African continent, to its poets, researchers, scientists, architects, engineers, teachers: the chance to write the curriculum of 21st-century pedagogy – a pedagogy that recognizes its deficiencies; that transforms them into strengths; that confronts the problems posed by wars, deaths, migrations, environmental destruction, violence against women and sexual minorities, people who identify as LGBTQ, outcasts. The pedagogy of a new humanism, of *being human as praxis*.[20]

Manifesto of Atelier IV

Let us tear down the curtain that masks what is possible. The powerful, the masters of Capital and Empire, tell us that the dystopia that we live is the norm and make us believe that they reign over time. Paraphrasing Frantz Fanon, we say the time has come to "shake off the great mantle of night which has enveloped us."[21] We want to bring about utopian thinking, understood as the force and energy of revolt, as the presence of and the invitation to dreams of emancipation, and as an act of rupture: the courage to think beyond the bounds of what appears "natural," "pragmatic," "reasonable." We do not seek to construct a utopian community but to reactivate the creative power of dreams of disobedience and resistance, of justice and liberty, of happiness and kindness, of friendship and wonder.

The world is dislocating our lives and the threats are growing. Everything is obliged to enter into the great global, racial, criminal, misogynist supermarket and become a commodity. Cultural appropriation masks itself in the clothing of diversity. History is becoming a vast store of bric-à-brac, and the postcolonial an enchanted world where one goes shopping for images, sounds, memories, bodies, and objects to fill cultural institutions as one sees fit, with no acknowledgment of the buried histories, bruised memories, and forgotten genocides.

By an insufferable reversal, the oppressors present themselves as victims. Once a handful of people took it upon themselves to declare History finished, everything became open to manipulation. Once the end of history is declared, there is no longer any need for peace; we are free to enter into a permanent state of war. Time is said to have stopped; history is no longer thought of as a process of contestations and aspirations, but as a moment trapped in an eternal repetition – an eternal return of the same. Historical revisionism produces new amnesias. On the one hand, widespread anti-intellectualism caters to the basest tastes; on the other, disincarnated art passes itself off as subversive. The very notion of "decolonization" is in the process of losing its meaning.

Nonetheless, everywhere a new day is dawning, spaces are opening up, voices are being raised, and the old term "solidarity" is starting to produce sense [*faire sens*] again. In this context, we want to restore power to dreams and hopes, to give them an open space on this earth, where the present can leap into the future. The fear of being dismissed as crazy will not force us to abandon utopia. Chatty subversion is of no interest to us. On the contrary, we are open to a thousand small acts, to the actions that everywhere organize resistance and transmission and that diffuse knowledge and awareness across temporalities and into spaces other than those of the masters.

In such reconfigurations, the figure of the Maroon, the one who refuses the long night of oppression, strikes us as primordial. The Maroons have bequeathed us the lesson of escape: escape, if only for an hour, if not a day, if not years – escape in order to create, in defiance of every expectation, a space of freedom. To make the Maroon into a fixed icon would already amount to betraying their memory. Such is the danger that awaits every figure of freedom, and we would soon run the risk of seeing this figure looking down at us from the pediments of museums. We give life back to the Maroon by requiring ourselves to be always in motion, always on the move, always in the process of inventing new, free territories. The night welcomes our dreams and opens for us unexplored paths …

We claim the right to be incomplete and contradictory. We want to creatively redefine the visual traces of history, to explore for the purpose of analyzing the present and imagining the future.

Our utopia must remain a goal that is never reached; it must bring forth a state of permanent curiosity.

Atelier IV – June 10–12, 2017
Commissioner: Françoise Vergès
Collège d'études mondiales, Cité internationale des arts & La Colonie
Bénédicte Alliot, Kader Attia, Paola Bacchetta, Jean-François Boclé, Odile Burluraux, Jephthe Carmil, Gerty Dambury, Myriam Dao, Lucie Dégut, Alexandre Erre, Fabiana Ex-Souza, Nathalie

Gonthier, Yo-Yo Gonthier, Antoine Idier, Marta Jecu, Léopold Lambert, Jean-Claude Carpanin Marimoutou, Myriam Mihindou, Kat Moutoussamy, Frédéric Nauczyciel, Pier Ndoumbe, Pascale Obolo, Yohann Quëland de Saint-Pern, France Manoush Sahatdjian, Melissa Thackway, Françoise Vergès, Mawena Yehouessi, Mikaela Zyss.

The Bewitchment of History
Mohammed Dib's *Who Remembers the Sea*

Soraya Tlatli

Soraya Tlatli *teaches literature and philosophy at the University of California, Berkeley. She specializes in francophone literature, psychoanalysis, and twentieth-century Continental philosophy. She has published many articles and books to date, including* La folie lyrique: essai sur le surréalisme et la psychiatrie *(Paris: L'Harmattan, 2004) and* Le psychiatre et ses poètes: essai sur le jeune Lacan *(Paris: Tchou, 2000). She is currently working on a book about the configuration of death in twentieth-century Algerian literature and ideology.*

An ancient and silent cataclysm having torn us from ourselves and the world, only a new cataclysm could restore us. But until then, we were to pursue our existence according to the order that was handed down to us, our disaffected destiny, grown cold, drained of its power, run aground deep inside each one of us.[1]

In what follows, I will develop the philosophical implications of this passage from Mohammed Dib's *Who Remembers the Sea*. The "ancient and silent cataclysm" – which dispossesses an entire collectivity, "ourselves" [*nous-mêmes*] – just like the "new cataclysm" – redemptive, prefiguring a dynamic of repossession, leading toward a different "ourselves" – can indeed be interpreted as symbolic ways of accounting for the violent conquest of Algeria and the war of national liberation (1954–62): a dynamic of being torn from oneself and returning to a collective self.[2] In this sense, one could say that the cataclysm is the key: the allegory of the war. And, to be sure, *Who Remembers the Sea*, published the same year that the Algerian War ended, 1962, is a fictional attempt to express the war's unheard-of violence through the use of an absolutely new style, profoundly at odds with the literary realism that had characterized Mohammed Dib's work until that point. "But until then," he continues, "we were to pursue our existence according to the order that was handed down to us, our disaffected destiny, grown cold, drained of its power, run aground deep inside each one of us." The description of this "order that was handed down to us," in the predestined perpetuation of an inhuman law, and the rebellion against this order make up the majority of the novel, indicating, it would seem, that the liberating potential of the "new cataclysm" allows for liberation from the yoke of coloniality.

This inhuman order – the war – as well as the rebellion are not the objects of realist description, for the reader is never confronted with a conventional war, nor with a precise territory, Algeria, whose name is never mentioned in the body of the text. One thus finds oneself faced with a new mythology of the war waiting to be deciphered. But how is one to interpret it? Dib invents a new mythology that makes recourse to the immemorial and the unprecedented alike; he drops us into the middle of a city that has fallen under the dominion of minotaurs and mummies. In this city, matter [*la matière*] is endowed with a life of its own. New buildings draw together, encroaching upon residents who desperately try to reach an underworld [*un sous-monde*] – an underground city – to escape the cruelty and resist. And, while this is going on, "iriace" birds, mocking and insolent, swarm in a perpetual frenzy above the residents: humans persecuted by telluric, avian, and mythic forces. Faced with such spectacular, imaginative abundance, unique in Algerian literature, one experiences a strong temptation to read allegorically, in the traditional sense of the term. One might well argue that this is an allegorical representation of the Algerian War. Persecuted by walls that never stop closing in on them, prey to the tremendous cruelty of minotaurs and iriace birds, forced to seek shelter beneath a city beset by all the forces of evil: the residents would thus be the members of the Algerian resistance. In such a reading, we would be dealing with a fictional version of the final throes of the Algerian War, conceived in a symbolic manner. At the same time, however, Dib's choice never to represent but instead to express the psychic horror of the Algerian War suggests that he wanted to endow his text with metaphysical depth. It therefore becomes necessary for us to examine the meaning of the allegory, which his novel invites us to consider in a new way. *Who Remembers the Sea* is indeed rooted in the Algerian War, and thus in history. I will attempt to show that, depending on the conception of history and of allegory that one has in mind, the very meaning of the text changes: on the one hand, and according to a traditional reading, the text could refer to the national history in the making; on the other, and according to the Adornian and Benjaminian conception of allegory, the text opens onto a new dimension: the violent processes of war and decolonization understood as the interruption of the course of history in the indistinguishability of life drives from death drives.

Allegory in the Debate over Postcolonialism

In the field of postcolonial studies, the term "allegory" refers in the first instance to the definition that Fredric Jameson proposes in *The Political Unconscious* – that is, the necessity of interpreting postcolonial literary works in relation to their intimate connection to the allegory of the nation. In the debate that Jameson's postulation of a causal link between postcolonial writing and national allegory provoked, the vigorous critique leveled by Aijaz Ahmad stood out in particular.[3] More recently, in 2012, Neil Lazarus attempted to defend the political and hermeneutic value of Jameson's use of allegory in *The Postcolonial Unconscious*. It is a continuing debate that inflects the very nature of postcolonial studies. Without entering into the details, I would like to emphasize that in all three cases – in Jameson, Ahmad, and Lazarus – the notion of allegory refers exclusively to the nation. The novel thus finds itself in a particularly "third-world" bind: the obligation to prefigure the emergence of the nation. An impressive number of Maghreb novels have been analyzed according to this interpretive grid. This has incited another, equally vigorous debate, denouncing any hermeneutic bias that reduces a novel to the message it transports at the expense of its literality [*littéralité*]. Nonetheless, this typical understanding of allegory as a vehicle for a national – if not nationalist – ideology is not convincing for works such as Dib's, where the imagined universe defies circumscription. These works present us with a new universe to decipher – a new universe that impoverishes rather than enriches the allegory of the nation in the Maghrebin novel. After sketching an analysis of Dib's novel, I will present the radically different interpretation of allegory elaborated by Theodor W. Adorno in "The Idea of Natural-History,"[4] and by Walter Benjamin in *Origin of the German Trauerspiel*.[5]

"Terrible and Legendary"

In his postface, Dib expresses his motivation for creating what he describes as the "terrible and legendary" fictional framework for his novel: "The sudden consciousness that came to me of the limitless character of the horror and, at the same time, of the extremely rapid erosion that it produced, was undoubtedly at the source of this writing of vision and foreboding.... Horror never grows more profound; it only repeats itself" (121). How is one to write about the Algerian War? While "our century, tortured, martyred, cries out its suffering and its despair, this erosion has gone on spreading.... How can one speak of Algeria after Auschwitz, the Warsaw ghetto, and Hiroshima? ... A little spilled blood, a little mangled flesh, a little sweat: there exists no more desperately dull [*terne*] spectacle" (121). Here, the refusal of mimesis ("there exists no more desperately dull spectacle") goes hand in hand with a project that is both aesthetic and ethical and that, in the scope of its theoretical ambition, exceeds both the realist enterprise (a description of the various twists [*péripéties*] of the Algerian War) and the linear sequence of historical events into which the Algerian War is inscribed. To break away, to escape the exhaustion [*l'usure*] induced by the repetition of historical tragedy that marks the twentieth century, one must flush out "the evil" at the source: "I understand then that the evil is not to be surprised amidst its ordinary enterprises, but elsewhere, in its true lair: man – and in the dreams, the deliria, that he feeds blindly" (122).

The apposition between man, on the one hand, and "the dreams, the deliria," on the other, will reverse itself in the sense that the latter phenomena, as we shall see, are no longer anchored in an individuality. What matters for Dib, then, is moving beyond the dimension of individual and collective trauma that war writing ordinarily evokes. His project is unique in the sense that it seeks to escape the memory of a violent past that haunts us into the present, so that it may produce something radically new [*un nouveauté radicale*] – for this reason, it presents the war not as a part of the course of history, but rather as the radical interruption thereof. A literally unheard-of endeavor: "For anyone who really cared to listen, there were other sounds to hear than the footfall of blood following its course" (4). Let's listen to those "other sounds."

The war that Dib describes is strange indeed, for it is less the stage of corporeal violence tied to singular individuals than the attempted fusion of history and nature through the creation of a new mythology and the clash of exceptional forces. We are thus confronted with a different reality – unknown to us, and for this reason unsettling. The war whose depiction one expects has been replaced by a nightmarish universe: mysterious monsters invade the city and its subterranean passages, while a new mythology emerges that mixes the well-known figure of the minotaur with the unknown figure of the "iriace" bird – a bird of prey. In parallel with this invention of a new mythology, the war's most extreme manifestations are the transformations to which matter has been subjected: the walls tighten around the city, cause buildings to burst; basalt, in turn, covers the walls while, underground, a world of resistance comes into being. Another city is created beneath the city: "The city was buried in basalt, … the basalt had covered it over…. The walls were constantly tying themselves into inextricable knots, mindless of what became of their captives" (9).

A peculiar logic thus falls into place: that of a series of unconscious drives which nonetheless cannot be referred back to a specific subject. The narrator had warned us from the narrative's beginning: "Our fate is decided between words without weight or color, gestures that no memory, no clay, no reflection ever captures. With us, outside us" (4).

This passage can be read as a *mise en abyme* of Dib's own project: to try to fix in writing and recollection an experience that is said [*qui se dit*] with words without weight or color, and that demands new words – a new mythology. The "other world" to which he refers here can be interpreted as the oneiric world, the unconscious, the other scene said to constitute who we are. But, contrary to what the postface seems to suggest, what one has here is not an individual unconscious, but rather a generalized scene of disquieting uncanniness [*scène généralisée de l'inquiétante étrangeté*] – namely, the abolition of the barriers between subjectivity and the object.[6] The state of the city is inseparable from the affect it produces in its residents, who can no longer be distinguished from it – who are no longer distinct from the forces that oppress them: the movement of the stone invading the city, even filling the throats of living beings, conjures up the nightmare of being absolutely walled off that looms over the whole narrative. The fact of being seized by stone further reinforces the difficulty of deciding between the categories of the living and the dead, the animate and the inanimate. Furthermore, the identification with deadly violence is so powerful that the book's message is also the nihilistic acknowledgment of such a fusion: to do away with the other is to risk erasing oneself in their disappearance. "'What should be done?' 'Demolish everything'" (115). For the other is so inseparable from the ego [le moi] that to demolish oneself is also to demolish the other, and conversely:

> There is no space, or almost none, between us and our city, we are neither there nor elsewhere, we are ourselves the city, or else it's us. Who is the other? No matter, we'll never know.... What is in us is in it as well, and it's terrible enough that one can pull from oneself so many resources, set oneself so many traps. (88)

Here, the war is no longer conceived in terms of a deadly confrontation between a constituted self or a specific collectivity, on the one hand, and the enemy, on the other. What matters, instead, is acknowledging an impossible sharing [partage], as well as a fusion of the ego [le moi] and the other [autrui]. Certainly, the initial violence of the Algerian War is what produces this fusion for Dib. And it is certainly such inextricability – the dangerous non-separation that leads to the symbolic death of the two entities, that leads to generalized destruction – which the narrative produces through its recurring figures of encirclement, of the basalt progressively moving in, of the moving walls that accompany the feeling of death, of the premonition of death that the narrative traverses while, drop by drop, the "footfall of blood follow[s] its course." Dib constructs his novel to produce a space where the distinctions between the ego and others, inside and outside, the city and the underground, can no longer exist, with the result that one loses touch with the foundation on which mental health is built: the barrier that differentiates my subjectivity from the surrounding world. At that point, how is it possible to situate limits?

This text is very violent. But what kind of violence are we dealing with exactly? A violence tied to the specific category of fright [effroi] – a fright that I will characterize as mythic. Here, the peak of violence lies in rendering alterity inactive. Dib's whole narrative obeys a dual process: on the one hand, alterity is suppressed; on the other, things are not recognized in their singularity – the city, the speaking, the invaders with names from science fiction. Topographical space is itself subjected to this process which consists in making the familiar strange and the strange familiar: the symbols of the other's sovereignty are enveloped in the symbolic body and annihilate it. This undifferentiation of ego, objects, and the other [*autrui*] rests on a deeper process of fusion and undifferentiation: nature sharing the attributes of history and, conversely, history appearing under the mask of nature. And it is just such an imbrication of history and nature that is presented by first Benjamin and then Adorno, in their respective essays. Indeed, it seems that the long habit of reading certain Maghrebin novels of the fifties and sixties as allegories of the nation has obfuscated a basic dimension of allegory: namely, how allegory stages the entanglement of history with nature – what Adorno calls the "natural-history."

The Bewitchment of History

The concept of natural-history (*Natur-Geschichte*) flickers in and out of Adorno's corpus. It was only conceptualized once, during a lecture Adorno gave in Frankfurt on July 15, 1932. That said, it long remained "obscene" in the etymological sense: off stage [*hors scène*]. Published only posthumously, the lecture maintained a hidden existence for all of the philosopher's existence: a text kept secret during his life. According to certain theorists, however, the early concept constitutes the luminous core of his future work. By a curious sort of mirroring, Adorno acknowledged the scope of its philosophical power not in his own thinking, but in the thought of Benjamin. In the eulogy that he wrote for Benjamin ten years after his death, Adorno makes the concept of "natural-history" into the centerpiece of his friend's philosophy:

> The totality of his thought is characterized by what may be called "natural history" (*Natur-Geschichte*). He was drawn to the petrified, frozen, or obsolete elements of civilization, to everything in it devoid of domestic vitality no less irresistibly than is the collector to fossils [*sic*] or to the plant in the herbarium.... He is driven not merely to awaken congealed life in petrified objects ... but also to scrutinize living things so that they present themselves as being ancient, "ur-historical" and abruptly release their significance.[7]

In what follows, I propose to reconstruct the echoes of their mutual correspondence on the subject of natural-history. Nonetheless, to grasp the implications of the philosophical blow that Adorno attempts to deal out in his 1932 text, it is necessary to briefly situate the discipline of natural history. In the classical sense – Greek and Latin – the term designates research in the natural sciences, or even "the report of an inquiry into nature."[8] Such study, which excludes the work of interpretation (*Deutung*) from its domain, considers its object, nature, in its static dimension – which is to say, a-temporally. It was not until the beginning of the eighteenth century that the discipline began to incorporate the dimension that it had ignored until then: the historical dimension. The historicity of the object "nature" thus only became an active participant in its conceptualization with the philosophy of the Enlightenment.[9] For his part, Adorno tries to break with both of these understandings of natural history by inscribing history and nature into a dialectical process in which each element cannot help but refer to the other.[10] The same problematic will form the heart of the *Dialectic of Enlightenment*,[11] where "nature and history are not fused with each other, rather they break apart and interweave at the same time in such a fashion that the natural appears as a sign for history and history, where it seems to be most historical, appears as a sign for nature."[12] With respect to this relation between history and nature, Adorno says he has in mind "a sort of bewitchment of history." Indeed, only then is the historical "pass[ed] off" as the natural.[13] That would thus be the mutual bewitchment of history and of nature.

This concept has a precise signification for Adorno. In the first place, such a relation to a nature loaded with history means that we interpret nature in its ephemerality – that is, we ascribe it a historicity. Unlike what happens in all scientific understandings of nature, ephemerality here is not an indicator of the fact that nature goes through an evolution; rather, the point is that the signification of nature's historicity becomes perceptible under the sign of the ruin.[14] The ruin places nature in history. And it is here that Benjamin's philosophical intervention becomes crucial. For the apprehension of nature in its historical dimension – that is, as transitory, as ephemeral – is precisely what Benjamin calls allegory.

For Benjamin, allegory's theme is history. This conception of history is particularly fruitful, for it allows one to incorporate questions about the relationship between history, nature, and mythical power into one's understanding of colonial violence, and thereby allows one to conceptualize such violence differently. In "The Idea of Natural-History," Adorno references Benjamin's *Origin of the German Trauerspiel*, the text which in his opinion elevated allegory to the status of a philosophical object. Indeed,

Adorno notes that, according to Benjamin, "in nature the allegorical poets saw eternal transience [*Vergängnis*], and here alone did the saturnine vision of these generations recognize history." When history comes on to the scene in the German baroque drama, "it does so as a cipher to be read. 'History' is writ across the countenance of nature in the sign language of transience."[15]

Allegory according to Benjamin and Adorno

History and nature are imbricated then, but in what way are they joined? According to Adorno, Benjamin developed an understanding of temporality grounded in the transitory. Such ephemerality and transitoriness are precisely what make the connection between history and nature possible. For Benjamin, nature presents itself as ephemeral (*vergänglich*) in its transitoriness. Doomed to decline, it presents itself as history; the temporality in which nature participates is thus not fundamentally different from the temporality of history: "'History' is writ across the countenance in the sign language of transience." History here does not exclusively refer to concrete history – that is, history as a sequence of historical events. Rather, it is a question of thinking the junction of two temporalities that previously were presented as distinct: that of history and that of nature. "Whenever a historical element appears," Adorno writes, "it refers back to the natural element that passes away within it. Likewise the reverse: whenever 'second nature' appears, when the world of convention approaches, it can be deciphered in that its meaning is shown to be precisely its transience."[16] This conjunction of history and nature operates exclusively in the allegorical mode.

All the novelty of this understanding of allegory lies in the entwinement of history and nature that Benjamin describes thus:

> [I]n allegory there lies before the eyes of the observer the *facies hippocratica* of history as a petrified landscape. History, in everything untimely, sorrowful, and miscarried that belongs to it from the beginning, is inscribed in a face – no, in a death's head.... This is the core of the allegorical vision, of the Baroque profane exposition of history as the Passion of the world – meaningful only in the stations of its decline.[17]

At stake, then, is a radically new interpretation of allegory, since allegory, while marking history's irreversible movement through "the stations of its decline," is no longer grounded in the traditional distinction between the sensible and the intelligible. Traditionally, allegory presents an abstract entity in a concrete form – the allegory of the nation, for example. Similarly, the difference between allegory and symbol lies in the nature of the articulation that joins the sensible and the intelligible. The articulation is motivated in the case of the symbol; it is unmotivated, Benjamin claims, in allegory. Moreover (and this constitutes his principal contribution), Benjamin introduces a temporality specific to the allegorical, which presents history under a specific emblem: the death's head, cadaverous rigidity. "If nature has at all times been subject to the power of death," Benjamin writes, "it is also at all times allegorical."[18] It contains a historical moment. Allegorical language "is the language of the creature who, having lost Paradise, wanders endlessly in the labyrinth of Creation in the hopes of recovering by itself the key to meaning [sens] ... But nothing emerges to guarantee the objectivity of these significations."[19]

Allegory is unmotivated and thus requires an understanding of history as irresolute. The world of baroque drama, analyzed through the lens of its major feature – allegory – is characterized by an absence of motivation. One could say that such irresolution is brought to the point of greatest luminosity by Dib who presents a world at once apocalyptic and potentially redeeming. The whole dynamic of *Who Remembers the Sea* is no different: make the cataclysm into the simultaneous movement of death and renewal. What Dib's narrative brings into sharp relief is how mythic violence destroys the psychic identity that allows me to differentiate myself from the other, that allows me to singularize myself. Such recognition of individuality is precisely what is lost in Dib's exposition of the violence of war, which, for this reason, renders living beings not mortal, not mortal targets, but dehumanized, unable to present themselves as their own [*se poser comme propre*] or to remember on their own [*se souvenir en tant que propre*], separated from the other. The text produces a unique kind of fright, occasionally counterpoised only by the sea and its power.

The Sea

The sea is presented throughout the text in the unrelenting breaking of waves that carries us away. The sea is the only available refuge from the psychic violence; it is at once a maternal force (mother/

sea [*mère/mer*]) and a sentinel of memory, and of history, a piercing invocation. The breaking of the waves rocks both the narrator and the reader in a hypnotic movement. "One often forgets that the sea, above all, is ageless; in this resides its strength" (11). The sea is nonetheless charged with history. But this history is its own, not that of the humans whom it rocks. Its history is the history of nature. In this sense, it would seem to fall within Adorno's concept of natural-history. The text produces a kind of fright which only the infinite breaking of waves seems to counterbalance. To the sea falls the charge of memory, a power of remembrance issuing from an immemorial being. The sea returns; it reappears in the narrator's nocturnal dreams and contributes to the peculiar temporal rhythm of this story, which is animated not by the single temporality of events but by that of a mythic nature.

"At times there still comes to me a sound of something shattering, of muffled singing, and I let my thoughts wander, I remember the sea" (120).

A redemptive power, a maternal power which once "embraced the feet of man, remembering back to when it had carried him" (9), the sea also reigns as a transcendence: "the wisdom of the sea always wins out in the end over man's little displays" (121). Paradoxically, as the power of memory, the sea "is ageless; in this resides its strength" (11). It is thus a memorial power that issues from an immemorial being. The sea remembers the humans and bears their memory, and not the contrary. Indeed, *Who Remembers the Sea* proceeds by means of the ablation of subjectivity, since the pronoun "who" [*qui*] is a ruse [*leurre*]. It is not anchored in an actor; it refers to no individuality – at best, it points to an anonymous and indistinct collectivity. This very indistinction calls into question the pronoun's precision; it runs aground rather than finds itself in the sea that holds all its memory. One might then think that, as an a-temporal memory, the sea incorporates into itself humanity's entire past. Its history. When they are read as part of traditional allegories, the figures of the sea and the cataclysm would thus seem to refer to diametrically opposed significations: on the one hand, the sea as a symbol of redemption, the bearer of an ageless history; on the other hand, the cataclysm as a symbol of humanity's disappearance. However, if one considers these two elements in greater depth, a different, subjacent dynamic emerges: neither sea nor cataclysm is considered exclusively in their naturalness [*naturalité*]. In them, history and nature are confused and profoundly imbricated.

We often speak of the Algerian War imagistically – indeed, in the terms of cataclysm. My whole intention consists in eliminating this symbolic imagery that weakens the force of Mohammed Dib's statements. When Dib speaks of an "ancient and silent cataclysm" that had "torn us from ourselves and the world," and of the need for a "new cataclysm" as the only thing that might return us to ourselves, he is not speaking symbolically about the horrors of war, but about a cataclysm. There is no doubt that much would be gained by reading this cataclysm allegorically, in the sense put forward by Adorno (following Benjamin): nature's telluric powers are confronted with history in such a way that they become imbricated in it. It was my intention to show that Dib's writing brings us face to face with a deadly union of history and nature, where history is envisaged under the sign of death through the natural figure of the cataclysm – an allegory, in Adorno's and Benjamin's sense.

This constellation of texts continues to have something essential to say to us, in my opinion. For Dib, the violence of war certainly involves psychic fright, a fright entirely driven by "disquieting uncanniness." When introducing the problematic of allegory in Benjamin's work, I noted that his version of disquieting uncanniness is even more radical than the psychoanalytic version that Freud offers.[20] Benjamin's uncanny manages to intimately combine what good sense encourages us to separate: history and nature. If, as I have attempted to sketch, this imbrication does indeed take place in Dib's text, then the time has come to subject colonial times to the scrutiny of a new reading, as befits a negative imagination [*une imagination négative*] anchoring itself in prior destruction, an imagination gesturing toward the creative capacity of the death drive. This is how I would interpret the novel's final, enigmatic lines.

> Exploding one after the other, the new constructions all went up in smoke, to the very last one, following which the walls fell apart and collapsed: the city was dead, its remaining inhabitants standing in the middle of the ruins like desiccated trees, in the pose in which the cataclysm had surprised them, until the arrival of the sea, whose tumult had long been heard. (120)

What Dib offers us in the domain of fiction – what psychoanalysis would call the creative capacity of the death drive[21] – is deeply anchored in the Adornian and Benjaminian notion of allegory, where it is effectively a question of projecting oneself "towards an immemorial past by the royal road of an eros-thanatos."[22] The sea is the royal road to this fusion of an eros-thanatos. Since it issues from the imbrication of nature, life, and history, what this conception of allegory proposes is the imbrication of the life drive and the death drive, which cease to be distinguishable. Put differently, to claim that history and nature are joined amounts to no longer distinguishing between the power of these two drives. It is just this fright that characterizes Mohammed Dib's text and its extraordinary hold on its readers.

Currency, Sovereignty, Development
Revisiting the Question of the CFA Franc

Ndongo Samba Sylla

Ndongo Samba Sylla *is a developmental economist. After having worked as a technical advisor to the Presidency of the Republic of Senegal, he is now responsible for programming and research at the West African office of the Rosa Luxemburg Foundation (Dakar). The author and editor of many works, he has published on fair trade, labor markets in developing countries, social movements, democratic theory, and economic and monetary sovereignty, among other topics.*

The current debate about the CFA franc strangely recalls the intellectual context in the run up to the period of African independence. At the time, there were, on one side, those who demanded immediate independence and planned on moving toward political integration on Pan-Africanist lines. On the other side, there were the "gradualists" and those who wanted to remain within the bounds of the "French community."

Now, 60 years later, one sees, *mutatis mutandis*, the same stances being taken. On one side, there are the "abolitionists" – that is, those who desire the abolition of the system of political, economic, financial, and monetary relations known as the CFA franc. This camp brings together three profiles: sovereigntist, Pan-Africanists, and heterodox economists.

On the other side, there are the "conservatives" – that is, those who are for the maintenance of the CFA franc system, for either self-interested, ideological, or pragmatic reasons. This camp brings together the representatives of the dominant classes and those with interests abroad: the French government and its experts, orthodox economists, political authorities (African heads of state, finance ministers, senior officials, etc.), monetary authorities (governors and executives of central banks, experts working for community institutions ...).

This essay is an introduction to a debate that, while not new, is again making news in francophone countries. At the same time, it takes a position in favor of liberating African countries from the FCFA system.

Some Historical Context

The CFA franc is a late avatar of the monetary relations that link France and Africa. In this tumultuous history, 1820 is a year of symbolic importance, coinciding with the introduction of the écu in the geographic space that would later become Senegal.[1] Relations took a consequential new turn on December 21, 1853, when the Bank of Senegal was created by decree of Napoleon III. The bank's capital, which was entirely in the hands of French colonists, derived in part from the compensation that the French state had offered French slaveowners after the formal abolition of slavery in France in 1848.[2] Dissolved in 1901, the Bank of Senegal was reborn in the period 1901–55 under the name Banque d'Afrique-Occidentale [Bank of West Africa; BAO]. Following the law of January 29, 1929, this private bank found itself entrusted with issuing the franc that circulated within the French colonies of Sub-Saharan Africa. It exercised this responsibility under the supervision of the Bank of France. The BAO's successors would include the Institut d'émission de l'Afrique Occidentale Française et du Togo [lit. the note-issuing institution of French West Africa and Togo] (1955–9) and the Banque centrale des États de l'Afrique de l'Ouest [Central Bank of West African States, BCEAO] (1959–present).

The franc was introduced in Sub-Saharan Africa as an instrument of colonial domination. To take the exemplary case of the western Volta (now located in Burkina Faso), the franc was imposed progressively and at the expense of the vibrant pan-African commercial networks based upon the use of cowries, which served simultaneously as a unit of account, a means of payment, and a store of value.

The cowries came from the Indian Ocean. They arrived in Africa via European merchants who exchanged them for African products. They served as a means of payment, just like gold, pieces of silver, salt bars, brass rods, pearls, textile moneys, etc. During the eighteenth century especially, they started being adopted by African traders and itinerant merchants above all .

In 1907, following the war of colonial conquest that had begun in 1898 in the western Volta, the colonial government of francophone West Africa prohibited the importation of cowries, as well as the use of cowries for the payment of colonial taxes. These authoritarian measures were not enough to break the monetary resistance [*résistance monétaire*] of the region's populations. In 1925, with the adoption of the new Code de l'indigénat [lit. "native code"], not accepting the franc in commercial transaction became a crime punishable without trial.[3]

The influence of cowries dwindled immediately following the Second World War, notably with the creation of the CFA franc. They had been defeated by the growth of trade with the metropole. In francophone Africa, therefore, what anthropologists call "monetary transition" was achieved with violence and over time – monetary resistance lasted 50 years. There was nothing spontaneous about the adoption of the franc. It had to be imposed upon Africans, and above all on the African merchants who were active in small-scale commerce and whose resistance to the franc routinely provoked the ire of colonial administrators.[4]

The Pillars of the FCFA System

The CFA franc – originally the "Franc of the French Colonies in Africa" [*franc des colonies françaises d'Afrique*] – was officially created on December 26, 1945, to facilitate France's economic activities in its colonies in Sub-Saharan Africa. From its birth, its function as an instrument of extracting economic surplus always went hand in hand with its function as an instrument for controlling and subjugating African peoples. Despite the fact that, in other experiences of decolonization, the acquisition of national independence typically led to the adoption of a national currency, this was not the case in many francophone countries. For these countries, attaining state sovereignty presupposed the preservation of a set of neocolonial relationships in cultural, diplomatic, military, economic, commercial, financial, and monetary domains.

With the period of independence, the acronym FCFA changed its designation. It acquired two meanings: franc of the Financial Community of Africa [*franc de la communauté financière africaine*], the money that today is common to the eight countries of the West African Economic and Monetary Union (Union économique et monétaire ouest-africaine, or UEMOA: Benin, Burkina Faso, Ivory Coast, Niger, Senegal, Togo, Mali – which left the group in 1962 and rejoined in 1984 – and Guinea-Bissau – which joined the group in 1997); and the "franc of Financial Cooperation in Central Africa" [*franc de la coopération financière en Afrique centrale*], the money that today is common to the six countries of the Economic and Monetary Community of Central Africa (Communauté économique et monétaire de l'Afrique central, or CEMAC: Cameroon, the Central African Republic, the Republic of the Congo, Gabon, Chad, and Equatorial Guinea – which joined the community in 1985).

From its inception to the present, however, the pillars of the FCFA system have remained the same:

- a fixed rate of exchange with the euro (previously, with the French franc) that is set at 1 euro = 655.95 CFA francs;
- France's guarantee of the so-called unlimited convertibility of CFA francs into euros;
- the centralization of exchange reserves: external assets are first centralized at the level of the two central banks (the Central Bank of West African States, and the Bank of Central African States [*Banque des États de l'Afrique centrale*, BEAC]) which, since 2005 and 2007 respectively, have been obliged to deposit half of their net external assets in so-called operational accounts [*comptes d'opérations*], specially run by the French Treasury. In the immediate aftermath of independence, they had been obliged to deposit 100 percent of their net external assets (65 percent between 1973 and 2005). This mechanism was established in exchange for France's "guarantee" of so-called unlimited convertibility;
- the free transfer of capital within the franc zone.

In essence, the debate about the CFA franc is organized around two principal questions. The first is of a political nature and can be formulated thus: is the CFA franc really an African currency (that is, a currency sovereignly administered and controlled by Africans for their own benefit), or is it rather an instrument of neocolonialism wielded by France? Implicitly, this is a question about the democratic legitimacy of the CFA franc: is it an asset or a handicap for the African countries that have it in common?

The Question of Monetary Sovereignty

Is the CFA franc a sovereign African currency? There are two perspectives one can take in attempting to respond to this question: the first is political, the next is economic. In the former, one speaks of monetary sovereignty from a legal/institutional point of view, while in the latter one inquires instead into the independence of monetary policy.[5]

From a political perspective, the CFA franc is a currency used by Africans; it is not a currency controlled by Africans. It is rather an instrument of neocolonialism wielded by the French government. Several facts support this claim.

First, it is necessary to emphasize French influence at the level of the two central banks (BCEAO and BEAC). In its capacity as the guarantor of the convertibility of CFA francs into euros, France has representatives on the governing bodies of both central banks (notably, on the administrative council and the committee of monetary policy). Given that all members must agree for the statutes of either central bank to be modified, the presence of France's representatives on these bodies implicitly grants France veto power with respect to all essential questions, even if ordinary decisions are made on the basis of a simple majority of votes. While the two central banks are independent with respect to African governments – having no obligation to report to them – they are not with respect to the French Treasury. From this perspective, if one were to insist on strict accuracy, the Central Bank of West African States and the Bank of Central African States should be called: Central Bank of the States of the Franc Zone in West Africa [*Banque centrale des États de la zone franc en Afrique de l'Ouest*] and Bank of the States of the Franc Zone in Central Africa [*Banque des États de la zone franc en Afrique centrale*].

Second, foreign exchange policy (the determination of the exchange rate regime and the external value of CFA francs) falls, in principle, under the authority of the French Treasury as the presumed guarantor of the currency. In this manner, France effectively adjudicated to itself the power over whether to devalue the CFA franc or not – as can be seen in the January 1994 devaluation, and in the devaluation to determine the CFA franc's nominal anchor.

This last point was brought to the fore when France abandoned the franc for the euro. With disappearance of the franc, it was necessary to find a new nominal anchor for the CFA franc. France exercised its sovereignty by anchoring the CFA franc and the Comorian franc to the euro in an agreement with the authorities of the European Union.

Formalized by the EU Council's November 23, 1998 decision, this agreement stipulates that the European Union's Economic and Financial Committee must be informed before any change in the exchange rate of CFA francs to euros can be made. Moreover, it stipulates that France is obligated to inform the Economic and Financial Committee, the Commission, and the European Central Bank of any plans to modify "the nature or scope" of the agreements concerning exchange regime matters between France and the countries of the franc zone in Africa. In this manner, the decision gave material form to the tutelage France and the European Union exercised over the FCFA system.

Third, monetary signs (banknotes and coins) are made in France by the printers of the Bank of France. To be sure, the large majority of African countries with so-called national currencies do not produce their monetary signs themselves. However, in the case of the countries of the FCFA zone, one cannot help but wonder why more than 70 years of "monetary cooperation" with France has not enabled FCFA countries to develop the means for producing coins and banknotes. Nor can one help wondering about the absence of international solicitations for bids on the contracts, despite the considerable sums involved.

Finally, it must be said that France has rarely tolerated dissidence with respect to the FCFA system. Proof of the extremely political character of the FCFA system is that, between 1960 and 2012, roughly 40 percent of attempted *coups d'état* recorded on the African continent took place in countries of the franc zone.[6]

While abolitionists tend to insist on the different dimensions of French monetary tutelage, African conservatives typically attempt to brush them aside by arguing that the CFA is an African currency ... since it is accepted by the people. As for French conservatives, their dominant rhetoric maintains that the CFA franc belongs to the Africans, and that France is acting like a big brother by providing support to the countries that share its use. Indeed, from the perspective of the Institut Montaigne, a think tank close to President Macron, today's CFA franc is nothing more than an instrument of development aid, graciously conferred by France upon the Africans.[7]

From an economic point of view, monetary sovereignty refers to a state's ability to use monetary policy to attain given domestic objectives, especially in relation to production and employment. According to the heterodox macroeconomic approach known as Modern Monetary Theory, the concept of "sovereign currency" refers to currencies such as the dollar, the yen, and the pound sterling – that is, national currencies with floating exchange rates.[8]

Taken individually, the member states of the FCFA zone are not sovereign in a monetary sense, since they have made a decision to fuse together in a large monetary bloc. In their case, the question is thus whether monetary policy is autonomous for each of the two FCFA blocs. The answer is no.

In economics, there is a well-known principle that you cannot have a fixed exchange rate, the free circulation of capital, and monetary autonomy all at the same time. You can only have two of these three possibilities at one and the same time. Since a fixed exchange rate with the euro and the free circulation of capital are two of the four pillars of the FCFA system, it follows that the FCF"s two blocs do not have monetary autonomy. These central banks are obligated, *nolens volens*, to adapt to the monetary policy of the European Central Bank. Put differently, the choice was made to pursue a monetary policy that responds to the changing circumstances of the euro zone, rather than of the countries of the two FCFA blocs. Put still another way, some of the poorest countries on the planet, such as Niger and the Central African Republic, are subject to a monetary policy that better reflects the fluctuations of the euro zone than the fundamentals of their own economies and the urgent demands of the moment.

The FCFA zone has the unique distinction of being the oldest integrated monetary zone still in existence (the sterling area and the escudo monetary zone no longer exist); it is unprecedented in the sense that very rarely does one see two monetary zones operating in accordance with the same principles band together through a fixed rate of exchange with another monetary zone. Most economists would agree with the proposition, backed by empirical evidence and good sense, that no single foreign exchange regime is suited for all countries or all times.[9] Nonetheless, the anachronistic persistence of the FCFA system seems to imply that a single foreign exchange regime is indeed optimal *ad vitam aeternam* for a certain number of African countries.

Before finishing with this first aspect of the debate, it is important to revisit the claim that France is the "guarantor" of the CFA franc

– which is to say, France would guarantee the so-called unlimited convertibility of CFA francs into euros. During his November 28, 2017 visit to Burkina Faso, Emmanuel Macron made the following statement about the CFA franc: "France is not its master; it is its guarantor."

Emmanuel Macron has it all wrong: in practice, France is the master of the CFA franc, it is not its guarantor. The system of operational accounts was conceived so that France would, for all intents and purposes, never be obliged to reach into its pockets to "guarantee" the convertibility of CFA francs.[10] When the African countries have sufficient foreign exchange reserves, France's guarantee is superfluous. When, however, they do not have enough – which happened once (in 1993) – France chooses to devalue the currency. An insurer is someone who promises to provide financial assistance should the dreaded event for which one pays an insurance premium take place. This role has never been filled by France. In addition, if one trusts a recent analysis by Standard & Poor's communicated by the press, the French Public Treasury has not agreed to advances for either central bank since 1994.[11]

Based on this fact, the following question inevitably poses itself: what justifies French tutelage over the FCFA system, given that, in practice, France does not "guarantee" the convertibility of this currency? Perhaps, one day, conservatives will deem this question worthy of an answer.

Nonetheless, this generally concealed fact allows one to see why Macron sidesteps the true stakes of the issue when he pretends to offer countries dissatisfied with the FCFA system the opportunity to leave. To be fair, if any member were to leave the system, that member should be France, first and foremost. Such a "Frexit" is one of the major demands put forward by certain Pan-Africanist movements who have mobilized around the issue of the CFA franc. In principle, it requires African countries to decide as a group to abolish the conventions underlying the operational accounts that bind them to the French government.

On the Economic Impact of the CFA Franc

The other side of the debate over the CFA franc concerns its economic impact: is the CFA franc an asset or is it a handicap for African economies? Let's begin by noting four major characteristics shared by the countries belonging to the FCFA zone.

The first is their meager productive dynamism: over the long term – over the last 60 years – the countries of the FCFA zone have experienced low mean rates of annual growth. With the exception of Equatorial Guinea, which is an oil-exporting country, and Mali, the other countries in the zone have reported an average growth in per capita GDP of less than 2 percent for the years between independence (or their entry into the FCFA zone) and the present. Of the 14 countries, 10 fall into the category of least developed countries (LDC), while the 4 non-LDCs (Cameroon, Congo, Ivory Coast, Gabon) have seen their real per capita GDP decline in absolute terms with respect to their historical peaks in the 1970s and 1980s (see the table in the appendix).

The second is that the countries of the FCFA zone exhibit the weakest socioeconomic indicators in the world. For example, the bottom four entries on the United Nations' Human Development Index for 2016 are countries in the FCFA zone – namely, Burkina Faso, Chad, Niger, and the Central African Republic.[12]

The third is their low degree of structural transformation: all countries in the FCFA zone are, without exception, exporters of raw materials.[13]

Finally, trade across the franc zone remains very modest, despite 72 years of monetary integration: commercial exchanges between countries of the franc zone represent less than 10 percent of all their commercial exchanges.[14]

To be sure, the CFA franc is not the source of all the economic troubles that afflict the countries that share its use. Nor do those who despise monetary domination argue that the abolition of the FCFA system would magically solve all the difficulties that these countries face. This is because opponents of the CFA franc do not consider currency outside its various articulations with other instruments of economic policy and the economic strategies pursued by states. Nor do they think about currency without putting it in relation to other aspects of imperialist domination. Herein lies their difference from the conservatives, who tend to conceive currency as an essentially technical issue and, more precisely, as a veil ... having no real effect on production ... over the long term! The limits of this intellectual perspective have been exposed in the most flagrant manner by the global financial crisis of 2007–8.[15]

The FCFA system bears its share of responsibility for the economic situation of its African countries, and does so for three reasons: (1) it is a system of financial repression; (2) it is a dysfunctional economic arrangement; and (3) it is a mechanism for extracting surpluses.[16]

System of financial repression

In the capitalist world-system, money is located at production's *starting point* as well as being its *object*. To produce, it is necessary to have access to capital, and therefore to credit. The aim of production is to accumulate a monetary surplus; the priority is not the satisfaction of social needs. Hence the famous formula M – C – M': money (to produce) – commodities (that are sold to obtain) – more money. In the capitalist world-system, the growth of production requires the availability of credit, which is the creation of supplementary means of payment.

It is necessary to recall this basic teaching of the monetary theory of production, since one often hears conservatives claim that FCFA zone countries' major problem is not money, but rather the weakness and non-diversified character of their production. This type of reasoning amounts to exonerating the monetary system (and the foreign exchange regime) of any responsibility for the meager structural transformation of African economies, and consists, in practice, in putting the cart before the horse. Without credit, without the creation of money, how can one conceive capitalist-style accumulation?

The paradox of the FCFA zone is that its economies are under-financed in a context of excessive liquidity in the banking system – that is, in a situation in which banks have excessive reserves at the central bank.[17] In 2014, the ratio of credits to the economy in relation to GDP corresponded to the 1991 measure in both zones.[18] Not only has there been stagnation with respect to the level of credit, but the better part of bank loans are short term and awarded to the tertiary sector. Prioritized sectors such as agriculture and the secondary sector's small- and medium-sized enterprises and industries have limited access to bank financing.[19]

To such problems, one must add the prohibitively high cost of credit in the FCFA zone. According to the Bank of France, the interest margins of the banks (the difference between the return on loans and the average costs of the resources) is of the order of 9 percent, which is higher than the global average of 5 percent, and higher than what is seen in countries such as South Africa and Morocco.[20] This fact contradicts the conservatives' argument that the flipside of the modest inflation in FCFA zone countries is a cost of credit that is lower than elsewhere in real terms. Moreover, it is enough to point out that the banks of the FCFA zone have among the highest rates of profitability in the world[21] – quite an achievement when one considers the modest amount of bank financing reported in most countries of the zone!

The best illustration of the FCFA system's deficiencies with respect to the allocation of credit is provided by the following comparison: while the employees of the BCEAO (roughly 2,500) had been able to benefit from a volume of credit of 52.2 billion CFA francs in 2016,[22] in the same year outstanding credit in the economy of Guinea-Bissau reached 63.6 billion CFA francs.[23] Is it possible to develop a modern economy with this level of indebtedness? Is it normal that a country of 1.8 million inhabitants receives a volume of credit comparable to that extended to the employees of a central bank, where the population is 700 times smaller?

Dysfunctional economic arrangement

As an economic arrangement, the FCFA system is dysfunctional in three respects. First of all, the choice of a fixed foreign exchange regime ends up privileging external equilibrium at the expense of internal equilibrium. This trade-off – which implies monetary policy's lack of autonomy – is questionable for economies that need to grow and diversify their production as well as create decent employment opportunities. It is even more questionable in light of the extreme volatility of the economies of the FCFA zone, a volatility provoked by political, economic, and environmental/climatic shocks.

One advantage of a floating exchange regime over a fixed exchange regime is that a floating regime is better able to absorb shocks without excessively impacting production and employment. In the economic literature, one reads that fixed rates of exchange allow for low inflation while having the disadvantage of being associated with increased volatility in the areas of production and employment. By contrast, floating rates of exchange generally produce more inflation and less volatility in production and employment.[24]

Next, the flipside of the anti-inflationist obsession is economic growth that falls below what FCFA zone countries are capable of.[25] In any case, since the introduction of the euro, one has observed that per capita revenue in FCFA zone countries has grown an average of 1.4 percent per year, compared with 2.5 percent in the rest of Sub-Saharan Africa.[26]

Finally, the policy of foreign exchange is inconsistent with other instruments of economic policy: to have a strong currency is akin to subventioning imports and taxing exports. In the case of FCFA zone countries, pegging the franc to a strong currency like the euro penalizes the exportation of anything except raw materials. Indeed, maintaining an exchange regime as inflexible as the CFA franc in a context of commercial liberalism is a kind of double penalty (a decrease in tariff and non-tariff protection for domestic goods exposed to foreign competition, on top of an increase in the rate of exchange) which forces economies into the trap of specializing in primary products [*la spécialisation primaire*].

Mechanism of extraction

In a context of weak productive dynamism (a fact which implies that the rest of the world is responsible for, and controls, a large part of the production observed in FCFA zone countries), the free transfer of capital combined with a fixed exchange rate facilitates the legal and illegal extraction of colossal sums from the continent. A perfect example is Equatorial Guinea. On paper, it is the richest country in Africa in terms of GDP per capita. In 2014, net income payments of this country to the rest of the world were equivalent to almost half of its GDP.

To conclude this point, one must say that the limits of the FCFA system that we observe today had already been identified in work that Samir Amin published in 1972 – a sure sign, if one needed it, of the monetary immobility of the FCFA zone countries. Samir Amin had been solicited by the then president of Nigeria, Hamani Diori, who was in favor of reforming the system despite opposition from France, Ivory Coast, and Senegal.[27]

The Specious Argument of Economic Stability

The conservatives' main argument is that the CFA franc provides economic stability. By "economic stability," they mean that the external and the internal values of the CFA franc are stable.

In a situation where the commercial exchanges of African countries are chiefly with the euro zone, and where their principal exports are denominated in euros, the fixed exchange rate between the CFA franc and the euro confers considerable advantages, notably in terms of reduced uncertainty and lower transaction costs. That said, in a context where African countries trade less, in relative terms, with Europe and more with China, India, and each other, and where their principal exports are denominated in dollars, the advantages of pegging the CFA franc to the euro are less certain. All things being equal, the exports of African countries, with the exception of raw materials, are only competitive when the dollar appreciates in relation to the euro. Since its creation, however, the euro has tended to appreciate in relation to the dollar. This considerably inhibits the exportation of goods (raw materials excepted) from FCFA zone countries and stimulates their imports – a point that is even conceded by a fringe of conservatives:

> Given that the CFA franc is evolving with the euro, its fluctuations are less the reflection of changes in the competitiveness of its African countries than of changes in the euro zone. Moreover, an overly strong euro might penalize exports from the African countries, which might instead have need of a weaker currency to improve their competitiveness ... The export sector of the African countries of the franc zone nonetheless continues to be dominated by hydrocarbons, minerals, agricultural raw materials, whose prices are generally denominated in dollars. In this context, the evolution of the euro has a limited impact on the competitiveness of such sectors. By contrast, a strong euro tends to penalize the development of a local manufacturing sector, since the strength of the currency allows for low-cost importation of manufactured products from abroad.[28]

In other words, the "external stability" of the CFA franc is only relative: its parity vis-à-vis the dollar is not fixed despite the fact the dollar remains the principal currency of international trade, as well as the currency in which the debts of African states are denominated. Moreover, having their currency pegged to the euro no longer adequately reflects the geography of commercial flows in African countries and encourages an economy based upon external consumption rather than on local production.

With respect to the "internal" value of the CFA franc, it is undeniable that the countries of the FCFA zone have significantly lower levels of inflation than most African countries. But the flipside of such performance is production and employment growth that remains below its potential level. Is it normal that, for the last 60 years, a country such as Ivory Coast has seen an evolution of consumer prices that, on average, falls below the evolution observed in countries such as Botswana, China, South Korea (the three countries with the highest recorded rates of economic growth in the period 1960 to 2000) and the United States?[29]

Conservatives often claim that price stability allows populations to preserve their purchasing power. In principle, this is entirely possible. In reality, this has not been the case for the FCFA zone countries, whose populations have become poorer. How can low inflation preserve the purchasing power of working-age persons without jobs, or of those whose nominal incomes have been stagnating for decades, especially when such a situation is a result of deflationist monetary and foreign exchange policies?

A particularly illustrative case is the example of Guinea-Bissau. This lusophone country joined the UEMOA in 1997, its peak year in terms of real per capita GDP. Over the course of 19 years, real per capita GDP has fallen 22 percent from its 1997 peak (see the table in the appendix).

In this case as in others, it is absurd to claim that belonging to the FCFA zone protected the population's purchasing power. The only logically defensible argument – which is nonetheless controversial – is that the FCFA zone countries would have been in an even worse situation without the CFA franc. In Guinea-Bissau's case, this would imply that real per capita GDP would have fallen more than 22 percent over the period, had the country not entered the CFCA zone. From such a counterfactual, one can at least derive the following logical conclusion: until now the CFA franc has been a currency for the worse, not for the better.

Conclusion

At the margins of, and beyond, current mobilizations seeking the abolition of the CFA franc, three developments suggest that the system has no future. The first is the proposal of a single currency for the Economic Community of West African States (ECOWAS). One can certainly argue about this proposal's timing and pertinence, and about whether it is realizable within the 2020 horizon. In this context, it is nonetheless useful to emphasize that that the anglophone countries have sent a clear message to their francophone neighbors in the FCFA zone. For example, the Nigerian president, Muhammadu Buhari, has listed the UEMOA countries' divorce from the French Treasury as a prior condition for a single currency.[30]

The second development stems from the impending end of oil in Central Africa. Not having diversified economically, the economies of Central Africa are very dependent on oil; without it, they will see their foreign exchange reserves shrink.[31] With exchange reserves dwindling over the long term, it is not realistic to expect France to come to the rescue, given that France does not in fact guarantee the CFA franc. For Central Africa, the longer it takes to leave the CFA franc system, the more painful the crash will be. The longer they remain in the system, the fewer chances these countries will have to diversify economically. The less diversified their economies are, the greater the threat of economic implosion.

Lastly, there is the demographic dynamic. In 1950, the population of the countries that now belong to the FCFA zone equaled roughly 80 percent of the French population (30 million versus 41 million). In 1980, the population of FCFA zone countries had already exceeded the French population (59 million versus 54 million). In 2015, the figures were 162 million and 64 million, respectively. This demographic uncoupling will grow more accentuated over the course of this century. In 2100, the French population is projected to be roughly 74 million (0.7 percent of the world population), versus a population of roughly 800 million projected for the CFA franc zone. It is difficult to imagine that the small country that France will become will be in a position to "guarantee" the currency of the African countries. Since 1945, France has kept up the pretention of "guaranteeing" the CFA franc, since it never thought that these countries would develop to the point of needing to do without its "guarantee"!

The moral of this story is easy to summarize: the institutional anachronism represented by the FCFA system still owes its exceptional longevity to African leaders' lack of vision and ambition.

Étienne de la Boétie's audacious, shocking hypothesis of "voluntary servitude" is often mobilized by abolitionists to describe the behavior of the elites of francophone Africa.[32] However, in light of the comfort and wellbeing associated with this situation of apparent servitude, it would be doubtless more accurate to speak, with Joseph Ki-Zerbo, of a "sweet alienation" [*aliénation sucrée*].[33]

Appendix

The evolution of real per capita GDP in the countries of the FCFA zone and in the former countries of the franc zone

	Period of observation	Rate of real per capita GDP growth over the period of observation (%)	Year of peak per capita GDP	Peak value of real per capita GDP in inflation-adjusted 2010 dollars (A)	Value of real per capita GDP for the year 2016 in inflation-adjusted 2010 dollars (B)	(A−B)/B (%)
Countries for which the peak in income takes place prior to 2010						
Gabon	1960–2016	1.41	1976	19,493	9,569	50.9
Central African Republic	1960–2016	−1.09	1977	625	326	47.9
Niger	1960–2016	−0.81	1965	716	388	45.8
Equatorial Guinea*	1985–2016	10.20	2008	20,334	12,029	40.8
Ivory Coast	1960–2016	0.47	1978	2,392	1,563	34.7
Guinea-Bissau*	1997–2016	−1.30	1997	731	572	21.7
Cameroon	1960–2016	0.73	1986	1,727	1,357	21.4
Togo	1960–2016	0.84	1980	683	558	18.3
Republic of the Congo	1960–2016	1.20	1984	3,292	2,798	15.0
Countries for which the peak in income takes place after 2010						
Benin	1960–2016	0.85	2016	837		
Burkina Faso	1960–2016	1.80	2016	644		
Mali*	1984–2016	2.00	2016	743		
Senegal	1960–2016	0.02	2016	1,093		
Chad	1960–2016	0.38	2014	967		
Former members of the franc zone						
Algeria	1960–2016	1.2	2016	4,846		
Morocco	1966–2016	2.8	2015	3,205		
Tunisia	1965–2016	2.7	2016	4,265		
Vietnam	1984–2016	4.8	2016	1,770		

* For these countries, the year in which observation begins corresponds to the year of entry (or re-entry) into the FCFA zone. For the other countries, the observation begins with the first year for which there is statistical data about the real per capita GDP.
Source: World Bank Development Indicators, consulted October 30, 2017.

Bibliography

Abensour, Miguel. "Du bon usage de l'hypothèse de la servitude volontaire?" *Réfractions*, no. 17 (2006): pp. 65–84.

The African Development Bank Group, the African Unity Commission, and the United Nations Economic Commission for Africa. *African Statistical Yearbook: 2009*, www.afdb. org/fileadmin/uploads/afdb/Documents/Publications/African_ Statistical_Yearbook_2016.pdf.

Agbor, Julius. "The Future of the CEMAC CFA Franc" (Washington, DC: The Brookings Institution, 2012).

Amaïzo, Yves Ekoué. *Naissance d'une banque de la zone franc: 1848–1901. Priorité aux propriétaires d'esclaves*. Paris: L'Harmattan, 2001.

Amin, Samir. *L'éveil du Sud: l'ère de Bandoung, 1955–1980. Panorama politique et personnel de l'époque* (Paris: Le Temps des cerises, 2008).

Bank of France. "Rapport annuel de la zone franc." Banque de France, January 2, 2009, www.banque-france.fr/sites/default/ files/medias/documents/zone-franc-rapport-annuel_2009.pdf.

BCEAO. "Chronologie des événements marquants de l'histoire de la BCEAO et de l'UEMOA." BCEAO, 2012. www.bceao.int/IMG/ pdf/chronologie_des_evenements_marquants_de_l_histoire_de_ la_bceao_et_ de_l_umoa.pdf

———. "États financiers de la BCEAO au 31 décembre 2016." BCEAO, April 5, 2017, www.bceao.int/IMG/pdf/bceao_-_etats_ financiers_ au_31-12-2016_vf_sans_couleur_.pdf.

Devarajan, Shantayanan, and Dani Rodrik. "Do the Benefits of Fixed Exchange Rates Outweigh Their Costs? The Franc Zone in Africa," NBER Working Paper no. 3727 (Cambridge, MA: National Bureau of Economic Research, 1991).

Diop, Samuel, "L'évolution du système bancaire en zone franc." *Techniques financières et développement* 4, no. 121 (2015): pp. 59–69.

Doumbia, Soumaila. "Surliquidité bancaire et sous-financement de l'économie: une analyse du paradoxe de l'UEMOA." *Revue Tiers Monde*, no. 205 (2011): pp. 151–70.

Edwards, S., and E. L. Yeyati. "Flexible Exchange Rates as Shock Absorbers," NBER Working Paper no. 9867 (Cambridge, MA: National Bureau of Economic Research, October, 2003).

"Francophone Africa's CFA Is under Fire," *The Economist*,

January 27, 2018, www.economist.com/news/middle-east-and-africa/21735636-some-credit-french-backed-common-currency-fostering-stability-others.

Frankel, Jeffrey A. "No Single Currency Regime is Right for All Countries or at All Times." NBER Working Paper no. 7338 (Cambridge, MA: National Bureau of Economic Research, 1999).

Institut Montaigne. "Prêts pour l'Afrique d'aujourd'hui?" Institut Montaigne, September 2017, www.institutmontaigne.org/ressources/pdfs/publications/prets-pour-afrique-ajourdhui-rapport.pdf.

Keen, Steve. *Debunking Economics: The Naked Emperor Dethroned?* Revised and expanded edn. (London: Zed Books, 2011).

Ki-Zerbo, Joseph. *À quand l'Afrique? Entretien avec René Holenstein*. Lausanne: Éditions d'en bas, 2013.

Linge, Idris. "Standard & Poor's livre son point de vue sur le Franc CFA, ses éléments positifs et négatifs, au-delà de son impopularité." Agence Ecofin, December 9, 2017, www.agenceecofin.com/gouvernance/0912-52757-standard-poors-livre-son-point-de-vue-sur-le-franc-cfa-ses-elements-positifs-et-negatifs-au-dela-de-son-impopularite.

Mitchell, William, L. Randall Wray, and Martin Watts. *Modern Monetary Theory and Practice: An Introductory Text* (Callaghan: Center of Full Employment and Equity, 2016).

Mundell, Robert A. "Money and the Sovereignty of the State," in *Monetary Theory and Policy Experience*, ed. Axel Leijonhufvud (London: Palgrave, 2001).

"Nigeria Wants Single Currency for ECOWAS Slowed Down," *Premium Times*, October 25, 2017, www.premiumtimesng.com/news/headlines/247135-nigeria-wants-single-currency-ecowas-slowed.html.

Pettifor, Ann. *The Production of Money: How to Break the Power of Bankers* (London: Verso, 2017).

Saul, Mahir. "Money in Colonial Transition: Cowries and Francs in West Africa." *American Anthropologist* 1, no. 106 (2004): pp. 71–84.

Sylla, Ndongo Samba. "Émerger avec le FCFA ou Émerger du FCFA?" in *Sortir l'Afrique de la servitude monétaire: à qui profite le Franc CFA?* ed. Kako Nubukpo, Bruno Tinel, Martial Ze Belinga, and Demba Moussa Dembele (Paris: La Dispute, 2016).

———. "Quelle intégration monétaire post-FCFA au service de la souveraineté démocratique et de la solidarité panafricaine?" Paper presented at "Samedis de l'économie" organized by ARCADE and the Rosa Luxemburg Foundation, Espace Harmattan, Dakar, Senegal, December 16, 2017.

Tinel, Bruno. "Le fonctionnement et le rôle des comptes d'opérations entre la France et les pays africains," in *Sortir l'Afrique de la servitude monétaire: à qui profite le Franc CFA?* ed. Kako Nubukpo, Bruno Tinel, Martial Ze Belinga, and Demba Moussa Dembele (Paris: La Dispute, 2016).

United Nations Conference on Trade and Development. *State of Commodity Dependence 2016* (New York: United Nations, 2017).

United Nations Development Program. *Human Development Report 2016: Human Development for Everyone* (New York: UNDP, 2016).

Wray, L. Randall. *Why Minsky Matters: An Introduction to the Work of a Maverick Economist* (Princeton University Press, 2016).

Zimmermann, C. D. "The Concept of Monetary Sovereignty Revisited." *European Journal of International Law*, no. 24 (2013): pp. 797–818.

Statistical sources

Bank of France. Statistical Series on the Franc Zone, www.banque-france.fr/en/banque-de-france/about-banque-de-france/franc-zone-and-development-financing/statistical-series-franc-zone.

United Nations. World Population Prospects, 2017, https://population.un.org/wpp.

World Bank. World Development Indicators, https://databank.worldbank.org/source/world-development-indicators.

Part V

Memories of the World, Memory-World

Séverine Kodjo-Grandvaux

Séverine Kodjo-Grandvaux *is a philosopher and scholar associated with the research center Laboratoire d'études et de recherches sur les logiques contemporaines de la philosophie (LLCP) at the University of Paris 8 Vincennes-Saint-Denis. She is the author of* Philosophies africaines *(Paris: Présence africaine, 2013), and the co-editor of the volume* Droit et colonisation *(Brussels: Bruylant, 2006). She is the former Editor-in-Chief of the culture pages of the magazine* Jeune Afrique, *and is currently a journalist for* Le Monde.

If to hold oneself in esteem is to make meaning [*faire sens*],[1] then memory, as the construction of a story and the elaboration of a past worthy of preservation participates in the need for recognition that lies at the foundation of self-esteem.[2] In reality, to make memory [*faire mémoire*] is both to be a producer of meaning – by selecting what not to abandon to oblivion, we choose what in History, in our experience, in what we live through, we take to be crucial to our existence – and, from a collective point of view, to participate in the dispute over meaning through which each civilization forges itself. This constructive relationship to the past is not only what makes self-fashioning and self-reinvention possible, it is also what allows one to build a future for oneself. However, when the histories, pasts, or cultures of individuals do not appear in the grand narratives of nations or the world, it is assumed that what belongs specifically to them, what they have inherited, and what, in part, they are, holds no significance for the national communities or for the humanity to which they belong. It is not just that individuals are stripped of their capacity to make meaning within narratives that have been violently imposed upon them, it is that the two fundamental modalities of structuring individual and collective experience, identification and relation, become problematic and undermine their self-esteem. It is impossible for them to identify with the national narrative, and they find themselves cut off from the community to which, at least legally, they belong.

How is self-fashioning possible when one does not appear in collective memory? When one's past has been effaced or is considered foreign to the very national community that it helps to constitute? When the link to one's history has been broken – for example, at the moment when one's ancestors were torn from their homeland and deported to another continent? How can one manage an experience of memory that is doubly missing (missing from one's heritage, and missing from the narrative of the nation)? How to manage the experience of transgenerational memory that is equally capable of transmitting an experience of domination as it is one of submission, an experience of self-hatred as it is one of arrogance, an experience of denial as it is one of resilience and resistance? Whether we live in a former colony or a formerly colonial society, we inherit a history of violence with consequences and responsibilities that differ depending on whether we belong to the former or the latter. Citizens of former colonial powers who are not descendants of victims of the crimes against humanity represented by colonization and the slave trade are asked to assess their own responsibility for the perpetuation of this unique system of domination. The persistence of racism and unequal relations between the West and Africa demonstrates the degree to which the coloniality [*colonialité*] of being, of power, and of knowledge is transmitted and perpetuated. For those who are perceived as descendants of Africans, fashioning a memory means rewriting themselves into the History from which they were excluded and, beyond History, into the entire fullness of their humanity. This shared past obliges us to try to comprehend what makes community [*fait communauté*] and to try to understand the members we must bring together. How can we integrate those who were excluded from the founding narrative into its structure without resorting to the destructive violence of assimilation that dissolves the difference of those I initially perceive as other – which orders them to erase their own memories, together with their histories, their cultures, and their languages, so that others can be imposed upon them?

Unlike the historical approach, memory work [*le travail mémoratif*] is a social practice characterized by the affective and intimate tie that it forges with a particular past. It threads us into a weave of episodes, or else a filiation, that elucidates our contemporary moment, finding in earlier events the origin of who we are – the origin that will found our being. Memory is what draws things and people closer. At times, it ends up recalling – that is, making present – a traumatic past whose opacity weighs on me and holds me down, and whose force I would like to attenuate. Rather than refusing the trauma, at such moments I must work toward an acceptance that allows me to move past the trauma to a remove at which it cannot take hold of me and arrest my life force, my *élan vital*. By such efforts, I open up avenues of resilience and for reconstructing what I am. When memory is forced upon me, when it is manipulated and does not recognize me as part of the national narrative – or when it insists on the positive value of what devastates me or those close to me – then it annihilates me in my very being, since I am penetrated by an element with which I can have no intimacy. This practice is nothing more and nothing less than a rape of the imaginary [*un viol de l'imaginaire*]. When sites of memory [*lieux de mémoire*], such as the street names, metro stations, memorials, and statues that make up our public space in Europe and Africa, pay homage to colonial explorers or soldiers, slaveowners, or colonial politicians, I am forced into intimacy with historical actors complicit in crimes against humanity. Obliged to suffer an arrogance typical of victors, I am expected to manifest solidarity with the historic past which killed my ancestors, carried them into slavery, and dominated them – a history that, seeing as it was a crime against humanity, killed a part of us all. Or else I am asked to accept and perpetuate the legacy of the economic and political system that separated humanity into a zone of being (the West) and a zone of non-being (the rest of the world that the West authorized itself to debase). Adorning such figures with an explanatory phrase does not suffice to attenuate the trauma violently renewed by the memory of colonial arrogance. On the contrary, if we desire to heal the suffering caused by that past so that we might at long last live in societies that take care of their members, then it is important for us to understand that the work of memory must also be a project of humanization – that is, a movement toward being-more [*vers le plus-être*]. When there is no disjunction, but rather a real intimacy, between a memory and a being, then we realize our humanity, because this memory contributes a presence that fulfills and becomes a vital force [*qui accomplit et devient force vitale*] in that it is of the order of a positive relation. This kind of memory binds the living to one another and to earlier generations. Michel de Certeau and Paul Ricœur have shown us the degree to which writing history and producing a work of memory amount to paying homage to the dead and providing them with a public sepulcher – and the degree to which, by this gesture, they accord a place to the living.

Making memory [*faire mémoire*] means undertaking a work of mourning whose therapeutic dimension is essential in order for the repossession of oneself to be possible – notably by means of reconnecting with what has been unjustly depreciated, devalorized, and struck out in partial recollection. And also by recovering the humanity that is one's own, but that was denied in the extreme situations of possession/dispossession of a body being violated, reduced to slavery, beaten to death; of a body devalorized for its different appearance; of a body debased so as to deprive one of oneself. Physical domination is reinforced by symbols, and shapes imaginaries – for example, origin stories:

> [T]here exists no historical community that has not been born out of a relation that can, without hesitation, best be likened to war. What we celebrate under the title of founding events are, essentially, acts of violence legitimated after the fact by a precarious state of right [*un État de droit précaire*]. What was glory for some was humiliation for others. To celebration on one side corresponds execration on the other. In this way, symbolic wounds calling for healing are stored in the archives of collective memory.[3]

For this reason, the heritage must be inventoried.

Making memory means repossessing oneself, appreciating one's history, being master of what is said about oneself [*du discours sur soi*]. All that is part of the work of constructing one's identity. It is a place where I can select from my trajectory what makes meaning for me and, from a collective point of view, what makes meaning for those close to me. Memory is a social practice that makes the construction of communities possible and that allows us to conceive what we wish to join together: if making memory is an occasion to speak oneself [*se dire soi*], it is also an occasion to speak the other [*dire l'autre*]. "The duty of memory," Paul Ricœur notes, "is the duty to do justice, through memories, to an other than the self."[4] In a de-colonial project, the duty of memory is to understand that the history of Europe – and of European thought – does not belong exclusively to Europeans; Africa and its diasporas are also its co-authors. This obliges us to interrogate abuses (memories that have been thwarted, manipulated, violated, etc.) and work toward the construction of a world-memory [*mémoire-monde*], since at last we will have accepted the idea of humanity itself – humanity not as an empty concept, but as an idea that we set ourselves to bringing about. This begins with humbly accepting that we can inhabit different imaginaries, that we can offer the other [*l'autre*] the best of what we have produced, that we can borrow what others have created and what will allow us to realize ourselves, with the *sine qua non* that we are no longer in a relationship of commerce or domination. For that to be possible, we must rethink the relation, construct egalitarian human relationships, and ask ourselves how we might achieve a relationship to the past that will allow us not only to preserve different customs, traditions, universes of signification, etc., but also to create, to bring forth, to reinvent ourselves.

This world-memory incites us to world-making [*à vouloir faire monde*]. If we want to fully realize our being-in-the-world [*notre être-au-monde*], it is not enough to be in the world; in addition, one must be *with* the world – that is, think and act *with* others. Technological development gives us the impression – owing in particular to the Internet's omnipresence in our lives – that it is easier to travel today than it was before. From the multiplication of information channels, we similarly infer that we are now more connected to one another. At the same time, however, the West (United States, Europe) has withdrawn into itself to an extraordinary degree: once again prey to nationalist – when not supremacist – demons, these societies do not face a crisis of migrants [*crise des migrants*] but a crisis of reception [*crise de l'accueil*]. One is forced to concede that, despite our technological progress, we do not know how to make world more intensively, on the grounds that we refuse to feel our proximity to others [*d'autrui*]. We refuse their presence, and we refuse to be present for them. Presence, François Jullien explains, "at the same time as it given to us in immediacy ..., is what we nevertheless must conquer – and to which we have to *gain access*."[5] And Jullien adds: "technology, by increasing presence, atrophies it."

We must relearn to live together and to create the "in-common" [*l'en-commun*]. And we must thereby recall the lesson of *ubuntu*, that social cogito. *Ubuntu* teaches that the community is not the sum of scattered individuals; on the contrary, by virtue of the bonds it creates and nourishes, the group amplifies the power to act. The community is not a given, but rather a construction that, over the course of its evolution, must unceasingly be fed and reinforced through an openness to new elements. This practice is grounded in the in-common that one constructs. It presumes the development of an ethics of participation and solidarity. Community-making [*faire communauté*] is re-membering. It reassembles disparate members around a set of values, possessions, or a History that one chooses to share. Consequently, world-making becomes the collective construction of a memory of the in-common – a memory added to our own without replacing it. Memories are not mutually exclusive: the memory of the in-common can be added to the memory of self [*la mémoire de soi*], which leads us to forge the synthesis of a reconciled memory – the only one that allows everyone to develop their full potential and to realize what they are. This implies neither that we always agree with others, nor that we pursue consensus at all costs, but that we reflect on how we might invest the tension to make it a positive and not necessarily a destructive force. Keep in mind that in certain situations dissensus can be beneficial, particularly for combatting totalitarian tendencies. Then we must ask ourselves the question: How can memory reunite the different and the multiple without dissolving them in the common? How can what produces dissensus participate in the construction of the in-common? If the memory of the in-common is a memory of tension and attention, how might we manage the tension in which we live? How might we inhabit it?

Above all, world-making means making a place habitable. Contrary to what we would like to think, however, what makes our world what it is is less humans and their activities than plants and the photosynthetic process that transforms solar energy into living matter. We belong not only to humanity but to the living [*au vivant*] as well. We do not inhabit the earth so much as we inhabit the atmosphere, which is the cosmic fluid we produce in collaboration with plants. World-making means inhabiting a world that is mine, because it makes meaning for me and because it permits me to reaffirm my *belonging* to a world that also *belongs to me* and in which I fully participate, since I co-produce it with others and with the whole of the living. But that is not all. This world is vaster still. I must expand it to the scale of the cosmos and understand that every world-memory is a cosmic memory. Until now, our ecological and geographical thinking and our definitions of the various geo-disciplines [*des géo-savoirs*] have focused on the earth.

But we have forgotten our planetary condition – the fact that we are part of the cosmos, and that the Earth could not exist outside of it. This process unfolded in the West over the course of what's called Modernity, a period which "has identified itself with the call of the Earth and the oblivion of the stars, with the even deeper affirmation of the Earth as the definitive horizon of our existence and of our knowledge."[6] Without the sun, however, there would be no life. We must rethink heliocentrism from a philosophical point of view and understand that we are solar beings [*des êtres solaires*]. Just as we are lunar beings [*des êtres lunaires*]: the moon influences our production of melatonin, for example, and thus impacts the quality of our sleep, and it affects the development of plants. The moon is responsible for variations in the color and smell of trees, and in how their sap tastes. Astrophysicists have demonstrated that we are all star dust, that we are the children of stars which exploded and thereby produced the chemical elements out of which both we and our world are composed. "The stars are our distant ancestors," Trinh Xuan Thuan tells us, "and we all share the same cosmic genealogy."[7] To speak of cosmic memory is not a metaphor. Everything that lives on earth has an astral nature. There is a material and ontological continuity between the Earth and the rest of the universe; the Earth is a celestial body. We must exit the night in which we are sealed to think the light, the sun, the moon, the stars – for no planet is autonomous. And of our philosophy we must once again make a cosmology.

Our roots are less in the earth than in the cosmos, a fact which denies the legitimacy to any thinking of verticality and which calls for a more englobing perspective, a thinking of immersion. We do not find ourselves in a world that lies outside of us; we are fully in this world. To be immersed is not to be inside something surrounding us; it is to participate in that something that is in us. To inspire [*inspirer*] is to bring the world into oneself. To expire [*expirer*] is to project oneself into the world. Immersion is an action of reciprocal co-penetration; it reveals "the limits of the notions of place or environment – which continue to represent the relation between the living being and the world exclusively under the aspects of *contiguity* and *juxtaposition*."[8] On the contrary, everything is in everything else and each thing is also its contrary, just as Chinese philosophy teaches. Every action is thus interaction. There is no emergence that is not co-emergence. *Pratītya-samutpāda*, a Sanskrit expression meaning "being by co-emergence," transcribes this reality: nothing exists in and of itself, and nothing can be its own cause. Interdependence is such that we must rethink immersion and mixture from a philosophical point of view. This cosmology of mixture obliges us to summon a "we" and to rethink relation in opposition to the borders that separate and no longer relate – in defiance of the walls being built, because:

> to recognize that the world is a space of immersion means ... that there are no real or stable frontiers: the *world* is the space that never lets itself be reduced to a house, to what is one's own, to one's digs, to the immediate. Being in the world means to exercise influence especially outside one's own space, outside one's own habitat, outside one's own niche. It is always the totality of the world one lives in, which is and will always be infested by others.[9]

This cosmic memory obliges us to recognize that world-making is only possible when we open our community to the other, to the stranger, and when we grasp the intimate connection that binds the human community to the rest of the animal, vegetable, and mineral world; to the invisible – ancestors and future generations; and to the stars of our universe and of other universes – the astrophysicists' multiverses. World-making means understanding that human rights cannot be separated from the right to a healthy environment and thus to the right of nature [*droit de la nature*]; it means committing ourselves to the process of transforming our social and political organizations so as to multiply those benefitting from the right to nature [*droit à la nature*], as well as the right to democracy. It is entirely possible to imagine democratic processes that include future generations as well as our ancestors. Making memory collectively in a just manner means integrating the past – our ancestors – into a democratic political form. As Valérie Cabanes notes, so-called first peoples:

> when they succeed in preserving their culture in a territory that they have occupied from time immemorial, are known to interact with the living in a manner that preserves or regenerates it. Through their social organization, they also show us that values such as sharing, solidarity, goodwill, and tolerance are necessary for humans, not just for them to care for one another, but also for them to respect the entirety of living beings and live in harmony with them. Ultimately, these peoples privilege two complementary levels of governance: community-based management [*la gestion communautaire*] and respect for universal rules. They thereby urge us to question our own modes of government, which are constructed at a very different level: at the level of the state.

The state, by contrast, is suspicious of communitarian aspirations and impedes the development of a holistic vision of the world.[10]

In this, the West stands to learn from the Asian, South American, and African civilizations that have opted for a biocentric philosophical vision, deeming it necessary to under-utilize the productive potential of nature, since the planet belongs to the whole of the living. And it is similarly invited to move beyond the anthropocentrism of its humanism.

Close observation of the living teaches us that the world beyond the human is not without meaning. Animals are capable of observing their environment, of representing it to themselves, of interpreting it, and of adapting their behavior in accordance with it. Just like humans, vegetables (plants, trees, etc.) are endowed with memories; they are able to communicate with one another as well as with what surrounds them. Fruit trees transmit olfactory messages as invitations to bees, thereby making pollination possible. Trees transmit electrical messages too through the intermediary of a kind of nerve cell at the ends of their roots. Vegetables make decisions that allow them to resolve problems. Rethinking "a relational ecology of selves that constitutes the cosmos"[11] requires moving beyond the human universe and directing one's attention to forms of living thought [*pensées vivantes*] and to the other beings, different from oneself, that people the world. During the second half of the twentieth century, African philosophy constructed and defined itself in opposition to African cosmologies and to animism. And yet it could be extremely productive to re-explore such traditional philosophies, since, as Felwine Sarr notes:

> the conception of the universe that manifests itself in the diverse forms of African knowledge and practices is that of a cosmos considered as a great living being. This living being is a whole of which humankind is only one expression, one living being among others.... Humankind is considered a symbolic operator connecting the heavens to the earth.... The ritual restoration of the world constitutes one of the most meaningful symbolic acts of humankind's realization of this responsibility.[12]

Traditional African philosophies could certainly provide us with the rich material we need to approach a posthumanist form of thought. Such thought – and this is not a paradox – would permit us to realize our humanity in the sense that what becoming human or being more human [*être plus humain*] comes down to is aiding in the growth of life, in the expansion of every vital force. One of the consequences of such posthumanist thought is the repudiation of the possibility of their existing a zone of non-being such as colonialism had constructed, since such a zone of non-being is a zone of less-being [*moins-être*] where life's burgeoning is blocked. To succeed in world-making is to find one's place in a cosmology of emergence and to bring about the world's humanization – not just for humans, but for the whole of the living. It is in such a cosmology of emergence that "the push toward more being is carried out. Its horizon is what Léopold Sédar Senghor, always a Teilhardian, consistently refers to as 'Civilization of the universal.'"[13] But this universal is not the homogenizing and destructive universal of colonialism. On the contrary, it is a cosmic, plural universal. Here, too, the lesson is grounded in the observation of the living. It shows us that, while there is only one principle, this principle both engenders, and can only be spoken, in the plural: there is a cosmic principle that refracted itself and engendered the world; the living, for its part, only offers itself in its plurality. In contrast to the colonial and imperial "One," which is the "One" of the same, the cosmic "One" is the "One" of the different. The universal is fundamental – it is the origin of our world, of the cosmos – but it only offers itself in its plural. It is a "pluriversal" [*un pluriversel*]. As a consequence, our horizon, that toward which we should strive, is the in-common. This obliges us to draw up an ethics of the relation that strengthens being and permits us to fully realize ourselves – which is to say, leads us not toward a having-more [*un plus-avoir*] but toward a being-more [*un plus-être*]; that permits us, in a word, to realize ourselves spiritually. It is thus a question of privileging the relation that allows one to be connected [*relié*] without being tied down [*lié*], that is emancipatory and not suffocating:

> We can, Teilhard de Chardin tells us, follow the path of egoism which consists of thinking that movement has attained its end with one's self (whether one is an individual or a nation). This egoism, parent of all "ethnocentrisms," carries within itself domination and colonization.
>
> We can, on the other hand, fully grasp the meaning of "being born and developing *as a function of a cosmic stream*" and thus see the responsibility of having to continue the effort to bring about more life, more Being, by extending towards ever-greater unity the "generative forces of the world."[14]

Being aware of our cosmic dimension obliges us to pursue world-making, to construct the in-common and weave our differences together so that we may strengthen our vital force. And, as Teilhard de Chardin counsels, it obliges us to "open our hearts wide to the call of the world within us."[15] This vitalist philosophical ontology, which is equally present among the Bantu, the Dogon, the Serer, etc., charges us to adopt an ethics of action according to which acting must help to augment the force of life – evil being that which diminishes the *élan vital*.

Realizing one's humanity means stepping outside one's ego to be available for world-making. Because I am bound to the other, I let myself be overcome [*déborder*] by the other. As François Jullien puts it: "I no longer place the Other as an 'object,' for conquest or possession ...; instead, I construct the Other as a 'subject' facing me, at once an instance of initiative and a source of humanity like me, since, before the other, I find that I have *overcome* [*débordé*] myself."[16]

Being human no longer means being terrestrial, but rather being cosmic and confronting oneself with a cosmic memory that is both panoptic and a-topic [*panoptique et a-topique*]. This memory is panoptic because, as Éric Letonturier says, it obliges us "to live the world in its full diversity, according each place, each being, the importance and dignity that it is due, while simultaneously resituating it in a vast network of spatio-temporal correspondences, mutual recognition, and shared responsibility where it acquires its full meaning."[17]

Such memory is a-topic because, being in everything, it is in no place in particular. Furthermore, it is utopic because the consideration of plurality for the purpose of world-making and creating a memory-world out of tension and attention means fashioning a memory that will permit us not to repeat the past, but to engage in creation by joining the future and the past in the present. In fact, futurity is included in the apprehension of the historic past. Memory is something that one fashions as a function of the meaning one gives to one's present. Meaning comes from a future that tells us what to retain of our past and how to build on the rubble so we may reinvent ourselves. There is a continuum of psychological experience between the past and the future, which we must, to the degree it is possible, try to invest in a positive way. Memory-making, in this regard, means carrying within oneself an active utopia. It means reading the past in relation to a desirable future that one wishes to offer oneself, in relation to a project. With respect to slavery, I can retain of the Africans who suffered it either the image of victims whom a master eventually emancipated, or I can retain the image of victims who, by multiplying forms of resistance and strategies of response and attack, displayed a resilience that allowed them to liberate themselves and force the masters to abandon their ignominious practice. The implications for self-esteem and respect for the other are different depending on the option one privileges. Such utopian memory takes up the past anew: it distances itself from the curated remembrance [*le souvenir entretenu*] of the past to facilitate the appearance of the new. Letting go is what makes repetition [*la reprise*] possible; it is a critical operation that allows one to escape the pitfalls of commemoration.

For Kierkegaard, recollection [*le re-souvenir*] "is discarded clothing which, however lovely it might be, no longer suits one," while repetition [*la reprise*] "is clothing that never becomes worn, that fits snugly and comfortably, that neither pulls nor hangs too loosely."[18] Unlike recollection – which is a repetition backward that attempts to find again what once was, and thus places us from the beginning in the iteration and the fixed – repetition is "recollection forwards." It inscribes us into a movement turned toward the future that allows for personal appropriation, a recreation that gives us the possibility of a new birth, of a re-birth. By thus working on ourselves, we acquire the force to free ourselves from the traumas and burdens of the past that impede our progress. Such memory work provokes an inner movement toward a better grasp of the self. It alone will allow us to return to and be with our selves:

> I am myself again. The machinery has been set in motion. The traps in which I had been caught have been hewn asunder. The magic spell that had been placed on me so that I could not come to my senses has been broken. No one raises his hand against me now, my freedom has been secured, I am born again to myself.[19]

Finally, one arrives at "stillness where one hears oneself speak, even if the movement takes place only within."[20] In the African context, this might be translated by a repetition [*reprise*] of precolonial bodies of knowledge – that is, by a new reading which culminates in the transformation and enrichment of knowledge and the repetition of traditions. Such memories in motion survey what the past offers and select what parts of it to actualize in light of the future that they choose to give themselves. By this very action, they realize a universe of signification and allow me to make meaning.[21]

Utopian memory is the site of self-fashioning: it transforms life into existence, unfolding it and re-unfolding possibilities with it. To ex-ist [*ex-ister*], as Jullien explains, is to hold oneself "*outside* what conditioned and contained one's life within boundaries to which one did not even know oneself was subjected."[22] Jullien clarifies: "In this way one can, by disengaging one's life, 'maintain oneself outside' the enclosure [*clôturation*] of the world and nonetheless remain in the world, ex-isting in the proper sense – *or else* one can let one's life slip by and wall itself up within the narrow horizon of what makes world [*ce qui fait monde*]."[23] Utopian memory encourages us to listen for the self, to be awake in order to wake up to ourselves, and to pay attention to the life that wells up within us, as well as to the "silent transformations" at work inside us.[24] It is a question of "find[ing] a philosophy of movement in which – in a universe constantly in the process of renewing itself – the human comes about and becomes himself via his creative action."[25] From such a perspective, time can no longer be understood in a linear fashion, but must be grasped in a more expansive manner that permits a circular causality, where, as cybernetics teaches, effects may precede causes – to the detriment of all developmentalist and progressivist thought. This kind of time superposes and grounds different temporalities in a creative *durée*. Cosmic temporality does not function according to a before and after, and has no beginning. This asks us to conceive of a memory that is open to time and space, a memory which establishes both notions on a new foundation, which renounces the spatialization of time, and which privileges the agglomeration where past, present, and future are mixed together and where the future is already here – full of possibilities and impossibilities for us to realize. This memory shatters the notion of place – it has no place, it is u-topian. The *durée* on which such memory is founded, as theorized by Bergson and picked up by Senghor, "is communicated to us through the vital knowledge we have of it, in the intuition that sets us immediately at the heart of the object, grasped as an organic totality."[26] Living the world intensively, being intensely *with* the world, means being in the movement of the world, in the e-motion [*l'é-motion*] that Senghor advocates. The act of knowing must not stand still. On the contrary, it can only be accomplished in movement.

It is a question of revalorizing intuition, which allows us to know the world "vitally."[27] The greater part of Western modernity established itself in opposition to such intuition: it not only objectified the world during the mechanist revolution of the seventeenth century, it separated nature and culture and, in the same gesture, created the zone of non-being where the people of non-Western civilizations lived in what one considered to be a state of nature. Thus, a *humanitas* was created in opposition to an *anthropos* fit for domination – a humanity that extracted itself from nature and from the living. A veritable "physiocide" took place, the repression of the living, a refusal to recognize nature or the cosmos's claim to any philosophical dignity whatsoever.[28] As Philippe Descola observes: "This way of representing the human environment in all its exteriority was of course indissociable from the movement to mathematize space that in the same period was being promoted by geometry, physics, and optics, ranging from Copernicus's decentralizing of the cosmos to Descartes's *res extensa*."[29] By objectifying nature and the world, one transformed it into a resource and authorized oneself to possess it, to become a landowner, to behave as if one were its "master and possessor"; one embarked – with all possible hubris – on the savage business of conquest. It was a question of colonizing both the Others and the Earth. One of the justifications of colonization found in legal textbooks was the failure of local populations to exploit the land. By the same rationale, one took possession of the land and of the human beings who inhabited it, contributing to the new era in the offing: the Anthropocene. The objectivation effected by an all-powerful subject – the subject which extracts itself from the world and creates the figure of the Other that colonial ethnology will curate – could not have been produced without immobilizing the march of the world. It is the work of what Senghor calls the "reason-eye," [*la raison-œil*] which, analytical, fixes what it sees. World-making requires not only being-in-the-world. To cease to have a purely external relationship to things, one must be born to the world [*naître au monde*] and let one's body speak. This means reconnecting with the "reason-embrace" [*la raison-étreinte*], which, synthetic, comprehends rather than separates, and which places us at the heart of an object that is no longer defined by its duality with the subject. "The immediate embrace of an undivided whole in an act of sheer intuition: this is how embrace-reason operates. It does not, therefore, place the object in front of itself; rather, it places itself in the object, marrying its flux. We might say that it dances rather than thinks the object."[30] This is, as Souleymane Bachir Diagne explains, the "true path of knowledge"[31] that allows Senghor to formulate "the notion of a 'corporeal cogito,' as a movement among the movement of things."[32] For Senghor, "rhythm is the vital element *par excellence*."[33] Rhythm is "the architecture of being, the internal dynamism that gives it form, the system of waves that it transmits for the reception of *Others*, the pure expression of the vital force. Rhythm: it is the vibratory shock, the force that, through the senses, seizes us at the root of being."[34]

From this perspective, "to know" [*con-naître*] the world is "to be born" [*naître*] to the world, as well as "to be born" [*naître*] with the world, in its very movement. Such cognizance is what permits the memory-world, which is at once a-topic and u-topic, for the same reason that it is cosmic. Under way on open waters, it inscribes us into the fullness of the world, the very fullness treated by animist philosophy. If we desire to be born to the world, we must therefore turn our backs on the cold reason that developed an arid scientific discourse and repeat – in a Kierkegaardian sense – the poetic discourse of the cosmogonies and the first ecologies. And if poetry was the only thing capable of disclosing and helping us to receive the beauty and the light of the world? Would that not be the most audacious form of world-making?

Cum patior Africa
The Political Production of Regimes of "the Nigh"

Nadine Machikou

Nadine Machikou is Professor of Political Science and a researcher at the Center for the Study and Research of Political and Administrative Dynamics at the University of Yaoundé 2, as well as a member of the LASPAD, a research center on Africa and African diaspora, at the University of Gaston Berger in Senegal. After a thesis on the construction of decision-making support in health policy and research into the political economy of public reform, the governance of environmental policy, and the evaluation of various kinds of public policy, she has turned her attention to political sociology. Her recent research focuses on the state and the community management of security issues, particularly in relation to the struggle against the Islamist Boko Haram sect in Cameroon.

Might Africa be the privileged site for a moral economy of compassion? "The most troubled continent in the world" despite its extraordinary wealth – to borrow a phrase from Richard Dowden[1] – its sufferings seem to offer to others a privileged object for compassion, just as compassion appears to be a central category in how Africa is grasped, described, and thought. A source of concern for itself and for others, Africa is subject to a compassionate governmentality [*gouvernementalité compassionnelle*] characterized by a desire to put an end to its sufferings, improve its lot, and assure its prosperity. Here, governmentality is understood as a large, technological ensemble whose purpose is to organize the wellbeing of populations;[2] it is grounded in a manner of governing observable in micro-apparatuses [*micro-dispositifs*], while also establishing the basis for how the suffering of Africans is depicted and framed (in the categorial sense).[3] This concern for poor Africans, however, also marks a significant shift in the economy of power: historically, the poor, the sick, and the needy have been targeted by and inscribed within relationships of power born of the development of a globalizing and quantitative concern for the population, a political concern which Michel Foucault traced back to the pastoral power of the Middle Ages.[4] With the weakening of ecclesiastical institutions, this power tasked with the "salvation" of the individual spread to the state in its modern form. Progressively, salvation assumes a worldly form, with the objectives of promoting health and wellbeing on earth.[5] It is in this sense that compassion for Africa is a principally biopolitical inclination, while also constituting an indispensable index for the continent's presence/absence in the world. This voice of virtue[6] within the endogenous and exogenous apprehension of the continent belongs to what Joan Tronto called the "support of life,"[7] and forms the basis for what Laurent Thévenot calls a "regime of familiarity" [*régime de familiarité*][8] and that we, for the sake of etymology, will call a "regime of the nigh" [*régime du proche*].[9]

Tracible to the Latin phrase *cum patior*, "compassion" is in fact intimately bound to an experience of suffering – it is a matter of *suffering with the other*. It expresses itself in a passion nonetheless capable of disinterestedness or altruism (in this, compassion is unlike pity, which otherwise is often close to it). Without wanting to add an additional layer to a tradition of Africanist thought that already seems saturated with emotions,[10] one could say that compassion is creative and productive; it intimates a path toward a "higher state of understanding" that allows one to grasp the sense of the real in all its thickness and depth. As a form of intuitive reasoning, it is grounded in a cognitive process – that is, a means of understanding – and constitutes a schema for accessing the real.[11] *Cum patior* is a suffering with the other that is produced within an "ethical interpellation of the face-to-face"; the experience of compassion constitutes a bond characterized by an ethics of the face and by a responsibility for the other person [*autrui*], in the sense put forward by Emmanuel Levinas.[12] The latter characteristic is also underscored by Philippe Corcuff, who notes that the regime of compassion is grounded in

> the fact of being "seized," in practical terms and even without reflection, by a feeling of responsibility vis-à-vis another person's distress, in the

proximity of bodies and face-to-face. It means taking action in a mode strained between measure and the absence of measure [*entre mesure et dé-mesure*]. At first, it presupposes a minimal kind of measure, which lies in the recognition of the other person's distress, but it is carried beyond all measure towards the total gift [*le don total*] to the other. The measures that justice commonly employs, on the other hand, are there to temper the measurelessness of the singular relation (why privilege one other person over everyone else?).[13]

Logically, the suffering that provokes such emotion is a social construction and not merely a natural given.

Is it a feeling of guilt or of responsibility (or both) that allows one to share the suffering of Africa? Called upon by the misery of Africans, does one feel a duty to share it or, in Levinas's sense, is one taken hostage by a suffering to which one is then obligated?[14] Being conscious of the pain and the vulnerability of the other, the experience of compassion is also a competence;[15] it produces respect and attention by pressing for ethical action to be taken out of concern for the other [*autre*] and in the name of a responsibility for other persons [*autrui*]. As Levinas notes, the pain of suffering is also the possibility of a cry, a groan, or a sigh, "the original call for aid, for curative help, help from the other me whose alterity, whose exteriority promises salvation."[16] While Hannah Arendt mocks compassion as a "feminine virtue" to be excluded from public space – and while others characterize it as a self-evident, laughable sentiment, politically insignificant and of no consequence, an emotion that should stay outside politics which is best stripped of all affective content[17] – the argument of this contribution to The Ateliers is, by contrast, that compassion is an emotion that structures political relations with Africa.

Making a distinction between immediate affective reactions and intellectual evaluations is, as Christophe Traïni proposes, essential for producing a general and radical decolonization of the emotions.[18] One must search such emotions for their motivations, since the regimes of proximity (or "of the nigh" [*du proche*]) with Africa have in part been constructed upon them – in the name of compassion, on the fiction of an elsewhere, of a remoteness, brought near [*proche*] by the force of sentiment. This commerce of proximity leads to the crystallization of sentiments of familiarity that cannot be grasped as part of a unitary exchange between the world – above all the Western world – and Africa, but must be grasped instead as intricated within a tangle of multiple networks and motivations. To be sure, Africa is not the only target of the rhetoric of good intentions saturating international politics. In an era when moral judgments weigh down the fabric of the world, it is difficult, as Monique Canto-Sperber writes, "to justify any international action, whether it has to do with the relations between states, with the world economy, or with the criminal prosecution of political leaders, without invoking the values of justice or citing the ambition to construct a better world."[19]

In this world of emotions, the temptation of a history of compassion [*histoire compassionnelle*] is perilous, owing to the traps of historicization and periodization (can one clearly determine for how long Africa has been an object of compassion?).[20] If the presence of Africa in the world is, as we suggest, characterized by a governmentality of compassion, we hereby make the choice to base our analysis on the modern era by identifying three privileged domains of projects built on compassion [*entreprises compassionnelles*]: the benefits of salvation and civilization, aid for development, and humanitarian intervention. It follows that, far from any form of rigidification, a history of the present time of compassion should be constructed on the basis of the historicity of projects of compassion across time, which infinitely reproduces its effects in the present, as is figured by Michel Serres's metaphor of folded time [*temps plié*]. It is a question of a time that "folds or twists," like a crumpled handkerchief at the bottom of a pocket, because it is made up of ruptures and moments of arrest, wild acceleration, and collapses, of lacunae and rips.[21] The challenge of analyzing the dynamics by which Africa becomes the recipient of compassion stems from time's uncertain, unstable, and non-linear contours. This time that "folds or twists" (since, like every historical event, compassionate governmentality is "multi-temporal") draws "from the obsolete, the contemporary, and the futuristic" and "reveals a time that is gathered together, with multiple pleats."[22] In the spirit of the metaphor of folded time, in which, like a sheet of paper folded in two, the two ends are brought very close together, we have chosen to focus on two pivotal moments of compassionate expression: the end of the nineteenth century and the end of the twentieth century, which we will examine through the lens of that particular form of objectification that the notion of a regime of historicity authorizes. This approach aims to reconstruct the continuity of these two moments by tracing the common thread of compassionate governmentality, underscoring the fact that, while each may be unique, "regimes of the nigh" have in their contemporary form been constructed along a path formed by the sedimentation of markers of compassion.

In an uncertain regime of proximity with Africa, a "regime of the nigh," one thinks of the biblical parable of the good Samaritan, an exceptional figure of the neighbor [*prochain*], and thus of the near relation [*proche*], who, moved by compassion, stops on the road traveled by the suffering human. This encounter has also entered the Christian perspective on the neighbor who stops at the sight of the suffering of the other, confronts it, and is moved to make a compassionate gesture. Guarding oneself from being taken in by what is evident at the present time, one might adopt a long-term historical perspective (precolonial, colonial, postcolonial) to rediscuss the historicity of the modalities by which Africa was perceived to suffer and by which compassion manifested itself. Do these three times correspond to individual regimes of historicity in Hartog's sense?[23] Put differently, if mobilizing in the name of African suffering has now been naturalized, it is thanks to the efforts of entrepreneurs of compassion, whose privileged domains are bringing Africa the benefits of salvation and civilization, securing aid for development, and organizing humanitarian interventions. To be sure, there is a common thread running from one era to the next, a domination whose forms add compassion to other motivations for dominating Africa. Accordingly, this thread will be reconstructed by means of an archeology of the act and the discourse of compassion as found in an archive that is deliberately heterogeneous: drawn from the dissemination of compassionate expression across three sites – namely, the benefits of salvation and civilization, aid for development, and humanitarian intervention.

It seems that compassionate governmentality targeting Africa is a dialectic that can be grasped by two independent routes. When thinking about the compassion felt for Africa and about the capacity for people to put themselves in its place and bear its suffering, there are effectively two options: the path of denouncing compassionate imperialism, and the path of rehabilitating a compassion of peers.

Of a Regime of Compassionate Imperialism Whose Essence Is Vertical ...

How does one suffer on behalf of Africa? In the name of what? Such questions lead us to examine the logics by which the world is seized "in practical terms and even without reflection, by a feeling of responsibility vis-à-vis another person's distress, in the proximity of bodies and face-to-face."[24] Compassionate alterity [*l'altérité compassionnelle*], grounded in emotion and reason, constitutes the foundation of a longstanding apparatus [*dispositif*] of power that produces (alongside other effects) the legitimacy of victimhood.

Emotion as a sediment of an apparatus of power

The compassionate authority that cuts across and works over the continent cannot be separated from the regimes of justification that legitimate the continent's suffering.[25] Such authority is old and multidimensional, as an archeology of colonial discourse will attest. While the colonial ambition stretches far into the past, it was only at the end of the nineteenth century that it became clearly tied to a project of modernization (or of civilization). In a poem first published in *McClure's Magazine* in February 1899 with the title "The White Man's Burden," Rudyard Kipling, future Nobel laureate in literature and fervent defender of colonization, calls on the white man to civilize, administer, and attend to the needs of colonized populations, in the name of a "burden" and a duty grounded in his superiority and his progressive civilization. He says,

Take up the White Man's Burden –
The savage wars of peace –
Fill full the mouth of Famine
And bid the sickness cease.[26]

Faced with ungrateful colonized populations – the "fluttered folk and wild," "half-devil and half-child" – the white man is encouraged see to his task with care and altruism, hiding his exhaustion and accepting "The blame of those [he] betters / The hate of those [he] guards." This invitation to sacrifice is anchored in "the great contemporary colonial period, at a time when all actors – soldiers, missionaries, bureaucrats, and merchants – are persuaded of the superiority of western civilization and convinced of their duty to disseminate progress unto the very ends of the earth."[27] The same aspiration had, 14 years earlier, seized Jules Ferry, who, speaking before the Chambre des députés on July 28, 1885, paid homage to the work of Savorgnan de Brazza:

He's an apostle; he pays with his own person, he marches towards a goal that is placed very high and very far off; he has wrested [*conquis*] from the populations of equatorial Africa a personal influence unlike anyone else's; but who can say whether one day, in the institutions that he established, which have just been consecrated by the European Areopagus and which henceforth belong to France – who can say whether one day the black populations, having at times been corrupted, perverted by adventurers, by other travelers, by other explorers who are less scrupulous, less paternal, less enamored with persuasion than our illustrious Brazza – who can say whether one day these populations won't attack our institutions?" Then, he reassures us that the "rebel tribes" are in need of western assistance, since: "One must openly state that, in effect, the superior races have a right [*un droit*] vis-à-vis the inferior races. I repeat, the superior races have a right, because they have a duty [*un devoir*]. They have the duty to civilize the inferior races."[28]

The compassion that underlies the duty of bringing civilization poorly conceals France's desire for grandeur vis-à-vis its European rivals:

To shine without acting, without getting involved in the affairs of the world, keeping one's distance from the maneuverings of Europe, to regard the Orient as a trap, as an adventure – for a great nation to live in this way, you had better believe me, means abdication, and, sooner than you can believe, it will mean descending from the first rung to the third or the fourth.[29]

For Ferry, France has the duty to "carry its language, its customs, its flag, its arms, its genius" anywhere it can. If this position is not shared by all,[30] it nonetheless remained dominant and laid the basis for a doctrine of colonization, which, despite the schools, hospitals, and bridges, followed a trajectory of brutality, inhumanity, and racism.[31] This tendency to valorize colonization lies at the center of the teaching of history (in school textbooks) – nor has it lost its adepts. It is premised in a simple chain of reasoning: colonization was what allowed the valiant nurses and teachers to lead Africa out of the long night and, even if certain profiteers and adventurers benefitted, on the whole colonization remained a financial sacrifice for colonizing states. From this perspective, preying on the colonies is seen as the action of only a few, while the majority paid for civilizing Africa. The historian Jacques Marseille assures us that colonization was bad business for France,[32] providing a "scientific" argument to the apostles who tout the inestimable contributions of colonization,[33] and who believe that decolonization left the third world at an impasse.[34] Like a stubborn fact of life, this tendency reappears at the highest echelons of the state in the form of the memorial law presented by Michèle Alliot-Marie, Minister of Defense under President Jacques Chirac.[35] As it happens, Article 4, paragraph 2 rules, "educational programs specifically recognize the positive role of France's presence overseas, especially in North Africa, and give the history and sacrifices made by French soldiers from these territories the eminent place they deserve." The article provoked backlash from historians[36] and jurists before finally being abrogated by decree on February 15, 2006, despite Article 1 which affirms: "The nation expresses its gratitude to the women and men who participate in the work [*l'œuvre*] accomplished by France in the former French departments of Algeria, Morocco, Tunisia, and Indochina as well as in the territories formerly placed under French sovereignty." This regime of justification legitimating colonization as the materialization of a compassionate sentiment is also employed by François Fillon, who, at the beginning of his international campaign, hammered home: "No, France is not guilty of wanting to share its culture with the peoples of Africa, Asia, and North America" – buttressing his position in a speech at Sablé on August 28, 2016, by referring to "the millennium-long history of France and of its greatness; the first reason for my candidacy ... when the other candidates neglect the history of France." Before Fillon, such rhetoric was repeatedly used by Jean Marie le Pen and even Nicolas Sarkozy when he spoke in Dakar on July 26, 2007.

The compassionate authority at the heart of, and resulting from, the colonial enterprise can also be observed in the domain of another expression of civilization: development. The state aid that gives substance to this compassionate governmentality is based on the paradigm of helping poor countries catch up with their peers who belong to the first circle of prosperity, and is sometimes understood as a form of reparation for colonial misconduct.[37] In both the Western and the Eastern blocs, by means of socialism or liberal capitalism, international cooperation on behalf of development provided gifts, loans, and other forms of technical support as powerful catalyzers of this affection. In the eyes of certain analysts, Sub-Saharan Africa was the region where state aid for development played the most consequential role (which distinguishes the region from the Maghreb, Asia, and Latin America). After colonial states achieved independence, aid for development was introduced to support numerous public investments, to assist technical cooperation, and sometimes also to pay the salaries of public officials in the many states that were in crisis or else bankrupt, owing to reverses in the prices of imports and exports, an incapacity to cover public deficits with fiscal receipts, or, more generally, poor governance. The catechism of the World Bank, the ideal type of "lender," was constructed at the intersection of "1) the economic theory of welfare in partial equilibriums as formulated according to models of economic dependency, and 2) liberal economic policy."[38] The perfected paternalism of the World Bank rests on three more or less implicit principles – namely, "the introduction of the liberal norm of the non-interventionist state and, most notably, the norm of free exchange; the quest for parsimony at all costs; and the will to circumscribe the political."[39] Grossly simplistic in its analysis of the role of the state, the World Bank's approach imposes untenable policies of stabilization and structural adjustment that aggravate the distress of African states (reduction in the number of public officials, drastic shrinking of salaries, privatization of large stretches of state portfolios, and the handling of debt by means of international negotiations). The lenders end by noting:

> the rise in criminality, the increasing use of violence to economic ends, and the collapse of numerous states. It highlights the transgressions brought about by the state's inability to protect property rights, ensure a working judiciary system, maintain stable rules, etc. It recognizes that corruption does not have the same consequences everywhere in the world and that its presence is less significant than its forms and meanings.[40]

The verdict is implacable:

> Despite its importance for the economies of these countries, state aid for development has not prevented their failure. Hasn't it, in a certain sense, failed in its mission? Despite the severe consequences that they have entailed for the poor, the politics of liberalization and the policies of "structural adjustment" that followed them are today producing economic results. The continent is showing a return to growth through exports; opening up economically is bearing fruit. It is also witnessing the beginning of endogenous growth. It nonetheless remains the case that there has not been a reduction in poverty. Worse, a considerable portion of educated young people cannot find employment and is compelled to migrate or to traffic illegally in goods. From a social point of view and with respect to the morale of the populations, the onset of policies of structural adjustment have had a very negative role.[41]

The intervention of funding bodies [*bailleurs de fonds*] in Africa has helped to structure and consolidate informal economies and encouraged the privatization and the criminalization of contemporary political regimes. According to the historian Philippe Hugon, the aid given to Africa may alleviate the conscience of the rich, but mostly it is a more or less conscious pillage of the continent. In 2014, 15 NGOs calculated that, for the $134 billion that enter Africa each year, $192 billion leave, leaving a net loss of $58 billion.[42] On this basis, it would be a mistake to consider that aid for development answers to altruistic and disinterested objectives (the idealist tendency conceives it as a moral imperative based in concerns about guaranteeing human dignity).[43] In its realist orientation, aid for development is an instrument of power and of security for every state seeking, in the first instance, to increase its wealth and strength: "Aid thus forms a part of an interested partnership by which donors authorize financial commitments for the purpose of conquering markets, maintaining and expanding their zones of influence, and promoting the interests of their ruling classes."[44] When it is bestowed in a privileged fashion upon fragile or failed states, aid is bound together with interests of hegemony and security (whether from a bilateral[45] or multilateral[46] perspective). In American foreign policy, for example, aid is clearly an apparatus of "strategic defense," as Lael Brainard shows.[47] In many cases, recipient countries are given little leeway for expressing their preferences about the forms that aid for development takes or the sectors that it targets. At times, they find themselves receiving assistance with no relevance for their priorities for development.[48] Nonetheless, the debate on aid is renewed year after year – even if the sums distributed and the impulse to take action in the name of international solidarity, in the struggle against misery, or in response to planetary crises (global warming and environmental protection, epidemics, terrorism, mass migration, etc.) have all remained constant.

In its humanitarian aspect, aid is the materialization of a universal compassion and an unavoidable part of the situations produced by the crises and conflicts that are so common on the continent. The appearance in French of the word "humanitaire" – *humanitarian* – goes back to the first half of the nineteenth century; it refers, as both an adjective and a noun, to all that aims for the good or the interest of humanity. Closely related to philanthropy, humanitarian action is understood as the effect of treating humans humanely [*humainement*], of seeking their wellbeing. This is the sense that Rony Brauman, a professional in the humanitarian field, gives the word. "Humanitarian action," Brauman writes, "is an action that seeks, without discriminating and by peaceful means, to preserve life out of a respect for dignity, to restore to human beings their capacities of choice."[49] To a great extent, Africa has been the target of all kinds of assistance that,

> inserting themselves at various levels of an international aid apparatus [*dispositif international de l'aide*], are governed by a certain set of principles and undertaken (in the name of what are considered universal values) for the benefit of populations whose conditions of existence, owing to acts of nature (catastrophes) or to the actions of other humans (domestic or international armed conflict) have been thrown into crisis and who find their physical integrity and even survival jeopardized.[50]

Additionally, the face of the humanitarian target is essential: the Black child on the cover of many works, or as an illustration accompanying numerous articles and other working guides. From the Red Cross model to the colonial health service model, the religious and compassionate tendency of humanitarian action is well known,[51] and, as Pierre de Senarclens notes, this tendency is "constitutive of the social tie. It expresses itself emblematically in the protection that parents provide their children. It is associated with pity, or rather with compassion, which also gives form to the relationships of mutual identification that one finds undergirding solidarity between human beings – the basic solidarity without which there is no organized society."[52]

No matter whether it is administered by states, global coalitions of agencies, or international organizations of collective actors or individuals, humanitarian aid is operationalized by a plurality of agents, and notably by doctors, nurses, rescue workers, and members of the armed forces. The market in suffering is doing well, as the asymmetry between the needy and aid professionals attests: high salaries, "guarded compounds, fancy vehicles and advanced communications systems are highly visible. In war zones, they have become symbols of power, wealth, and superiority. They separate aid providers from aid recipients in terms of wealth and options."[53] Far from the religious principle of unostentatious generosity,[54] humanitarian actions are widely mediatized for highly complex motives ... The humanitarian space is traversed by public and private organizations, both national and international, and often operating according to different mandates. Care, food, protection from violence, and compassion are materialized through logistical and technical means. In this domain, the Nigerian Civil War

(1968–70) remains a pivotal moment for structuring the "sans-frontiérisme" (literally, "without-borders-ism") that lays claim to a duty of compassion (a humanitarian duty to intervene that attenuates the cardinal principle of the sovereign equality of states).

Humanitarian crises present the challenge of coordinating food and medical aid, relocation of populations, material reconstruction, institutional support, social reorganization, and transitional justice. Rescuing victims has sometimes provided justification for humanitarian intervention, as well as for a state interventionism with strong imperialist overtones (in these cases, humanitarian aid becomes part of state foreign policies). The state humanitarian [*humanitaire d'État*] very often combines humanitarian action with military action as part of an imperialist militarization of assistance, at times far removed from principles of humanity, impartiality, neutrality, independence, free consent, unity, or universality. In addition, the risks that come with replacing a state's own capacities with humanitarian interventions sometimes lead to the institutionalization of emergency policies that completely undermine the durability of the desired transformations.[55] Intervening to protect human dignity from the violence of other humans or the violence of nature becomes a part of a regime of justification, which, often enough, provokes ethical dilemmas at odds with the principle according to which "all suffering, no matter where it occurs, calls for a response; one cannot see the reasons why this response need be tied to the political action or inaction of the powerful in this world."[56]

As one can see, the territories that compassion draws offer a caricatural picture of a world divided between victims and do-gooders. They continuously trade blame over who is responsible for the suffering. Resorting to the crucible of nature, the gods, the cruelty of humans or governments (read: corrupt and incompetent leaders), they call for an emotional separation: "Africa should take care of itself!" is enjoined in an attempt to cut ties to Africa (consider, for example, Western far right movements that prefer to look to their own suffering rather than to the suffering of others). While Bernard Lugan (a historian with ties to extremist politics) calls on the West to abandon all its complexes,[57] Daniel Lefeuvre denounces a "repentant propaganda" [*propogande repentante*][58] backed up by "the preaching of sectarians of colonial repentance founded upon ignorance, mystifications, and errors – even upon untruths."[59] Colonial memory together with the violence of humans and nature have supplied a decisive argument for the construction of the kind of thinking proper to victimhood [*la pensée victimaire*].

A Suffering that Produces Legitimate Victimhood

The surging of compassion is always accompanied by a large movement of victimization: an ambiguous symptom of both refusing and accepting to take suffering and pity upon oneself. As Guillaume Erner explains, human beings have, in practice:

> lived with pain for centuries, resigned and powerless. With the rise of democracy, suffering became at once insupportable and scandalous. This fact, so self-evident as to appear anodyne, bears witness to radical changes in the way we conceive of human beings and society. Having become our last absolute, the refusal of suffering organizes our society according to a new set of values. One no longer believes in the good faith of conquerors; history has also become the history of the defeated. In the secular world, victims incarnate the new form of the sacred, a form which prohibits sacrilege and justifies sacrifice.[60]

The story of African victimhood is relatively rudimentary; it is characterized by a dissatisfaction with the condition of Africans and by the creation of a set of responsibilities. At times bipolar, the story brings the exaltation of Africa's qualities, merits, wealth, and advantages together with the injustice of its situation, basing itself on what Achille Mbembe calls the three canonical meanings [*significations canoniques*] of the African experience. The first concerns separation from oneself, "which is supposed to result in a loss of familiarity with the self, to the point that the subject, having become estranged from him- or herself, has been relegated to a lifeless form of identity: the spectacle of drawing and quartering."[61] The second has to do with disappropriation [*désappropriation*], which is an expropriation and material dispossession (straddling subjection through others' falsification of oneself and an ontological impoverishment). The last meaning carried by such self-writing [*écriture de soi*] is degradation, in the sense that the condition of servitude is "supposed to have plunged the African subject not only into humiliation, debasement, and nameless suffering but also into a zone of non-being and social death characterized by the denial of dignity, heavy psychic damage, and the torment of exile."[62] At times, the woes of Africa get summarily attributed to colonization, to unjust debt, to inopportune aid or wars provoked and sustained by the West; rarely are they attributed to the responsibility of Africans themselves. Neglected in the past, the painful memory of the suffering of Africans during slavery and under colonialism is today increasingly sacralized for the benefit of investments by entrepreneurs specializing in the memory of Africa; they have rallied around the talking points [*argumentaires*] of scholars (especially historians) and militants who call for recognition and reparation.

The dialectic of compassion creates a disagreement that gives rise to an "initial twist that institutes politics as the deployment of a wrong or of a fundamental dispute."[63] As a consequence, the injunction to fly to the rescue of the suffering continent has essentially constituted Africa as a "continent of victims" and led to the belief that the world has duties [*devoirs*] vis-à-vis Africa, while Africa has rights [*droits*] vis-à-vis the world. This thinking lays the basis for a series of struggles and demands for the recognition of suffering and the institution of policies of reparation. The adoption of a law declaring slavery and the slave trade "crimes against humanity" in May 2001 marked a real turning point in that it cleared the way for legal demands for reparation.[64] Although only one provision of the final law concerns such legal action, Article 5 of the draft bill had anticipated reparations: "There is instituted a committee of qualified persons charged with determining the harm suffered, and with examining the conditions of due reparation with respect to this crime." This article of the draft bill would be abrogated by the Law Committee of the French National Assembly so that the text could be unanimously adopted – despite strong protest by the Representative Council of France's Black Associations (CRAN) who demanded the recognition of the imprescriptability of the aforementioned crimes. In the wake of this decision, during the third World Conference Against Racism organized by the United Nations, which took place between August 31 and September 8, 2001, in Durban, South Africa, the suffering of Africans was once again recognized, in the thirteenth point of the final *Declaration and Programme of Action*:

> We acknowledge that slavery and the slave trade, including the transatlantic slave trade, were appalling tragedies in this history of humanity not only because of their abhorrent barbarism but also in terms of their magnitude, organized nature and especially their negation of the essence of the victims, and further acknowledge that slavery and the slave trade are a crime against humanity and should always have been so, especially the transatlantic slave trade, and are among the major sources and manifestations of racism, racial discrimination, xenophobia and related intolerance, and that Africans and people of African descent, Asians and people of Asian descent and indigenous peoples were victims of these acts and continue to be victims of their consequences.[65]

The *Declaration* identifies colonialism as a source of racism and racial discrimination, and states that the suffering inflicted by the colonizer has led to persistent social and economic inequalities.

This commitment is made with the goal of rendering concrete a notion of "human family" based upon equality, dignity, and solidarity. Special and repeated mention is made of "the people of Africa in their continuing struggle against racism, racial discrimination, xenophobia and related intolerance." Similarly, the member states

> recognize the sacrifices made by [the African people], as well as their efforts in raising international public awareness of these inhuman tragedies. [They] also affirm the great importance [they] attach to the values of solidarity, respect, tolerance and multiculturalism, which constitute the moral ground and inspiration for [their] worldwide struggle against racism, racial discrimination, xenophobia and related intolerance, inhuman tragedies which have affected people throughout the world, especially in Africa, for too long.[66]

The 160 states represented by the *Declaration*, together with NGO-observers, draw links between racism, poverty, underdevelopment, marginalization, social exclusion, and economic disparities. Furthermore, the *Declaration* urges the United Nations, other international organizations, and states to actively commit themselves to "redress the marginalization of Africa's contribution to world history and civilization by developing and implementing a specific and comprehensive programme of research, education and mass communication to disseminate widely a balanced and objective presentation of Africa's seminal and valuable contribution to humanity."[67] Of the *Declaration*'s several invocations, the reference to Africa is without a doubt the one that enjoys the greatest consensus, for, faced with recognizing the suffering of the Palestinian people, the United States and Israel were obliged to leave the conference.

The inevitable question of reparation is posed by Africans from the continent and in diaspora. It is organized around two connected demands: slavery should be officially recognized as constituting a crime against humanity and, on the same grounds, the victims of this dark period of human history should be restored their rights "by creating for their benefit either a fund for compensation, or a program of economic recovery for their countries of origin, or both."[68] The vice president of the Republic of Zambia, Enoch P. Kavindele, would say:

We have come to Durban to liberate ourselves from historical injustices committed against mankind in the form of slavery and servitude and now to emphasize that slavery should not be remembered as an appalling tragedy, but also as a factor that for centuries deprived Africa of her human and natural resources. We must accept the fact that it is the resources plundered over centuries, the oppression and displacement of human capital, which have seriously impaired African development to this very day.... The Berlin Conference of 1886 on the partition of Africa drew its moral authority from the fact that people who lived in the African continent were too inferior to be consulted when arbitrary boundaries and ownership of their native lands were being decided.... Africa requests for an audience, so that the world can honour and take responsibility for the memory and recognition of the crime of slavery and colonialism in recent history. Failure that [sic], Black people will continue to be viewed as property, whose value fluctuates according to the law of demand and supply.... The cry for Africa is that all the victims of all abuses of human rights in the recent past and the very recent times have been [sic] adequately redressed for the wrongs of the past, but Africa remains suffering and bleeding from the aftermath.... Zambia ... calls for the establishment of an international compensation scheme for victims of the slave trade and a development reparation fund to provide additional resources for the development process in countries affected by colonialism.[69]

Stafford Neil, Jamaica's representative at the conference, extended the painful legacy to include the African diaspora in the Caribbean and the Americas, the result of a transatlantic trade that lasted three centuries and enriched numerous companies and individuals. For him, moving toward reconciliation

is not to catalogue the abuses or highlight the human suffering endured during that era, but to point the way to reconciliation and atonement. The proposals relating to reparations that have been made to this Conference are directed towards this purpose. These proposals are not intended to be divisive or confrontational, but rather form part of a process to heal the wounds of the past. Indeed we believe that reparations equally serve the interests of the descendants of the victims, as well as the descendants of the oppressors. It is a means by which both may be able to confront the past without guilt or bitterness.[70]

Held responsible for Africa's innumerable torments, the countries of the Global North responded by "agreeing to assist countries affected by slavery with development" – without, however, providing specifics.[71] Notable exceptions were the United Kingdom and the Netherlands, who "recognized that slavery was an abomination and that their countries 'regret' this period of their history for which they are ready to offer an 'apology.'"[72] Amos de Brondesbury, the United Kingdom's minister for Africa, invoked the friendship between peoples and the need to leave Durban with the commitment to "look[...] unflinchingly at the past," while at the same time joining the European Union in profoundly deploring "the human suffering, both individual and collective, caused by slavery and the slave trade. They are among the most dishonourable and abhorrent chapters in the history of humanity. Such acts of acknowledgement, regret and condemnation will allow us to move forward in a spirit of hope and give us the basis on which to continue to tackle contemporary problems."[73]

The Minister of Luxembourg, Lydie Polfer, however, added the qualification:

> This Conference cannot do justice to the victims. But it does confront states with their political responsibilities. It is our duty to identify the mechanisms in our past which led to racism and to seek out their afterlives in our present. It is our duty to clarify the principles behind the struggle against intolerance – its most insidious forms included, since they are precisely the forms that we carelessly transmit. The duty to remember is a work of liberation, because it helps us gain awareness of the horrors and the guilt that haunt us. Solidarity with people from countries which were victims of racist practices of government calls out to be affirmed as such.[74]

Polfer nonetheless relativizes Western responsibility by recalling that

> solidarity is universal; it is independent of bilateral agreements.... That today we might conceive a country having the right to mobilize international solidarity for the purpose of reclaiming its past, restoring the mutilated memory of victims, working on its identity – in the same sense that it does in the context of the struggle against poverty – seems to me to belong to the same spirit that drove the international community to list development as a human right.[75]

No matter what terms are used, development as a humanitarian action is "indissociable from western capitalist hegemony at the end of the twentieth century."[76] The duty of compassion thus refers to past suffering, but there is a well-established connection to contemporary suffering, which is presented as a logical consequence of the earlier. It is in this way that the posture of victimhood extends to the structural causes [*les ressorts structurels*] behind the international community's political and economic relations with Africa. One of the privileged arenas for the promotion of Africa's suffering is debt, unjustly used as a mechanism for reducing African countries to servitude. The Committee for the Cancellation of Third World Debt singles out the 19 richest countries belonging to the Paris Club. The intervention of the International Monetary Fund as issuer of the letter of intent is also denounced for the fact that the IMF pushes states to adopt extreme budgetary rigor. The compassionate authority of the West, which is rooted in a productive political emotion, has affected Africa's ability to think and project itself.

When it comes to the relationship between one's own suffering and the suffering of geographic neighbors [*des proches*], the thinking proper to victimhood draws abundantly from a specific schema of distantiation. In effect, since compassion is constructed at a distance, it is effectively on the basis of fictions and other myths about what Africa is (the power of representations should not be neglected in this compassionate governmentality) that Africa has progressively distanced itself from the obligation of compassion. It is by these means that a second path, breaking from the regime of compassionate imperialism grounded in the asymmetric alterity of its protagonists, becomes possible and necessary. This second path is the rehabilitation of a regime of the nigh [*régime du proche*], re-established upon the principle of compassionate self-sufficiency.

... towards a regime of compassionate self-sufficiency whose essence is horizontal

It is essential that Africa's capacity for compassion be rethought and rehabilitated. In reference to contemporary societies characterized by the institutionalization of compassionate politics, Myriam Revault d'Allonnes points to the emergence of "the compassionate man" [*l'homme compassionnel*],[77] while Clifford Orwin affirms that compassion has become a cult object for subjects with "moist eyes."[78] The fact that compassion has become a marker structuring Africa's presence in the world deserves to be turned around. It is essential to observe that, by inscribing compassion within (and beyond) the scope of a decolonial thinking that invites us to leave behind the monopolistic and obligatory reference to the West

– including in the analysis of how Africa is seized by compassion – one produces the possibility for a subversion of compassion (1) which is centered around "care" for equals (2).

Africa's subversion of compassion through self-care

Decolonizing compassion also means making compassion into a political act of subversion. It is a question of breaking with a compassion that views its object from on high, which is essentially charity-empathy: compassion as a perverted form of pity. This is the compassion Hannah Arendt rejects when, repeatedly and with great admiration, she cites Machiavelli's famous statement that one "should learn to not be good." Compassion should be concealed within one's heart and within the private sphere, far from the bright light of the public, for the purest form of this "beautiful and noble passion" is, as Arendt indicates, incarnated by Jesus Christ. Objecting to any proposal for relegating compassion to the private sphere, we affirm that the compassionate emotions and actions provoked by Africa's misfortunes, being creative and productive, represent a condition that reconfigures the three frontiers of morality (and, as a consequence, the boundaries of regimes of the nigh). These frontiers run between politics and morality, the universal and the particular, and, finally, between the public and the private. It is precisely this beautiful and noble "passion" that Africans feel for Africans which should be rehabilitated. This passion is grounded in regimes of the nigh that constitute and legitimate themselves by means of goodwill and sympathy for Africa or the "African," whose worlds it aims to sustain, perpetuate, and repair.

Such are the terms in which the subversion of compassion is expressed. It sees itself as a reversal of the established order, a refusal to obey the rules of compassionate interaction, a (re)definition of morality (as a distinction between good and evil, and definition of the just), and an obligation to attend to neglected realities – and, doubtless, thereby to the reasons behind their neglect.[79] The subversion of compassion is founded upon a duty of humanity [*humanité*] toward the neighbor [*le proche*] – in the imperatives to restore their autonomy and dignity. At times, it takes the form of an obligation to refuse the commiseration of others and the expression of their compassion. Whether or not it is meant explicitly, such a process amounts to the affirmation and legitimation of the self and of its capacities. It relativizes the difficulties and suffering that Africa faces, but it also recalls the continent's powers and advantages. The refusal expresses itself as much in feigning not to hear the West and contesting its reading of African reality as it does in offering a diagnostic analysis of the continent's problems, or in putting forward proposals for their resolution different from those made by others. The subversion of compassion can also be read in terms of what Mbembe calls a "liturgical construction" [*construction liturgique*] based in "self-(re)writing."[80] One can think of this evolution in terms of a movement from a government of bodies to a government of the self – or, more precisely, Foucault's notion of *care of the self*.[81] The importance that one's self-image and the gaze of others assumes accentuates the rational interiorization of compassion for one's self and one's neighbors [*ses proches*]. Subjectivity or subjectivation (particularly in the context of suffering) is essential for understanding the room for maneuver that the African subject has when faced with the "good" that the other wants for him or her. Doubtful about the other's desire for his or her wellbeing, the African subject may choose not to adopt the prescriptions offered, or else refuse to be helped. As Alain Ehrenberg observes, in a society of generalized autonomy, "where individual responsibility for one's own life forms the backdrop of social life, socialization consists of ruling schemas that allow, oblige, and drive every individual, regardless of their position in the social hierarchy, to be the agent of their own transformation."[82] He notes that three social schemas combine to produce the permanent transformation of the self, the development of social and relational competencies, and support for life trajectories. These schemas allow one to act spontaneously in the appropriate manner, mindful of prescriptions and of self-care. Ehrenberg adds that "in a sociality where what matters is being the agent of one's own transformation, social inequalities undergo a profound change: the opposition winner/loser comes to dominate the opposition dominant/dominated, characteristic of industrial society. The equality that counts is an equality of capacity, which is a life-long equality."[83]

What Ehrenberg describes forms the basis for the subversion of compassion. Whether the stakes are existential or phenomenological, this subversion applies to the way in which the subject is led to construct a transitive relation with the self or the ego [*le moi*] as an outcome of knowledge. In *Security, Territory, and Population*, and "Governmentality," Foucault shows that care for the bodies of individuals arises and manifests itself in different modalities from one time to another: hence the need to historicize the techniques and instruments of government. By situating the instruments and apparatuses [*dispositifs*] of government, one can see that such care corresponds to specific modes of governmentality. This care is not to be set apart from what takes place at the heart of political apparatuses. Self-care concerns the work that everyone is led to undertake for themselves and for the city. Basically, "the place allotted to self-knowledge becomes more important. The task of testing oneself, examining oneself, monitoring oneself in a series of clearly defined exercises, makes the question of truth – the truth concerning what one is, what one does, and what one is capable of doing – central to the formation of the ethical subject."[84]

Starting with conceptions of pleasure in Antiquity, Foucault is led to reflect on the morality that underlies them, and on how individuals cultivate such morality, so that exhibiting temperance means "being under one's own command," and to demonstrate a "culture of the self." Self-care belongs to the arts of existence – which is to say, "those intentional and voluntary actions by which men not only set themselves rules of conduct, but also seek to transform themselves in their singular being, and to make their life into an *œuvre* that carries certain aesthetic values and meets certain stylistic criteria."[85] Formulated as an ethics of the subject, self-care participates in the return of the practical subject (in the place of the subject subjected to power). Whether self-care is characterized by the "measuring of what one is capable of," or by the free and virtuous relationship one cultivates with oneself and with others, the consequences for one's relationship to one's own suffering are clear.[86] To make a practice of oneself [*se pratiquer soi-même*] and to govern one's own suffering or the suffering of friends or family is to express a sensibility for oneself and for others and to show a capacity of self-control by dominating one's desires and pleasures. By doing so, one takes care of others. Here, one can draw a parallel with the notion of "care" developed by the feminist theorist Joan Tronto. For Tronto, care is associated with goodwill and sympathy for others as they are practiced in social life: "A species activity that includes everything that we do to maintain, to continue, and to repair our world so that we can live in it as well as possible. That world includes our bodies, our selves, and our environment, all of which we seek to interweave in a complex, life-sustaining web."[87] By drawing on Foucault's idea of counter-conduct [*contre-conduites*], one can grasp the reversal of subjectivation and thus the subversion of compassion which at times rests on a universalist interpretation of human dignity and an indignation at how Africa is treated.

Indignation is mobilizing, particularly with respect to Pan-Africanism. Pan-Africanism is a movement that arose at the beginning of the twentieth century,[88] but that also participates in an older dynamic, which:

> initially emerged with opposition to the slave trade, to slavery, and to their consequences for the legal status of Black people, for the image of Africa in the world, and for the fate that the great powers of the period envisioned for Africans and their continent. By rejecting the slave system, Africans in both Africa and the diaspora affirmed that all peoples were equal and that Africans had the right to live in freedom and dignity like other human beings.[89]

Such protest was intellectual and political, and it would utterly transform the histories of nations and the continent. This was the case for those who undertook the subversion of compassion: figures such as John Nkologo Chilembwe, a pastor from Malawi (at the time, Nyasaland), who, well before the beginning of the First World War, called for fundamental changes regarding questions of colonial administration. These included access to land for African peasants, who had often been dispossessed and reduced to serfdom, as well as changes to the system of taxing by hut (the obligation to work for free for three months on a large European plantation).[90] Chilembwe would take a stand in open opposition to British colonization, before vanishing on February 3, 1915, in circumstances that have yet to be clarified. The Nigerian Nnamdi Azikiwe, in a collection of speeches given between 1927 and 1960,[91] as well as the Ghanaian Kwame Nkrumah, in his 1961 "Statement of African Ideology,"[92] are not silent about their conviction that Africa does not need others; they demand effective independence, including in the way the continent's situation is viewed. A work of memory is what the young poet Léopold Sédar Senghor calls for in his text "On the Appeal from the Race of Sheba":

> Car le cri montagnard du ras Desta a traversé l'Afrique de part en part comme une épée longue et sûre dans l'avilissement de ses reins
> Il a dominé la rage trépignante crépitante des mitrailleuses, défié les avions des marchands
> Et voici qu'un long gémissement plus désolé qu'un long pleur de mère aux funérailles d'un jeune homme
> Sourd des mines là-bas, dans l'extrême Sud.[93]

> [For the mountain cry of the Ras Desta has gone through and through Africa like a long firm sword through the rottenness of its loins.

It has sounded above the trembling stuttering rage of the machine guns, defied the aeroplanes of the merchants
And, listen, the long groaning, more desolate than a mother's long wail at the burying of a young man,
Muffled, from the mines there in the farthest South.][94]

Senghor's denunciation of the physical and moral humiliation of the Black condition during the Second World War and in the work camps takes place in the context of his promotion of negritude, which he understands as "the Black world's set of civilizational values." His work aims to guide the Black soldier out of oblivion by praising his sense of honor and courage, his dignity, his attachment to brotherhood.

Seized by a spirit of revolution, Thomas Sankara of Burkina Faso would regularly insist on an aspiration to autonomy and dignity. One of his most powerful interventions occurred on October 4, 1984, when he addressed the 39th session of the United Nations General Assembly to express the double aspiration, in the name of the people of Burkina Faso together with "all those who suffer, wherever they may be," for an "Africa for the Africans."[95]

In a similar spirit, Nkrumah writes:

> I believe strongly and sincerely that with the deep-rooted wisdom and dignity, the innate respect for human lives, the intense humanity that is our heritage, the African race, united under one federal government, will emerge not as just another world bloc to flaunt its wealth and strength, but as a Great Power whose greatness is indestructible because it is built not on fear, envy and suspicion, nor won at the expense of others, but founded on hope, trust, friendship and directed to the good of all mankind.... For centuries, Europeans dominated the African continent. The white man arrogated to himself the right to rule and to be obeyed by the non-white; his mission, he claimed, was to "civilize" Africa. Under this cloak, the Europeans robbed the continent of vast riches and inflicted unimaginable suffering on the African people. All this makes for a sad story, but now we must be prepared to bury the past with its unpleasant memories and look to the future.[96]

Autonomy of compassion is achieved by means of Africa's capacity to find its own solutions to its problems, a program that Nkrumah identifies with African unity. Having been impoverished by others, Africa, Nkrumah maintains, faces "the paradox of poverty in the midst of plenty, and scarcity in the midst of abundance. Never before have a people had within their grasp so great an opportunity for developing a continent endowed with so much wealth. Individually, the independent states of Africa, some of them potentially rich, others poor, can do little for their people."[97] This reversal strengthens Africa's capacity to speak to the world as an equal, such equality being a central objective of Pan-Africanist thought. As Nkrumah insists, "We have to prove that greatness is not to be measured in stockpiles of atomic bombs."[98]

The self-care that lies at the core of the subversion of compassion is attained through a process of radical dignification, as Aimé Césaire explained in the context of a French debate about reparations. Can one fix the price of suffering? No, Césaire responds:

> It's irreparable.... Reparation is a matter of interpretation. I know the Western world too well: "All right dear friend, how much? I'll give you half of that to pay off the slave trade. Okay? It's a deal!" Then it's over: they repaired the matter. But for me it's utterly irreparable. I don't really like the term "reparation." It implies that repairing the matter is possible.[99]

While Césaire recognizes that the West owes a moral debt to Africa, this debt consists in "provid[ing] aid to countries as they develop, help[ing] them thrive. It owes us this aid, but I don't believe that a simple check can pay for reparations. It's a question of aid, not a contract. It's purely moral."[100] The subjectivation at work does not produce a singularization of African suffering. Nor does it reduce the restoration of Africans' dignity to the terms of a reparation which, as the poet says, would encourage the West to regard Africans as "a bunch of beggars" who, centuries after the fact, plead not in moral but in financial terms for the crime committed against them to be compensated:

> I think we should help one another, and all the more so when one party is to a certain extent responsible for the misfortune of the other. I don't want this to become a series of trials, indictments, committees, compensation payments, etc. How much would it be? So many different figures have been put forward ... We can't give in to a sense of victimhood. This isn't an easy task. We've been educated and taught to see the world in a way that leaves us free of responsibility. Have we ever been responsible for ourselves?[101]

Sententiously, Césaire concludes, "We've always been the subjugated, the colonized. This has marked us."

As a desire for autonomy and self-preservation, the subversion of compassion also draws from Afrocentrism and Afro-optimism, which have been experiencing a comeback since the early 2000s.[102] Progressively, one has gone from *Hopeless Africa*[103] to *Resurgent Africa*, on account of the fact that nearly all of the continent's multilateral debt has been forgiven, that its rates of growth have at times been exceptional, and that, for the first time, its governments have been able to raise funds on the international financial markets at low interest rates. Even if such enthusiasm has largely evaporated, there are many who, like Macky Sall, are not giving up. During the 16th Francophone Summit in Madagascar in 2016, Sall said, "You know, as for myself, I'm an Afro-optimist. And I also want Africa to be respected for what it is. This is to say that, today, Africa has made efforts in democratization."[104] At the time, Sall remained an Afro-optimist despite the waves of Black migrants that, crashing into the Mediterranean, were statistically going to their deaths, and despite the innumerable victims of malaria, of Ebola hemorrhagic fever, of HIV/AIDS, of terrorist movements like Boko Haram or al-Shabaab, etc. Such massive, continental suffering spares few, and even the islands that do escape are tarred by an image of destitution.

The self-care that is a subjectivation and recentering on oneself comes about by means of a rehabilitation of the capacity and authority to show compassion for one's nearby peer [*pair proche*].

Towards the African, that neighbor: contributions of "care"

The legitimation of victimhood is also a pact between suffering and exploitation founded on "the intuition that there is a relationship between the misery of the poor and the egoism" of others[105] – it cannot last long, hence the movement to rehabilitate Africa's capacity for compassion. This capacity is rooted in a regime of horizontal compassion: the compassion of peers and equals. Responsibility for the other is directed first toward the neighbor [*proche*] before extending to the human in the name of a shared humanity.[106] Compassionate subjectivation is the affirmation of a solidarity for friends in the following sense:

> How selfish soever man may be supposed, there are evidently some principles in his nature, which interest him in the fortune of others, and render their happiness necessary to him, though he derives nothing from it except the pleasure of seeing it. Of this kind is pity or compassion, the emotion which we feel for the misery of others, when we either see it, or are made to conceive it in a very lively manner.[107]

It need not be an exaltation of a mythic and illusory "African solidarity," but rather manifests itself through public policies focused on what vitally belongs to the human:

> It is not the love of our neighbor, it is not the love of mankind, which upon many occasions prompts us to the practice of those divine virtues. It is a stronger love, a more powerful affection, which generally takes place upon such occasions; the love of what is honourable and noble, of the grandeur, and dignity, and superiority of our own characters.[108]

The affinity with the grief of those with whom he or she is closest, in a geographic sense of the word, constitutes the African as a neighbor; his or her compassion can construct itself on the basis of care in the definition of Fisher and Tronto given above.[109] Compassion for one's peers can construct itself as "support for life."[110] It must target zones of vitality beyond anatamo-politics and biopoitics,[111] and more generally the politics of life.[112] The latter play a decisive role in society as well as in one's own life: for Agata Zielinski,

> the solicitude that I provide, the solicitude from which I benefit, care given, care received. Those whom I care for, those who care for me – searching for examples outside the sphere in which we habitually look for care or forms of care: health and education. Where one can see that the aim of *care* is to nurture relations: "with and for others, within fair institutions," to employ Ricœur's definition of ethics.[113]

The subversion of compassion forms the basis for a renewal of politics similar to what Jean-Jacques Rousseau called compassionate democracy. Much more than a utopia, compassionate public policies can be materialized on African soil. It would begin with redefining the dimensions of the welfare state, which is a state of public goodwill, by committing it to a path of compassion politically grounded in public action whose specificity lies in seeking out what is vital in the human being and preserving it. To return to what is vital for the human being is, in a certain sense, to rehumanize politics. The aim of this return to essentials is to privilege the dignity of the human person. Such a utopian prospect would lead to the elaboration of "dignity-oriented" national budgets, setting aside a special place for dealing with suffering. At the heart of such policies, the ethics of care for the other affirms "the importance of caring for and attending to others, especially those whose lives and wellbeing depend on a particular form of attention, provided continually and on a daily basis"[114] – the most vulnerable.

As a whole, compassionate governmentality that targets Africa represents the disarticulation and the marginalization of Africa because it keeps the continent's suffering at a distance. This distantiation, which stems from a disagreement about the causes of suffering, not only produces a second-order division between Africa and everywhere else, it also introduces an ontological break grounded in "the question of equality with respect to the advent of an incommensurable wrong perpetrated against the have-nots [*sans-parts*] demanding their share [*leur parts*]."[115] A "have-not," Africa thought that the other, out of respect for a universal frame which makes every human responsible for their neighbor, would share, bear its suffering, and, at times, call out loudly for help. On the other hand, the evolution toward a subversion of compassion makes possible a rehabilitation of apparatuses [*dispositifs*] of compassion, which need no longer represent the "defeat of politics" [*déroute du politique*] but may, in fact, constitute the restoration of the soul of politics.[116] As an act, but also as an object, compassion can thus re-present, signify, and totalize a set of social relationships that permit the restitution of Africa's dignity.

The Sahara

A Space of Connection within an Emergent Africa, from the Anthropocene to the Spring of Geo-Cultural Life

Benaouda Lebdai

Benaouda Lebdai is a professor of colonial and postcolonial African literature at the University of Le Mans in France, as well as a literary columnist. He has published a dozen books and more than 50 articles on writers working on both sides of the Sahara. His research treats the relationships between literature and history; between literature and memory; questions of migration, exile, and gender; as well as the genre of autobiography. He has organized numerous international conferences in France, the United States, Tunisia, Morocco, and Algeria. He is, among other achievements, the author of La Représentation de l'Histoire dans les littératures et les arts africains *(Algiers: ENAG, 2017).*

The Sahara is the largest desert in the world, 8 million square kilometers running East to West across the top of Africa. Historically, this space has never been treated with indifference, nor can it, at the beginning of the twenty-first century, be brushed aside with the back of the hand, as if it were simply empty or, at most, a destination for tourists hungry for adventure and an exotic change of scenery. The Sahara is divided territory; it is shared between ten countries with officially recognized borders defined on the basis of a partition introduced during colonization. As a space of exchange, the Sahara has contributed extensively to fashioning contemporary Africa's religious, cultural, and political life. The Sahara's strategic situation, we can infer, justifies a digression in these Dakar reflections for the purpose of emphasizing the signification its geography has for the economic, political, and cultural debates that animate contemporary Africa whenever the conversation touches on the continent's evolution or future. My participation in the debate over the "politics of the living" has led me to think that any attempt to marginalize this rich space would be harmful and reinforce the racialization [*la racialisation*] of Africa. This judgment is grounded in the fact that a thorough understanding of the cultural, economic, and political aspects of the Sahara is essential in order for the populations found on both sides of the desert to be valorized within a perspective that reconciles Africa with its own history. When we are faced with the urgent need to discuss the future of the world's oldest continent, we accordingly find ourselves solicited by this space, for it harbors immense wealth fundamental for the future of humanity. My general procedure will be to examine the image that the Sahara has evoked over time, in history on the one hand and in literature on the other, so that I may show how any posture of indifference with respect to this so-called desert space would be a strategic error for Africans in our globalized world in motion. Building on these analyses, my contribution will treat strategies for exploiting the Sahara for the benefit of the men and women of this continent, using the frame of the African Union to treat the question of borders.

The Sahara, Space of Exchange

The historians are unequivocal: the Sahara was never ignored by the ancestors of the Africans, whether they came from the North or the South. During Antiquity, the Sahara was present in Greek texts, owing to Ptolemy and Herodotus who described it as an inhabited desert – a space rich not only in history, but also in mythology, art, magic, and, of course, commerce. The frescoes of Tassili in Algeria attest to a past that was dynamic and vigorous on every level. The frescoes of the Tassili plateau and of the Hoggar mountains were studied by Henri Lhote in *Le Hoggar, espace et temps* and by Théodore Monod in *Vie et mort au désert*. In the nineteenth century, René Caillié became the first French traveler to traverse the Sahara starting from Algiers; he recounted his illuminating journey in *Travels through Central Africa to Timbuctoo*, a city described as overflowing with gold owing to its thriving commerce. Henri Duveyrier and Camille Douls also recounted their voyages across the desert, just like André Gide, who drew from their example to write *The Fruits of the Earth*. Antoine de Saint-Exupéry was fascinated by the Sahara, which he incorporates into *The Little Prince* and *Southern Mail*. Pierre Benoît places a mysterious, mythical, millennium-old city of the "Grand South," home of the queen Antinea, at the center of his marvelous text *Atlantida*. For Isabelle Eberhard, the great Swiss adventuress, the desert was a refuge; her texts reveal its importance for her – she described its vitality until her tragic death in Aïn Séfra in the Algerian Sahara. The desert has inspired poets, painters, and priests such as Charles de Foucauld, who discourses on it philosophically in *Carnets de Tamanrasset* and *Esquisses sahariennes*. Novelists too – from Louis Gardel (*Fort Saganne*) and Edmond Jabès (*Intimations in the Desert*) to J. M. G. Le Clézio (*Desert*) and Paul Bowles (*The Sheltering Sky*) – have presented the Sahara as a stage for every dream and every fantasy. The desert has always elicited attraction and fascination, and for this reason every attempt to define this geographic space cannot help but be restrictive. European interest in the Sahara seems to me particularly important to emphasize here, since Europeans have described not only its various sites but also the people who live there.

On the African side, the Sahara was never considered "uncrossable." Robust ties have existed between North Africa and Sub-Saharan Africa from time immemorial. The British writer Basil Davidson describes Berbers using horses and chariots for the purpose of trading with tropical regions well before 500 BCE. He writes that "Timgad and Volubilis had been Roman forerunners of Sijilmasa and the great Arabo-Berber entrepôts of later times."[1] Indeed, it is reported that, until the thirteenth century, merchants from Tahert in Algeria and Sijilmasa in Morocco traded with the peoples of West Africa. With the arrival of Arab conquerors in Africa in the seventh century, cultural, religious, and demographic exchanges intensified, as is shown in the accounts of Arab travelers such as Ibn Battuta and Leo Africanus. From the vantage of Sub-Saharan Africans, Islam came from the desert and spread along with the gold trade in Mali, but also Ghana, Senegal, Sudan, and Niger. In *Folia orientalia*, the historian Tadeusz Lewicki provides a repertory of unpublished documents pertaining to the first trans-Saharan commercial exchanges conducted by Ibadi merchants from M'zab. For centuries, then, the Sahara was a space of human and cultural transhumance. During the colonial period, the exchanges between the people of the Sahel and the people of the North were brutally interrupted for the sake of a colonial strategy based on the motto "divide and conquer." The colonial system thus transformed the Sahara into a frontier separating two Africas, and this was how Africa came to be racialized [*s'est racialisée*], divided into white Africa and Black Africa.

The Sahara, Literary Visions

In my attempt to valorize the Sahara and to demonstrate the role it plays in geopolitics, it is helpful to examine it through the literary visions of the African writers on both of its sides, whose representations reflect the views of the region's peoples. Writings by poet travelers searching for the absolute cast the Sahara as a space of friendship [*espace d'amitié*] between Africans. The Sahara is present in literary texts that describe the affective and emotional potential of its two shores and that show legitimate interest through narrative discourses that tell of the obsession with the desert. Examples include *Terre desséchée* by Martine Djoup of Cameroon; *Saison de la migration vers le nord* (translated as *Season of Migration to the North*) by Tayeb Salih of Sudan; *Sahel! Sanglante sécheresse* by Alpha Mandé Diarra; *Que revienne la rosée sur les oasis oubliées* by Albakaye Kounta; *Le désert inhumain* by Mamadou Soukouna; *Le jeune homme de sable* by Williams Sassine; *Le devoir de violence* (translated as *Bound to Violence*), a novel that retraces the history of Africa from 1202 to 1947, by Yambo Ouologuem of Mali; *Makarie aux épines* by Baba Moustapha of Chad; *À l'orée du Sahel* by Youssouf Gueye of Mauritania; *Two Thousand Seasons* and *Why Are We So Blest?* by Ayi Kwei Armah of Ghana; *Les bouts de bois de Dieu* (translated as *God's Bits of Wood*) by Ousmane Sembène; *Gens de sable* by Catherine N'Diaye; *Cycle de sécheresse* by Cheikh C. Sow; *Amkoullel, l'enfant Peul: mémoires* (translated as *Amkoullel, the Fula Boy*) by Amadou Hampâté Bâ; *Une hyiène à jeune* by Massa Makan Diabaté; *Ségou, les murailles de terre* and *Ségou, la terre en miettes* (translated as *Segu* and *The Children of Segu*, respectively) by Maryse Condé of Guadaloupe, a novel in two volumes that retraces the author's roots in Africa and in the desert. And then there are the Algerian texts: one might refer to *La traversée du désert* by Mouloud Mammeri; *Le vent du sud* by Abdelhamid Benhadouga; *Timimoun* and *Cinq fragments du désert* by Rachid Boudjedra; *Un été africain* and *Le désert sans détour* by Mohammed Dib; *L'invention du désert* by Tahar Djaout; as well as the poems of Kateb Yacine.

These texts show that the space of the Sahara is absent neither from African literatures nor from the imaginary of Africans. Four major themes recur with persistence: history, geophysics, politics, and poetics. Travels, exchanges, and characters, both historical and invented, weave together stories and epics narrated with a profound sense of belonging. In *The Children of Segu*, Maryse Condé describes the trade that reaches beyond the desert, invoking prized imports such as Muslim gowns, caftans, boots, Moroccan furniture, and "Arab surgeons well-versed in the art of operations and amputations" that Amadou brought over from Morocco and Egypt.[2] Condé has a gift for making historical information into an ally for her imagination as a novelist, vividly describing the merchants of Fez, Marrakesh, Algiers, Tripoli, and Tunis who cross the desert to Segu carrying salt bars and sesame seeds. She portrays rich merchants such as Abdullahi, "the furnishings of [whose] hut were varied and luxurious ... Besides the divans covered with heavy cotton fabrics, there were deep-pile woolen carpets."[3] Everyone who visits his house in Segu appreciates and admires the fineness of the cloth. The stories recount journeys being made in both directions. Indeed, the appeal of contrasts provokes exchange, as in cooking, where Condé invokes reciprocating contributions to the meal: "Two sheep would be sacrificed and roasted on a spit, dripping with spices and meat juices. Pans of millet couscous would be passed around, some of them flavored with dates the way Mustapha's mother, Fatima the Moroccan, liked to make it."[4] Condé's narration of the exchange between the people of the two regions is all the more valuable for the fact that she treats the Islamization of Sub-Saharan Africa with a certain neutrality – although references to slavery are by no means lacking. In the first volume of *Segu*, for example, Tiekoro cannot believe what he sees in the new region: "Islam was new to the region, brought there by the Arab caravans like some exotic merchandise!"[5] The slave trade with the north, which in any case paralleled "the trade in kola, gold, ivory and salt," is denounced.[6]

Amadou Hampâté Bâ, by contrast, describes a peaceful adherence to Islam: "Tierno Kounta had me pronounce the shahada, or Islamic profession of faith ... This is how he received my conversion to Islam, a conversion that would be my decision to renew on my own volition once I reached adulthood."[7] The writer-storyteller belongs to the Sufi brotherhood, the Tijaniyyah, and narrates, for example, how the training and "techniques of auditory memorization learned in Qur'anic school" also helped him to remember the legends and stories told by the griots.[8] The Sudanese novelist

Tayeb Salih describes the desert in positive terms and shows its philosophical resonances through Mustafa Sa'eed's grandfather in *Season of Migration to the North*, where he offers a poetic vision of the desert as a space of transcendence. Mustafa Sa'eed, the novel's hero, returns south, through the dunes to the fertile and welcoming oases, finding a land of plenty, forgiveness, and peace after peregrinating across industrialized Europe as an "Arab-African."[9] The desert is also a blessing in the folktales and legends that celebrate its contributions to civilization and the tranquility it provides. The tale of *Tara ou la Légende d'El-Hadj Omar* begins thus: "This is the legend of El-Hadj Omar, the great Black Sheikh who taught Islam according to the Tiyaniyyah rite to the African population."[10] El-Hadj Omar crossed the desert in 1846, passing through Fouta-Toro, Boundou-Kangari, Kong Haoussa, Katchéna, the lands of the Tuaregs and of the people of Fezzan, which shows that the geographic space had already been mastered. The tale *Sara Ba* defines the Sudan as the cradle of Black civilizations, where Islamic faith is ecstatic; for this reason, many poets invoke the Sahara in conjunction with Islam. Birago Diop, storyteller and poet, writes in "Desert":

Dieu Seul est Dieu. Mohamed Rassoul Allah!
La voix du muezzin bondit sur les dômes,
S'enfle, s'étend, puis s'éteint au loin, là-bas
Lentement se courbent les corps, les corps
de nos hommes ...
Sur le désert et dans l'infini des âges.[11]

[God Alone is God. Muhammad Rusul Allah!
The muezzin's voice rebounds over the domes,
Swells, spreads, then falls silent in the distance, below
bodies slowly bend, the bodies of our men ...
Over the desert and into the infinity of ages.]

Nonetheless, the Sahara is also perceived in a very negative manner, which demonstrates that the connection existed even if it was perceived differently. Novelists who advocate the search for an authentic African identity explore this historic aspect of the desert. In practice, this entails a rejection of Islamization, which is presented as a form of colonization. Such is the case for Ayi Kwei Armah and Yambo Ouloguem, two of the fiercest critics of the Sahara as a gateway for Islam. In their visions, Islam came from the Sahara: it disrupted local animist beliefs and drove the African people from its "way," as the Ghanaian Armah once formulated it. The two writers denounce the African travelers who departed with Black slaves. Accordingly, the desert becomes the "Saharan sea," just like an ocean: both are home to every possible danger.[12] Rebelling against this intrusion, the Ghanaian novelist rails against all religions that, no matter which sea they crossed, invaded Sub-Saharan soil: "We are not so warped in soul, we are not Arabs, we are not Muslims to fabricate a desert god chanting madness in the wilderness, and call our creature creator. That is not our *way*."[13] Armah sees trans-Saharan commercial exchanges as being harmful for the populations of West Africa. In *Two Thousand Seasons*, he is scathing, sharp, biting, and critical of a commerce that had such disastrous consequences. In this novel in the form of an African fable, Armah denounces perversity and exuberance; his vision of the desert is of a gate through which the evil that weakens the mind and body enters. He writes that "white men from the desert had made a discovery precious to predators and destroyers: the capture of the mind and the body."[14] He describes the thousands of small luxury items brought down from the north of the desert to seduce and weaken the locals – fabrics in a thousand colors, spices of a thousand fragrances – to seduce them and take their gold. According to the novelist, the desert travelers interested in trade are effectively indistinguishable from destroyers: "the predators consistently reduced these men first to beasts, then to things – beasts they could command, things they could manipulate, all in the increase of their power over us."[15] Armah denounces dagga, a drug introduced to the people of the Sahel to weaken and harm them. He describes the Askaris, soldiers who "from morning till sleep ... were either at some sport, eating, drinking, copulating, smoking, or defecating."[16] The wildest scenes of corruption, sex, and war – all presented in a vivid, visual style – border on xenophobia, and Armah's narration is structured by an extreme hatred of the other.

For his part, the Malian Ouologuem pushes the negative vision of the Sahara further still. Indeed, he denounces the historic frauds of the men who came from the desert. In response to the Arab historians who speak of *Tarikh al-fattash* (the opening) and *Tarikh al-Sudan* (the route of Sudan), in *Bound to Violence* Ouologuem depicts the history of Saifs in the African empire of Nakem, south of Fezzan, after the conquests of Uqba ibn Nafi. He invokes transhumant slaves crossing the desert. He speaks of massacres and violence and describes struggles for power. He portrays the story of Saif Isaac al-Heit, "the terrible," who crossed the desert in defiance of "the Berbers, the Moors, and the Tuareg," to become the Caliph of Nakem, south of the desert.[17] Ouologuem throws himself into the work of demystifying folk beliefs; he denounces the "vice and corruption" of the Arab conquerors.[18] He deploys vivid metaphors to describe the invasion: "a she-dog baring her white fangs in raucous laughter."[19] From the Malian novelist's perspective, the African personality was perverted by the religions that arrived from abroad – all the more so since after the period of desert crossings came the period of ocean crossings. The two novelists' bitter critiques are directed not only at the "invaders," but also at Africans who were slavers, conscienceless traitors whose greed drove them to sell their souls. Hence, their vision of the Sahara amounts to a rejection of a space both perceive less as a tie [*un lien*] than as a barrier, a perspective which reinforces the colonial system's achievement of making the desert into a frontier in the service of colonial politics.

The Sahara, Geophysical Space

In the dawning twenty-first century, the economic potential of the Sahara is infinite; post-Independence Africa should recognize this and so take an interest in the geophysics of this shared space. The people of the region are confronted with the hard, physical reality of a desert spreading ever farther, provoking severe droughts. African writers feel themselves solicited by such climatic changes, since they often use their fiction to denounce the poverty of the region and the hard life led by the Sahel's inhabitants. The desert is a place where life threatens to become extinct, where the harmattan, that warm wind from the desert, is growing more and more harmful: "it blows," Maryse Condé writes, "driving the Fulani and their herds ever further towards the water holes. Then stone disappears, vanquished by sands."[20] The hard life is described and denounced: "No song of bird is heard, no snarl of wild beast. It is as if there were no life apart from an occasional glimpse of the river, like a mirage born of loneliness and fear."[21] Overcome by the injustice of nature, Alpha Mandé Diarra does not hesitate to assume an apocalyptic tone in *Sahel! Sanglante sécheresse*; for him, the horror presses at the gates to the desert: "A field of fossils. All the trees took on the color of whitened bone; everything was lifeless. And the starved bodies of the survivors, scraping by in unimaginable destitution, cachectic like angry wild dogs, prepare themselves – having no other escape – to take their places in this cemetery out of prehistory [*ce cimetière de la préhistoire*]."[22] Efforts to infuse life strike one as ridiculously insignificant: "When you leave Segu you are on the edge of the desert. The earth is the color of ochre and burning hot. The grass, when it manages to grow at all, is yellow. But usually there is nothing but a desolate stony crust."[23] Williams Sassine refers powerfully to the "violence of the desert," where drought is the synonym of death, where humanity and nature are the same thing: "Not a single word escaped his dry lips opened like fissures in the chalky ground during the dry season."[24] In *Cycle de sécheresse*, Cheikh C. Sow takes stock of the impact of droughts on human bodies. He describes the consequences of hunger, thirst, misery:

> Never, perhaps, had the nuns in the mission seen bodies so thin, so desolated. Nevertheless, they had seen, even prior to the period of drought, the several faces that misery draws on man. Living faces more terrible than those of the dead, since the face of the departed no longer stirs like the one stalked by insidious death. What to make of this woman, this empty body, these features which look as if they were erased? By what unfathomable secret was this woman still alive? And how did this tottering body still manage to stand up and walk?"[25]

Such droughts are a source of anxiety for the poet and novelist Kateb Yacine, as when he captures the distress of the people of the desert in the following lines from his long poem *L'œuvre en fragments*:

> La sécheresse
> La méprisante
> Le pays de la peur
> ... La haute vision de feu fume et se pulvérise
> ... Hallucinée.
> La pierre claque.[26]
>
> [The drought
> The contemptuous
> The country of fear
> ... The exalted vision of fire smokes and becomes powder
> ... Hallucinated
> The stone rings out sharply.]

Mohammed Dib, for his part, denounces this aspect of desert desolation in his novel *Le désert sans détour*: "Space itself without beginning or end seems to take up [*reprendre*], seems to let loose [*répandre*] the question. Torrid sky, torrid earth, torrid air between. Uncertain horizon and dry odor of stone in a world that consumes itself in its own flame. A world: a desert, and the fever of the desert."[27]

Clearly, to suppose that the Sahara is ignored by Africans is an error, since drought is a preoccupation of the people who live there, a worry echoed by novelists from both sides of the Sahara. The crucial problem is the erosion of the soil and the expansion of the desert north and south brought about by climate change. Indeed, the desert is spreading, advancing, occupying more space, which is a serious concern for the states of the Sahel and of the north, and a major problem raised by scientists and politicians. In his work *Pour l'Afrique, j'accuse*, René Dumont warns decision-makers to take action before it is too late because, as he says, the "desert is advancing."[28] He shows that the situation is driving the people of the desert to move elsewhere, into exile. He also denounces rich countries with their perpetual preference for monocultures that ruin the soil. Harmful to the social fabric, these monocultures are what Dumont calls "cultures of exportation" [*cultures d'exportation*] – crops which, like the peanut, are detrimental to the cultivation of vegetables for local consumption.[29] The West's responsibility is thus a burning issue; the locals grasp the source of their unhappiness, whence the necessity of "de-neocolonizing" [*dé-néocoloniser*] Africa. The Sahara must be defended and protected by all Africans for the benefit of Africans.

The Black and white racial division of Africa should be rejected; numerous thinkers from both sides of the Sahara decry the failure of certain intellectuals to become conscious of this fact. Indeed, incontestable ties exist between the two sides of the Sahara. This is what the Nigerian writer Chinua Achebe means when, in *Morning Yet on Creation Day*, he refers to the perception of a racialized Africa as a political aberration. The historian Ibrahima Baba Kaké offers a pertinent perspective: "One is accustomed to considering North Africa and Sub-Saharan Africa as two distinct worlds ... Those who thus separate Africa in two different entities produce historical nonsense."[30] The writer Boubou Hama sings of the meeting of civilizations that the desert enabled. The desert was the tie and must remain so in spite of past missteps, since it was out of such exchanges that new "human material" [*matériau humain*] was created: the Songhai people, a happy amalgam of cultures found on both sides of the Sahara.[31] For Hama, to ignore the Sahara and treat North Africa as a world apart is to find satisfaction in a colonial logic, to refuse to leave such logic behind, and thereby to approve of the perspective whose racist implications harm Africa as a whole. The African Union shows the alternative.

As the writers of the North and the South emphasize, the Sahara is neither a frontier nor an abstraction, and its historical dimension does not leave indifferent those who know it. The desert is alive, the source of tumultuous passions with respect to History, metaphysics, the religious. These were passions of exceptional force, for the desert expanse could not stop humans even when crossing it amounted to no small feat. The desert should be a catalyst, a challenge, the site of an encounter. The desire of the people and governments on both sides of the Sahara to be together – to re-establish the relations that their ancestors initiated and that the colonial system interrupted – is visible today. It can be seen in the route from Algiers to Timbuktu that was re-established after Algerian independence, and in the Trans-Saharan Highway from Algiers to Lagos that was inaugurated in 2011. Nor should one forget the project of laying fiber-optic cable across the Sahara. Such trans-Saharan routes, which "permitted a significant commercial traffic between the two sides of the Sahara in the past," have been re-established, adding to intra-African air routes between Casablanca and West Africa and between Algiers and the countries of the Sahel.[32] In our rapidly changing world, with an Africa embracing movement in order to find its place and assert its presence globally, valorizing the Sahara becomes an absolute necessity. What lies beneath the Sahara gives hope to peasants, as one of Sassine's characters says: "Somewhere *there is* gold, diamonds, and oil," but also uranium, iron, gas.[33] The mines are known to be rich; exploiting them for the benefit of Africans and not for the benefit of multinationals should help to stem the migration of young people to the West by creating jobs around the mineral deposits. The whole of Africa should take such measures into account, for there are many things that foreign powers covet, and China is no exception. Non-African powers will only act for their own benefit.

There is no mistaking the fact that, today, oasis cities are growing larger and larger. A dozen have more than 100,000 inhabitants. Their growth owes to the fact that the nomads are becoming sedentary, even if many remain faithful to their traditions. Counting all nationalities together, the Sahara has more than 6 million inhabitants, which means that one must cease to regard this space as an arid frontier, particularly when alternative strategies for development are available. Indeed, the cities of the Sahara should become centers of employment for the whole of Africa – all the more so since the region's underground aquifers are gigantic. The residents of the Sahara have known about the aquifers since the dawn of time. As Rachid Boudjedra notes, "Certain oases receive water by means of one hundred to two hundred kilometers of tunnels that carry it from water tables located, paradoxically, below irrigable gardens. Excavated tunnels [*galeries creusées*] have existed for centuries."[34] Such ancestral know-how should be taken up once more with today's technology so that farmsteads might be created for the youth. Political wills will band together to create these sites of agricultural life – nor is such an idea a chimera or a mirage. The Sahara should return to its initial mission of providing a space of life, exchange, sharing, and commerce: it represents an exceptional chance and possibility for ending the scourge of migrations to a Europe that is shutting its doors. The African Union should apply itself to the task, and the surrounding states should pursue the economic development of the Sahara. It is true that today the Sahara has become a base for banditry, drug trafficking, and Islamic terrorism; these sad realities globalize this space negatively. My point is that, thanks to the natural wealth awaiting exploitation, it is now time to "positivize" the Sahara for the sake of achieving a balanced globalization and of transforming the desert not into a transit zone for migrants, but into a destination for young Africans coming from both its sides, as well as from elsewhere. In the face of the global challenge of climate inequality, the Sahara could transform itself into an employment area [*bassin d'emploi*] for thousands of young people, and a resource for the provision of voltaic energy. In addition, such action could play a major role in the struggle against climate inequality; through the creation of a green belt like the one developed by Algeria and Morocco, through the creation of agricultural oases, the battle could be won. The Sahara's mineral and natural resources must bring stability to its human resources situated outside the region. If, at the moment of its formation, the Sahara was, as Boudjedra puts it, "a cosmic tumult. An accumulation. An overload and a disintegration. And all of these at the same time. The dunes, the rifts, and Hoggar, that intolerable quarrel of geography, topology, and topography. Nowhere is chaos as chaotic as it is there!"[35] – then there is certainly no ruling out the possibility of it becoming a site of upheaval once again, and for the better. Boudjedra also notes that the desert, with its prehistoric frescoes, is the largest natural museum in the world, and that its majesty and timeless cultural richness should be translated into employment for the benefit of young people in this promising sector. In the beginning of the twenty-first century, overcoming the climatic afflictions of the desert is the essential concern and primary interest of all states sharing the Sahara, all of whom have a stake in making it a haven of peace, human richness, economic growth, and cultural activity. This space of life should become desirable by becoming a region of employment for young people, just as in the dreams of African writers from both sides of the Sahara. In this context, let us remember that Africa is not "an object of intellectual curiosity; it is above all a space where populations are every day fighting for their survival."[36] It is in this sense that the Sahara will have an "exemplary fate" for the benefit of all people everywhere.[37]

Bibliography

Achebe, Chinua. *Morning Yet on Creation Day* (London: Heinemann, 1975).
Armah, Ayi Kwei. *Two Thousand Seasons* (London: Heinemann, 1979).
Bâ, Amadou Hampâté. *Amkoullel, the Fula Boy*, trans. Jeanne Garane (Durham, NC: Duke University Press, 2021) Google Play Books.
Boudjedra, Rachid. *Cinq fragments du désert* (Arles: Actes Sud, 2007). First published 2001 by Barzakh (Algiers).
——. *Timimoun* (Paris: Denoël, 1994).
Condé, Maryse. *The Children of Segu*, trans. Linda Coverdale (New York: Ballantine, 1990).
——. *Segu*, trans. Barbara Bray (New York: Viking, 1987).
Davidson, Basil. *The Africans: An Entry to Cultural History* (London: Longmans, 1969).
Diarra, Alpha Mandé. *Sahel! Sanglante sécheresse* (Paris: Présence africaine, 1981).
Dib, Mohammed. *Le désert sans détour* (Paris: Sindbad, 1992).
——. *Un été africain* (Paris: Plon, 1986).
Diop, Birago. "Désert." *Éthiopiques*, no. 66–7 (2001).
Dumont, René. *Pour l'Afrique, j'accuse* (Paris: Plon, 1986).
Hama, Boubou. *L'empire songhay, ses ethnies, ses légendes, et ses personnages historiques* (Paris: Oswald, 1974).
Kaké, Ibrahima Baba. *Combats pour l'histoire africaine* (Paris: Présence africaine, 1982).

M'Bokolo, Elikia. *L'Afrique au XXe siècle: le continent convoité* (Paris: Études vivantes, 1980).
N'Diaye, Catherine. *Gens de sable* (Paris: POL, 1984).
Ouologuem, Yambo. *Bound to Violence*, trans. Ralph Manheim (New York: Harcourt Brace Jovanovich, 1971).
Salih, Tayeb. *Season of Migration to the North*, trans. Denys Johnson-Davies (London: Heinemann, 1969).
Sassine, Williams. *Le jeune homme de sable* (Paris: Présence africaine, 1979).
Socé, Ousmane. *Contes et légendes d'Afrique noire* (Paris: Nouvelles Éditions latines, 1962).
Sow, Cheikh C. *Cycle de sécheresse* (Paris: Hatier, 2002).
Yacine, Kateb. *L'œuvre en fragments* (Paris: Sindbad, 1986).

Migrations, Narrations, the Refugee Condition

Dominic Thomas

Having received his doctorate in French from Yale University, **Dominic Thomas** *is currently Director of the Department of French and Francophone Studies at the University of California, Los Angeles. He is the author and editor of several books on comparative literature and postcolonialism, including* Black France: Colonialism, Immigration, and Transnationalism *(Bloomington: Indiana University Press, 2007) and* Africa and France: Postcolonial Cultures, Migration, and Racism *(Bloomington: Indiana University Press, 2013).*

> *In nature there are two approaches to dealing with flooding. One is to build a dam to stop the flow. The other is to find the right path to allow the flow to continue.... The nature of water is to flow. Human nature too seeks freedom and that human desire is stronger than any natural force.*
> Ai Weiwei[1]

How many times have we heard people say that most stories have already been told? How are we to *rethink, narrate, pronounce* the words that accompany images in which we do not figure? In a context where certain contemporary populations are said to have lived "in a symbiotic relationship with nature for thousands of years" – populations regarded as "not [having] fully entered into history"? Populations whose official history has always been told by others? "I came to tell you," Nicolas Sarkozy proclaimed in Dakar in 2007, "that this African part and this European part of yourselves form your torn identity."[2] The former president seemed to be invoking an imbrication and entanglement of these spaces; his paternalistic remarks, however, formed part of an ongoing historical continuity, running from Valéry Giscard d'Estaing's project for "massive remigration" (1970s) to Michel Rocard's formula: "We cannot shelter all the misery of the world. France should remain a land of political asylum ... but nothing more" (1989). Nor should we forget Jacques Chirac's reference to "the noise and the smell" (1991) and, more recently, in an allusion to the small boats transporting migrants from the Comoro Islands to Mayotte, the new French President Emmanuel Macron's claim that "the *kwassa-kwassa* is seldom used for fishing, it carries Comorans. That's different." But the perfect incarnation of the banalization of racist and xenophobic speech is President Donald Trump himself. In Trump's various pronouncements, the criminality and propension for rape of undocumented, Mexican "bad hombres" are essentialized; people from countries with Muslim majorities are inextricably linked to terrorism; and new immigration policy is justified by the need to fight back against immigrants from "shithole countries."

How is one to combat this logic of *vilification* and *devalorization* which foments and intensifies racial hatred, and which necessarily produces a growing *insensitivity* toward migrants? How might art and literature offer new axes of reflection with respect to the *planetary condition and politics of the living*? How might they humanize the migrants? How might they give a name to these bodies and faces, which, anonymous and interchangeable, are most often reduced to statistics? How might art and literature offer them an identity and narrate a biography, provide us with the names, tell us *who* they are, *from where* they come, and *what* they are searching for – while at the same time rousing consciences and sparking political action?

Migrations: The Wretched of the Mediterranean

We constantly come across articles about the "wretched of the Mediterranean," and the gates of fortress Europe have perforce become the meeting place for a sub-class of persons originating from various regions of the world. The situation is all the more paradoxical – as Claire Rodier has clearly shown – since, "at the very moment that the economic, social, and environmental gulf separating the two shores of the Mediterranean is deepening," Europe has begun to "organize" and, with increasing frequency, "prohibit the mobility of populations."[3] The permanent quality of the "threat" that clandestine migration to Europe represents helps to legitimate the process by which member states adopt fiercely reactive, preventative policies aimed at eliminating or reducing the migratory pressure. Today, these efforts lie at the core of xenophobic discourses and hostility toward immigrants – all linked to a nativism which has become conventional, and which authorities appropriate and manipulate for their own benefit. According to the Italian sociologist Alessandro Dal Lago, this discourse feeds a "tautology of fear," as we have recently seen in various elections in Great Britain, Holland, France, Germany, Austria, Hungary, and Poland.[4] In the United States, the preoccupation with securing the border is now a major political issue. In Australia, the zero-tolerance turnback policy "No Way" has been in operation for several years with the slogan "No Way: You will not make Australia home."

But, as Claire Rodier points out, the question of migrants

> does not affect the European Union first and foremost, despite what the official line would have us believe. It first strikes the hundreds of thousands of persons who are forced to leave their countries to escape war, bad treatment, or conditions of existence that barely suffice for survival, and who come up against the impossibility of reaching a safe haven [terre d'accueil] by legal means.[5]

Interviewed about her 2013 book *Xénophobie Business*, Rodier stressed the values of empathy, precisely because any attempt to cross the ocean in small, overcrowded rafts "surpasses the understanding." As she explained:

> one cannot erect a barrier on the route of migrants who have no other options. And the fact that they have no other option is demonstrated by the incredible risk they are taking. Such a thing so exceeds our understanding that it is rather our comprehension that ought to be clarified by this situation. There is indeed a side of this that is so absurd that one can only try to imagine solutions other than simply building walls and letting people die on our doorsteps – or out of our sight, and once it's out of our sight, we quickly forget all about it.[6]

Narrations of Precarity

Known for his dissident and activist works, the Chinese artist Ai Weiwei has produced a large œuvre about the refugee crisis across the world, a body of work which notably includes the 2017 documentary *Human Flow*. From March 2017 to January 2018, an exposition on the theme "Law of the Journey" was held in the buildings of the Národní Galerie v Praze (National Gallery of Prague).[7] In a statement tied to the exposition, Ai Weiwei declared, "There's no refugee crisis, but only a human crisis ... In dealing with refugees we've lost our very basic values." The exposition's central piece is a massive installation: an inflatable Zodiac raft nearly 40 meters long, suspended from the ceiling in the Big Hall, and filled with several hundred plastic figures. This sea of faces literally floats above a sea of words, the floor beneath being covered with texts on exile, immigration, and identity from an impressive array of writers and intellectuals, including Václav Havel, Franz Kafka, Samar Yazbek, Edward Said, Hannah Arendt, among others. The faces aboard the raft are impossible to distinguish: their interchangeability serves to show that at stake is a potentially infinite multiplication of bodies. However, what is most alarming, most troubling, may not even derive from the anonymity with which we are confronted, but rather from the fact that these bodies are already swollen [*gonflés*]: a premonition of death *to come* [*une mort* à venir] for this mass that seems to have *no future coming* [*ne semble pas avoir d'avenir*]. A premonition of drowning, the death that awaits, *pre-carcasses* confronting an ocean that threatens to swallow them up, impatient for its turn to swell these bodies, the wretched of the sea who will end up running aground on the coasts of a walled Europe, which long ago raised the drawbridge and shut its eyes – since, unfortunately, that's "the cynical reasoning practiced by Europe, whose principal response to the plight of refugees consists in encircling itself in a *cordon sanitaire* so as to keep them at a distance."[8]

This enormous rubber installation, to which the migrants cling with all their energy, is itself vulnerable too, and, instinctively, we know that it will likely succumb to tears. Its precarity is also that of the adventurous passengers, who are just as fragile as the material that sustains their hope, of which we have no knowledge. The sea of words forms a striking contrast with the vocabulary of the administrative machine and its documents, which are decidedly half-hearted in their expression of compassion, and where numbers reign.[9] The meeting of two opposing currents will produce eddies in the water, just as, confronted with this dissociative record and this incompetence or incapacity for compassion – what Achille Mbembe calls a "violence of ignorance" – we also find ourselves faced with an "ignorance that allows one to justify neglect and indifference, the fact that one finds nothing unusual about treating us in a way one would treat no one else."[10] Before this reality and the terrifying living conditions of the migrants, we are speechless: the words always seem insufficient, unsuited for the expression of our thoughts. Art and literature can together perform the work of moral imagination: broaching dilemmas, pushing us to reflect on these questions and compile solutions, making us uncomfortable, but also humanizing the protagonists. Artists and writers might play the role of catalysts in the cultivation of a real political will, providing the necessary preconditions for discussions and for a meaningful debate capable of pushing forward a focused examination, to introduce real changes in mentalities and in the way of seeing things. Clearly, such procedures draw upon emotional intelligence and human empathy, since, as the South African poet Antjie Krog so admirably put it: "To be vulnerable is to be entirely human. It is the only way one can bleed into the other."[11]

The question of empathy and of relationality lies at the core of the debate, for "the refugee crisis is not about refugees. It is about us."[12] In the article he published in the British newspaper the *Guardian*, Ai Weiwei explains how his own history has helped him not only to assume a critical perspective on migration policies, but also to take action in solidarity with migrants and their cause: "From my youth, I experienced inhumane treatment from society.... As a result, I remember experiencing what felt like endless injustice.... I share this personal background because it sheds light on my emotional connection to the current global refugee condition." As early as 1973, the playwright Joby Bernabé, in his piece *Kimafoutiésa*, invented two characters, Bumi and Dom, for the purpose of talking about BUMIDOM [Bureau pour le développement des migrations dans les départements d'outre-mer, the French state agency regulating migration from overseas departments], while the Martinican writer Daniel Boukman, in *Les négriers* (1972), drew an equivalence with slavery; later, Simone Schwarz-Bart, in her 1987 play *Ton beau capitain* [translated into English as *Your Handsome Captain*], examined exile and Haitian migrations. These "ambiguous adventures" [*aventures ambiguës*] that Cheikh Hamidou Kane had spoken about during the period of African independence, already structured the novels of the colonial period, such as Ferdinand Oyono's *Chemin d'Europe* [translated as *Road to Europe*] (1960), or Ousmane Sembène's *Le docker noir* [*The Black Docker*] (1957) and *La noire de …* [*Black Girl*] (1962), as well as Ousmane Socé's *Mirages de Paris* (1937) and Bernard Dadié's *Nègre à Paris* (1959).

Later, in a context of postcolonial migrations, the same questions are revisited in Alain Mabanckou's *Bleu-Blanc-Rouge* [*Blue White Red*] (1998), Abdourahman Waberi's *Aux États-Unis d'Afrique* [*In the United States of Africa*] (2005), Salim Jay's *Tu ne traverseras pas le détroit* (2001), Mahi Binebine's *Cannibales* (2005), Nathacha Appanah's *Tropique de la violence* [*Tropic of Violence*] (2016), and Patrick Chamoiseau's *Frères migrants* [*Migrant Brothers*] (2017).

"The tragedy of modern man is not that he knows less and less about the meaning of his own life, but that it bothers him less and less," and "The salvation of this human world lies nowhere else than in the human heart, in the human power to reflect, in human humbleness, and in human responsibility," Václav Havel proclaims in one of the citations that accompany Ai Weiwei's exhibition. As the novelist Alain Mabanckou writes, "The road to Europe has also fed the artist's imagination as well as several writers from the Black continent, most notably from the 1990s on ... These novels are like alarm bells. They feature marginal characters trapped on the Black continent and mired in their illusions, and who, for the most part, end up at an "impasse."[13]

The Refugee Condition

As early as the eighteenth century, the philosopher Jean-Jacques Rousseau wrote in his *Discourse on the Origin of Inequality*:

> The first person who, having enclosed a plot of land, took it into his head to say *this is mine* and found people simple enough to believe him, was the true founder of civil society. What crimes, wars, murders, what miseries and horrors would the human race have been spared, had someone pulled up the stakes or filled in the ditch and cried out to his fellow men: "Do not listen to this imposter. You are lost if you forget that the fruits of the earth belong to all and the earth to no one!"[14]

For Achille Mbembe, "the government of human mobility might well be the most important problem to confront the world during the first half of the twenty-first century," and the question of borders – and thus of circulation – underscores not only our "planetary entanglement" but also, and above all, the danger of "enclosure" that threatens to produce '"an increasingly ... gated world, with myriad enclaves, culs-de-sac and shifting, mobile, and diffuse borders."[15] The question of *defrontierization* forces itself upon us – above all for the African continent, where it offers the possibility of a *retopographication* of the borders drawn at the Congress of Berlin at the end of the nineteenth century. It also offers an occasion for reflecting further on the mechanisms driving displacements and circulations beyond borders and across very different cultural spaces, and, at the same time, for examining "the equality and reciprocity of freedoms in a context where citizenship's juridical-political function is above all to fabricate and reproduce differences – racial differences included."[16]

Reality and perception are formed by cognitive, social, and emotional experiences that are often manipulated by far-right movements; both nourish the platforms of traditional parties that have integrated them into their programs. According to François Gemenne:

> we are no longer in the managerial logic operating "between humaneness and firmness" which had long dominated the regulation of migration and whose only horizon was the closing of borders. Now, it is the border itself that defines the shape of the social project.... The migration question is a fundamental ideological indicator, because it enquires into our relationship to the other: is the person standing on the other side of the border a foreigner, or are they one of us?[17]

Such debates have acquired a strong political and emotional flavor, and it is difficult to refute the other side's arguments – especially after the introduction of mechanisms that, "by converting a bureaucratic task into a political objective," legitimate and "further politicize the suppression of illegal immigration."[18] For the anthropologist and sociologist Didier Fassin, today there is "a way of seeing the world in terms of distance, since the closer lives are the more precious they become, and conversely. The three to five thousand people who die each year in the Mediterranean excite less emotion."[19]

Unfortunately, what was once considered extremist now enjoys widespread acceptance, often forms an integral part of how the majority of people think, and finds itself appropriated or assimilated by political leaders from across the political spectrum. Compassion and sensitivity are signs of weakness. Angela Merkel's policy of openness toward migrants and asylum-seekers, and her slogan "Wir schaffen das" (We can do it), are responsible for the depreciation of her political capital. Indeed, the German chancellor was not only obliged to defend her empathy, but forced to go back on her migration policy and suffer the consequences in political terms. Ai Weiwei summarizes this situation better than I know how:

Establishing the understanding that we all belong to one humanity is the most essential step for how we might continue to coexist on this sphere we call Earth. I know what it feels like to be a refugee and to experience the dehumanization that comes with displacement from home and country. There are many borders to dismantle, but the most important are the ones within our own hearts and minds – these are the borders that are dividing humanity from itself.[20]

Part VI

Humanity and Animality
(Re)thinking Anthropocentrism

Bado Ndoye

Bado Ndoye *is a scholar specializing in phenomenology, epistemology, and the history of science. After a decade teaching philosophy in secondary school, he is now a lecturer at Cheikh Anta Diop University in Dakar. His research focuses mainly on Husserlian phenomenology, the history of science, and political philosophy.*

Since Descartes, Reason and the autonomy of the modern subject have constituted the metaphysical foundation upon which the distinction between humanity and animality has been grounded, a foundation which has authorized the de facto exclusion of animals from the sphere of ethics. From the seventeenth century onward, this mechanist paradigm has been the favorite target of the "Romantic" understanding of nature which expresses itself through the rejection of the argument that a monopoly of sensibility [*sensibilité*] characterizes humanity, to the detriment of the animal. On the other hand, if it is shown that the animal is endowed with sensibility and experiences pain, then the question is raised about the principle that warrants excluding it from the sphere of ethics. But how are we to conceive of opening this sphere to the animal and to forms of life that, by themselves, are incapable of ascending to the status of subject of law [*subjet de droit*]? If we treat all forms of life equally (which amounts to denying humanity any ontological privilege), do we not risk losing sight of the urgent duty incumbent upon humanity to serve as guarantor for the order of nature? For this reason, I propose the following hypothesis: if life attains its fullest development only in humanity, then a "weak anthropocentrism" is required that will figure man [*l'homme*] as the form of life to which the duty to protect life falls.

If it is true that the principal philosophical category to characterize the emergence of modernity in the seventeenth century is the subject as problematized by Descartes and his heirs, this is because the category of the subject translates all the logics at work in European societies of that time into the conceptual domain. Thus, for the humanism that takes shape beginning in the Renaissance, what gives man his intrinsic dignity and sets him apart from other beings within the animal kingdom is also what lifts him above the sphere of things, in which he nonetheless participates owing to the materiality of his body. Being a subject allows man to transcend his corporeal condition and to participate in a higher order, where he comes to know himself as mind [*esprit*]. As a result, the body that inscribes and situates him in the sensible is no longer perceived as a simple physical object, but rather as a *lived body* [*un corps vécu*] in which a subjectivity is incarnated – that is, a mind [*esprit*] capable of turning back on itself and, as it were, keeping itself at a distance. On account of this, it confronts a world that it comes to perceive as an outside object. By means of such distinctions, it knows itself to exist in a manner different from the simple, mute presence of the objects that can no more than one-sidedly occupy space. It exists not only in the sense that it is conscious of what it is, but also because the reflexivity by which it grasps itself is mediated by other consciousnesses that it comes to see as its fellows and with whom it forms communities.

What the concept of the subject problematicizes is thus, on the one hand, an awareness of the radical difference specific to man, and, on the other, the constitution of a human community reaching well beyond the tight circle of direct acquaintances, since it covers all those with whom such originary empathy on the basis of corporality is possible. As a consequence, one can see that the major heuristic function of the concept of the subject is to grant man a dignity that distinguishes him from the rest of nature and makes of him a specific kind of being – a dignity grounded in the fact that he is the only being endowed with reason, which singles him out among the living as the sole bearer of inalienable rights.

Nevertheless, it would be a historical mistake to believe that modernity invented the idea of man's superiority over the animal.

Descartes has been quite unjustly pilloried on this point. One need only recall the famous passage from the Bible: "Be fruitful, and multiply, and replenish the earth, and subdue it: and have dominion over the fish of the sea, and over the fowl of the air, and over every living thing that moveth upon the earth" (Gen. 1:28, King James Version). As everyone knows, in the spiritual universe of the revealed religions, the existence of reason in man [*l'homme*] is the sign of his resemblance to God, who created him in His image – an indication of the ethical community by which men are distinguished from animals. Commenting on the fundamental prohibition that defines humanity – "Thou shalt not kill!" – Saint Augustine writes:

> When we read "Thou shalt not kill", we are not to take this commandment as applying to plants, for these have no sensation. Nor does it apply to the non-rational animals which fly, swim, walk or crawl, for these do not share the use of reason with us. It is not given to them to have it in common with us; and, for this reason, by the most just ordinance of their Creator, both their life and death are subject to our needs.[1]

What is new with the Moderns is that they strip this thesis of its theological baggage by secularizing it. Starting with the Moderns, the new criterion of ontological difference becomes autonomy, derived from the fact that man, as a being endowed with reason, can give himself ends to work toward – a horizon of sense – and act in conformity with them. This is very clear in Kant. Of course, the animal will subsequently find itself all the more excluded from such an ethical community owing to the fact that the seventeenth century, under the influence of Cartesian mechanist philosophy, will theorize the notion of an "animal-machine" that is incapable of feeling the least pain since it lacks that which uniquely allows for the sensation of anything whatsoever – namely, the soul which Descartes will make the property [*le propre*] of man.

Beginning in the eighteenth century, the mechanist paradigm according to which the animal is perceived as the expression of the most radical alterity becomes the target of the "Romantic" understanding of nature. The latter will find expression in Rousseau's work through the rejection of the criterion of Reason, and of the monopoly of sensibility that some had wanted to make a distinguishing characteristic of man. Indeed, it is Rousseau who writes:

> It seems, in effect, that if I am obliged not to do any harm to my fellow man, it is less because he is a rational being than because he is a sentient being: a quality that, since it is common to both animals and men,

should at least give the former the right not to be needlessly mistreated by the latter.[2]

At the origin of the human soul, Rousseau sees two principles that precede reason: on the one hand, the necessity of self-preservation, and, on the other hand, the natural sentiment one has watching any sensitive being suffer or perish, irrespective of whether it is a man or an animal. If it is shown that the animal is endowed with sensibility and that it suffers, the question becomes: on what grounds does it merit effective exclusion from the sphere of ethics? If the injunction to always treat man [*l'homme*] as an end and never as a means stems solely from the fact that man is a subjectivity and experiences pain, why should the animal (or at least certain, higher animals) – in this regard, not meaningfully different from man – be excluded from the sphere of ethics?

The seventeenth century would come up with 1,001 ways to justify this exclusion. We all know the notorious distinction between "human suffering" and "the mere pain of animals," the latter being purely physical since it only affects the body – for, as Descartes established: "We know for certain that it is the soul which has sensory perceptions, and not the body. For when the soul is distracted by an ecstasy or deep contemplation, we see that the whole body remains without sensation, even though it has various objects touching it."[3] The most common interpretation of Cartesianism has consisted in saying that, within the paradigm of man's divided nature, the dualism of soul and body can only be to the latter's disadvantage: on the one hand, there is a body of little value and, on the other, a spirit [*esprit*] capable of sublimating this material part, which, if it is affected, is so only because spirit can sidestep and reappropriate the affectation in the mode of conscious reflexivity. Conversely, the body without the soul cannot, properly speaking, be host to any experience – which amounts to saying that the animal's pain is not, in a strict sense, pain at all. As one can see, this way of distinguishing between pain and suffering leads to a vision of suffering as disincarnate, reduced to its representation, which alone gives it an ethical and ontological value. In other words, the only suffering worthy of note is suffering that can be reappropriated reflexively and eventually put into words. Such an opposition cynically forgets forms of suffering that cannot be formulated and that, for this reason, leave the subject directly exposed to its immanent suffering.

If this paradigm has proven itself inadequate to the needs of our time, it is because the division it once invoked to justify itself

– namely, the mechanist understanding of nature, and of man as outside it – has literally collapsed. Moreover, most of the specific differences for which humanity might have claimed a certain exceptionality have since faded. On the other hand, as soon as sensibility and not autonomy represents the criterion of evaluation, a new scale of good and evil comes into being, its span following the curve of such sensibility. This is how one has articulated the need to transition from an anthropocentric to an ecocentric ethics, in which the criterion of evaluation expands to include all living beings, in accordance with their degree of sensibility. Encompassing humanity alongside animals, plants, and nature in general, the outlines of a new space for ethical evaluation become visible, shaking philosophical reflection's inherited frames to their very foundations.

Previously, nature was seen only as a reservoir of energy and resources, whose stocks one inspects in accordance with the mercantilist demands of a capitalist economy that is interested in little except gain and immediate profitability. One of the greatest merits of the new ethics of the earth is that it opens ours eyes to the fact that the division between nature and culture at the basis of our technical civilization, a division which seems so obvious to us, is not the only possible configuration, as the famous work of Philippe Descola indicates.[4] Well before modern science disenchanted the world, many varieties of "continuist metaphysics," including versions found in the West, emphasized man's native belonging to nature. If we are drawn to such thinking today, it is certainly not out of an interest in reconnecting with ancient philosophies of nature. Rather, it is because such thinking indicates what our modernity most desperately needs: a new philosophy of nature.

That said, the question remains about how we are to leave anthropocentrism behind without allowing the notion of respecting life to dissolve into a sentimentalism that, by being applied to anything and everything, is just as vague as it is ineffective. Let's ask the question in another way: what are some concrete ways in which we can integrate the animal into the sphere of ethics, given that it cannot, by means of its sensibility alone, raise itself to the status of a bearer of rights? Indeed, what does it mean to be an ethical subject for a being that is trapped behind walls of silence and, for this reason, cannot claim any right for itself? My hypothesis is that an attenuated form of anthropocentrism is needed here: a "weak anthropocentrism" that will amount to recognizing the moral value of other natural beings, but that will only be able to do so if man is allowed to retain his special status as guarantor of the natural order, and thus as a point of reference. To defend this thesis, it is necessary to make an important conceptual distinction between two categories that are important in ethics: the "moral agent" and the "moral patient." To ask whether the animal has a moral status and may be included in the sphere of ethical evaluation is first and foremost to ask whether it can be a moral agent, a moral patient, or both at once. The moral agent is a figure whose behavior can be subjected to moral evaluation, and hence whose actions can be judged and qualified as good or bad – which presupposes that it is responsible for its acts. The moral patient, by contrast, is the figure for whom moral evaluation applies to the way it is treated. The line demarcating the two categories establishes a symmetry between actions produced and actions suffered; whence follow the specifications of being an agent – that is, a subject – or else being a patient: the one whom, in a certain sense, the action takes as an object. For example, a "normal" human adult is both a moral agent and a moral patient: the actions he or she produces, together with the actions he or she suffers, can be morally evaluated. Babies, children, and the mentally handicapped, by contrast, are not moral agents because they are not, no longer are, or have yet to become responsible for their acts. By the same logic, it is clear that certain animals can also be moral patients: it is immoral to cause them unjustified suffering, even though they cannot on their own lay claim to any right whatsoever.

With this conceptual distinction in place, it remains necessary to show that, owing to the special status conferred to man by his ontological status, it becomes possible to leave behind what one has called the "paradigm of life" – a paradigm that one finds at the core of the most radical and fundamentalist theories of *deep ecology*. According to such theories, once it is shown that a certain continuity exists between the most elementary forms of life and the highly complex form that expresses itself in man, one is obliged to conclude that the latter enjoys no special ontological privilege. Taken to its most radical extreme, this is the argument put forward by Bertrand Russell:

> There is no impersonal reason for regarding the interests of human beings as more important than those of animals. We can destroy animals more easily than they can destroy us; that is the only solid basis of our claim to superiority. We value art and science and literature, because these are things in which we excel. But whales might value spouting, and donkeys might maintain that a good bray is more exquisite than

the music of Bach. We cannot prove them wrong except by the exercise of arbitrary power. All ethical systems, in the last analysis, depend upon weapons of war.[5]

Russell is certainly correct to say that man's superiority lies solely in the power of destruction, of which he enjoys the monopoly – certainly not in any intrinsic superiority that his interests may have over those of the animals. Indeed, a good bray, from the donkey's point of view, may well be worth a Bach sonata. In other words, our ethical system is nothing other than a sublimation of the absolute power that man wields over animals. Or so one might think. For it is just this destructive force of which man alone is capable that makes him responsible for all living beings, a responsibility of which he alone is aware, and, as a consequence, which he alone must bear – as is taught by the celebrated Qur'anic verse in which God charges man with the responsibility of being his successor [*lieutenant*] on earth.[6] This mission invests man with a terrible power: he can disobey and spread disorder and bloodshed across the earth. And yet, this duty, which he is nonetheless free to neglect, consists precisely in being the guarantor of life on earth – as is taught in another verse that serves to rein in such freedom by means of the prohibition: "[D]o not take the life God has made sacred, except by right."[7] One may ask what justice is to be found in taking the life of an animal solely for our own pleasure ...

Since it is in man that life awakens to itself and becomes conscious of what it is, I do not consider it legitimate to deny man the privilege of enjoying the special status that obliges him to be its guardian. For that to be possible, it is necessary to move from a paradigm that places all forms of life on equal footing to a paradigm of *existence* that is only expressed in man's ipseity. By this means, one escapes the aporias produced by that form of biological totalitarianism that levels the whole of being on the plane of immanence, and that forbids one to envisage the possibility of any transcendence whatsoever. Indeed, if we follow biologism's lead by reducing the body to chemistry, and thought, in accordance with a strict naturalism, to a mere arrangement of neurons – showing no consideration for the spiritual signification that it might possess as a *lived body* (that is, as a *Leib* in Husserl's sense) – we are effectively depriving ourselves of the possibility of thinking questions of value and of respect for human or animal life, and thus of its sacredness. For, after all, such sacredness does not and cannot derive from empirical characteristics that one might read directly off the body. A radical empiricist could perfectly well maintain, for example, that, since the sacredness of life is not a fact given by the senses, our uses of this word are simply *flatus vocis*. But, even if one admits that a culture of immanence adhering to the "paradigm of life" might have a practical interest in respecting life, if only to preserve the species, it is nonetheless the case that such a culture cannot exhibit *unconditional* respect for life as such. This is because, flattened out on the plane of immanence, life would hold no mystery for such a culture and could no longer be raised to the status of an ideal. By contrast, only mystery – that is, only that portion of night which inspires the fear of touching something sacred – can command respect unconditionally. I will not mention the fact that biologism, coupled with a celebration of telluric forces, has already produced a monster: Nazism.

It will thus be understood that what is at stake in this defense of a "weak anthropocentrism" is not just whether or not the animal has rights, but, ultimately, a respect for the inviolability of the human body: for, under pain of self-contradiction, one cannot champion the cause of life as it is manifested in the animal and at the same time disdain it in man. These two demands go together, and it is perhaps because we have yet to take the first seriously that we continue to take the second for nothing. Kundera expresses this demand in the form of an ethical test:

> True human goodness, in all its purity and freedom, can come to the fore only when its recipient has no power. Mankind's true moral test, its fundamental test (which lies deeply buried from view), consists of its attitude towards those who are at its mercy: animals. And in this respect mankind has suffered a fundamental debacle, a debacle so fundamental that all others stem from it.[8]

The Tree Frogs' Distress

Lionel Manga

An economist by training and an adept of transversality, **Lionel Manga** *is the author of* L'Ivresse du papillon. Le Cameroun aujourd'hui: ombres et lucioles dans le sillage des artistes, *an essay on the art of sculpture in Cameroon (Servoz: Edimontagne, 2008). Voluntarily assuming the state of a free electron, he has contributed in recent years to several journals and magazines, such as* Mouvement *or* Riveneuve Continents, *and has lectured at Quai-Branly to commemorate 50 years of African independence.*

After coming down from the trees in a sylvan environment of the East African Rift 6 million years back, the *sapiens sapiens* heirs of *Orrorin*, the first documented biped, have spread themselves across all the lands they found since their departure from Africa roughly 100,000 years ago.[1] The youngest child of burgeoning life [*du foisonnant vivant*], our species is still the only one not confined to a single ecological niche, and at the same time endowed with a voluminous brain liberating it from genetic determinism. Evolutionary crisscross: as reason's principal organ grew, prompting a de facto expansion and improvement of human capacities to act and interact with the environment and thereby enlarging the species' range from epoch to epoch, the determinative power of the program coded in its genome by the arrangement of chromosomes along chains of DNA waned dramatically. Out of an appanage consisting of a panoply of tools in silex, of fire for at least the last 100,000 years, and then, starting 70,000 years ago at the latest, of articulated language, and by means of the "hominization differential" for which Michel Serres has invented the elegant neologism "hominescence,"[2] the odyssey of those-who-walk-upright on the surface of the Earth has progressed across the territories of the ecumene once occupied by its ancestors the other animals, monopolizing one after the other, blazing its own trail under the sign of cultural diffraction at a distance of 8 light minutes from the sun.

All of this is borne out most directly by the spectrum of almost 6,000 languages still in use – in their babelian profusion and over which UNESCO watches so jealously, having been designated by the international community to guard the diversity that is emblematic of the species' altricial character, each language conveying its unique representation of the nature where it slowly emerged alongside the mixed, itinerant experience of its speakers, generation after generation. The consequences of the irresistible extension of human domain on the planet, the effects of our proliferation to the detriment of our precursors in the ecumene, assume dramatic, alarming, proportions, and scientists are now obliged to speak of a sixth mass extinction: this chilling and apocalyptic proposition nonetheless captures the full extent of the anthropic attacks that the biosphere suffers at every scale, at every latitude of the globe, and, owing to the unheard-of rhythm of biological depletion, to a truly unprecedented degree. Translated into the jargon of thermodynamics, the odyssey of the Biped – differentiated at the dawn of history into such a great variety of avatars, not all of whom belong to the same class – has entered a phase of pronounced entropy, and the water level is now dangerously high.

Traps

To adequately gauge the dimensions and the implications of this event, it is not unhelpful to know that the five previous biological mass extinctions have been attributed to and correlated with periods of intense volcanism – traps, instigators by chain reaction of major disruptions, such as the disappearance of the dinosaurs 65 million years ago at the Cretaceous–Tertiary boundary: it paved the way for mammals as if to say "beat-it-big-lizard-so-I-can-get-in."[3] In the noted absence of a phenomenon of trap-like magnitude, the desolation that afflicts the Earth is attributed to a range of externalities of human origin, dating back to the dawn of the Industrial Revolution, which, being based on fossil energy, has accordingly acquired the problematic status of a geological force.

At this point, Paul Crutzen, Nobel laureate in chemistry, states that we have entered the Anthropocene. Since when? The debate rages on. If, with respect to the range of externalities, responsibility for the situation is undeniably shared, the principal agent behind this vast and perilous alteration of the world's magnificence nonetheless remains the promethean hubris of which capitalism, in its multiple guises and its modern ubiquity, is the crowning historic expression. For this reason, I myself prefer to speak about the megalocene [*la mégalocène*], for the purpose of emphasizing the psychic source of such catastrophic excess. It is in fact less the human species – Anthropos, *as such* – that has led us to our perilous situation in 2017 than it is the specific mental and cultural configuration of a group of altricials [*altriciels*] whose stalwarts, hardened in their denial, perceive the calls for a civilizational change of direction since the 1992 Rio de Janeiro Earth Summit as nothing but puerile alarmism incited by international leftism.

Knowing themselves exposed and on the front line, directly targeted by the greens and by the tactical remonstrations of ecologists and other fanatics standing in the way of shamelessly turning a profit at the expense of the planet, these experienced predators have not hesitated to incite a counterattack by fomenting climate skepticism, assisted in their aims by a solid group of scientists who, in all likelihood, provide their services free of charge. This lobby keeps busy stirring up trouble in the public at large, and disparaging initiatives like the COP 21. As for the repeated calls of alarm sounded over the last quarter-century by its homologues in the ranks of anxious lucidity, it dismisses them as so much hysterical screaming, unworthy of attention. Trapped in a position that is as anachronistic as it is obscurantist, and whose stratospheric arrogance we won't even mention, this clique of contemptibles can now boast of the fact that the United States has withdrawn from the Paris Accords waving the banner of Donald Trump – which is no mean triumph to add to its grating hit parade. The US withdrawal is a powerful demonstration of the clique's influence, which must also be regarded as its genuine capacity for harm given the mounting stakes and challenges, the principal being to incite this global conspiracy to confront the future, at times compounded, consequences of our past actions – a conspiring [*conspiration*] that one must understand in the double sense of respiring together [*respirer ensemble*] and conjuring [*conjuration*] the ambient and boundless Ugliness.

Fragile, Handle with Care!

It is possible to see, in the diverse, global corpus of tales and legends in which animals are the main protagonists, the archive of a time immemorial when the animals and the Biped lived in due symbiosis, on the same plane of immanence, the accidental or intentional breakdowns of this mutuality, if not harmony, being generally presented in a negative light. Many animals in Africa are tutelary/totemic figures in the manner of Kulu, the tortoise, among the Fang people of Central Africa, or else Kakou, the spider, among the Ewe of West Africa. The place of the jaguar is no different among the Aztecs. Whatever the geographic latitude, in other words, the Biped has long taken stock of the existence and proximity of other species, whether animal or vegetable, to the point of entering into agreements of friendly understanding [*entente cordiale*] with them. In "Njeddo Dewal, Mother of Calamity," it is under a sacred jujube tree that bears fruit in all seasons and even in the worst droughts that Bâgoumâwel, the tale's predestined hero, sits to await revelation – before trusting his fate to a frog and a swarm of bees.[4] All of which goes to say, humans are not cut off from the other kingdoms; besides, the intrinsic plasticity of the real authorizes all sorts of marvelous translocations, possibilities which the dogma of strict separation nonetheless denies. Even if one takes them as idealizations, such classical stories reveal a holistic, comprehensive understanding of the world, where everything depends on everything else, from the tiny blade of grass to the bulky hippopotamus. In the end, the subtle interdependence that one observes at every scale generates a tangled complexity with a fractal structure.

Territorial expansion and rapid growth of the newcomers' demographic are the basic principles of a successful colonization pursued at the violent expense of those who first occupied the site. In this respect, the sinister red list prepared by the Convention on the International Trade in Endangered Species of Wild Fauna and Flora (CITES) is a macabre, accusatory record of the monopolization of the planet that commenced nearly 6 million years ago, as well as of the dominant position that hominins of the *sapiens sapiens* vintage have enjoyed in the ecumene. Having appeared 350 million years ago during the Devonian, amphibians are now up against the wall:

in these days of entropy, 32 percent of 3,900 amphibian species are in danger of extinction, as opposed to 12 percent of birds and 23 percent of mammals. The former would thus be entirely justified in bringing the Biped before a court of universal jurisdiction for abuse of power and other crimes associated with the spectacular disdain that animals, having become our radical non-self in the theatre of appearances, manage to elicit in us, perched on the pedestal of arrogance. Given the retroactions in gestation deep inside the bowels of Gaia's impressive thermodynamic machinery, the final cost of this pedestal may prove high indeed. The tree frogs' distress sends a signal that we would do best to heed: fragility is in great danger, the two biotopes where their lifecycle from tadpole to adult takes place – the aquatic and the terrestrial – having deteriorated owing to perilous changes.

Who will plead the case for the animals catalogued on CITES's red list? "You lack a single being, and all is unpeopled": referring to matters of the heart, Lamartine's aphorism nonetheless holds 1,000 percent for biodiversity. Without the giraffe, without the elephant, without the polar bear, without the tiger, without the puma, without the snow leopard, without the pangolin, without the golden toad (and the list goes on), will the Earth of tomorrow still be the same Earth? Should we just make our peace with these extinctions as localized and inexorable events, intrinsic to the dynamic of the living? With each species struck from the catalogue of diversity, the biosphere loses a precious degree of freedom, a path opened up by the non-inert several million years ago is closed off by the actions of the Bipeds with the big brains, or at least of a fraction of them – nor is there any reason to feel particularly proud about it. Is it not paradoxical and troubling, to say the least, that the fine film of life that appeared on the surface of the Earth 3.9 billion years ago has been so mistreated in the physico-chemical domain, while, over the same period, laboratories devoted to technology and artificial intelligence hustle behind their closed doors to augment humans and to develop "solutions" for the crisis to come – solutions from which Earthlings with limited purchasing power will be excluded?

This bizarre asymmetry should set us to thinking – even if the transhumanist coterie enthroned atop mountains of dollars in Silicon Valley is convinced that it is on the right track and that it holds the keys to the unprecedented future now taking shape before our very eyes. Just listen to what a professional lookout resting on a major body of philosophical work has to say, breathless with anticipation:

> Our world and we are going through a crisis spanning millennia; we are suffering from the pains of a childbirth without equivalent in what we have been calling history for not too long; we may be giving birth to another humanity. Nothing can arouse our concern more than this arrival.... Thus the road in front of us doesn't resemble any of the ones History has followed, so it can hardly serve as a support for us.[5]

With these words, the luminous Academician and evil sage of Stanford has formally emancipated us, but he has also warned us not to deceive ourselves about the nature of the present fork in the road. To mark and date this coming future [*cet à-venir*] of an absolutely, radically new kind, in language and with words, the former naval officer turned philosopher – owing to his basic loathing of aggression – has even forged an elegant neologism: "hominesence," where, as in luminescence, arborescence, and efflorescence, the suffix's seeming inchoateness indicates the beginning of a process. Here, Serres suggests, "autohominization enters into practice."[6] Our species is just as contingent as any other: it emerged on a continental plate that, unlike its fellow, wandering pieces of the tellurgic puzzle, had been stationary since the break-up of Gondwana 30 million years ago – on a site that today's mass-produced world maps refer to as Africa. Presently, we have arrived at the point of being able to fashion ourselves by means of a sort of iterative loop that integrates feedbacks cycle after cycle, knowing that biological systems are characterized by self-organization and mounting complexity, for we have begun using our various technological aptitudes to intervene in what the very long course of natural selection has made of us.

The Cannon Ball

The late Reverend Father Meinrad P. Hebga, one of Cameroon's first Jesuit scholars and a foremost specialist in the traditional beliefs of the Bassa people, a man of commendable intellectual curiosity reinforced by a reasoned concern for personal fulfillment, says in effect that seasonal reunions of initiation were occasions par excellence for neophytes of every age group to get to know their neighbors [*leurs proches*] in the animal, vegetable, and mineral kingdoms.[7] Was this with the intention of establishing and maintaining harmonious relations with them? For the purpose of becoming good neighbors? Or more than that? We may safely assume so, since, until someone convinces us otherwise, it represents the very minimum of goodwill in a shared house, among people(s) of decent upbringing, in the manner of a collective artists' residence, to know who is who and what he or she is doing there, prior to anything at all beginning between you. The library of the "Others" is rife with the records of libations and prayers performed by hunters in non-Western societies, as well as in the first days of agriculture, on the threshold of the Neolithic. In a universe characterized by subtle intricacies, where relation and reciprocity are fundamental terms, such cynegetic flows, calibrated to suffice for nourishment and nothing more, to simply restore the forces expended, necessarily had a symbolic counterpart: hunters would provide symbolic compensation for the trouble caused by their periodic depletions of a stock of resources which none of them had constituted and which seemed to renew itself without outside intervention. As remarkable as it was prodigious and mysterious, at the time such providence was well worth a propitiatory gesture, certified by longstanding tradition and handed down from generation to generation – a rule of conduct which joins up with the ideal of a serene community and which says, in effect, there's no such thing as a *free lunch*.

A cannon ball thundering across a battlefield does not sweat the details and sweeps away anything that might stand in its way. If Heinrich Mann used the metaphor to describe Napoleon, it applies equally well to the Eurocentric project of taking hold of the Earth that Christopher Columbus's voyage inaugurated in 1492. According to Peter Sloterdijk, this project would have been neither possible nor imaginable in the absence of a specific historical complex of insanity and disinhibition – one which Sloterdijk indexes to the fact that the West, enthralled by its own achievements, saw modernity's inaugural period as an epiphany of Reason triumphing *ad vitam* over medieval obscurities and superstitions. This effusion of pride skates around the Atlantic slave trade, and hovers about the ash heaps left by the unfortunate women sent to the stake over the course of three centuries, under the sham pretext that they were witches and "kept the Sabbath" with the devil. Rigorously following the Cartesian law of the excluded third, and venerable master René's principle by which an object must be isolated to be known, the promethean Western Subject headed for Olympus where gods and goddesses reside and, hoping to dispossess Zeus of his throne, has left a centuries-long wake behind the infernally blinkered Odyssey of its postcolumbian presence in the world. The desolation that today affects the world's magnificence is tribute to all such isolating gestures.

Precolonial Africa's comprehensive charters of the real imagine a period of general anomie whose description, in contexts today fallen into obsolescence, echoes the entropic phase that our fossil civilization has been traversing since the thundering alarm that Rachel Carson sounded across the United States in 1961 about the strangely "silent spring." One thinks of the Bassa myth of the Restoration, whose central maxim states that the world is the fall of a chimpanzee: it is thrown off balance and it restores itself.[8] *Idem* for the "Njeddo Dewal, Mother of Calamity," the initiatory tale mentioned above. The intellectual proximity that exists between such "animist" poetics and a major discipline in the scientific field of complexity – namely, thermodynamics – would seem to confirm Claude Lévi-Strauss's passing observation in *The Raw and the Cooked* that the idioms of the cultures he is studying seem to contain a knowledge about the properties of the world that is far more elaborate than what is articulated by positivist axioms. To my knowledge, no discussion has arisen around Lévi-Strauss's furtive claim, so troubling for the legions of scholars committed to reductionism – indeed, the latter point may explain the former. For their part, the Mwaba-Gurma of northern Togo think that we are in the world in order to express ourselves, and they maintain that, once heat gains the upper hand in a situation, the ad hoc application of cold water will temper it.[9] This metaphorical truism conceals a sophisticated *Weltanschauung*, and Albert de Surgy, who authored an illuminating monograph on the topic, advises those who would seek to understand/situate it in all its richness to equip themselves with a prior knowledge of linguistics and molecular biology.

Extended Commensality

In the nineteenth century, the geographer and anarchist Élisée Reclus suggested that humanity was nature becoming conscious of itself. With equal reason, one might replace "nature" with "universe." So that tomorrow we will not have to compose a poignant requiem for the tree frogs, we had best respond to the contingent amphibian's present decline – and all the more so because its extinction would set in motion a domino effect within the biosphere that, given the crucial place such fragile species occupy in the tangled, topological space of predator–prey interactions, would result in the cataclysmic collapse of animal populations. In the oblique light of this circular statement, we, contingent Bipeds who have appeared on Earth, have a decisive responsibility toward the fragility of the living [*du vivant*] to take up and fulfill: protect them. You could even call it a crucial public health project in the service of our planetary civilization, presently under the sway of algorithms.

The future will only arrive under the sign and the banner of an active finesse, of restraint held up as an ethics of life. The challenge is quite simply cosmic: it is a matter of making poetics and politics coincide on the planet, for the sake and wellbeing of the living. *In fine*, we are ourselves its caretakers; though one might not suspect it, Reclus in fact intimates nothing less from between the lines of his nineteenth-century aphorism: how things stand on this massive body wandering through the galaxy is primarily incumbent on us. We too are fragile, no less than the tree frogs: contingency is thus urgently called upon to take note of this generic quality presiding over the set of animals, bearing the seal of extended commensality, since, after all, we breathe the same oxygen produced by plants, which, diffuse as it is, nonetheless remains an essential "food" – even more important than other, much more solid forms of nourishment. Is this not, along with sensitivity [*le sensible*] and fragility, a universal that transcends all cultural rifts and frontiers, and that sutures incommensurabilities? The agony of the scorpion's sting does not depend on the victim's skin color, nor the contents of the victim's wallet, nor the victim's weight or biography. Those bound by commensality [*des commensaux*] owe one another aid and protection.

The state of the planet now gives more than sufficient evidence of the deadly, delirious turn taken by the hominization differential, which the incorrigible Michel Serres in his luminous work calls "hominescence." It is im-per-a-tive that we right this cursed swerve, before irreversibility soon enters the equation and gains the upper hand – with, for the moment, unpredictable but doubtless catastrophic consequences. It is a categorical imperative that we reformulate the terms of altricial presence in the ecumene before we reach the point where all we can do is bite our nails to the quick and cry our eyes out. Considerable economic and political forces have arrayed themselves behind the banner of supremacy. Like a high mountain range, they block a change of direction that would jeopardize their status, the privileges and spoils that fall to the owners and brokers of the historic pillage of the world, which they enjoy at all latitudes of the North and South. The endless bla-bla of procrastination has been inappropriate since the day before yesterday, seeing that it is now years since the clear-thinking scientific community's well-founded anxiety started to forecast the imminent danger looming at every scale and in every clime, and given the devastating rise in entropy currently taking place on our Earth, a planet caught in the iron cage of untended capitalism's limitless cruelty and riven by the sharp stake to which the series of active and vital egoisms add up.

The stakes are too high for the fate of the Earth to be left solely in the hands of politicians, scientists, investors, and all those more or less composite bodies that have constituted themselves as apparatuses of power, as special interests defending precise parameters of influence in the global arena of appearances. We must instead break down barriers. We must reconnect what was, and what remains, separated by the tyranny of analytical reason. We must start today by turning our backs on cognitive dissonance. Lose no time in fomenting active constellations of collective intelligence. Working at every scale, push these collectivities to transcend the impenitent divisions of the existing orders that block the actualization of future possibilities residing in the present. Open up new Northwest Passages to join these shared concerns – concerns which, until now, have been mutually ignorant of one another, each tossing separately in the wake of the History that six centuries of dramaturges wrote to glorify themselves. Do away with borders. Bring them down without fear and without reproach, for the purpose of inventing a New World together. Confront the stubbornness of the real's rough patches. Face down the redhibitory tendency of obtuse conservatisms to oppose translations into different contexts, an adventure they regard as a bit too risky. From the historical perspective laid out here, there is no way to avoid taking a minimum of risks. We must venture outside our comfort zones. It will not be easy: faint-heartedness suits us quite well – and staying put in our blind bubble, even better.

To Speak and Betray Nothing?

Rodney Saint-Éloi

Rodney Saint-Éloi *is a poet, writer, essayist, and publisher. In 2012, he received the prestigious Charles Biddle Award for his contribution to the artistic and cultural development of Quebec. Inducted into the Académie des lettres du Québec, today he manages the publishing house Mémoire d'encrier that he founded in Montreal in 2003.*

I come from Haiti.
    Allow me to summon a fragmented vision, like a slightly dissonant creole drum. The drum is what you see before you. But inside, there is a little drum, which beats the rhythms of the heart. And this little drum, that marks out the silence, is very discreet. Nobody sees it or feels it, except in the tremor of tropical nights. I am in the middle of a paradox. I hope you will excuse my birth, my vision of the world, and my civilizational vices. I inhabit a real that abuts misfortune. People wait for hurricanes. The hurricanes arrive and people their sight. What dominates is not man, with his will to power, but the abundance of misfortune, the daily misfortune – the earthquake that is predicted, postponed, and back again. Nature escapes humanity's grasp. The human escapes nature's grasp. The living [*le vivant*] seems dead. And such impossibilities make life a marvelous and beautiful thing. Magic, the connection with spirits, the connection with the vibrant – that is, the living, the vegetal, the animal, the earth. All of it is both fragile and precious.

How am I to speak without betraying these possibilities/impossibilities?

How am I to speak?

Which language?

What is mine in these wounded, fragmented, diffracted, murdered memories, if not oblivion, absence, denial?

I want to say

I want to speak

I seek an action verb

I belong to all these histories, even those that alienate me

I belong to all these histories, even those that murder me

I claim the history of my executioners alongside the history of my drownings

Packed in my shadows, they are set to devour me or to comfort me

How can I say all that at the same time

Today, the most innocuous questions seem to catch me in their trap. I no longer know how to speak. Nor, however, am I silent. I no longer know how to communicate my being in speech, to tell my stories so that my traces, in me, what is mine, can be expressed, in order to get to the bottom of things.

In Cavaillon where I was born in the south of Haiti, I have a tree and a river that tenderly watch over me. The tree is sacred, an *arbre-reposoir*. Here today, I am very far from that childhood altar which saved me from the world.

I migrated very early to Port-au-Prince, to the city, so that I could become what was expected of a man: a man of cities; a man who is respected; a man who studies algebra, geometry, and French grammar.

Afterwards – to get ahead, as they say – I was obliged to throw myself into the struggle to exist, to work, to participate in human folly, to do as they do, to turn the cogs of the machine.

Then, to forget everything that I lost, and everything that I denied: my creole language, my roots, my totems, my intimate spaces, my natural territory, the most thriving part of myself; and then, to protect myself from folly, I chose exile and solitude.

In Montreal, I live in a confusion of geographies and languages.

I was talking with a kind official who worked for an employment center in Montreal.

I will relate the conversation.

Hello, sir.

Hello.

How long have you been in Montreal?
Six months.
Where are you from?
From Haiti.
What is your profession?
I am a writer. I am a publisher.
No. I am asking about your profession.
I am a writer.
In Haiti.
Yes.
Here, being a writer is different.
Is that so!
Yes ..., the official responds.
With the help of the Internet, I was obliged to prove to him that I am a writer. The proof is that I have published in France and in Belgium. Others talk about me, in the French journal *Notre librairie*. And that Belgian students read the world in a text that I had written.

At that, the official began to apologize profusely.
Another conversation that I would like to report.
It took place at the Montreal airport, in May, 2001.
A woman welcomes me.
Her job: immigration agent.
Why did you come here?
I was invited to a conference.
Where are you going to stay, sir?
At a hotel.
Do you have proof?
Here's the invitation with all the details, lodging and *per diem*.
Well then!
...
Sir, I am obligated to confiscate your passport.
But, ma'am, what am I without my passport?
Nothing. You are nothing, she answers.

The next morning, I called the airport's immigration office. I am told that it was an error on the official's part: she should not have kept my passport. I am asked to come back to the airport to pick up my passport.

These conversations bring me back to myself, to my legitimacy as a human living in the land of the other, and to my numerous losses: of myself, of my narratives, of the very nature of my existence.

So, how am I to speak?

How am I to (re)ground my identity?
How am I to (re)visit the cities of the world?
Who am I in Montreal when my life is already elsewhere, far off in another city where my human memory constituted itself?
Who am I in Port-au-Prince, where my creole name is Pèpi?
Who am I in Dakar, where my Serer name is Wagane?
Who am I in Mingan, where my Innu name is Utshimau Minush?
No one asked me to speak.
No one knows my voice.
The one and only question that returns again and again: *where are you from?*
I am always afraid of this distancing: *where are you from?*
I grew up in a dictatorship.
And I will surely die in exile.
I chose neither to grow up in a dictatorship nor to die in exile.
How am I to speak without betraying myself?
How am I to construct myself without jettisoning these cities, these languages, these imaginaries?
Still, as a child I had solved the problem.
All it took was a song for the time of confusions to pass
And everything departed in the radiant wing beat of an imagined butterfly
Or else in a jet airplane shooting through the clouds
And thus one started to sing in chorus
M *prale o zanana*
...
I'm off to the land of pineapples
...
In practice, Ozanana – the land of pineapples – does not exist.
Childhood meant inventing your own lands
Breaking free of constraints of forms and territories
Nor was the sky an exception to the rule
In the fable everything is safe
The sky becomes a house
doll, tree, ripe fruit
As in a work of naïve art, in the Haitian style
The world passed before our abundant eyes
We could name or rename each thing
And we could dream with things
As we were dreaming, we had achieved unawares
The greatest revolution of the century
That is, nourished UTOPIAS

Having become a big person
To escape the narrowness of the land
To flee the dictatorship of the grief
To isolate myself from the rumbling of truths and dictatorships
I hid between the dreams
And I held a long conversation with the stars
I imagined myself as each element
I was wind sky
I was clouds ships
I was seas waves
How big the world was
Do not betray the word …
Do not betray the voices that people the world in us

I am here in Dakar in a dense and beautiful network of filiation. I want to mention Jean-Fernand Bierre, Félix Morisseau-Leroy, Roger Dorsinville, Gérard Chenet, Lucien Lemoine, and Jacqueline Scott Lemoine. Gérard Chenet is the only one living today. These men and women, who came from Haiti, hoped for a new humanity when they set foot on the soil of Senegal. They saw Africa as the land of all possibilities. They came to dwell in the land of their ancestors to fertilize the soil of Negritude, their history's shining legacy.

I say, Honor goes to these men
I say, Honor goes to these women.
Who did not invent anything.

I say, Honor goes to these poets and to these storytellers: Jean-Fernand Bierre, Félix Morisseau-Leroy, Roger Dorsinville, Gérard Chenet, Lucien Lemoine, and Jacqueline Scott Lemoine – who gave a meaning, a trajectory, an understanding of the world, and a horizon to my dreams of existing, of narrating the world, and of dying.

I want to speak without betraying these voices that have come before me.

The Paths of the Voice

Ibrahima Wane

Ibrahima Wane *holds a doctorate in modern literature, and a doctorate in arts and humanities. He is a lecturer of African oral literature at Cheikh Anta Diop University in Dakar (UCAD). In addition, he is Director of Doctoral Research in African Studies at UCAD's Department of Arts and Humanities, and is the first Vice President of the Euro-African Network for the Study of Epics (REARE). His work focuses on popular poetry and music in West Africa, literature in African languages, urban culture, and the political imaginary.*

The place of the arts in social life amply demonstrates what aesthetic pleasure is for the human condition. Though made to please, such expressions are no less factors in the production of meaning. Particularly eloquent is the case of music, which, by combining contention and contentment [*en conjugant argument et agrément*], makes it possible to enunciate and "engrave ideas in the body's memory."[1] This manner of apprehending and expressing the real is what makes song the most popular and most powerful of all discursive models. This is why it has always occupied a place at the heart of the strategies of resistance, accommodation, and negotiation that West African societies have employed each time they are confronted with transformations and challenges.

Music represents one of the few domains to have escaped the authoritarianism that the colonial project engendered. The subversion of the political-administrative organization, the social-economic fabric, and the education system, whose effects spared so few domains of public life, had less of an influence on popular art. Military and religious fanfares, the philharmonic symphonies and orchestras, all of which became prominent features of the cultural landscape in the colonies, did little to sway the orientation of the local music scene. What does the music of Ismaël Lô, Mory Kanté, Oumou Sangaré, and Jalbia Kouyateh owe to French culture? Regarded as the seminal achievements of African modernity, the creations of these musical icons announce themselves as issuing, first and foremost, from the source constituted by the tradition.

At the height of the colonial occupation, the voice of the griots and of other popular composers continued to raise up and reverberate with the hymns of the most intractable adversaries to foreign domination. Carried by musical masterpieces, such linguistic productions were in this way able to commit the memorable to record. Far from falling silent, they instead became witnesses to the exactions of the colonial administration (forced labor, capitation tax, war effort).[2] These pieces have proven to be pockets of resistance, outliving the entities, institutions, and individuals that once secreted them.

At the dawn of independence, it was only natural that song [*la chanson*], above all – being the privileged form by which peoples celebrate their capacity to act – assumed the task of relating the pride and faith that had animated the builders of the "new nations." Since, it has been the same tunes, flying under different flags, that have peopled the African West. Indeed, such classics, which preserve the memory of these peoples' collective experience (*Kelefa Saane, Maan Saane Sise, Allah la ke, Ceddo, Lagiya, Taara* ...), ignore the borders that have carved and classed communities according to exogenous criteria: francophone countries, anglophone countries, lusophone countries. By archiving the significant events of each epoch, they form a thread that one can follow back in time and deploy to reconstitute the past over the long term.

The *yela*, the panegyric song of Haalpulaar griots, raises monuments to all the heroes who shaped the history of Futa Toro[3] and Bundu.[4] Its repertory has continued to evolve over time; it has grown richer through the incorporation of history. After having celebrated the Denianke heroes (sixteenth to eighteenth centuries), for example, the *yela* idealized the Almamys that assumed power with the creation of the Bundu kingdom at the end of the seventeenth century, and the Torodbe revolution in Futa Toro at the end of the eighteenth century. From that moment onward, the *yela*'s themes have been the warrior's sword and the saint's book. The musician Baaba Maal, the artist who took on this inheritance, immortalizes Koli Tenguella, the founder of the Denianke kingdom (in the song "Ngawla"), and Samba Gueladio Djegui, the prototype of the warrior-leader ("Dogata"), at the same time that he celebrates Sulayman Bal, the leader of the marabout elite that instituted theocracy in Futa ("Muudo Hormo"), and El Hadj Omar Tall, who promoted jihad in West Africa ("Taara").

Youssou N'Dour, who recuperates Wolof epic songs, reconciles his society's two poles in the space of a song that celebrates the military achievements of the Epicurian Ceddo prince Birima and expresses awe before the miracles of Mouridism's founder, Cheikh Amadou Bamba ("Birima").[5] The same spirit of combination suffuses the texts of hip hop. In the music of Positive Black Soul, references range from Sundiata to Sankara. In the space of a verse, the rappers move between multiple times, places, and milieus, convoking Mandela, Lumumba, Nkrumah, Cheikh Anta, Cheikh Ahmadou Bamba, Aline Sitoe Diatta ...[6] And the breviary of Daara J. is just as cosmopolitan.

Through the exploration of this pantheon, the past is recomposed, its different sequences put in order. The respective contributions of the military nobility, the religious leadership, and the contemporary political and intellectual elite are condensed, organized, and offered as a viaticum to assist the processes of constructing the present and the future. The people's history and horizon are made to interact, the representation of the past intervening principally in the way in which its future is conceived.

This capacity to select and reconstitute makes song a site of movement, a space for re-examining cultural heritages. Continually updating the melopoeia, tales, epics, myths, and proverbs by which society recounts and reproduces itself, song comes to function as a refuge for cultural expressions that are relegated to the margins of social exchanges.

The patrimony survives through the adaptations of contemporary artists. The pieces are exhumed and enriched by the new performances of which they are the objects. The "conservationist" is thus a creator: their œuvre is the product of a loan [*emprunt*] to which they have lent their own traits [*empreinte*] – that is, a work at the junction of authenticity (by virtue of its rootedness) and originality (by virtue of the personal touch that it bears).

Emerging out of this process, song could never be a site of self-flagellation; rather, it was the echo of a full expression of self-respect. The "hits" of West African music, most of which are new takes on centuries-old classics, prove that modernity occurs through a reappropriation of the tradition.

After vying with one another in their covers of Latin American hits and their command of imperfect Spanish, local artists returned to their culture, having understood that "retracing one's steps is also a way of making progress." Foreign musical instruments, once mastered, are tamed and put in the service of local languages and rhythms. Ablaye Ndiaye Thiossane, Sorry Bamba, and Kanté Manfila, among others, drew contemporary taste to the melopoeia of the Wolof, the Dogon, the Mandinka ...

The melding of words and notes means that questions about the use of everyday language, of the mother tongue, as a medium and instrument of creation and expression are, on the whole, poorly posed. Only the popular arts escape "the deliberate disassociation of the language of conceptualization, of thinking, of formal education, of mental development, from the language of daily interaction in the home and in the community."[7] Pulaar, Soninke, Bamanankan, Diola, and Mandinka are delicately poured into the scores of urban music where, fully unfurling themselves, they serve as a site for the production of meaning. Songs make the words of these languages sound and resound far beyond the source of their emission. For, unlike the book which only speaks to those who come calling, songs impose themselves on everyone. They invite themselves into every social group, and thus manage to reach the members of the community in all their diversity.

The acoustic effects created with the resources of the voice (intonation, cadence, rhythm ...) emphasize semantic features that can reach even foreign ears. On the relationship between music, language, and the voice, Roland Barthes says, "Now, my Evaluation of music passes through the voice, and very precisely the voice of a singer whom I knew and whose voice has remained in my life an object of enduring love and of recurrent meditation, often carrying me, beyond the music, towards the text and the language."[8]

Language is not a barrier but an interface, a space of dialogue and exchange; the listener can, while appreciating the sonorities, also access the substance of the message, since the disc is the space of translation par excellence. The verses, transposed onto different media and into different linguistic universes, discover other career paths. And the booklet reveals the song's capaciousness. For, transcribed on paper, the text's brevity is astounding. Its handful of lines reveal all of music's magic by making manifest the depth that discursive materials acquire through the way they are articulated and presented.

Artists are pedagogues who, in order to transmit their ideas and feelings, subject speech to the demands of the melodic line and manage to make a certain intensity of signification correspond to a condensation of linguistic statements. Such subtlety is what allows the public to listen and relisten to their work with pleasure, since "the work is found only in the active encounter of an intention and an attention."[9] The singers José Carlos Schwarz, Alpha Blondy, Salif Keïta, and Malouma, among others, owe their reputations as "revolutionaries," "Pan-Africanists," "engaged artists," etc., less to the length of their texts than to the echo of their choruses, which tell of Africa's achievements and challenges better than any other discourse. The depth and impact of their compositions stem from their evocative power and their performative value.

Owing to the abundance of its productions and to the constancy of the artists' audiences and commitments, music is one of the places where Africa's destiny has occasioned the most profound reflection and modeling. Indeed, song is probably the artistic form to have profited most from technological development, from the invention of the transistor to the digital revolution. Because they modified the conditions of production and distribution, these developments appeared as threats for other inherited forms of immaterial culture. The media of mass communication make it possible to reclaim and amplify various elements of the oral performance that make up the work – that is, "what is communicated poetically, in the here and now: the sonorities, the words and phrases, the rhythms, the movements, the visual and situational aspects."[10]

The power of dissemination that allows these works to orient the collective imaginary and channel its energy means that artists exercise a non-negligible influence on public space. Feeling themselves invested with authority and responsibilities, artists – charismatic figures – extend and accompany their œuvres with citizens' initiatives and actions, and, more and more, find themselves at the center of social and political transformations. The expressive space of the "lead vocal" increasingly overflows their albums' musical banks. Now the singer tries to seize the microphone from politicians who are decried for their unbridled appetites and their apathy. Possessed of aura and inspiration, artists are less and less willing to limit themselves to producing emotions, and demand to be recognized as bearers of a vision and trustees of a mission.[11]

Notes

From Thinking Identity to Thinking African Becomings

1 Paulin Hountondji, "Philosophie et politique: pour une discussion avec Lansana Keita," *Afrique et Développement* 29, no. 1 (2004): pp. 99–100.

   [Translator's note] Throughout, unless a specific translation into English is specified, translations from foreign-language titles are my own.
2 Aimé Césaire, "En guise de manifeste littéraire," *Tropiques*, no. 2 (April 1942).
3 Edmund Husserl, "The Vienna Lecture," in *The Crisis of the European Sciences and Transcendental Phenomenology*, trans. David Carr (Evanston, IL: Northwestern University Press, 1970) p. 275.
4 "Only fools and oysters adhere" is Valéry's oft-cited formula.
5 In *Cultivating Humanity: A Classical Defense of Reform in Liberal Education* (Cambridge, MA: Harvard University Press, 1977), Martha Nussbaum demonstrates that this form of Eurocentrism is predicated upon a simplification of cultures, whose reality is always complex, and which, as cultures, always entail conflict, pluralism, resistance, contestation, and movement. As Amartya Sen, winner of the Nobel Prize in Economics, recently wrote: "If the values that privilege the innovation, respect, and compassion necessary for a better understanding of the Other and of different societies are fundamentally 'western,' then there is every reason to be worried."
6 Hountondji, "Philosophie et politique," pp. 99–100.

7 Tanella Boni's magnificent poem "The Children of Icarus Watch the Stars" stands as an epitaph for the young martyrs of emigration. There one reads this affirmation of a different identity: "I am Icarus I take flight / and keep this life without tomorrow for yourself" – Tanella Boni, *Chaque jour l'espérance* (Paris: L'Harmattan, 2002) p. 148.

8 For the text in question, see Léopold Sédar Senghor, "Pour une coopération entre l'islam et le christianisme," in *Liberté 1: Négritude et humanisme* (Paris: Seuil, 1964) pp. 304–7.

9 Translation adapted from Souleymane Bachir Diagne, "A Secular Age and the World of Islam," in *Tolerance, Democracy and Sufis in Senegal*, ed. Mamadou Diouf (New York: Columbia University Press, 2013) p. 45.

10 Quoted, in French, by Senghor in "Pour une coopération entre l'islam et le christianisme," p. 307.

11 Léopold Sédar Senghor, "Les fondements de l'africanité ou négritude et arabité" (Cairo University, February 1967) and "Être arabe en assimilant toutes les civilisations méditerranéennes avec les africaines" (University of Algiers, February 1967), both in *Liberté 3: Négritude et civilisation de l'Universel* (Paris: Seuil, 1977).

12 G. W. F. Hegel, *Lectures on the Philosophy of World History, Introduction: Reason in History*, translated by H. B. Nisbet (Cambridge University Press, 1975) p. 172.

13 On this topic, we must honor and continue the pioneering work of John Hunwick and Rex Sean O'Fahey who, for many years, have untiringly published the titles of millions of African manuscripts written in Arabic or written using Arabic characters. See J. Hunwick and R. S. O'Fahey, eds. *Arabic Literature of Africa*, 5 vols. (Leiden: Brill, 1993–2015).

14 In 2004, the weekly *Jeune Afrique, l'intelligent* (nos. 2266, 2270, 2273) conducted an investigation into racism in the Maghreb, which reminds us that a multicultural politics in the region must become more attentive than it is today to the Black cultures who give it the appearance that it has.

15 *Bilâd as-Sudan* is the complete expression.

16 Indeed, one must not simplify things by presenting them as a quasi-fated clash of identities. In an excellent piece in which the different actors each provide their point of view, Samantha Power has managed to recover the situation's lost complexity ("Dying in Darfur: Can the Ethnic Cleansing in Sudan Be Stopped?" *The New Yorker*, August 30, 2004). In particular, the article reminds us of the multiplicity of identities in the region, their fluidity, the tradition of intermarriages, etc. This did not stop the crisis from quickly drawing a line between "Arabs" and "Africans," the latter referred to with a term considered insulting: *zurga*, "blacks."

17 Mira Nair's magnificent film *Mississippi Masala* recounted for the

screen this identitarian catastrophe that represented one of the worst moments in the late Amin Dada's disastrous regime.
18 Please refer to two presentations delivered at the General Assembly of CODESRIA held in Kampala from December 8 to 12, 2002: Wilson Kaplan, "Identity Mobilization and Conflict in Nigeria's Oil Communities: A 'Civic' Appraisal of the 'Ethnic,'" and Dickson Eyoh, "The Ethnic Question in African Democratization Experiences." Permit me also to refer to the study I prepared for UNESCO titled *Quelle sécurité pour les africains? Cadres éthiques, normatifs et éducatifs pour la promotion de la sécurité humaine en Afrique*, 2003.
19 CODESRIA has done pioneering work with the creation of the journal *Identité et politique*, which provides a space for dialogue between Africa and Asia.

Notes for a Maroon Feminism

1 I would like to thank Elsa Dorlin, Jules Falquet, Cédric Molino-Machetto, and Françoise Vergès for their attentive reading of this chapter and for their suggestions. That said, I am the only one implicated by the positions it develops.
   [Translator's note] This translation follows the historian Alvin O. Thompson in translating *marronnage* as "marronage" to avoid confusion with the several English senses of "marooning."
2 Orlando Patterson, *Slavery and Social Death: A Comparative Study* (Cambridge, MA: Harvard University Press, 1982).
3 See Sterling Lecater Bland, ed. *African American Slave Narratives: An Anthology* (Westport: Greenwood Press, 2001), and Charles T. Davis and Henry Louis Gates, Jr. *The Slave's Narrative* (New York: Oxford University Press, 1985).
4 "Women formed part of the rebel stronghold located in the heights of the Cahos Mountains, close to the shores of the Artibonite River, where the slave leaders Toussaint-Louverture and Jean Jacques Dessalines stored their weapons and spoils, and planned and executed their fighting strategies": Bernard Moitt, *Women and Slavery in the French Antilles, 1635–1848* (Bloomington: Indiana University Press, 2001) pp. 127–8.
5 *Palenques* in Colombia, Peru, and Cuba; *quilombos* in Brazil; *cumbes* in Venezuela; *maroon communities* in Jamaica, etc.
6 Richard Price, ed. *Maroon Societies: Rebel Slave Communities in the Americas* (Baltimore: Johns Hopkins University Press, 1979).
7 Aimé Césaire, *Toussaint Louverture: la Révolution française et le problème colonial* (Paris: Présence africaine, 1981) pp. 243f.
8 Monique Wittig, *The Straight Mind, and Other Essays* (Boston: Beacon Press, 1992).

9 A large number of Maroon communities were named after women, including Magdalena, Maria Angola, and Maria Embuyla in Colombia; Guardamujeres in Cuba; Nanny Town, Molly's Town, and Diana's Town in Jamaica; and Mulatto Girl's Town and Bucker Woman's Town in the United States.

10 For this reason, the character Beth in Toni Morrison's novel *Beloved* constitutes one of the most beautiful of all Maroon women's tragic figurations. The novel is inspired by the true story of Margaret Garner. Also see Marie-Christine Rochmann, *L'esclave fugitif dans la littérature antillaise: sur la déclive du morne* (Paris: Karthala, 2000), and Marie-Ange Payet, *Les femmes dans le marronnage à l'île de la Réunion de 1662 à 1848* (Paris: L'Harmattan, 2013).

11 See Stephanie M. H. Camp, *Closer to Freedom: Enslaved Women and Everyday Resistance in the Plantation South* (Chapel Hill: University of North Carolina Press, 2004); Arlette Gautier, *Les sœurs de Solitude: femmes et esclavages aux Antilles du XVIIe au XIXe siècle* (Presses universitaires de Rennes, 2010); Jesus García, *Africanas, esclavas y cimarronas* (Caracas: Fundación Afroamérica, 1996); Sonia Maria Giacomini, *Femmes et esclaves: l'expérience brésilienne, 1850–1888* (Paris: iXe, 2016); Jean Fouchard, *Les marrons de la liberté* (Paris: Édition de l'École, 1972); and Moitt, *Women and Slavery in the French Antilles*.

12 As Vergès argues, even if there is a distinction to be made between English and French colonies (the former having chosen the intensive, controlled reproduction of slaves as their means of renewing their supply of labor), one must nonetheless acknowledge that, up until their respective abolitions and the end of the illegal transatlantic trade in slaves, the wombs of African women were in practice drained [*ponctionné*], a fact which makes forms of slavery based upon the trade in Black bodies into economies for the extraction of the living. See Françoise Vergès, *Le ventre des femmes: capitalisme, racialisation, féminisme* (Paris: Albin Michel, 2017) pp. 95–106.

13 Drawing on the work of Eugene Genovese, bell hooks notes the specificity of the historical American situation. "African men were not taught to see themselves as the protectors of *all* women" (italics added): it was not before many years – many centuries – of slavery had passed that slave men came to see their masculinity constructed along the lines of white patriarchy, a model predicated on the idea that all Black women were *property* to be protected. This creolized Black patriarchy (that no longer had anything African about it) was at once encouraged and discouraged by the example of white slaveowners, for whom all Black women were their rightful property. The idea of a male leadership with the aim of protecting all Black women in Maroon societies is thus based on two problematic hypotheses. The first supposes that Black men adhered to the model of white patriarchy

in their marronage (the class of women being thereby considered the property of the class of men). The second supposes that the participation of Maroon women in their own liberation was minimal and therefore insignificant. With respect to the first hypothesis, however, bell hooks has demonstrated that it was less the case that white slaveowners discouraged the imitation of their form of patriarchy than it was that such imitations were rendered impossible by the fact that the cultural references of white patriarchy were untranslatable into the terms of traditional African patriarchy. "Throughout the years of slavery," bell hooks writes, "individual black men rallied to the defense of black women who were important to them. Their defense of these women was not motivated by a sense of themselves as the natural protectors of all black women." With respect to the second hypothesis: as the second half of this essay will show, women did indeed engage in numerous forms of resistance, both on the plantation and in marronage. See bell hooks, *Ain't I a Woman: Black Women and Feminism*, 2nd edn. (New York: Routledge, 2014) pp. 34–55; and Eugene Genovese, *Roll, Jordan, Roll: The World the Slaves Made* (New York: Vintage, 1976).

14 Gautier, *Les sœurs de Solitude*, 33.
15 See the chapter "Women and Manumission" in Moitt, *Women and Slavery in the French Antilles*.
16 The politics of emancipation had different legal bases in different colonial empires. As Arlette Gautier notes, even if French colonies did not seek to acquire breeding slaves [*des esclaves reproducteurs*], it was nonetheless possible to institute versions of a natality politics [*des politiques de natalité*] in Guadaloupe. There, women were made to "desire maternity" with the promise of being granted "savanna freedom" once they had given birth to a certain number of children (Gautier, *Les sœurs de Solitude*, 100). Mary Caroline Cravens observes that, for the Dutch East India Company in Cape Town, the value of slave women was determined less by their capacity to reproduce the slave population than by their labor power (as was the case for men) and their sexual value. The manumission of slave women – despite representing the majority of manumissions at the Cape Town Slave Lodge – was rare: simply producing children was not enough to earn emancipation; other factors were taken into account, such as whether one was creole or whether one was a native of Africa (Cravens, 114).
17 The slave garden was a small parcel of land that the owner allocated slaves so that, once their day's work was finished, they might grow food to feed themselves. On the topic of "slave gardens" in Martinique and Guadaloupe, see Caroline Oudin-Bastide, *Travail, capitalisme et société esclavagiste: Guadeloupe, Martinique (XVIIe–XIXe siècles)* (Paris: La Découverte, 2005) esp. p. 188: "As it happened, the rise of such self-employment within slave society upset its basic principles,

since it encouraged access to money and to certain forms of property. Holding such possessions was in total contradiction with the provisions of Article 28 of the Code Noir, which stipulated that slaves could possess nothing that did not belong to their masters and that 'everything that they acquired through their own industry, through the generosity of others, or otherwise, no matter the circumstances, became the full property of their masters.'"

18 Angela Davis thus opposes the idea, widely held at the time (E. Franklin Frazier, *The Negro Family*, published in 1939; the 1965 Moynihan Report on the Black family), according to which the Black family bore the trauma of a matrilocal structure produced by a slave system that had destroyed the power of men and fathers. The solution, it was claimed, lay in restoring male authority! See *Women, Race & Class* (New York: Random House, 1981) pp. 18–19.

19 It is in such terms that Angela Davis discusses the relationship of enslaved women to domestic labor, and especially to the slave garden: "In the infinite anguish of ministering to the needs of the men and children around her..., [the slave woman] was performing the *only* labor of the slave community which could not be directly and immediately claimed by the oppressor. There was no compensation for work in the fields; it served no useful purpose for the slaves. Domestic labor was the only meaningful labor for the slave community as a whole ... Precisely through performing the drudgery which has long been a central expression of the socially conditioned inferiority of women, the Black woman in chains could help to lay the foundation for some degree of autonomy, both for herself and her men" (Davis, *Women, Race & Class*, 17).

20 For example, in South Carolina between the years 1732 and 1782, roughly half of all fugitive slaves whose birthplace was known were born in the "New World": Philip D. Morgan, "Colonial South Carolina Runaways: Their Significance in Slave Culture," in *Out of the House of Bondage: Runaways, Resistance and Marronage in Africa and the New World*, ed. Heuman Gad (New York: Routledge, 2016) p. 59. Listed alongside fugitive slaves are also Native Americans, "engaged whites," etc.

21 Gautier, *Les sœurs de Solitude*, 40.

22 Ibid., 61–2.

23 Ibid., 44.

24 Ibid., 45.

25 Terminologically, the "appropriation" of women refers to Colette Guillaumin's theses on materialist feminism: for her, appropriation corresponds to a "sexage" that can be compared with – though not reduced to – the logic of appropriation at work in plantation slavery, where the enslaved experience not only the exploitation of their labor power but the constitution of their entire being as a body-for-another

[*corps-pour-autrui*] (see Hourya Bentouhami and Nacira Guénif-Souilamas, "Avec Colette Guillaumin: penser les rapports de sex, race, classe. Les paradoxes de l'analogie," *Cahiers du genre* 63, no. 2 (2017): pp. 205–19).

26 On the relationship between the filibuster and resistance to slavery, one might refer to Robert Wedderburn, a mulatto who grew up in Kingston, Jamaica. After becoming a sailor in the Royal Navy and being employed as a filibuster, he defended the right of slaves to kill their masters, to appropriate their lands, and to rename themselves. See Peter Linebaugh and Marcus Rediker, *The Many-Headed Hydra: The Hidden History of the Revolutionary Atlantic* (London: Verso, 2000) pp. 298f.

27 This holds despite the fact that marronage assumed a great variety of forms. There was, for example, a negotiated marronage in which Maroons would sign treaties with colonizers or white planters, and which might oblige Maroons to participate in militias hunting fugitive slaves. With respect to Maroons who actively participated in the repression of men and women who remained slaves, we can say that they are not "Maroons" in the sense we have in mind: they do not produce an interruption in the notion of race.

28 A circulation, that is, whose path need not be determined in advance.

29 On this understanding of marronage as beginning on the slave ship with the path of suicide, and the associated idea that vagabond souls return to the ancestors, see Marcus Rediker, *À bord du négrier: une histoire atlantique de la traite* (Paris: Seuil, 2013).

30 Patterson, *Slavery and Social Death*.

31 The production of the color line, and notably the polarization "white/Black," has a long history rooted in the discourses of scientific anthropology; in travel narratives; in legal, medical, and psychiatric texts; in politics of citizenship and nationality; etc. See Jean-Luc Bonniol, *La couleur comme maléfice: une illustration créole de la généalogie des Blancs et des Noirs* (Paris: Albin Michel, 1992).

32 Moitt, *Women and Slavery in the French Antilles*, 134.

33 While it is true that, in slave societies, not every person perceived as Black is a slave, nor every white person necessarily free in the sense of the property owner – for, in practice, plantations employed poor whites as workers – it was nonetheless the case that every person perceived as Black ran the risk of being taken for a slave, and particularly for a fugitive slave, and for this person there was always the possibility of being seized by slave hunters. In fact, any white person might stop a Black person and verify his or her identity – an authority which the latter was obliged to submit to and which invested the former with the unofficial role of policing the Black community. As Françoise Vergès points out, Black and white are social constructions and not natural characteristics: they imply a set of color distinctions within

a hierarchical system of classification where variations in "skin" stand for an array of moral, intellectual, and aesthetic distinctions. Nevertheless, the social character of this difference must be understood in relation to "what happens in the biological sphere" where, as Jean-Luc Bonniol argues, such "practices have repercussions (in the sense that the social structuration of reproductive encounters may shape the genetic heritage of populations), and where reproduction must take place in such a way that the discourse of race continues to be relevant": *La couleur comme maléfice*, 2. See also Françoise Vergès, "'Le Nègre n'est pas. Pas plus que le Blanc': Frantz Fanon, esclavage, race et racisme," *Actuel Marx* 38, no. 2 (2005): pp. 45–63.

34 From this perspective, we might consider the continuum of sexual exchange that Paola Tabet draws between exploited sex work and free sex work (what Guillaumin would call "appropriated" sex work) as having a particular resonance for slave women emancipated by mixed marriage. In their new condition, they experience what Tabet calls the conjugal amalgam [*l'amalgame conjugal*]: see Paola Tabet, *La grande arnaque: sexualité des femmes et échange économico-sexuel* ([1987] Paris: L'Harmattan, 2005); Jules Falquet, "La combinatoire *straight*: race, classe, sexe, et économie politique – analyses matérialistes et décoloniales," *Cahiers du genre* 4, no. 3 (2016): pp. 73–96.

35 Moitt, *Women and Slavery in the French Antilles*, 151.

36 Alvin O. Thompson, *Flight to Freedom: African Runaways and Maroons in the Americas* (Kingston: University of the West Indies Press, 2006) p. 32.

37 Ibid., 32.

38 See Frantz Fanon, *Black Skin, White Masks*, trans. Richard Philcox (New York: Grove Press, 2008) p. 57.

39 Simone de Beauvoir, *The Second Sex*, trans. Constance Borde and Sheila Malovany-Chevallier (New York: Vintage, 2011) p. 12.

40 The negotiation of peace treaties between Maroons and landowning planters often included the obligation to return any fugitive slave hoping to join the Maroon community to captivity. By the same token, free persons of color had to put themselves at the disposition of Black militias for the hunting of runaways.

41 Roger Caillois, *Man, Play and Games*, trans. Meyer Barash (Chicago: University of Illinois Press, 2001) p. 19.

42 Joseph Elzéar Morenas, *Précise historique de la traite des Noirs et de l'esclavage colonial* ([1828] Geneva: Slatkine, 1978) p. 322.

43 Homi K. Bhabha, *The Location of Culture* (New York: Routledge, 1994) p. 64.

44 Malcolm X, "Message to the Grass Roots: November 10, 1963, Detroit," in *Malcom X Speaks*, ed. George Breitman (New York: Grove Press, 1965) p. 10.

45 [Translator's note] The expression "Libres de couleur" can be read

differently depending on whether one construes "libres" as a noun or an adjective. On the one hand, "free persons of color"; on the other, "free *of* or free *from* color."
46 Vergès, "'Le Nègre n'est pas. Pas plus que le Blanc.'"
47 Thompson, *Flight to Freedom*, 34.
48 In this way, plantocratic societies opportunistically turned matrimonial mimeticism to their advantage. Marriage between slaves could be used as a tool to combat the depopulation of plantations, despite the fear that, "through the institution of marriage, the slave would hope to assimilate himself into the White community, all of whose customs he is obliged to respect without ever daring to imitate." See Gautier, *Les sœurs de Solitude*, 93.
49 See the proclamation of the governor general of the Danish West Indies, published in the June 17, 1786 edition of the *Saint-Croix Gazette*: "It is expressly forbidden to all and every one of the individuals who compose the people of colour, *free or slaves*, to wear jewelry of diamonds, gold or silver, except in a manner that is hereafter specified. It is likewise forbidden to wear silk and other clothing enriched with gold or silver, any dyed India cloth, cambric, muslins, gauze, linen and any kind of fine clothing and bombazine." Cited in Thompson, *Flight to Freedom*, 34 (italics added).
50 Thompson, *Flight to Freedom*, 37.
51 Quoted in Césaire, *Toussaint Louverture*, 277–8.
52 Quoted in ibid., 278.
53 For Hegel, the slave's labor, properly understood, consists in developing "a mind of one's own." Nonetheless, such "self-will" [*entêtement*] remains "a freedom which is still enmeshed in servitude." See Georg Wilhelm Friedrich Hegel, *Phenomenology of Spirit*, trans. A. V. Miller (New York: Oxford University Press, 1977) §196, p. 119.
54 Orlando Patterson, *Freedom in the Making of Western Culture*, Vol. I of *Freedom* (New York: Basic Books, 1991).
55 Harriet Jacobs, *Incidents in the Life of a Slave Girl: Written by Herself* ([1861] repr., New York: Oxford University Press, 1988) p. 68. See also Hazel V. Carby "'Hear My Voice, Ye Careless Daughters': Narratives of Slave and Free Women before Emancipation," in *African American Autobiography: A Collection of Critical Essays*, ed. William L. Andrews (Englewood Cliffs, NJ: Prentice Hall, 1993) p. 96.
56 Thompson, *Flight to Freedom*, 74.
57 Angela Davis indeed contests the idea that the quasi-systematic practice of rape on plantations can be explained as a way of preserving the sexual decency of white women.
58 C. L. R. James, *The Black Jacobins: Toussaint L'Ouverture and the San Domingo Revolution*, 2nd revised edn. (New York: Vintage, 1989) p. 361.

59 Quoted in Moitt, *Women and Slavery in the French Antilles*, 128–9.
60 Elsa Dorlin, *Se défendre: une philosophie de la violence* (Paris: La Découverte, 2017).
61 Moitt, *Women and Slavery in the French Antilles*, 144.
62 Ibid., 144.
63 Oudin-Bastide, *Travail, capitalisme et société esclavagiste*.
64 See Samir Boumediene, *La colonisation du savoir: une histoire des plantes médicinales du "Nouveau Monde" (1492–1750)* (Vaulx-en-Velin: Les Éditions des Mondes à Faire, 2016) p. 351.
65 Karla Gottlieb, *The Mother of Us All: A History of Queen Nanny, Leader of the Windward Jamaican Maroons* (Trenton: Africa World Press, 2000) p. 50.
66 Achille Mbembe, "Nécropolitique," *Raison politique* 21, no. 1 (2006): pp. 29–60.
67 See bell hooks, *Ain't I a Woman*, 23: "Transplanted African women soon realized that they were seen as 'surrogate' men by white male slavers. On any plantation with a substantial number of female slaves, black women performed the same tasks as black men; they plowed, planted, and harvested crops." On how the anxieties that plantation slave labor provoked in white masters contributed, in the case of Black women, to a gender ambiguity that facilitated capitalist exploitation, see Brian L. Moore, B. W. Highman, Carl Campbell, and Patrick Bryan, *Slavery, Freedom and Gender: The Dynamics of Caribbean Society* (Kingston: University of the West Indies Press, 2003) p. 212.
68 See Ronald Cummings, "Jamaican Female Masculinities: Nanny of the Maroons and the Genealogy of the Man-Royal," *Journal of West Indian Literature* 21, no. 1/2 (2012): pp. 129–54.
69 See Roger Bastide and Germaine Dieterlen, eds. *La notion de personne en Afrique noire* (Paris: L'Harmattan, 1993).
70 See the 2017 conference presentation "Décoloniser la danse" by the choreographer and curator of the festival "Danses et continents noirs," James Carlès.
71 See Terri L. Snyder, *The Power to Die: Slavery and Suicide in British North America* (University of Chicago Press, 2015) p. 39. On the importance of suicides where one's death forms a community, consider the case of the Maroons on the island of Saint-Jean. In November 1733, faced with the impossibility of succeeding in their revolt, the Maroons of Saint-Jean committed suicide "together": their bodies were discovered arrayed such that each held a revolver to the temple of his or her neighbor and companion. See Elsa Dorlin, "Les espaces-temps des résistances esclaves: des suicidés de Saint-Jean aux marrons de Nanny Town (XVIIe–XVIIIe siècles)," *Tumultes* 27, no. 2 (2006): pp. 37–51.
72 Dénètem Touam Bona, *Fugitif, où cours-tu?* (Paris: Presses universitaires de France, 2016) p. 82.

73 Étienne Balibar, *Equaliberty: Political Essays*, trans. James Ingram (Durham: Duke University Press, 2014).
74 This is why it was not rare to observe pregnant women escaping together with their children, as Beth does in Toni Morrison's *Beloved*. This is attested by the archives that Bernard Moitt consulted in his research. See Moitt, *Women and Slavery in the French Antilles*, 134.
75 "In the seventeenth and eighteenth centuries, slave women in the French Antilles generally ran away alone or in groups, mostly with other women and not with their husbands. This led Jean Fouchard to conclude that 'female slaves organized their marronage only among women'": ibid., 135.
76 Ibid., 136.
77 [Translator's note] Keep in mind that, while the English word "maroon" and the French word "marron" both designate fugitive slaves and their descendants in the Caribbean, both words are also names for colors. If the referent is the same in the first case, it is not the same in the second. In English, maroon is a dull dark red or purplish color. By contrast, in French (and Spanish), the color *marron* is a chestnut brown.

Africa and the New Western Figures of Personal Status Law

1 Daniel Gutmann, *Le sentiment d'identité: étude de droit des personnes et de la famille* (Paris: LGDJ, 2000).
2 Pierre Legendre, *De la société comme texte: linéaments d'une anthropologie dogmatique* (Paris: Fayard, 2001) p. 61, and Pierre Legendre, *Sur la question dogmatique en Occident* (Paris: Fayard, 1999) p. 40.
3 Alain Supiot, *Homo juridicus: On the Anthropological Function of the Law*, trans. Saskia Brown (New York: Verso, 2006) pp. 29–40.
4 Michela Marzano, *Penser le corps* (Paris: Presses universitaires de France, 2002) pp. 120–4; Jean-Louis Baudouin and Catherine Labrusse-Riou, *Produire l'homme: de quel droit? Étude éthique et juridique des procréations artificielles* (Paris: Presses universitaires de France, 1987); Muriel Fabre-Magnan and Philippe Moullier, *La génétique, science humaine* (Paris: Belin, 2004).
5 Laurent Alexandre, *La mort de la mort* (Paris: JC Lattès, 2012); Jean-Michel Besnier, *Demain les posthumains* (Paris: Hachette, 2009), and *L'homme simplifié* (Paris: Fayard, 2012); Ronald Dworkin, *Playing God: Genes, Clones, and Luck* (Cambridge, MA: Harvard University Press, 2002); N. Katherine Hayles, *How We Became Posthuman* (University of Chicago Press, 1999); Béatrice Jousset-Couturier, *Le transhumanisme: faut-il avoir peur de l'avenir?* (Paris: Eyrolles, 2016).

6 See the issue "Vers de novelles humanités? L'humanisme juridique face aux nouvelles technologies," *Archives de philosophie du droit* 59 (Paris: Dalloz, 2017).
7 Stéphanie Hennette-Vauchez, "Corpus iuris: jusnaturalisme et réinventions du corps par le droit (1970–2007)," in *La tentation du corps*, ed. Dominique Memmi, Dominique Guillo, and Olivier Martin (Paris: Éditions de l'École des Hautes Études en Sciences Sociales, 2009) pp. 199–219, esp. 206ff.
8 Jean Déprez, *Droit international privé et conflits de civilisations: aspects méthodologiques (les relations entre systèmes d'Europe occidentale et systèmes islamiques en matière de statut personnel)*, Vol. CCXI of *The Collected Courses of the Hague Academy of International Law* (The Hague: Brill, 1988); Marie-Claude Najm, *Principes directeurs du droit international privé et conflit de civilisations: relations entre systèmes laïques et systèmes religieux* (Paris: Dalloz, 2005); Pierre Mercier, *Conflits de civilisation et droit international privé: polygamie et répudiation* (Geneva: Droz, 1972); Khalid Zaher, *Conflit de civilisations et droit international privé* (Paris: L'Harmattan, 2009).
9 Samuel P. Huntington, *The Clash of Civilizations and the Remaking of World Order* (New York: Simon & Schuster, 1996).
10 Marie-Angèle Hermitte, "Le corps hors du commerce, hors du marché," in "La philosophie du droit aujourd'hui," *Archives de philosophie du droit* 34 (Paris: Sirey, 1988): p. 323.
11 Legendre, *Sur la question dogmatique en Occident*, 347.
12 The recent history of surrogate motherhood in French jurisprudence is an excellent example of the effect state intervention [*volontarisme*] has on family law. With the judgments *Mennesson* and *Labassée* of April 6, 2011 (*Revue critique de droit international privé* [2011]: p. 711, note Petra Hammje; *Revue trimestrielle de droit civil* [2011]: p. 340, obs. Jean Hauser), the French Court of Cassation initially prohibited the transcription into French civil status of any filiation issuing from a surrogacy agreement made abroad. The development of this contentious matter, which took place before the European Court of Human Rights, led the European judges to qualify the positions of the French magistrates. For the Court in Strasbourg, to prohibit the transcription of a filiation derived from a surrogate mother into a French civil status record amounted to an infringement of Article VIII of the European Convention on Human Rights (The European Court of Human Rights, June 26, 2014, no. 65192/11, *Mennesson v. France, Revue critique de droit international privé* [2015]: p. 1, note Hugues Fulchiron and C. Bidaud-Garon; *Revue trimestrielle de droit civil* [2014]: p. 616, note Jean Hauser). The decision of the European Court could not but affect French jurisprudence. With two judgments dated July 3, 2015, the plenary meeting of the Court of Cassation granted the transcription of foreign birth certificates for children born

under surrogacy agreements for the first time (*Revue trimestrielle de droit civil* [2015]: p. 581). In France, such jurisprudential liberalism with respect to surrogacy has recently been compounded by a series of judgments made on July 5, 2017, allowing a child born under a surrogacy agreement to be adopted by the non-birth mother named in the agreement (*Revue Dalloz* [2017]: p. 1737, note Hugues Fulchiron).

13 Conseil d'État français, May 31, 2016, *Revue trimestrielle de droit civil* (2016): p. 843, note Jean Hauser; *Revue Dalloz* (2016): p. 1470, note Marie Christine de Montecler; *Revue Dalloz* (2016): p. 1477, note Bernard Haftel. Despite the prohibitions named in Articles L. 2141-2 and L. 2141-11-1 of the Public Health Code, in deciding on this contentious matter the Conseil d'État français granted post-mortem medically assisted procreation to a foreign couple living in France, basing its decision on Article VIII of the European Convention of Human Rights. In this case, after the death of her Italian husband from cancer, a Spanish woman had requested the transfer of her husband's gametes to Spain (a country that permits post-mortem insemination) for the purpose of medically assisted procreation. Here, the granting of post-mortem insemination to the Spanish woman finds its justification principally in an appeal to affective concerns rather in reference to any legal orthodoxy.

14 Companies like Facebook and Apple have offered to finance – at the cost of some 16,000 euros – the freezing of their female employees' oocytes. The thought behind the offer is that, no longer handicapped by the pressure of maternity, female employees will invest themselves more profoundly in their professional activities. Indeed, the biomedical procedure should give working women the power to suspend their maternity as long as they wish. Cf. Françoise Marmouyet, "Congélation d'ovules: la proposition de Facebook et Apple fait debat," *France 24*, October 16, 2014, www.france24.com /fr/facebook-apple-congelation-ovules-sante-feminisme-parite-debat.

15 Philippe Malaurie and Hugues Fulchiron, *Droit de la famille*, 5th edn. (Paris: LGDJ, 2016) no. 1026, no. 1436.

16 Andreas Buscher, *La famille en droit international privé*, Vol. CCLXXXI of *The Collected Courses of the Hague Academy of International Law* (The Hague: Brill, 2000) pp. 24–6.

17 David F. Cavers, *Contemporary Conflicts Law in American Perspective*, Vol. CXXXI of *The Collected Courses of The Hague Academy of International Law* (The Hague: Brill, 1970) pp. 104–21; Joseph Story, *Commentaries on the Conflicts of Laws, Foreign and Domestic, in Regard to Contracts, Rights, and Remedies, and especially in Regard to Marriages, Divorces, Wills, Successions, and Judgements* (Boston: Hilliard, Gray & Co., 1834).

18 Friedrich Carl von Savigny (1779–1861) is a German jurist who

promoted the bilateral method. This method was practiced throughout Continental Europe and exported to Africa through Western colonization. In essence, this approach to dealing with international conflicts in the private sector takes the form of first identifying the legal relationship (the legal category of the conflict) and its spatial location (the connecting factor). See Friedrich Carl von Savigny, *Traité du droit romain*, Vol. VIII, trans. Charles Guénoux, 2nd edn. ([1860] repr. Paris: Éditions Panthéon-Assas, 2002).

19 Pasquale Stanislao Mancini, "De l'utilité de rendre obligatoires pour tous les États, sous la forme d'un ou de plusieurs traités internationaux, un certain nombre de règles générales du droit international privé pour assurer la décision uniforme des conflits entre les différentes législations civiles et criminelles," *Journal du droit international* (1874): pp. 220ff., esp. p. 298.

20 Yves Lequette, *Les mutations du droit international privé: vers un changement de paradigme?*, Vol. CCCLXXXVII of *The Collected Courses of the Hague Academy of International Law* (The Hague: Brill, 2017) esp. pp. 405–592.

21 Béatrice Bourdelois, "La famille du XXIe siècle et problématiques de conflits de lois," in *Mélanges en l'honneur du Professeur Pierre Mayer*, ed. Vincent Heuzé, Rémy Libchaber, and Pascal de Vareilles-Sommières (Paris: LGDJ, 2015) pp. 77ff., esp. 86–9.

22 Louis d'Avout, "La *lex personalis* entre nationalité, domicile et résidence habituelle," in *Mélanges en l'honneur du Professeur Pierre Mayer*, ed. Heuzé, Libchaber, and de Vareilles-Sommières, pp. 15–41.

23 Cheikh Anta Diop, *The Cultural Unity of Black Africa: The Domains of Matriarchy and of Patriarchy in Classical Antiquity* (London: Karnack House, 1989).

24 Voluntarism is a manifestation of legal liberalism. It grants subjects the power to choose the rules that will be applied to them in a legal proceeding. Voluntarism marks the arrival of a form of law "à la carte."

25 The rule of conflict is a technique for determining the spatial sphere of competence of each state in an international dispute. A rule of conflict is said to be "of material coloration" when the relevant state judge can select the applicable law from among the possibilities provided by his or her legislator. This technique is often a manifestation of a functionalism that aims to eliminate certain laws – and possibly certain African laws – judged undesirable for ruling on the international conflict. An illustrative example of this can be found in Article 202-1 paragraph 2 of the French Civil Code, which grants foreigners the power to enter into a same-sex marriage provided that their domicile is in France.

26 Cour de cassation française, première chambre civil, ruling no. 96, January 28, 2015. See Didier Boden, Sylvain Bollée, Bernard Haftel, Petra Hammje, and Pascal de Vareilles-Sommières, "Mariage de personnes de même sexe: exception d'ordre public," *Revue critique*

de droit international privé (2015): p. 400; Hugues Fulchiron, "Le 'mariage pour tous' est d'ordre public en matière internationale," *Revue Dalloz* (2015): p. 464. In this instance, the head of the Prosecution Department opposed the same-sex union of a Moroccan man and a French man by citing the following texts: Article 5 of the Franco-Moroccan Convention of August 10, 1981; Article 175-1 of the Civil Code; and Articles 422 and 423 of the Code of civil procedure. Dismissing the hierarchy of norms involved (the superiority of the aforementioned Franco-Moroccan Convention over the Civil Code with respect to Article 202 issuing from the law of May 17, 2013), the French Court of Cassation, to which the matter was referred, cited Article 4 of the Bilateral Franco-Moroccan Convention to call upon French regulations and, *in fine*, to grant the Moroccan man residing in France the power to marry a Frenchman. In practice, even if Article 4 of the aforesaid Franco-Moroccan Convention allows the French judge in question to apply his or her own law when Moroccan law is manifestly contrary to French policy [*ordre public*], the elevation of Article 202-1 paragraph 2 of the French Civil Code as a principle of international policy [*l'ordre public international*] seems specious. While certainly establishing a rule of conflict more substantial than processual, this text nonetheless does not, objectively speaking, presuppose its relevance for international public policy. Like Article 209 of the Civil Code, Article 202-1 paragraph 2 represents a galloping assault of French legal imperialism upon civilizations that oppose it. This text can be analyzed as a simple negation of the personal status of foreigners in the matter of marriage unions.

27 The American territorialist tradition, by inscribing personal status within the domain of domicile and not of nationality, would allow an African family living in the Unites States to enjoy a right of filiation through the mechanism of surrogacy.

28 Amplified by globalization, the market of filiation has given rise to procreative tourism in which certain Western legal orders (Italy, Spain, Belgium, Sweden, Switzerland, etc.) make their scientist policies available to all interested persons, irrespective of their nationality. By pursuing such a course, an African woman would currently be able to secure the freezing of her oocytes, thereby deferring her maternal intention. This will pose a problem for international private law, which will be tasked with coordinating African and the Western legal systems involved on how to recognize the child's filiation and whether the African state will grant nationality.

29 Valentin-Yves Mudimbe, *L'odeur du père: essai sur des limites de la science et de la vie en Afrique Noire* (Paris: Présence africaine, 1982) p. 96.

30 Bertrand Ancel, *Éléments d'histoire du droit international privé* (Paris: Éditions Panthéon-Assas, 2017) pp. 480–4.

31 Abd-El-Kader Boye, *Le statut personnel dans le droit international privé des pays africains au sud du Sahara: conceptions et solutions des conflits de lois. Le poids de la tradition négro-africaine personnaliste*, Vol. CCXXXVIII of *The Collected Courses of the Hague Academy of International Law* (The Hague: Brill, 1993); El Hadji Samba Ndiaye, "L'harmonisation du droit international privé en Afrique francophone du Sud du Sahara" (Ph.D. diss., Université de Rouen, 2014), www.theses.fr/2014ROUED008.
32 Michel Agier, *La condition cosmopolite: l'anthropologie à l'épreuve du piège identitaire* (Paris: La Découverte, 2013) pp. 137–52.
33 John Mbiti, *African Religions and Philosophy*, 2nd edn. (London: Heinemann, 1990); Alassane Ndaw, *La pensée africaine: recherches sur les fondements de la pensée négro-africaine*, 2nd edn. (Dakar: NEAS, 1997) pp. 89–94; Placide Tempels, *Bantu Philosophy*, English edn. (Paris: Présence africaine, 1969); Maurice Delafosse, *Haut-Sénégal-Niger*, Vol. III of *Les civilisations* (Paris: Émile Larose, 1912) pp. 160–85.

Rethinking Islam

1 Gilles Deleuze and Félix Guattari, *What Is Philosophy?* trans. Graham Burchell and Hugh Tomlinson (New York: Verso, 1994); Dominique Wolton, "Les contradictions de l'espace public médiatisé," in *L'espace public*, ed. Éric Dacheux (Paris: CNRS Éditions, 2008).
2 Hesna Cailliau, *L'esprit des religions: connaître les religions pour mieux comprendre les hommes* (Toulouse: Éditions Milan, 2003) p. 210.
3 Louis Gardet, *La cité musulmane: vie sociale et politique* (Paris: Vrin, 1954) p. 31, and *Les hommes de l'islam, approche des mentalités* ([1984] Brussels: Éditions Complexe, 1999) p. 74.
4 See Louis Massignon, *La passion de Hallâj, martyr mystique de l'islam*, Vol. III ([1975] Paris: Gallimard, 1990).
5 See Olivier Carré, *L'Islam laïque ou le retour à la Grande Tradition* (Paris: Armand Colin, 1993).
6 See Raymond Aron, "L'avenir des religions séculières," *La France libre* 8, no. 45 (1944): pp. 210–17; and Jean Baubérot, "Existe-t-il une religion civile républicaine?" *French Politics, Culture & Society* 25, no. 2 (2007): pp. 3–18.
7 See Nilüfer Göle, "Snapshots of Islamic Modernities," *Daedalus* 129, no. 1 (2000): pp. 91–117.
8 Henri Sanson, "Laïcité islamique en Algérie," *Revue des mondes musulmanes et de la Méditerranée* 29 (1983): pp. 55–68.
9 Italics added.

The Impossible Meeting

1 J. M. Coetzee, *Disgrace* (New York: Penguin, 2000) p. 4.
2 Ibid., 2.
3 Ibid., 16.
4 Ibid., 89.
5 Amos Oz, "Peace and Love and Compromise," in *Israel, Palestine and Peace: Essays* (New York: Harcourt, 1994) p. 77.
6 Coetzee, *Disgrace*, 91.
7 Ibid., 94.
8 Ibid., 164.
9 Ibid., 107.
10 Ibid., 78.
11 Ibid., 86.
12 Ibid., 121.
13 Elsa Dorlin, *Se défendre: une philosophie de la violence* (Paris: La Découverte, 2017) iBooks.
14 Mahmoud Darwish, "Counterpoint: For Edward Said," in *If I Were Another*, trans. Fady Joudah (New York: Farrar, Straus and Giroux, 2009) p. 183.

Circulations

1 United Nations, Department of Economic and Social Affairs, Population Division, "World Population Prospects," 2017; M. L. Flahaux and H. De Haas, "African Migration: Trends Patterns, Drivers," *Comparative Migration Studies* 4, no. 1 (2016): pp. 1–25; F. Natale, S. Migali, and R. Münz, *Many More to Come? Migration from and within Africa* (Brussels: Joint Research Centre, European Commission, 2018).
2 For details, see Peer Schouten et al. *"Everything that Moves Will Be Taxed": The Political Economy of Roadblocks in North and South Kivu* (Antwerp: Danish Institute for International Studies, 2017), https://ipisresearch.be/wp-content/uploads/2017/12/1801-Roadblocks-DRC-English.pdf.
3 See H. Laurens van der Laan, "Modern Inland Transport and European Trading Firms in Colonial West Africa," *Cahiers d'études africaines* 21, no. 84 (1981): pp. 547–75.
4 See Roland Poutier, "Le panier et la locomotive: à propos des transports terrestres en Afrique central," *Travaux de l'Institut de géographie de Reims* 83–4 (1993): pp. 41–61.
5 See Peer Schouten and Soleil-Perfect Kalessopo, *The Politics of Pillage: The Political Economy of Roadblocks in the Central African*

Republic (Antwerp: Danish Institute for International Studies, 2017), https://ipisresearch.be/publication/politics-pillage-political-economy-roadblocks-central-african-republic-2.

6 Hélène Blaszkiewicz, "La mise en politique des circulations commerciales transfrontalières en Zambie: infrastructures et moment néolibéral," *Geocarrefour* [online] 91, no. 3 (2017), http://journals.openedition.org/geocarrefour/10342.

7 Hannah Appel, "Offshore Work: Oil, Modularity, and the How of Capitalism in Equatorial Guinea," *American Ethnologist* 39, no. 4 (November 2012): pp. 692–709.

8 Denis Retaille, "L'espace nomade," *Revue de géographie de Lyon* 73, no. 1 (1998): pp. 71–82, 71.

9 Ibid., 74.

10 Carolina Kobelinsky, "Exister au risque de disparaître: récits sur la mort pendant la traversée vers l'Europe," *Revue européenne des migrations internationales* 33, no. 2–3 (2017): pp. 115–31.

11 Charles Heller and Antoine Pecoud, "Compter les morts aux frontières: des contre-statistiques de la société civile à la récupération (inter)gouvernementale," *Revue européenne des migrations internationales* 33, no. 2–3 (2017): pp. 63–90.

12 See Frédérique Fogel, *Parente sans papiers* (La Roche-sur-Yon: Éditions Depaysage, 2019).

13 Hélène Le Bail, "Les grandes villes chinoises comme espace d'immigration internationale: le cas des entrepreneurs africains," *Asie Visions*, August 19, 2009; Brigitte Bertoncello and Sylvie Bredeloup, "De Hong Kong à Guangzhou, de nouveau 'comptoirs' africains s'organisent," *Perspectives chinoises* no. 98 (2007): pp. 98–110.

14 Isabelle Delpla, "Vivre au pays vide?" *Critique* 860–1, no. 1–2 (2019): pp. 123–35, 133.

15 See Emanuele Coccia, "Gaia ou l'anti-Leviathan," *Critique* 860–1, no. 1–2 (2019): pp. 32–43.

On the Return

1 Aimé Césaire, *Notebook of a Return to My Native Land*, trans. Mireille Rosello and Annie Pritchard (Tarset: Bloodaxe Books, 1995) p. 113.

2 Valentin-Yves Mudimbe, *L'autre face du royaume* (Geneva: L'Âge d'homme, 1973) p. 11.

3 Stéphane Dufoix, *La dispersion: une histoire des usages du mot diaspora* (Paris: Éditions Amsterdam, 2011) p. 47.

4 Giulia Bonacci, *Exodus! Heirs and Pioneers, Rastafari Return to Ethiopia*, trans. Antoinette Tidjani Alou (Kingston: University of the West Indies Press, 2015).

5 Elikia M'Bokolo, foreword to ibid., 12.
6 Bonacci's *Exodus! Heirs and Pioneers* is a precious resource on the question of return within the Rastafari movement, and helpfully includes a complete cartography of the classical routes of return. For a precise treatment of the idea of "Black diaspora" in the Caribbean–American context, see Christine Chivallon, *La diaspora noire des Amériques: expériences et théories à partir de la Caraïbe* (Paris: CNRS Éditions, 2004).
7 The term "creolization" designates a central concept in the thought of Édouard Glissant – my use of it here draws from Glissant's analyses in *Introduction to a Poetics of Diversity*, trans. Celia Britton (Liverpool University Press, 2020). Creolization is a linguistic and cultural process in which utterly heterogeneous elements encounter one another, producing an unexpected, unforeseeable result. Creolization is "hybridity with an added value, namely unforeseeability": ibid., 8.
8 Ibid., 37.
9 On this topic, consult the geographical resources "géoconfluences" provided by the École normale supérieure de Lyon: http://geoconfluences.ens-lyon.fr/actualites/veille/migrations-intra-africaines.
10 "Yet, while many poor countries do their best to accommodate mass migrations, the nation-states of Europe prefer to say to life that it shall not pass. They who have migrated so much, shattered so many borders, conquered so much, dominated and still dominate, seek to entrench all human miseries, terrors and poverties at their place of origin": Patrick Chamoiseau, *Migrant Brothers: A Poet's Declaration of Human Dignity*, trans. Matthew Amos and Fredrik Rönnbäck (New Haven: Yale University Press, 2018) p. 25.
11 Paul Gilroy, *The Black Atlantic: Modernity and Double Consciousness* (Cambridge, MA: Harvard University Press, 1995).
12 Richard Marienstras, *Être un peuple en diaspora* (Paris: Les Prairies ordinaires, 2014).
13 "Majority implies a constant, of expression or content, serving as a standard measure by which to evaluate it. Let us suppose that a constant or standard is the average adult-white-heterosexual-European speaking a standard language (Joyce's or Ezra Pound's Ulysses). It is obvious that 'man' holds the majority, even if he is less numerous than mosquitos, children, women, blacks, peasants, homosexuals, etc.... Majority assumes a state of power and domination, not the other way around.... A determination different from that of the constant will therefore be considered minoritarian, by nature and regardless of number, in other words, a subsystem or an outsystem": Gilles Deleuze and Félix Guattari, *A Thousand Plateaus: Capitalism and Schizophrenia*, trans. Brian Massumi (Minneapolis: University of Minnesota Press, 1987) p. 105.
14 Édouard Glissant and Alexandre Leupin, *The Baton Rouge Interviews*

with Édouard Glissant and Alexandre Leupin, trans. Kate M. Cooper (Liverpool University Press, 2020).
15 See Paul Gilroy, *Postcolonial Melancholia* (New York: Columbia University Press, 2004).
16 Cheikh Anta Diop, *Black Africa: The Economic and Cultural Basis for a Federated State*, trans. Harold J. Salemson, expanded edn. (Chicago: Lawrence Hill, 1987) p. 18; translation modified.
17 Abdelmayek Sayad, *The Suffering of the Immigrant*, trans. David Macey (Cambridge: Polity, 2004).
18 Maurice Blanchot, *The Unavowable Community*, trans. Pierre Joris (Barrytown, NY: Station Hill, 1988) p. 46.
19 Ibid., 46f.
20 Ibid., 7.
21 Ibid., 8.
22 Maurice Blanchot distances himself from both of these conceptions of community. Among the various experiences of *forming bonds with* [*faire lien avec*], the events of 1968 brought to light another experience of community, one which "gave permission to everyone without distinction of class, age, sex or culture, to mix with the first comer as if with an already loved being, precisely because he was the unknown-familiar": ibid., 30.
23 For a genealogy of Afropolitanism, consult Patrick Ewondo's article "L'afropolitanisme en débat," in "Blackness," ed. Rémy Banzenguissa-Ganga and Thomas Fouquet, special issue, *Politique africaine*, 136 (December 2014): pp. 105–19.
24 "'Home' for this lot," Selasi notes, "is many things ... They (read: we) are Afropolitans – the newest generation of African emigrants, coming soon or collected already at a law firm/chem lab/jazz lounge near you. You'll know us by our funny blend of London fashion, New York jargon, African ethics, and academic successes. Some of us are ethnic mixes, e.g. Ghanaian and Canadian, Nigerian and Swiss; others merely cultural mutts: American accent, European affect, African ethos. Most of us are multilingual: in addition to English and a Romantic [*sic*] or two, we understand some indigenous tongue and speak a few urban vernaculars. There is at least one place on The African Continent to which we tie our sense of self: be it a nation-state (Ethiopia), a city (Ibadan), or an auntie's kitchen. Then there's the G8 city or two (or three) that we know like the backs of our hands, and the various institutions that know us for our famed focus. We are Afropolitans: not citizens, but Africans of the world": Taiye Selasi, "Bye-Bye Babar," *The LIP Magazine*, March 3, 2005, https://thelip.robertsharp.co.uk/2005/03/03/bye-bye-barbar.
25 A "subjective economy" is "an economy that solicits and produces processes of subjectivation" at a given historical moment. Cf. Maurizio Lazzarato, *The Making of Indebted Man: An Essay on the Neoliberal*

Condition, trans. Joshua David Jordan (Amsterdam: Semiotext(e), 2012) p. 37.
26 "One ever feels his two-ness, – an American, a Negro; two souls, two thoughts, two unreconciled strivings; two warring ideals in one dark body, whose dogged strength alone keeps it from being torn asunder": William Edward Burghardt Du Bois, *The Souls of Black Folk*, ed. Henry Louis Gates, Jr. and Terri Hume Oliver, Norton Critical Editions (New York: W. W. Norton, 1999) p. 11.
27 The exploitation of coltan mines in the Democratic Republic of the Congo is a striking example of such asymmetry.
28 Bertrand Ogilvie, *L'homme jetable* (Paris: Éditions Amsterdam, 2012); Achille Mbembe, *Critique of Black Reason*, trans. Laurent Dubois (Durham, NC: Duke University Press, 2017).
29 The African Summer School (ASS) was created by Fortuna Ekutsu Mambulu in Italy: www.africansummerschool.org. The fifth meeting of the ASS was organized by Fortuna Ekutsu Mambulu, Laura Fregi, and Prosper Nkenfack.
30 Appointed in 2013, Cécile Kyenge was the first Black woman to hold the office of minister in Italy.
31 José Do Nascimento, who regularly teaches at the ASS, distinguishes four conceptions of the African Renaissance: theological (based on Ka Mana's theology of reconstruction), developmentalist (as in the politics of Thabo Mbeki), Afro-cultural (as found in the Afrocentric thought of Ama Mazama and Molefi Kete Asante), and Promethean (as in Cheikh Anta Diop's Pan-African project). See José Do Nascimento, *Les chemins de la modernité en Afrique: pour changer l'Afrique, changeons de paradigme* (Paris: L'Harmattan, 2017).
32 Ibid., 411.
33 Ibid.
34 Diop, *Black Africa*.
35 The 2018 campaign for the Italian legislature had been the occasion of a wave of racist acts (see www.lemonde.fr/europe/article/2018/02/04/italie-ce-qu-il-faut-retenir-de-l-attaque-raciste-d-un-militant-d-extreme-droite_5251632_3214.html. The quotidian nature of such racial violence, brutally exemplified by the 2018 electoral campaign, was cited systematically in the contributions of several Afro-Italian students.
36 Frantz Fanon, *Black Skin, White Masks*, trans. Richard Philcox (New York: Grove Press, 2008) p. 89.
37 Specifically, it was the seventh edition of the "voyages of African integration" (VIA), established by the organization Hidaya – a different education in Pan-Africanism – at the invitation of Victoria Ahoueli and Jean-Paul Sagadou.
38 Léopold Sédar Senghor, "Vues sur l'Afrique noire, ou assimiler, non être assimilés," in *Liberté 1: Négritude et humanisme* (Paris: Seuil, 1964) pp. 39–69.

39 Achille Mbembe, *Out of the Dark Night: Essays on Decolonization*, trans. Daniela Ginsburg (New York: Columbia University Press, 2021).
40 Aimé Césaire, "Culture and Colonization," trans. Brent Hayes Edwards, *Social Text* 28, no. 2 (103) (Summer 2010) p. 130.
41 Ibid.
42 Ibid.
43 Achille Mbembe, "Le grand débarras," *AOC*, May 2018, http://aoc.media/opinion/2018/05/02/le-grand-debarras.
44 The Congolese Constitution currently in use, for example, stipulates the exclusivity of Congolese nationality (see Article 10 of the Constitution of 2006).
45 Glissant, *Introduction to a Poetics of Diversity*, 59.

Reopening Futures

1 See Jérôme Baschet, *Défaire la tyrannie du présent: temporalités émergentes et futurs inédits* (Paris: La Découverte, 2018).
2 For example, if one works on the history of the impact of the Atlantic trade on Senegal in the eighteenth century, one must bring together the dynamics of the Atlantic world (the history of Europe, of the rivalry between European powers, of Europe's "expansion," of commerce ...) with the dynamics of the local scene ("precolonial" kingdoms, social stratification, power games ...) so one can understand how societies reacted/responded to the trade, how they were impacted by the trade – how a type of power, how forms of domination, come into being; how they organize themselves and how they reproduce themselves.
3 Such a teleological vision, for example, justified colonialism by putting in place a horizon of expectations for the colonizers, which was to civilize other nations and conquer territories.

Un/learning

1 Russell Means, "Revolution and American Indians: 'Marxism Is as Alien to My Culture as Capitalism,'" July 1980, www.filmsforaction.org/news/revolution-and-american-indians-marxism-is-as-alien-to-my-culture-as-capitalism.
2 Thomas Sankara, "Appel de Gaoua sur la qualité de l'enseignement au Burkina Faso," speech given on October 17, 1986, transcribed by Max Vernet, www.thomassankara.net/appel-de-gaoua-sur-la-qualite-de-lenseignement-au-burkina-faso-17-octobre-1986

3 Laurence Caramel, "Éducation : L'Afrique toujours dans le peloton de queue," *Le Monde*, April 9, 2015.
4 GPE Secretariat, "Motiver les investissements dans l'avenir de l'Afrique," by Victoria Egbetayo, in Blog: Éducation pour Tous, January 25, 2018.
5 The website of the Global Partnership for Education is highly revealing in this regard: photos of young girls feature prominently on the majority of its pages.
6 GPE Secretariat, "Motiver les investissements dans l'avenir de l'Afrique."
7 Paulo Freire, *La pédagogie des opprimés*, trans. Melenn Kerhoas and Élodie Dupau (Marseille: Agone, 2021) p. 16.
8 See also David Ngamassu, "Problématique des grands groupes et didactique du français au Cameroun," *Corela* 3, no. 1 (2005), http://journals.openedition.org/corela/503.
9 Frantz Fanon, *The Wretched of the Earth*, trans. Richard Philcox (New York: Grove Press, 2004) p. 235.
10 Barbara Christian, "The Race for Theory," *Cultural Critique*, no. 6 (Spring 1987): pp. 51–63.
11 Ibid., 62.
12 Rabindranath Tagore, "My School," in *Personality: Lectures Delivered in America* (London: Macmillan and Co., 1918) p. 114.
13 Ibid., 118.
14 Matthew B. Crawford, *Shop Class as Soul Craft: An Inquiry into the Value of Work* (New York: Penguin, 2009; iBooks).
15 Frantz Fanon, *Black Skin, White Masks*, trans. Richard Philcox (New York: Grove Press, 2008) p. 203.
16 Jimi O. Adésìnà, "Re-Appropriating Matrifocality/Endogeneity and African Gender Scholarship," *African Sociology Review* 14, no. 1 (2010): pp. 2–19; Oyeronke Oyewumi, *The Invention of Women: Making an African Sense of Western Gender Discourses* (Minneapolis: University of Minnesota Press, 1997).
17 Frank Leon Roberts, Black Lives Matter: Race, Resistance, and Populist Protest, Fall 2016 syllabus, the Gallatin School of Individualized Study, New York University, New York, https://blacklivesmattersyllabus.com/fall2016.
18 See www.maorimovement.co.nz/using-maori-movement; see also www.apaonline.org/page/diversity_resources, which has gathered syllabi on a variety of topics, though it remains essentially North American in orientation.
19 I have participated in these workshops since their creation.
20 See Katherine McKittrick, ed. *Sylvia Wynter: On Being Human as Praxis* (Durham, NC: Duke University Press, 2014).
21 Fanon, *Black Skin, White Masks*, 235.

The Bewitchment of History

1. Mohammed Dib, *Who Remembers the Sea*, trans. Louis Tremaine (Washington, DC: Three Continents Press, 1985) p. 47. Hereafter, this edition will be cited parenthetically in the main body of the text.
2. On this topic, see in particular the edited collection by Benjamin Stora and Mohammed Harbi. This set of essays has the merit of presenting interwoven French and Algerian perspectives on the war: Benjamin Stora and Mohammed Harbi, eds. *La Guerre d'Algérie* (Paris: Fayard, 2010).
3. Aijaz Ahmad, "Jameson's Rhetoric of Otherness and the National Allegory," *Social Text*, no. 17 (Autumn, 1987): pp. 3–25.
4. Theodor W. Adorno, "The Idea of Natural-History," trans. Robert Hullot-Kentor, in Robert Hullot-Kentor, *Things Beyond Resemblance: Collected Essays on Theodor W. Adorno* (New York: Columbia University Press, 2006).
5. Walter Benjamin, *Origin of the German Trauerspiel*, trans. Howard Eiland (Cambridge, MA: Harvard University Press, 2019).
6. Sigmund Freud, "The Uncanny," in *The Standard Edition of the Complete Psychological Works of Sigmund Freud*, Vol. XVII, trans. and ed. James Strachey (London: Hogarth, 1955).
7. Theodor W. Adorno, "Portrait of Walter Benjamin," in *Prisms*, trans. Samuel and Shierry Weber (Cambridge, MA: MIT Press, 1983) p. 233.
8. Robert Hullot-Kentor, "Introduction to Adorno's 'The Idea of Natural-History,'" in Hullot-Kentor, *Things Beyond Resemblance*, 238. The evolution of the discipline that I chart follows the account Hullot-Kentor provides in his essay.
9. According to Robert Hullot-Kentor, natural history's double postulation – where the object is first static and thus historical – is best expressed in Kantian philosophy: "Kant was the first to write a scientific history of nature as a process of unending, infinite creation … Kant was also the most significant figure, perhaps the first, to promote the formal limitation of the ambiguity of the term *natural history*. He proposed that its meaning be restricted to the investigation of nature's self-development from primitive chaos to rational order": ibid., 239.
10. Adorno follows neither model because his idea is that the interaction between history and nature is of a dialectical order, such that what matters becomes comprehending "an object as natural where it appears most historical and as historical where it appears most natural": ibid.
11. Theodor W. Adorno and Max Horkheimer, *Dialectic of Enlightenment: Philosophical Fragments*, trans. Edmund Jephcott (Stanford University Press, 2002).

12 Adorno, "The Idea of Natural-History," 264. Indeed, in "The Idea of Natural-History," Adorno introduces what will occupy the center of the *Dialectic of Enlightment*'s problematic. On this point, Irving Wohlfarth notes that discontinuity ought to be thought of "as something situated between the natural, mythical-archaic material of history, of the distant past [*le passé révolu*] and what appears dialectically new ... The philosophy of history is constantly confronted with this kind of entanglement of what existed originally and the new that is in emergence." See Irving Wohlfarth, "Entendre l'inouï: 'La Dialectique de la raison' et ses sirènes," *Tumultes*, no. 17/18 (May 2002): pp. 57–89, 84.
13 Adorno, "The Idea of Natural-History," 265.
14 As Hullot-Kentor writes in his introduction to "The Idea of Natural-History," in Adorno's text "this form of memory is conceived as the problem of perceiving transience within meaning, that is, as revealing the content of second nature. Meaning is the ruins of nature: 'When the world of convention approaches, it can be deciphered in that its meaning is shown to be precisely its transience'": Hullot-Kentor, "Introduction to Adorno's 'The Idea of Natural-History,'" 245.
15 Quoted in Adorno, "The Idea of Natural-History," 262.
16 Ibid., 264.
17 Benjamin, *Origin of the German Trauerspiel*, 174.
18 Ibid.
19 Jacques-Olivier Bégot, "Sous le signe de l'allegorie: Benjamin aux sources de la Théorie critique?" *Astérion*, no. 7 (2010), http://journals.openedition.org/asterion/1573.
20 Freud, "The Uncanny."
21 Sigmund Freud, "Beyond the Pleasure Principle," trans. and ed. James Strachey, *The Standard Edition of the Complete Psychological Works of Sigmund Freud*, Vol. XVIII (London: Hogarth, 1955).
22 Wohlfarth, "Entendre l'inouï," 84.

Currency, Sovereignty, Development

1 BCEAO [Banque centrale des États de l'Afrique de l'Ouest – Central Bank of West African States], "Chronologie des événements marquants de l'histoire de la BCEAO et de l'UEMOA," BCEAO, 2012, www.bceao.int/IMG/pdf/chronologie_des_evenements_marquants_de_l_histoire_de_la_bceao_et_ de_l_umoa.pdf.
2 Yves Ekoué Amaïzo, *Naissance d'une banque de la zone franc: 1848–1901. Priorité aux propriétaires d'esclaves* (Paris: L'Harmattan, 2001).
3 Mahir Saul, "Money in Colonial Transition: Cowries and Francs in West Africa," *American Anthropologist* 1, no. 106 (2004): pp. 71–84.

4 Ibid.
5 See Robert A. Mundell, "Money and the Sovereignty of the State," in *Monetary Theory and Policy Experience*, ed. Axel Leijonhufvud (London: Palgrave, 2001), and C. D. Zimmermann, "The Concept of Monetary Sovereignty Revisited," *European Journal of International Law* 24, no. 3 (2013): pp. 797–818.
6 Ndongo Samba Sylla, "Émerger avec le FCFA ou Émerger du FCFA?" in *Sortir l'Afrique de la servitude monétaire: à qui profite le Franc CFA?* ed. Kako Nubukpo, Bruno Tinel, Martial Ze Belinga, and Demba Moussa Dembele (Paris: La Dispute, 2016).
7 Institut Montaigne, "Prêts pour l'Afrique d'aujourd'hui?" Institut Montaigne, September 2017, www.institutmontaigne.org/ressources/pdfs/publications/prets-pour-afrique-ajourdhui-rapport.pdf.
8 William Mitchell, L. Randall Wray, and Martin Watts, *Modern Monetary Theory and Practice: An Introductory Text* (Callaghan: Center of Full Employment and Equity, 2016).
9 Jeffrey A. Frankel. "No Single Currency Regime Is Right for All Countries or at All Times," NBER Working Paper no. 7338 (Cambridge, MA: National Bureau of Economic Research, 1999).
10 Bruno Tinel, "Le fonctionnement et le rôle des comptes d'opérations entre la France et les pays africains," in *Sortir l'Afrique de la servitude monétaire*, ed. Nubukpo et al. (Paris: La Dispute, 2016).
11 Idris Linge, "Standard & Poor's livre son point de vue sur le Franc CFA, ses éléments positifs et négatifs, au-delà de son impopularité," Agence Ecofin, December 9, 2017, www.agenceecofin.com/gouvernance/0912-52757-standard-poors-livre-son-point-de-vue-sur-le-franc-cfa-ses-elements-positifs-et-negatifs-au-dela-de-son-impopularite.
12 United Nations Development Program, *Human Development Report 2016: Human Development for Everyone* (New York: UNDP, 2016).
13 United Nations Conference on Trade and Development, *State of Commodity Dependence 2016* (New York: United Nations, 2017).
14 The African Development Bank Group, the African Unity Commission, and the United Nations Economic Commission for Africa, *African Statistical Yearbook: 2009*, p. 68, https://www.afdb.org/fileadmin/uploads/afdb/Documents/Publications/African_Statistical_Yearbook_2016.pdf
15 Steve Keen, *Debunking Economics: The Naked Emperor Dethroned?* Revised and expanded edn. (London: Zed Books, 2011); L. Randall Wray, *Why Minsky Matters: An Introduction to the Work of a Maverick Economist* (Princeton University Press, 2016); and Ann Pettifor, *The Production of Money: How to Break the Power of Bankers* (London: Verso, 2017).
16 On the last two aspects, see Sylla, "Émerger avec le FCFA ou Émerger du FCFA?"
17 Soumaila Doumbia, "Surliquidité bancaire et sous-financement de

l'économie. Une analyse du paradoxe de l'UEMOA," *Revue Tiers Monde*, no. 205 (2011): pp. 151–70.
18 See the statistical series produced by the Bank of France.
19 Bank of France, "Rapport annuel de la zone franc," Banque de France, January 2, 2009, pp. 82–3, www.banque-france.fr/sites/default/files/medias/documents/zone-franc-rapport-annuel_2009.pdf.
20 Ibid.
21 Samuel Diop, "L'évolution du système bancaire en zone franc," *Techniques financières et développement* 4, no. 121 (2015): pp. 59–69.
22 BCEAO, "États financiers de la BCEAO au 31 décembre 2016," BCEAO, April 5, 2017, p. 49, www.bceao.int/IMG/pdf/bceao_-_etats_financiers_ au_31-12-2016_vf_sans_couleur_.pdf.
23 See the statistical series produced by the Bank of France.
24 See, for example, S. Edwards and E. L. Yeyati, "Flexible Exchange Rates as Shock Absorbers," NBER Working Paper no. 9867 (Cambridge, MA: National Bureau of Economic Research, October, 2003).
25 Ibid.
26 "Francophone Africa's CFA Is under Fire," *The Economist*, January 27, 2018, www.economist.com/news/middle-east-and-africa/21735636-some-credit-french-backed-common-currency-fostering-stability-others.
27 Samir Amin, *L'éveil du Sud: l'ère de Bandoung, 1955–1980. Panorama politique et personnel de l'époque* (Paris: Le Temps des cerises, 2008) pp. 181ff.
28 Institut Montaigne, "Prêts pour l'Afrique d'aujourd'hui?" 96.
29 Ndongo Samba Sylla, "Quelle intégration monétaire post-FCFA au service de la souveraineté démocratique et de la solidarité panafricaine?" Paper presented at "Samedis de l'économie," organized by ARCADE and the Rosa Luxemburg Foundation, Espace Harmattan, Dakar, Senegal, December 16, 2017.
30 "Nigeria Wants Single Currency for ECOWAS Slowed Down," *Premium Times*, October 25, 2017, www.premiumtimesng.com/news/headlines/247135-nigeria-wants-single-currency-ecowas-slowed.html.
31 Julius Agbor, "The future of the CEMAC CFA Franc" (Washington, DC: The Brookings Institution, 2012).
32 Miguel Abensour, "Du bon usage de l'hypothèse de la servitude volontaire?" *Réfractions*, no. 17 (2006): pp. 65–84.
33 Joseph Ki-Zerbo, *À quand l'Afrique? Entretien avec René Holenstein* (Lausanne: Éditions d'en bas, 2013) p. 184.

Memories of the World, Memory-World

1 [Translator's note] The usual French translation of the English expression "to make sense" is "avoir un sens" – literally, "to have

a sense." "Faire sens" is sometimes heard in French, though it is considered an Anglicism. This trace of the other language should be kept in mind when reading this article. "Faire sens" not only echoes other key expressions like "faire monde" ("to make world") and "faire mémoire" ("to make memory"), it dramatizes the subtle difference between already *having* a sense and *making* one, with all the risks this implies for idiom and comprehension. To capture some of this distinction in English, "faire sens" is translated at times with "to make sense" and at others with the willfully non-idiomatic expression "to make meaning."

2 See Séverine Kodjo-Grandvaux, "Esteem for Self: Creating One's Own Sense / Carving Out One's Own Path," trans. Drew Burk, in *To Write the Africa World*, ed. Achille Mbembe and Felwine Sarr (Cambridge: Polity, 2022).
3 Paul Ricœur, *Memory, History, Forgetting*, trans. Kathleen Blamey and David Pellauer (University of Chicago Press, 2004) p. 79.
4 Ibid., 89.
5 François Jullien, *From Being to Living: A Euro-Chinese Lexicon of Thought*, trans. Michael Richardson and Krzysztof Fijalkowski (London: Sage, 2020) Google Play Books.
6 Emanuele Coccia, *The Life of Plants: A Metaphysics of Mixture*, trans. Dylan J. Montanari (Cambridge: Polity, 2019) p. 89.
7 Trinh Xuan Thuan, *Face à l'univers* (Paris: Autrement, 2015) p. 35.
8 Coccia, *The Life of Plants*, 38.
9 Ibid., 43.
10 Valérie Cabanes, *Homo natura: en harmonie avec le vivant* (Paris: Buchet/Chastel, 2017) p. 17.
11 Eduardo Kohn, *How Forests Think: Towards an Anthropology beyond the Human* (Berkeley: University of California Press, 2013) p. 17.
12 Felwine Sarr, *Afrotopia*, trans. Drew S. Burk and Sarah Jones-Boardman (Minneapolis: University of Minnesota Press, 2019) Google Play Books.
13 Souleymane Bachir Diagne, *Postcolonial Bergson*, trans. Lindsay Turner (New York: Fordham University Press, 2019) p. 45.
14 Souleymane Bachir Diagne, *African Art as Philosophy: Senghor, Bergson and the Idea of Negritude*, trans. Chike Jeffers (New York: Seagull Books, 2011) p. 161.
15 Pierre Teilhard de Chardin, *Human Energy*, trans. J. M. Cohen (New York: Harcourt Brace Jovanovich, 1971) p. 31.
16 François Jullien, *Une seconde vie* (Paris: Grasset, 2017) p. 150.
17 Éric Letonturier, "Utopies du cercle, panopties du eseau. Formes et topologies sociales de la communication," *Quaderni*, no. 30 (1996): pp. 23–39.
18 Søren Kierkegaard, *Repetition and Philosophical Crumbs*, trans. M. G. Piety (New York: Oxford University Press, 2009) p. 4.

19 Ibid., 76.
20 Ibid.
21 Bonaventure Mve-Ondo, À chacun sa raison: raison occidentale et raison africaine (Paris: L'Harmattan, 2013) p. 80.
22 Jullien, Une seconde vie, 23.
23 Ibid., 184.
24 Ibid.
25 Diagne, Postcolonial Bergson, 14.
26 Ibid., 13.
27 Léopold Sédar Senghor, Liberté 1: Négritude et humanisme (Paris: Seuil, 1964) p. 209.
28 See Iain Hamilton Grant, "Everything Is Primal Germ or Nothing Is: The Deep Field Logic of Nature," Symposium: Canadian Journal of Continental Philosophy 19, no. 1 (2016): pp. 106–24.
29 Philippe Descola, Beyond Nature and Culture, trans. Janet Lloyd (University of Chicago Press, 2013) p. 61.
30 Diagne, African Art as Philosophy, 101.
31 Ibid., 129.
32 Diagne, Postcolonial Bergson, 26.
33 Senghor, Liberté 1, 35.
34 Ibid., 211.

Cum patior Africa

1 Richard Dowden, Africa: Altered States, Ordinary Miracles (London: Portobello Books, 2008).
2 Michel Foucault, "The Political Technology of Individuals," in Technologies of the Self: A Seminar with Michel Foucault, ed. Luther H. Martin, Huck Gutman, and Patrick H. Hutton (Amherst: University of Massachusetts Press, 1988) pp. 145–62.
3 On these questions, see Michel Foucault, An Introduction, Vol. I of The History of Sexuality, trans. Robert Hurley (New York: Vintage, 1990), further developed in Foucault's lectures starting in 1976: "Society Must Be Defended": Lectures at the Collège de France, 1975–76, trans. David Macey (New York: Picador, 2003) pp. 239–63, and Security, Territory, Population: Lectures at the Collège de France, 1977–1978, trans. Graham Burchell (New York: Palgrave, 2009) pp. 1–27.
4 See the updated discussion that Philippe Büttgen provides in "Théologie politique et pouvoir pastoral," Annales. Histoire, Sciences Sociales 62, no. 5 (2007): pp. 1129–54.
5 See Pascale Laborier and Pierre Lascoumes, "L'action publique comprise comme gouvernementalisation de l'État," in Travailler avec Foucault: retours sur le politique, ed. Sylvain Meyet, Marie-Cécile Naves, and Thomas Ribémont (Paris: L'Harmattan, 2005) p. 37.

6 This expression is borrowed from Sandra Laugier's book *La voix et la vertu: variétés du perfectionnisme moral* (Paris: Presses universitaires de France, 2010).
7 Joan Tronto, *Moral Boundaries: A Political Argument for an Ethic of Care* (New York: Routledge, 1993) p. 122.
8 Laurent Thévenot, "Le régime de familiarité: des choses en personne," *Genèses* 17 (September 1994): pp. 72–101.
9 [Translator's note] The French adjective "proche" (near, close, proximate) is etymologically related to the noun "prochain" (fellow human, neighbor, brother). A similar relationship exists between the English noun "neighbor" and the adjective "nigh" (near, proximate, close). I have chosen the somewhat affected translation "regime of the nigh" over alternatives like "regime of the proximate" to emphasize such etymological resonances and to catch the echo of Leviticus 19:18, "Tu aimeras ton prochain comme toi-même" (Thou shalt love thy neighbor as thyself).
10 From one year to the next, the Dakar Workshops of Thought have taken emotions as their starting premise. Such emotional inflation is readily legible in contributions that invoke "melancholia," "anger," "goodwill," "shame," "self-esteem," "laetitia africana," etc. – often in a quasi-incantatory manner.
11 Practically speaking, we acknowledge the evolution of Léopold Sédar Senghor's provocative proposition: "Emotion is negro [*nègre*], just as reason is Hellenic [*hellène*] ... The very nature of emotion, of the Negro's sensibility, explains their attitude before the object, which is perceived with such an essential violence. It is an abandonment that becomes a need, an active attitude of communion, even of identification, should the action (I was going to say personality) of the object be strong enough. A rhythmic attitude. Let us hold on to that word": Léopold Sédar Senghor, "Ce que l'homme noir apporte" [1939], in *Liberté 1: Négritude et humanisme* (Paris: Seuil, 1964) p. 24. We also recall the clarification that the philosopher provided in the October 1956 issue of *Diogène*, where he maintained that "European reason is analytic through utilization, Black reason intuitive through participation."
12 Philippe Corcuff, "De la thématique du 'lien social' à l'expérience de la compassion: variété des liaisons et déliaisons sociales," *Pensée plurielle* 9, no. 1 (2005): pp. 119–29, 127.
13 Ibid., 128.
14 If Emmanuel Levinas did not explicitly use the term "compassion," he is nonetheless one of the most insightful theoreticians of compassionate action [*l'agir compassionnel*]. He extracted the virtue of recognizing suffering from the space of religious transcendence and made it a reasoned act and a philosophical category. See Emmanuel Levinas, *Entre Nous: On Thinking-of-the-Other*, trans. Michael B.

Smith and Barbara Harshav (New York: Columbia University Press, 1998) p. 93.
15 Like love, the virtue of compassion can be regarded as a competence according to what Luc Boltanski proposes in *L'Amour et la Justice comme compétences: trois essais de la sociologie de l'action* (Paris: Métalie, 1990).
16 Levinas, *Entre Nous*, 93.
17 See Robert Soloman, *In Defense of Sentimentality* (London: Oxford University Press, 2004) p. 43.
18 See Chistophe Traïni, "Registres émotionnels et processus politiques," *Raisons politiques*, no. 65 (2017): pp. 15–29.
19 Monique Canto-Sperber, *La morale du monde* (Paris: Presses universitaires de France, 2010).
20 The notion of historicity (and not simply of temporality) indicates the stakes of time and structures the objectification of the past (or its "experience," to use François Hartog's term). Hartog uses the expression "regime of historicity" to designate "a scholarly way of formulating the experience of time that, in its turn, provides a model for how we talk about and live our own time ... A regime of historicity opens up and circumscribes a domain of work and thought ... It gives rhythm to the writing of time, represents an order of time to which one might subscribe or, by contrast (and more frequently), from which one might want to escape, by attempting to elaborate another regime": François Hartog, "Temps et histoire. 'Comment écrire l'histoire de France,'" *Annales. Histoire, Sciences Sociales* 50, no. 6 (1995): pp. 1219–36, 1220. See also François Hartog, *Regimes of Historicity: Presentism and Experiences of Time*, trans. Saskia Brown (New York: Columbia University Press, 2015), and Reinhart Kosellek, *Futures Past: On the Semantics of Historical Time*, trans. Keith Tribe (New York: Columbia University Press, 2004).
21 Michel Serres and Bruno Latour, *Conversations on Science, Culture, and Time*, trans. Roxanne Lapidus (Ann Arbor: University of Michigan Press, 1995) p. 58.
22 Ibid., 60.
23 See Hartog, *Regimes of Historicity*.
24 Corcuff, "De la thématique du 'lien social' à l'expérience de la compassion," 128.
25 See, in particular, Luc Boltanski and Laurent Thévenot, *De la justification* (Paris: Gallimard, 1991), and Claudette Lafaye and Laurent Thévenot, "Une justification écologique? Conflits dans l'aménagement de la nature," *Revue française de sociologie* 34, no. 4 (1993): pp. 495–524.
26 Rudyard Kipling, "The White Man's Burden," in *The Cambridge Edition of the Poems of Rudyard Kipling: Collected Poems I*, ed. Thomas Pinney, Vol. I of 3 (Cambridge University Press, 2013) p. 528.

27 Paul Coulon, "Le fardeau de l'Homme blanc: *The White Man's Burden*," *Histoire et missions chrétiennes* 21, no. 1 (2012): pp. 3–4, 4.
28 Jules Ferry, "Les fondements de la politique coloniale," speech at the Assemblée nationale, July 28, 1885, www2.assemblee-nationale.fr/decouvrir-l-assemblee/histoire/grands-discours-parlementaires/jules-ferry-28-juillet-1885.
29 Ibid.
30 Such was the case with Georges Clemenceau, who said: "Look at the history of the conquest of the peoples that you call barbarian and you will see violence, rampant crime, oppression, blood flowing in waves – the weak laid low, tyrannized by the conqueror! ... How many atrocious, terrifying crimes have been perpetrated in the name of justice and of civilization. I do not understand why all of us here did not rise up in unison in forceful protest against your words." Quoted in Marc Fayad, "Jules Ferry, un athée qui se croyait de 'race supérieure,'" *Le Point*, March 17, 2014, www.lepoint.fr/histoire/ferry-jules-1832-1893-22-08-2013-1716224_1615.php.
31 See Bouda Etemad, *L'héritage ambigu de la colonisation: économies, populations, sociétés* (Paris: Armand Colin, 2012).
32 This argument is contested by Élise Huillery who, studying reconstituted financial flows between France and the colonies, established that "the gross budgetary flows from France to the colonies were meager: 1.3 billion 1914 francs over the course of fifty years – that is, 2.6% of France's GDP in 1914, military spending not included. After, it was essentially a matter of loans, most of which were repaid: over the same period French West Africa (AOF) transferred 572 million 1914 francs to France. The net amount of transfers from France to the AOF thus rose to 732 million over fifty years – that is, less than 0.1% of annual French GDP over the period. The AOF thus did not cost the French taxpayer much. Nor did it live principally by France's financial support. Net goods transferred from France represented roughly 6% of the annual budget of the AOF." See Élise Huillery, "Histoire coloniale: développement et inégalités dans l'ancienne Afrique Occidentale Française" (Ph.D. diss., École des Hautes Études en Sciences Sociales, 2008). See also Olivier Le Cour Grandmaison, *Coloniser, exterminer: sur la guerre et l'État colonial* (Paris: Fayard, 2005); Marc Ferro, ed. *Le livre noir du colonialisme* (Paris: Robert Laffont, 2003); or Henri Brunschwig's older work, *French Colonialism 1871–1914: Myths and Realities*, trans. William Granville Brown (New York: Praeger, 1964).
33 See Jacques Marseille, *Empire colonial et capitalisme français: histoire d'un divorce* (Paris: Albin Michel, 1964). Marseille's student, the historian of French colonization Daniel Lefeuvre, claims that colonization was a "barrel of the Danaïdes"; France was ruined in Algeria. Cf. Daniel Lefeuvre, *Pour en finir avec la repentance coloniale* (Paris: Flammarion, 2008). This polemical thesis has been widely contested.

34 Paul Bairoch, *Third World at an Impasse*, trans. Don Fillinger (New York: Prentice Hall, 1996). Bairoch's thesis strangely recalls the position of Levinas, who claimed that decolonization and de-westernization would produce disorientation. See Emmanuel Levinas, *Humanism of the Other*, trans. Richard A. Cohen (Chicago: University of Illinois Press, 2006).
35 Law no. 2005-158 of February 23, 2005: recognizing France's contribution to its overseas colonies and departments and providing compensation for repatriated French citizens. Article 4 concerning the beneficial effects of colonization was eventually amended.
36 Put in circulation on April 25, 2005, the petition "Colonisation: non à l'enseignment d'une histoire officielle" received the signatures of more than 11,000 teachers.
37 See Olivier Charnoz and Jean-Michel Severino, *L'aide publique au développement* (Paris: La Découverte, 2015) pp. 40–1, and William Easterly, *The White Man's Burden: Why the West's Efforts to Aid the Rest Have Done So Much Ill and So Little Good* (New York: Penguin, 2006).
38 Béatrice Hibou, *The Political Economy of the World Bank's Discourse: From Economic Catechism to Missionary Deeds (and Misdeeds)*, trans. Janet Roitman, Les Études du CERI, no. 39 (Paris: Sciences Po, January 2000), www.sciencespo.fr/ceri/sites/sciencespo.fr.ceri/files/etude39a.pdf.
39 Ibid.
40 Ibid.
41 Michel Griffon, "Les défis de l'aide au développement," *Revue Projet* 338, no. 1 (2014): pp. 54–61, 55–6.
42 See *Honest Accounts? The True Story of Africa's Billion Dollar Losses*, Curtis Research, July 2014, https://curtisresearch.org/wp-content/uploads/Honest-Accounts-report-v4-web.pdf.
43 See Roger C. Riddell, "Does Foreign Aid Work?" in *Doing Good or Doing Better: Development Policies in a Globalising World*, ed. Monique Kremer, Peter van Lieshout, and Robert Went (Amsterdam University Press, 2009) pp. 47–9; Peter van Lieshout, Robert Went, and Monique Kremer, "The Development Aid Split," in *Less Pretension, More Ambition? Development Policy in Times of Globalization* (Amsterdam University Press, 2010).
44 Gilles Carbonnier, "L'aide au développement une fois de plus sous le feu de la critique," *Revue internationale de politique de développement* 1 (2010): pp. 141–7, 142.
45 See Julien Meimon, *L'invention de l'aide française au développement: discours, instruments et pratiques d'une dynamique hégémonique*, Questions de recherche / Research in Question, no. 21 (Paris: Centre d'études et de recherches internationales, 2007).
46 See Teresa Hayter, *Aid as Imperialism* (Harmondsworth: Penguin, 1971), and Dambisa Moyo, *Dead Aid: Why Aid Is Not Working and*

How There Is a Better Way for Africa (New York: Farrar, Straus, and Giroux, 2009).

47 Lael Brainard, ed. *Security by Other Means: Foreign Assistance, Global Poverty, and American Leadership* (Washington, DC: Brookings Institution Press, 2006).
48 Easterly, *The White Man's Burden*. See also Céline Monga, *Nihilisme et négritude: les arts de vivre en Afrique* (Paris: Presses universitaires de France, 2009) and Stephen Browne, *Aid and Influence: Do Donors Help or Hinder?* (London: Earthscan Publications, 2006).
49 Rony Brauman, *L'action humanitaire* (Paris: Flammarion, 1995) p. 9.
50 Philippe Ryfman, *La question humanitaire: histoire, problématiques, acteurs et enjeux de l'aide humanitaire internationale* (Paris: Ellipses, 1999) p. 17.
51 See Thomas Aquinas, "Charity," trans. R. J. Batten OP, in *Summa Theologiæ*, Vol. XXXIV (Cambridge University Press, 2006); Jean Guillermand, "Les fondements historiques de la démarche humanitaire, le courant religieux," *International Review of the Red Cross* 76, no. 806 (April 1994): pp. 216–37; Yadh Ben Achour, "Islam et droit international humanitaire," *International Review of the Red Cross* 62, no. 772 (April 1980): pp. 56–69.
52 Pierre de Senarclens, *L'humanitaire en catastrophe* (Paris: Presses de Sciences Po, 1999) p. 29.
53 Mary B. Anderson, "'You Save My Life Today, But for What Tomorrow?' Some Moral Dilemmas of Humanitarian Aid," in *Hard Choices: Moral Dilemmas in Humanitarian Intervention*, ed. Jonathan Moore (Lanham: Rowman & Littlefield, 1998) p. 150.
54 "Thus, when you give alms, sound no trumpet before you, as the hypocrites do in the synagogues and in the streets, that they may be praised by men.... But when you give alms, do not let your left hand know what your right hand is doing, so that your alms may be in secret; and your Father who sees in secret will reward you": Matt. 6:2–4 (Revised Standard Version). In a secular philosophical version, Paul Audi praises Nietzsche's muted and modest application of compassionate sentiment: "It is necessary to be it without saying it, without glorifying it, and, above all, to do so while keeping distant from the suffering that one shares." Quoted in Paul Audi, *L'empire de la compassion* (Paris: Éditions Les belles lettres, 2011) p. 187.
55 See Rony Brauman, *Penser dans l'urgence: parcours critique d'un humanitaire* (Paris: Seuil, 2006).
56 Rony Brauman, "Les dilemmes de l'action humanitaire dans les camps de réfugiés et les transferts de populations," in *Des choix difficiles*, trans. Dominique Leveillé, ed. Jonathan Moore (Paris: Gallimard, 1999) p. 251. [Translator's note] This particular passage from Brauman's contribution does not appear in the English version of Moore's volume, published by Rowman & Littlefield in 1998.

57 Michel Leroy and Le Club de l'Horloge, *L'Occident sans complexes* (Paris: Carrère-Vertiges, 1987).
58 Lefeuvre, *Pour en finir avec la repentance coloniale*, 157.
59 Lefeuvre, 157.
60 Guillaume Erner, "Compassion et société des victimes," *Le Journal des Psychologues* 249, no. 6 (2007): pp. 45–6.
61 Achille Mbembe, "African Modes of Self-Writing," trans. Steven Rendall, *Public Culture* 14, no. 1 (Winter 2002): pp. 239–73, 241; translation slightly modified.
62 Ibid., pp. 241–2.
63 Jacques Rancière, *Disagreement: Politics and Philosophy*, trans. Julie Rose (Minneapolis: University of Minnesota Press, 1999) p. 13.
64 Law no. 2001-434 of May 21, 2005, still known as the "Taubira law."
65 World Conference Against Racism, Racial Discrimination, Xenophobia and Related Intolerance, *Declaration and Programme of Action* (New York: United Nations, 2002) p. 15. Available online at www.ohchr.org/Documents/Publications/Durban_text_en.pdf.
66 Ibid., 13–14.
67 Ibid., 89.
68 The United Nations, "Les états expriment leur position sur la question de réparation," press release no. DR/D/933, September 4, 2001, www.un.org/press/fr/2001/DRD933.doc.htm.
69 Enoch P. Kavindele, "Statement to the World Conference Against Racism, Racial Discrimination, Xenophobia and Related Intolerance," September 2, 2001, Durban, South Africa, transcript, www.un.org/WCAR/statements/zambE.htm.
70 Jamaica's ambassador suggests that "the international community could proceed by way of two forms of action. First, there should be an acknowledgement that slavery and the transatlantic slave trade was a crime against humanity. This would constitute an acceptable gesture in relation to the historical and ethical issue – an open and strong condemnation of the grave injustice and violation of the rights of the people of Africa. It would set the record straight in the context of universally accepted principles and provide a common judgment on a historical phenomenon of fundamental importance in shaping the modern world. In the second place, there should be economic measures in the form of policies and programmes at the international level that seek to remedy the negative consequences of the historic injustice – the destabilisation and underdevelopment of Africa and the degradation and psychic damage of the people of the Diaspora. What is important now is for the world community to accept the principle of equity compensating policies which can be applied to improve the development prospects of affected countries. Within this framework, a number of the possible initiatives could be more specifically identified, whether in the form of debt relief, resettlement grants, or programmes

for the development of human resources. This conference could take these important steps now, clearing a major hurdle and laying the basis in the long term for better understanding, goodwill and co-operation": Stafford Neil, "Statement to the World Conference Against Racism, Racial Discrimination, Xenophobia and Related Intolerance," September 2, 2001, Durban, South Africa, transcript, www.un.org/WCAR/statements/jamaE.htm.
71 United Nations, "Les états expriment leur position sur la question de réparation."
72 Ibid.
73 The United Nations, "Acknowledgement of the Past, Compensation Urged by Many Leaders in Continuing Debate at Racism Conference," press release no. RD/D/24, September 2, 2001, www.un.org/WCAR/pressreleases/rd-d24.html.
74 United Nations, "Les états expriment leur position sur la question de réparation."
75 Ibid.
76 Bernard Hours, "L'action humanitaire: thérapie et/ou idéologie de la globalisation?" *Sud/Nord* 17, no. 2 (2002): pp. 9–17, 9.
77 Myriam Revault d'Allonnes, *L'homme compassionnel* (Paris: Seuil, 2008).
78 Orwin shows that compassion is an object of struggle between the American left, which claims to hold a monopoly on it, and neoconservatives, who are desperately trying to take it for themselves. See Clifford Orwin, "Moist Eyes – From Rousseau to Clinton," *Public Interest* (Summer 1997): pp. 3–20, 20. In Canada, too, left and right make exclusive claims to authentic compassion, accusing their opponents of exhibiting a false compassion with devastating consequences. This struggle is analyzed by Roger Scruton in "Totalitarian Sentimentality," *American Spectator*, December 9, 2009 (https://spectator.org/40477_totalitarian-sentimentality). See also Kathleen Woodward, "Calculating Compassion," in *Compassion: The Politics and Culture of an Emotion*, ed. Lauren Berlant (New York: Routledge, 2004).
79 Sandra Laugier, "L'éthique du *care* en trois subversions," *Multitudes* 42, no. 3 (2010): pp. 112–25, 112.
80 [Translator's note] The paragraph containing the notion of a "liturgical construction" does not appear in Steven Rendall's English translation of Mbembe's "À propos des écritures africaines de soi." What follows is an English translation of the relevant passage in the French version: "It is thus by virtue of being psalmodized that a set of pious dogmas and empty dreams ended up imposing themselves upon common sense, to the point of being taken for *the* African discourse in general from that moment on. The central object of this discourse is identity in its double dimension, at once political and cultural.

Essentially, modern African inquiries into the facts of identity [*faits d'identité*] belong to liturgical construction and incantation rather than to historical criticism. These facts of identity are liturgical constructions to the degree that the discourse said to account for them boils down to three propositions repeated so incessantly that they become inaudible": Achille Mbembe, "À propos des écritures africaines de soi," *Politique Africaine* 77, no. 1 (2000): pp. 16–43, 17.

81 See, especially, Michel Foucault, "The Meshes of Power," trans. Gerald Moore, in *Space, Knowledge and Power: Foucault and Geography*, ed. Stuart Elden and Jeremy W. Crampton (London: Routledge, 2007) pp. 153–62; "The Subject and Power," in *The Essential Works of Foucault 1954–1984: Power*, trans. Robert Hurley et al., ed. James D. Faubion (London: Penguin, 2002) pp. 326–48; "The Ethics of the Concern of the Self as a Practice of Freedom," in *The Essential Works of Foucault 1954–1984: Ethics: Subjectivity and Truth*, trans. Robert Hurley et al., ed. Paul Rabinow (London: Penguin, 2000) pp. 281–301; and *The Care of the Self*, Vol. III of *The History of Sexuality*, trans. Robert Hurley (London: Penguin, 1990).

82 Alain Ehrenberg, "Épistémologie, sociologie, santé publique: tentative de clarification," *Mouvements* 49, no. 1 (2007): pp. 89–97, 92.

83 Ibid., 93.

84 Foucault, *The History of Sexuality*, Vol. III, 68.

85 Michel Foucault, *The Use of Pleasure*, Vol. II of *The History of Sexuality*, trans. Robert Hurley (New York: Vintage, 1990) pp. 10–11.

86 Foucault, *The History of Sexuality*, vol. III, 62. See also Foucault, "The Ethics of the Concern of the Self as a Practice of Freedom."

87 Berenice Fisher and Joan Tronto, "Toward a Feminist Theory of Care," in *Circles of Care: Work and Identity in Women's Lives*, ed. Emily K. Abel and Margaret K. Nelson (Albany: State University of New York Press, 1990) p. 40.

88 The term was first employed during the First Pan-African Conference of 1900.

89 Organisation internationale de la Francophonie, *Le mouvement panafricaniste au XXe siècle* (Paris: Organisation internationale de la Francophonie, 2013) p. 16.

90 Hervé Cheuzeville, "John Chilembwe, précurseur de l'Église et du nationalisme africains," Echos d'Afrique.com, May 28, 2011, www.echosdafrique.com/20110528-john-chilembwe-precurseur-de-l'eglise-et-du-nationalisme-africains.

91 Nnamdi Azikiwe, *Zik: A Selection from the Speeches of Nnamdi Azikiwe* (Cambridge University Press, 1961).

92 Kwame Nkrumah, *I Speak of Freedom: A Statement of African Ideology* (London: Heinemann, 1961).

93 Léopold Sédar Senghor, "À l'appel de la race de Saba," in *Hosties noires* (Paris: Seuil, 1948).

94 Léopold Sédar Senghor, "On the Appeal from the Race of Sheba," in *Prose and Poetry*, trans. John Reed and Clive Wake (London: Oxford University Press, 1965) p. 125.
95 UN General Assembly, 39th Session, 20th Plenary Meeting, UN doc. A/39/PV.20 (October 4, 1984), available at undocs.org/en/A/39/PV.20. In this intervention, Sankara borrows the title of the British missionary Joseph Booth's 1896 work *Africa for the African*, in which Booth recommends the return of African Americans to their continent of origin.
96 Nkrumah, *I Speak of Freedom*, xi–xiv.
97 Ibid., xiv.
98 Ibid.
99 Aimé Césaire, *Resolutely Black: Conversations with Françoise Vergès*, trans. Matthew B. Smith (Cambridge: Polity, 2020) p. 17.
100 Ibid., 17–18.
101 Ibid., 19.
102 See, especially, Mary R. Lefkowitz, *Not out of Africa: How Afro-Centrism Became an Excuse to Teach Myth as History* (New York: Basic Books, 1996); Molefi Kete Asante, *The Afrocentric Idea*, new edn. (Philadelphia: Temple University Press, 1998); Stephen Howe, *Afrocentrism: Mythical Past and Imagined Homes* (London: Verso, 1998); and Jean-Pierre Chrétien, François-Xavier Fauvelle-Aymar, and Claude-Hélène Perrot, eds. *Afrocentrismes: l'histoire des Africains entre Égypte et Amérique* (Paris: Karthala, 2000).
103 "Hopeless Africa," *The Economist*, May 13, 2000, www.economist.com/leaders/2000/05/11/hopeless-africa.
104 "Macky Sall: 'Je suis un afro-optimiste. Je souhaite que l'Afrique soit respectée,'" RFI, November 28, 2016, radio broadcast, available at www.rfi.fr/emission/20161128-senegal-sall-je-suis-afro-optimiste-je-souhaite-afrique-soit-respectee-elle-est.
105 Luc Boltanski and Ève Chiapello, *Le nouvel esprit du capitalisme*, new edn. (Paris: Gallimard, 2011) p. 437.
106 Aristotle speaks of a duty of solidarity between men for the sake of the virtue of generosity – which must be exhibited under certain circumstances (in accordance with the recipient's merit) – and for the sake of the virtue of friendship, which is not to be confused with philanthropy (see *Nicomachean Ethics*). The existence of a shared humanity has been developed in a notable fashion by Souleymane Bachir Diagne in "Faire humanité ensemble et ensemble habiter la terre," *Présence Africaine*, vol. 193, no. 1 (2016): pp. 11–19.
107 Adam Smith. *The Theory of Moral Sentiments* (London: Penguin, 2009) p. 13.
108 Ibid., 159.
109 Fisher and Tronto, "Toward a Feminist Theory of Care," 40. See also Carol Gilligan, "Le *care*, éthique féminine ou éthique féministe?"

Multitudes 37-8, no. 2-3 (2009): pp. 76-8. For a more sustained discussion, see Carol Gilligan, *In a Different Voice: Psychological Theory and Women's Development* (Cambridge, MA: Harvard University Press, 1982).
110 Joan Tronto, *Moral Boundaries: A Political Argument for an Ethic of Care* (London: Routledge, 1993) p. 122.
111 Foucault, "The Political Technology of Individuals," 145-62.
112 Didier Fassin, "Entre politiques de la vie et politiques du vivant: pour une anthropologie de la santé," *Anthropologie et Sociétés* 24, no. 1 (2000): pp. 95-116.
113 Agata Zielinski, "L'éthique du *care*: une nouvelle façon de prendre soin," *Études* 413, no. 12 (2010): pp. 631-41, 631-2.
114 Laugier, "L'éthique du *care* en trois subversions,"14.
115 Corcuff, "De la thématique du 'lien social' à l'expérience de la compassion," 122.
116 See Paul Audi, *L'empire de la compassion* (Paris: Encre marine, 2011).

The Sahara

1 Basil Davidson, *The Africans: An Entry to Cultural History* (London: Longmans, 1969) p. 211.
2 Maryse Condé, *The Children of Segu*, trans. Linda Coverdale (New York: Ballantine, 1990) p. 12.
3 Ibid., 25.
4 Ibid., 117.
5 Maryse Condé, *Segu*, trans. Barbara Bray (New York: Viking, 1987) p. 22.
6 Ibid., 45.
7 Amadou Hampâté Bâ, *Amkoullel, the Fula Boy*, trans. Jeanne Garane (Durham, NC: Duke University Press, 2021) Google Play Books.
8 Ibid.
9 Tayeb Salih, *Season of Migration to the North*, trans. Denys Johnson-Davies (London: Heinemann, 1969) p. 38.
10 Ousmane Socé, *Contes et légendes d'Afrique noire* (Paris: Nouvelles Éditions latines, 1962) p. 58.
11 Birago Diop, "Désert," *Éthiopiques*, no. 66-7 (2001): p. 1.
12 Condé, *Segu*, 45.
13 Ayi Kwei Armah, *Two Thousand Seasons* (London: Heinemann, 1979) p. 3 (italics added).
14 Ibid., 33.
15 Ibid., 29.
16 Ibid.
17 Yambo Ouologuem, *Bound to Violence*, trans. Ralph Manheim (New York: Harcourt Brace Jovanovich, 1971) p. 7.

18 Ibid., 18.
19 Ibid.
20 Condé, *Segu*, 44.
21 Ibid.
22 Alpha Mandé Diarra, *Sahel! Sanglante sécheresse* (Paris: Présence africaine, 1981) p. 12.
23 Condé, *Segu*, 44.
24 Williams Sassine, *Le jeune homme de sable* (Paris: Présence africaine, 1979) p. 40.
25 Cheikh C. Sow, *Cycle de sécheresse* (Paris: Hatier, 2002) p. 5.
26 Kateb Yacine, *L'œuvre en fragments* (Paris: Sindbad, 1986) p. 208.
27 Mohammed Dib, *Le désert sans détour* (Paris: Sindbad, 1992) p. 72.
28 René Dumont, *Pour l'Afrique, j'accuse* (Paris: Plon, 1986) p. 30.
29 Ibid.
30 Ibrahima Baba Kaké, *Combats pour l'histoire africaine* (Paris: Présence africaine, 1982) p. 175.
31 Boubou Hama, *L'empire songhay, ses ethnies, ses légendes, et ses personnages historiques* (Paris: Oswald, 1974) p. 9.
32 Elikia M'Bokolo, *L'Afrique au XXe siècle: le continent convoité* (Paris: Études vivantes, 1980) p. 84.
33 Sassine, *Le jeune homme de sable*, 41.
34 Rachid Boudjedra, *Cinq fragments du désert* ([2001] Arles: Actes Sud, 2007) p. 28.
35 Ibid., 21.
36 Dumont, *Pour l'Afrique*, 286.
37 Boudjedra, *Cinq fragments du désert*, 40.

Migrations, Narrations, the Refugee Condition

1 Ai Weiwei, "The Refugee Crisis Isn't about Refugees. It's about Us," *The Guardian*, February 2, 2018.
2 Nicolas Sarkozy, "The Unofficial English Translation of Sarkozy's Speech" [July 26, 2007], *Africa Resource*, www.africaresource.com/essays-a-reviews/essays-a-discussions/437-the-unofficial-english-translation-of-sarkozys-speech.
3 Claire Rodier, "Aux marges de l'Europe: la construction de l'inacceptable," in *Le retour des camps? Sangatte, Lampedusa, Guantanamo*, ed. Olivier Le Cour Grandmaison, Gilles Lhuilier, and Jérôme Valluy (Paris: Autrement, 2007) p. 138.
4 Alessandro Dal Lago, *Non-Persons: The Exclusion of Migrants in a Global Society*, trans. Marie Orton (Milan: IPOC Press, 2009).
5 Claire Rodier, "Fermer les frontières pour conjurer la peur: le réponse de l'Europe à la 'crise migratoire,'" in *Vers la guerre d'identités? De la fracture coloniale à la révolution ultranationale*, ed. Pascal Blanchard,

Nicolas Bancel, and Dominic Thomas (Paris: La Découverte, 2016) p. 179.
6 Claire Rodier, "Migrations: choix politique ou responsabilité collective?" *Les Matins*, hosted by Marc Voinchet; broadcast by France Culture, October 8, 2013, www.franceculture.fr/emissions/les-matins/migrations-choix-politique-ou-responsabilite-collective-1ere-partie-hommage.
7 See the time-lapse film of the installation's construction: Ai Weiwei (@aiww), "The Seventh Day of the Installation 'Law of the Journey,'" Instagram post, March 13, 2017, www.instagram.com/p/BRlm-vggoA7.
8 Claire Rodier, "Fermer les frontières pour conjurer la peur," 186.
9 On this topic, see Michel Agier, *Le couloir des exilés: être étranger dans un monde commun* (Bellecombe-en-Bauges: Éditions du Croquant, 2011), and Dominic Thomas, *Africa and France: Postcolonial Cultures, Migration, and Racism* (Bloomington: Indiana University Press, 2013).
10 See Calérie Marin La Meslée, "Achille Mbembe: L'insurrection se fera par l'éducation," *Le Point Afrique*, February 3, 2018.
11 "Être vulnérable c'est être humain à part itera. C'est la seule façon de pouvoir saigner dans l'autre": Antjie Krog, unpublished interview with the South African poet and novelist Denis Hirson, 1995.
12 Ai Weiwei, "The Refugee Crisis Isn't about Refugees. It's about Us."
13 Alain Mabanckou, *The Tears of the Black Man*, trans. Dominic Thomas (Bloomington: Indiana University Press, 2018) pp. 30–1.
14 Jean-Jacques Rousseau, *Discourse on the Origin of Inequality*, trans. Donald A. Cress (Cambridge: Hackett, 1992) p. 44.
15 Achille Mbembe, "Scrap the Borders that Divide Africans," *Mail & Guardian*, March 17, 2017.
16 Achille Mbembe, Michel Agier, and Rémy Bazenguissa-Ganga, "Mobilités africaines, racisme français," *Vacarme* 43, no. 2 (2008): pp. 83–5.
17 François Gemenne, "Bart De Wever a raison: il faut discuter de l'ouverture des frontières," *Le Soir*, January 25, 2018.
18 Alexis Spire, *Accueillir ou reconduire: enquête sur les guichets de l'immigration* (Paris: Éditions Raison d'Agir, 2008) p. 9.
19 Didier Fassin and Anne Laffeter, "Interview avec Didier Fassin: il y a chez Emmanuel Macron un désintérêt pour la question sociale," *Les Inrockuptibles*, January 27, 2018.
20 Ai Weiwei, "The Refugee Crisis Isn't about Refugees. It's about Us."

Humanity and Animality

1 Augustine, *The City of God against the Pagans*, trans. and ed. R. W. Dyson (Cambridge University Press, 1998) bk. I, ch. XX, p. 33.

2 Jean-Jacques Rousseau, *Discourse on the Origin of Inequality*, trans. Donald A. Cress (Cambridge: Hackett, 1992) p. 14. Rousseau is quite explicit about his intention to found a new philosophy of nature that breaks with mechanist imperatives of classical rationalism when he writes, "It is from the conjunction and combination that our mind is in a position to make regarding these two principles [i.e., interest in self-preservation and compassion for the suffering of other beings – P. G.], without the need for introducing that of sociability, that all the rules of natural right appear to me to flow; rules which reason is later forced to re-establish on other foundations, when, by its successive developments, it has succeeded in smothering nature": ibid., 14.
3 René Descartes, *Optics*, trans. Robert Stoothoff, in *The Philosophical Writings of Descartes*, Vol. I (Cambridge University Press, 1985) p. 164.
4 Philippe Descola, *Beyond Nature and Culture* (University of Chicago Press, 2013).
5 Bertrand Russell, "If Animals Could Talk" [1932], in *Mortals and Others: Bertrand Russell's American Essays (1931–1935)*, Vol. I, ed. Harry Ruja (London: Allen & Unwin, 1975) pp. 120–1.
6 Surah *The Cow*, verse 30: "When your Lord told the angels, 'I am putting a successor on earth,' they said, 'How can You put someone there who will cause damage and bloodshed, when we celebrate Your praise and proclaim Your holiness?' but He said, 'I know things you do not'" (Qur'an 2:30, Abdel Haleem 7).
7 Qur'an 6:151, Abdel Haleem 92.
8 Milan Kundera, *The Unbearable Lightness of Being*, trans. Michael Henry Heim (London: Faber & Faber, 1984) p. 289.

The Tree Frogs' Distress

1 See Bertrand Hirsch and Bernard Roussel, eds. *Le Rift est-africain, une singularité plurielle* (Paris: IRD Éditions/MNHN, 2009).
2 Michel Serres, *Hominescence*, trans. Randolph Burks (London: Bloomsbury, 2019).
3 See Vincent Courtillot, "Le point chaud de l'Afar," in *Le Rift est-africain, une singularité plurielle*, ed. Hirsch and Roussel.
4 Amadou Hampâté Bâ, *Contes initiatiques peuls* (Paris: Stock, 1994).
5 Serres, *Hominescence*, 9.
6 Ibid., 11.
7 Meinrad Pierre Hebga, *Sorcellerie, chimère dangereuse?* (Abdidjan: Inades éditions, 1979).
8 Nouck Bassomb, "Le mythe bassa de la Restauration chez les Bassa du Sud-Cameroun" (Master's thesis, University of Yaoundé, 1984).

9 Albert de Surgy, *La divination par les huits cordelettes chez les Mwaba-Gurma* (Paris: L'Harmattan, 1983).

The Paths of the Voice

1 Bob W. White, "Écouter ensemble, penser tout haut: musique populaire et prise de conscience politique en Congo-Zaïre," in *Musique populaire et société à Kinshasa*, ed. Bob W. White and Lye M. Yoka (Paris: L'Harmattan, 2010) p. 232.
2 Samuel P. Salo, "La chanson populaire, source de l'histoire coloniale au Moogo (Burkina Faso)," in *L'écriture de l'histoire en Afrique: l'oralité toujours en question*, ed. Nicoué T. Gayibor, Dominique Juhé-Beaulaton, and Moustapha Gomgnimbou (Paris: Karthala, 2013) pp. 239–40.
3 Futa Toro occupies the region to the north of Senegal and to the south of Mauritania.
4 The Islamic state founded by Almamy Malik Sy in Bundu at the end of the seventeenth century in the eastern part of present-day Senegal.
5 Cf. the remix from 1998: Youssou N'Dour and Le Super Étoile, "Birima," track 8 of *Spécial Fin d'Année*, Jololi, 1998.
6 Positive Black Soul, "Iyata," track 9 of *Run Cool*, EastWest, 2000.
7 Ngũgĩ wa Thiong'o, *Decolonizing the Mind: The Politics of Language in African Literature* (London: James Currey, 1986) p. 28.
8 Roland Barthes, "La musique, la voix, la langue," in *L'Obvie et l'Obtus: essais critiques III* (Paris: Seuil, 1982) p. 247.
9 Gérard Genette, ed. *Esthétique et poétique* (Paris: Seuil, 1992) p. 8.
10 Paul Zumthor, "Poésie et vocalité au moyen âge," *Cahiers de littérature orale*, no. 36 (1994): pp. 28–9.
11 The examples are legion. They reach from Ali Farka Touré, former mayor of the town of Niafunké in Mali, to Youssou N'Dour, who aspired to become president of the Senegalese republic in 2012, to the rappers who started the movement Y'en a marre and whose struggle for a change in political leadership [*alternance politique*] has inspired other young Africans (Les Sofas de la République in Mali, Le Balai citoyen in Burkina Faso, Filimbi in Congo …).

Index

absent community 103–9, 112
Achebe, Chinua
  Morning Yet on Creation Day 230
Adésinà, Jimi O. 138
Adorno, Theodor
  and allegory 153–4, 156
  Dialectic of Enlightenment 152
  "The Idea of Natural-History" 148, 152–3
  and natural-history concept 148, 151–3, 155
Africa
  depiction of contemporaneity of societies 119
  evaluation of social wellbeing 119
  independence of states 121
  population 86, 91
  return to *see* return to Africa
African Arabness 6, 15
African body
  territory of expression of in the West 58–61
African descent, claiming 113
African experience
  three canonical meanings of 206
African as a neighbor 218–19
African personality 4, 228
African presence 6
  affirming of, in a world of cultural diversity 17–18
"African Renaissance" 109
African Summer School 109
African thought 3–4, 9, 41–51
African Union 130, 232
Africanity (*africanité*) 4, 6, 10, 18
  Hegel's dismemberment of 14
  Senghor's convergence of Arabness and negritude in 14–15
Afrocentrism 23–4, 34, 217–18
Afro-cosmopolitanism 105–6
Afro-optimism 217–18
Afropolitanism 105–6
aging
  rich nations and accelerated 91
Ahmad, Aijaz 147
Ai Weiwei 237–8, 239, 241–2
aid
  development 201–3, 217
  humanitarian 203–5
Al-Afghani 7
Algeria 11
  secularism in 71

Index

Algerian War (1954–62) 145–6
  and Dib's *Who Remembers the Sea* 145–51
allegory
  and Adorno's "The Idea of Natural-History" 148, 153–4
  and Benjamin's *Origin of the German Trauerspiel* 148, 152–4, 156
  and Dib's *Who Remembers the Sea* 146–7, 148–51, 155–6
  difference between symbol and 154
  in the postcolonialism debate 147–8
Alliot-Marie, Michèle 201
Amadiume, Ifi 138
Amin, Samir 7, 169
amphibians 256–7, 260
Andrianampoinimerina, King 48
animality
  and humanity 245–52
"animal-machine" 247
animals 256–7
  exclusion from sphere of ethics 245, 247, 248
  extinction 256–7
  man's superiority over 246–7, 250–1
  as tutelary/totemic figures 256
  way to integrate into sphere of ethics 249–50
Anthologie de la nouvelle poésie nègre 5
Anthropocene 255
anthropocentrism 245–52
apartheid 76, 82, 92
Appiah, Kwame 4
Arab nationalism 7
Arab renaissance 4
Arab world
  European colonization 6
Arendt, Hannah 196, 212
Arkansas law (1859) 29

Armah, Ayi Kwei 226–7
  Two Thousand Seasons 227
Aron, Raymond 68
artists
  influence on public space 272
assimilation 102
"atavistic cultures" 98–9
Atelier, The 136, 139–41
  Manifesto of Atelier IV 142–4
"Atlantic triangle" 98
Augustine, Saint 247
Australia, and migration 237
Ay 46
Azikiwe, Nnamidi 215

Bâ, Amadou Hampaté 224, 225
Baldwin, James 137
Balibar, Étienne 35–6
Bank of Central African States *see* BEAC
Bank of France 159, 167
Bank of Senegal 159
Bank of West Africa (BAO) 159
Barthes, Roland 271
Bassa people 258, 260
Baubérot, Jean 68
BCEAO (Central Bank of West African States) 159, 161, 162, 168
BEAC (Bank of Central African States) 161, 162
Beauvoir, Simone de 24, 27
  The Second Sex 137
"becoming-woman" 27
becomings
  from thinking identity to thinking African 3–18
Benjamin, Walter 151
  and allegory 152–4, 156
  Origin of the German Trauerspiel 148, 152–4
Benkirane, Réda 69
Benoît, Pierre 223
Bentouhami, Hourya 19
Berber movement 15

Berger, Gaston 12
Bergson, Henri 191
Bernabé, Joby
   Kimafoutiésa 239
Bhabha, Homi 27, 28
Bible 247
bilateral method 61, 62–3
biologism 251, 252
Black Lives Matter Syllabus 139
Black nationalism 98
Black Panthers 137
Black paranoia 29
Blanchot, Maurice
   The Unavowable Community 103
Blaszkiewicz, Hélène 88
body double 25, 27, 28, 29, 32, 33, 34
Boni, Tanella 4
borders 99
   need for unfreezing of colonial 94
   reactivation of 92
   violence of 90–1
Botswana 170
Boudjedra, Rachid 232
Boukman (Maroon leader) 141
Boukman, Daniel
   Les négriers 239
Boulaga, Fabien Eboussi 138
Boum, Hemley 73–81
Bowao, Charles 4
Bowles, Paul 223
Brainard, Lael 203
Brauman, Rony 203–4
Brazza, Savorgnan de 199–200
Brazzaville, battle of 16
Brondesbury, Amos de 210
Buhari, Muhammadu 171
Burkina Faso 121, 166, 216

Cabanes, Valérie 186–7
Cabral, Amilcar 132
Cailliau, Hesna 67
Caillié, René 222
Caillois, Roger 27

Cameroon 258
Canto-Sperber, Monique 197
capitalism 123, 255, 262
care 214 *see also* self-care
Carson, Rachel 260
Cartesianism 247, 248, 259
Castoriadis, Cornelius 124
CEMAC (Economic and Monetary Community of Central Africa) 161
Central Africa
   end of oil in 171–2
Central African Republic 164, 166
Central Bank of West African States *see* BCEAO
Certeau, Michel de 182
Césaire, Aimé 36, 96, 111, 217
CFA franc 158–73
   and abolitionists 158, 163, 166
   anchoring of to the euro 163, 169–70
   and conservatives 158–9, 163, 166, 167, 169–70, 171
   creation of (1945) 160
   developments suggesting no future for 171–2
   dysfunctional economic arrangement 168–9
   economic impact of 165–9
   and economic stability 169–71
   and financial repression 167–8
   and foreign exchange policy 162–3, 168–9
   French influence 162–5
   historical context 159–60
   and inflation 170
   as instrument of neocolonialism wielded by the French government 162
   mechanism of extraction 169
   monetary sovereignty issue 161–5
   pillars of 160–1, 164
   see also FCFA zone
Chad 166

Chamoiseau, Patrick 99
Char, René 124
Chardin, Teilhard de 188–9
Charnay, Jean-Paul 67
Chilembwe, John Nkologo 215
China 170
Chirac, Jacques 236
Christian, Barbara 136
  "The Race for Theory" 136
Christianity 10, 12, 13
  respect between Islam and 13
  and secularism 69
  spread of in Africa 10
circulation(s) 85–95
  and creation of tunnels 87, 88
  distinction between migrations and 89
  and enclavement 87–90, 94
  and fabricating networks of alliance 89
  inequality 91–2
  obstacles 86
  violence of borders 90–1
  see also mobility
CITES 256, 257
citizenship
  cosmo- 114
  democratic/communitarian perspective 17
  democratic/liberal perspective 17
  and ethnicity 16–17
  juridical/political function 241
civil war 16
climate change 230, 255
clothing 47
CODESRIA 10
co-emergence 185–6
Coetzee, J. M.
  Disgrace 73–82
colonialism/colonization 4, 24, 47, 91, 192, 200–1
  absence and lack as central notions of 139
  of Arab world by Europe 6
  borders inherited from 94
  and compassion 199–201
  and education system 131
  forming ties and establishing relations 48
  and mobility/circulation 87
  and music 268–9
  negation produced by 6
  response to the negation produced by 4
  and the Sahara 223–4
  as a source of racism (*Declaration and Programme of Action*) 208
  struggle against 4, 132
  suffering of Africans during 206–7
  use of roadblocks 87
  see also decolonization; postcolonialism
commensality, extended 260–2
Committee for the Cancellation of Third World Debt 211
commodification 18
community
  absent 103–9, 112
  elective 104
  and identification 104–5
  making of (*faire communauté*) 184
  and Maroon feminism 24–5
  meaning of the term 103
  traditional 104
community-making 184
compassion 194–220
  African as a neighbor 218–19
  and an ethics of the face 195
  autonomy of 216–18
  and colonization 199–201
  as a competence 196
  as creative and productive 195
  decolonizing 196, 211, 212
  and development aid 201–3, 217
  governmentality of 197
  history of 197
  horizontal 218

compassion (*cont.*)
  and humanitarian action 203–4
  and past suffering 206–11
  and the politics of life 219
  privileged domains of projects built on 197
  rehabilitation of Africa's capacity for 218–19
  and responsibility for the other person 195–6
  structuring of political relations with Africa 196–7
  subversion of through self-care 212–18
  and victimization 205–11
compassionate alterity 198–9
compassionate democracy 219
compassionate governmentality 194–5, 197, 211, 219–20
compassionate self-sufficiency 211–12
compassionate subjectivation 218–19
Condé, Maryse 228
  The Children of Segu 225
  Segu 225
Congo 16, 63
Congo-Brazzaville 62
"constitutional patriotism" (Habermas) 17
Convention on the International Trade in Endangered Species of Wild Fauna and Flora *see* CITES
Coobah (Maroon slave) 31
Corbin, Henry 7
Corcuff, Philippe 195
cosmic memory 184–7, 188–9, 193
cosmocitizenship 114
counter-conduct (Foucault) 214
counterfactual reasoning 124
cowries 159–60
Crawford, Matthew
  Shop Class as Soul Craft 137
critical theory 133

Crutzen, Paul 255
cultural decolonization 93–4
cultural diversity
  affirming an African presence in world of 17–18
"cultural exception" 18
cultural nationalism 4, 18
cultural pluralism 9, 14–17
cultural resources
  a reconsidered relationship to one's 120–1
culture(s) 119, 186
  atavistic 98–9
  division between nature and 191, 249
  economic 123
  genuine 8
  oral 15
  Romantic/modern approaches to 100
"cultures of exportation" 230
cum patior Africa 194–220

Dal Lago, Alessandro 237
d'Allonnes, Myriam Revault 211
Darfur 15–16
Darwish, Mahmoud 82
Davidson, Basil 223
Davis, Angela 23
de la Boétie, Étienne 172
debalkanization
debt 211, 218
Declaration and Programme of Action 207–8
Declaration of the Rights of Man (1789) 36
decolonization 138, 143, 147, 160, 200
  of compassion 196, 211, 212
  cultural 93–4
  of the ego 132
  of knowledge 134
  of the mind 137
  struggle for 132
  territorial 94

deep ecology 250
defrontierization 240–1
degradation 206
Deleuze, Gilles 66
Delpla, Isabelle 95
democracy
 compassionate 219
 representative 121
 and secularism 68, 69, 71
Democratic Republic of the
 Congo
 militarization of roads 86–7
demography 91
Descartes, René 246, 247, 248
Descola, Philippe 192, 249
desert, African 89 *see also* Sahara
d'Estaing, Valéry Giscard 236
development aid 201–3, 217
Diagne, Ramatoulaye 4
Diagne, Souleymane Bachir 3, 192
Diarra, Alpha Mandé
 Sahel! 228–9
diaspora
 African 96–114
 Jewish 102
 meaning 97
 see also return to Africa
diasporic privilege 99–100
Diaw-Cissé, Animata 4
Dib, Mohammed
 Le désert sans détour 229–30
 Who Remembers the Sea
 145–51, 154–7
dictatorships, and secularism 68
dinosaurs, disappearance of 254
Diop, Alioune 5
Diop, Birago
 "Desert" 226
Diop, Cheikh Anta 14, 103, 109
 The African Origin of
 Civilization 6
Diori, Hamani 169
Diouf, Abdoul Aziz 55
disappropriation
 (*désappropriation*) 206

discourse
 ideological 66
 media 66
 political 66
 types of 66
Disgrace (film) 76
Disgrace (J. M. Coetzee) 73–82
Donner, Nicholas 88
Dorlin, Elsa 81
"double absence" 103
double consciousness 107
double presence
 and return to Africa 107–9,
 110
double/doubling 34 *see also* body
 double
Douls, Camille 222–3
Dowden, Richard 194
Du Bois, W. E. B. 107, 130
dualism 248
Dumont, René
 Pour l'Afrique, j'accuse 230
Duveyrier, Henri 222–3
dystopia 19, 140

Eberhard, Isabelle 223
Economic and Monetary
 Community of Central Africa
 (CEMAC) 161
Economic Community of West
 African States (ECOWAS)
 single currency proposal 171
economic culture 123
economic institutions 123
economism 119
economy
 crisis of neoliberal 122–3
 need for reinvention of 122–3
 as part of a larger social system
 122, 123
 principles of 122–3
education 129–44
 analyzing as colonial 131
 Ateliers and manifesto of Atelier
 IV 136, 139–41, 142–4

education (*cont.*)
  demand for decolonization of knowledge 134
  disjunction between school and life 137
  imagining the African campus 134–7
  and international "experts" 133
  lack of ideology and devitalization of 135–6
  "lagging behind" 130
  need to move beyond the "civilizing mission" ideal 138
  and obscurantism 130
  pedagogy of emancipation 131–4
  problems and challenges 130–1
  protests in South Africa (2016) 134
  recolonization of by economic and accounting vocabulary 133
  school enrollment 130
  and the state 133
  and transformation 131–2
  using the master's tools to demolish the master's house 137–8
educational vouchers 133
Ego 28
  decolonizing of 132
Egypt 69
  ancient 14
Ehrenberg, Alain 213
El-Hadj Omar 226
emancipation, pedagogy of 131–4
emigration 9
  lack of in Africa 86
enclavement 87–90, 94
Enlightenment 58, 152
entropy 254, 257, 262
equaliberty, and Maroon women 35–6
Equatorial Guinea 166, 169
Erner, Guillaume 206

ethics
  distinction between moral agent and moral patient 250
  exclusion of animals from sphere of 245, 247, 248
  of the face 195
  need for transition from an anthropocentric to an ecocentric 249
  ways to integrate the animal into the sphere of 249–50
ethnicity
  and citizenship 16–17
ethnocentrism 67, 188
euro 163
  pegging CFA franc to 163, 169–70
Eurocentrism 8, 119, 259
Europe
  colonization of Arab world 6
  and migration 236–7
European Central Bank 164
europhone intellectuals 11
existential insecurity 16
extinctions 254, 256–7

fabric 46–9
Fanon, Frantz 27, 29, 130, 132, 138
  Black Skin, White Masks 27
Fassin, Didier 241
FCFA zone 163, 164, 167–72
  characteristics shared by countries belonging to 165–6
  cost of credit in 167–8
  evolution of real per capita GDP *173*
  inflation 170, 171
  monetary immobility of 169
  population 172
  volatility of economies in 168
  see also CFA franc
feminism 132
  legal 25
  Maroon *see* Maroon feminism

Ferry, Jules 199–200
fidelity 7, 26
  to masters 27
  to tradition 7
Filali-Ansary, Abdou 4
Fillon, François 201
forest 140–1
Foucauld, Charles de 223
Foucault, Michel 32, 195, 213
  "Governmentality" 213–14
  Security, Territory, and Population 213–14
franc
  introduction of as an instrument of colonial domination 159–60
  see also CFA franc
Franc of the French Colonies in Africa *see* FCFA zone
France 236
  abandoning of franc for euro 163
  and CFA franc 158–72, 159, 172
  and colonization 200–1
  colonization of Algeria 14
  memorial law 201
  and migration 235–6
Francophone Summit (Madagascar) (2016) 218
"free persons of color" (*libres de couleur*) 28–9
Freemasons
  ambivalence toward by Muslims 68
Freire, Paulo 132
Freud, Sigmund 28, 156
Friedman, Milton 133
functionalism, legal 60
futures
  need for reinvention of economy 122–3
  need for reinvention of political forms 121–2
  need for reinvention of relationship with cultural resources/traditions 120–1

reopening 117–25
  uchronias and counterfactuals 124

Gallieni, Joseph 92
Gandhi, M. 47
Gardel, Louis 223
Gardet, Louis 67
Garvey, Marcus 98
Gautier, Arlette 23
gaze
  absent community and the 105
Gemenne, François 241
Ghana 110
  independence (1957) 6
Gide, André 223
Gilroy, Paul
  The Black Atlantic 100–1
Glissant, Édouard 98, 110
Global Partnership for Education (GPE) 130
globalization 4, 10, 123
Gnawa cultures 15
good Samaritan 198
governmentality, compassionate 194–5, 197, 211, 219–20
griots 269
Guadeloupe slave revolt (1802) 32
Guattari, Félix 66
Guinea-Bissau 168, 171

Haalpulaar griots 269
Habermas, Jürgen 17
Haiti 263–7
Hall, Stuart 138
Hama, Boubou 230–1
Haram, Boko 9
Hartog, François 118
Hausa women 23
Havel, Václav 240
Hebga, Reverend Father Meinrad P. 258
Hegel, G. W. F. 6, 9, 14, 24, 30
heliocentrism 185
heterotopias 140

hip hop 270
history 119, 120
　bewitchment of 145, 151–3
　natural 151–6
History of Spirit (Hegel) 6
hominescence (Serres) 254, 258, 261
hope
　return to Africa and geopolitics of 109–14
Hountondji, Paulin 3, 4, 8
"house Negro" 28
Hugon, Philippe 203
Human Development Index 166
human rights
　integralism of Western 59
humanism 246
humanitarian action/aid 203–5
humanity
　and animality 245–52
　extension of and consequences 253–4, 256
　and nature 260, 263
hunters 259
Husserl, Edmund 5–6
hybridity 15

identification
　and community 104–5
identitarian catastrophes 16
identitarian obsession
　and return to Africa 100–1
identity 110–11
　and African thought 4
　distinction from solidarity 110–11
　from thinking of to thinking African becomings 3–18
　re-founding of the self 6–7
identity politics 102
ideological discourse 66
illegal immigration
　struggle against 90–1
imaginary
　importance of in the creating of the real 124

imagined community 125, 131
immigrants/immigration
　European policies to combat 92
　struggle against illegal 90–1
　xenophobic discourses and hostility toward 236–7
　see also migration/migrants
India 47
inequality 35, 108, 122, 240
Institut Montaigne 163
integration 102
intellectuals, African 10–11
　europhone 11
　and religion 11
International Monetary Fund (IMF) 211
intuition, revalorizing of 191–2
Islam 6–7, 10, 12, 13, 14, 65–71
　ethnocentrism of scholarly discourses on 67
　in Maghreb 68
　and Occidentalism 70, 71
　relationship between religion and politics in 69–70, 71
　respect between Christianity and 13
　and Sahara 223, 225–7
　and secularism 67–71
　spread of in Africa 10
Ivory Coast 170

Jabès, Edmond 223
Jacobs, Harriet 31
Jacobs, Steve 76
James, C. L. R. 31
Jameson, Fredric
　The Political Unconscious 147
Jewish diaspora 102
Judaism 13
Jullien, François 183, 189, 191

Kaké, Ibrahima Baba 230
Kane, Cheikh Hamidou 239
Kant, Immanuel 247
Kavindele, Enoch P. 208–9

Kawlra, Aarti 136
Keïta, Lansana 8
Kepel, Gilles 11
Kierkegaard, Søren 190
Kipling, Rudyard
    "The White Man's Burden" 199
Kisukidi, Nadia Yala 96
Kodjo-Grandvaux, Séverine 179
Kouvouama, Abel 4
Krog, Antjie 239
Kundera, Milan 252

laicism (*laïcisme*)70
language(s) 254
    and music 271–2
"Law of the Journey" exposition (2017–18) 238–9
Lazarus, Neil
    The Postcolonial Unconscious 147
Le Clézio, J. M. G. 223
Le Pen, Jean Marie 201
Lebdai, Benaouda 221
Lefeuvre, Daniel 205
legal feminism 25
legal system, African 55, 56–7
    and bilateral method 61
    de-ideologization of 61
    hybridity of 63
    and *ordre public* 62–4
    and Western body 61–2
legal system, Western 55, 56, 63
    and body of African subject 57–61
    and personal status 57–8
Letonturier, Eric 189
Levinas, Emmanuel 195, 197
Lévi-Strauss, Claude 260
    The Raw and the Cooked 260
Lewicki, Tadeusz
    Folia orientalia 223
Lhote, Henri 222
liberty
    and equaliberty 35–6
    and Maroon women 30–4, 36–7

literacy 130
lived body (*corps vécu*) 246, 251
Lorde, Audre 137–8
Louverture, Toussaint 20, 29, 30, 36
Lugan, Bernard 205

Maal, Baaba 270
Mabanckou, Alain 240
Machiavelli 212
Machikou, Nadine 194
Macron, Emmanuel 165, 236
Madagascar 46
    and *Ay* 46
Maghreb 13, 15
    Islam in 68
Maghrebin novel 147, 151
Malcolm X 28
Mali 166
Mancini, Pasquale Stanislao 59
Mandela, Nelson 81, 132
Manga, Lionel 253
manumission 22, 26, 27, 30, 37
"Māori Movement" 139
Marie-Jeanne 23
Marienstras, Richard 102
Marley, Bob 129
Maroon communities
    Afrocentric culture 23–4
    circulation and exchange 24
Maroon feminism 19–37
    and collective emancipation 25
    and community 24–5
    as a feminism of survival 36
Maroon women
    abuses subjected to on plantations 31
    acceptance of death as punishment for resistance 24, 31–2
    commitment to escape 31
    and equaliberty 35–6
    and ethics of death 31
    higher regard for liberty than for life 30–4

Maroon women (*cont.*)
  and leadership 22
  and manumission 22, 26, 27, 30, 37
  mythical accounts 21
  public executions of 31–2
  role in camouflage tactic 20
  role of in marronage 20, 21
  stubbornness for freedom 30, 31–2, 36–7
  and suicide 31, 32
  use of poisoning to attain justice 32, 33
Maroons
  seen as direct threat to plantations 20
  war waged against 20
marronage 19–20
  abolitionism as a "liberation of liberty" 36
  and camouflage 35
  circulation of bodies and signs 24
  creation of communities of women 36–7
  dominance of patriarchal filiation in 21
  and lesbianism 20, 33
  strategies of war 20
  and struggle against recognition 24, 25–30
  way for Black women to contest denial of their femininity 33
  will to put an end to the doubling of one's life in slavery 34
  women's role in 20, 21
Marseille, Jacques 200
Marthe-Rose 32
Massignon, Louis 67, 71
Master–slave dialectic (Hegel) 24, 30
Mbembe, Achille 4, 32, 85, 206, 213, 238, 240
Means, Russell 129

media discourse 66
megalocene 255
Memmi, Albert 132
memory work (*travail mémoratif*) 181, 190
memory/memories 179–93
  cosmic 184–7, 188–9, 193
  duty of in a de-colonial project 182–3
  of the in-common 183, 184, 188
  integration of those who were excluded from national narrative 180–1
  making (*faire mémoire*) 182, 189
  making construction of communities possible 182
  as a project of humanization 181–2
  and self-esteem 179, 180, 190
  and self-fashioning 179, 180
  and slaves 189–90
  utopian 189–91, 193
  world- 183, 184–5
memory-world 179–93
Merkel, Angela 241
migration/migrants 88, 91, 93, 235–42
  anti-migration policing 99
  crisis 86
  depictions of precarity of in art and literature 237–40
  in the desert 89
  distinction between circulations and 89
  European restrictions on 236–7
  struggle against illegal 90
  to Africa 93
  to Europe from Africa 99, 231
  use of colonial technologies to regulate 91
  vilification of 236
  violence of borders 90
  "wretched of the Mediterranean" 236–7
  see also immigrants/immigration

mimicry 27–8, 34
mobility 85
    border crossings and danger of 87, 90–1
    challenge of removing the obstacles to 94–5
    and colonization 87
    and enclavement 87–90
    governing of as a global-scale challenge 92
    inequalities 91
    natural obstacles to 86
    need for Africa to forge a new politics of 93–4
    need for unfreezing of colonial borders 94
    obstacles to 88–9, 91
    and principle of sedentariness 95
    restricting of by roadblocks 86–7
    right to 86
Modern Monetary Theory 164
modernity 117, 185, 246
    and religions 13
Mohammad Abduh 7
Moitt, Bernard 36
Monod, Théodore 222
monotheism 9, 10
Morrison, Toni
    Beloved 34
Mudimbe, Valentin-Yves 96, 110, 138
    The Invention of Africa 138
multiculturalism 8, 10, 15, 16
    embracing of and building an African union 15
multiple identities
    and Afropolitanism 105–6
music 268–72
    escaping colonial authoritarianism 268–9
    and language 271–2
    song as a space for re-examining cultural heritages 270
Muslim Brotherhood 69
Mwaba-Gurma 260

nahda 6
Napoleon Bonaparte 29–30
nationalism 60
    Arab 7
    Black 98
    cultural 4, 18
nation-state, rethinking model of 122
nativism 237
natural-history (*Naturgeschichte*)151–6
    and Adorno 151–2, 153, 155
    and Benjamin 153
    and Dib's *Who Remembers the Sea* 155–6
nature
    division between culture and 249
    fragility of 256–7
    and humanity 260, 263
    need for new philosophy of 249
    objectifying of 192
N'Dour, Youssou 270
Ndoye, Bado 245
negritude 4, 14, 15, 216, 267
Neil, Stafford 209
neoliberalism 122, 133, 136
neo-Malthusian discourses 86
Netherlands 209–10
Niger 164, 166
Niger River Delta conflicts (1990s) 17
Nigeria 10, 17, 169
Nigerian Civil War 204–5
Njami, Simon 71
"Njeddo Dewal, Mother of Calamity" 256, 260
Nkrumah, Kwame 6, 110, 132, 215, 216–17
    "Statement of African Ideology" (1961) 215
nomadism 90
non-linear time 197
nudity 42, 46–7

oasis cities 231–2
obscurantism 130

Occidentalism 70, 71
oil
   end of in Central Africa 171–2
ordre public 62–4
Organization of African Unity 94
Orwin, Clifford 211
Ouloguem, Yambo 226–7
   Bound to Violence 227–8
Ousmane, Sèmbene 10, 239
Oyewumi, Oyeronke 138
Oz, Amos 75

Pan-Africanism 4, 98, 110, 158, 165, 215, 217
paradigm of life 250, 252
paranoia, Black and white 29
Paris Accords 255
Paris Club 211
patriarchy 14, 27, 135
Patterson, Orlando 30
pedagogy of emancipation 131–4
personal status 55–64
   and biomedicine 56
   body of the Western subject in Africa 61–4
   current status in the West 57–8
   and infinitude 56
   and nationality 58–9
   neo-functionalism and resolving conflicts over 57
   and new Western figures 55–64
   principal function 55
   shift from nationalism to territorialism 59–60
   territory of expression of the African body in the West 58–61
plantocratic slavery 21, 25–6, 32, 34
pluralism
   cultural 9, 14–17
   religious 9–14
   thinking and living 7–9
Polfer, Lydie 210
political discourse 66

political forms
   need for reinvention of 121–2
Positive Black Soul 270
positivism, Western 57
postcolonialism 17, 133, 142
   allegory in the debate over 147–8
posthumanism 56, 118, 187–8
postmodernity 118
poverty 8
   international concern for Africans 195
Présence africaine (journal) 5
Présence africaine (publishing house) 5–6
presentism 118, 120
privilege
   and return to Africa 99–100
   white 27

Queen Nanny 32, 33

Raharimanana, Jean-Luc 41
   Rano, rano 50
rationalism 69
Ravelona, J. A. 46
reason 118, 245, 246, 247
"reason-embrace" (Senghor) 192
"reason-eye" (Senghor) 192
re-birth 6
Reclus, Élisée 260, 261
recollection (Kierkegaard) 182, 190
Reconquista 13
refugee crisis 237–8
refugees 235–42 *see also* migration/migrants
"regime of the nigh" 194–220
religion(s)
   importance of respect between 13
   and intellectuals 11–12
   and modernity 13
   relationship with politics in Islam 69–70, 71
religious fervor 11, 12
religious identity 10

religious pluralism 9–14
religious violence 10
reparations 201, 217
  and slavery 207, 208–10
"replacement negro" 27–8, 32
Representative Council of France's Black Associations (CRAN) 207
researchers, African 133
Retaille, Denis 89, 90
return to Africa 96–114
  and absent community 103–9
  Afro-diasporic Renaissances 109–10
  and Afropolitanism 106
  and diasporic privilege 99–100
  and double presence 107–9, 110
  forms taken 112–13
  and geopolitics of hope 109–14
  history of idea of 98
  and identitarian obsession 100–1
  persistence of desire to 98
  practices 112–14
  and rhetorics of the majority 101–3
  and slaves 98
  and solidarities 110–12
  and suspicion 98–103
"revenge of God" 11
rhythm 192–3
Ricœur, Paul 182–3, 219
Rio de Janeiro Earth Summit (1992) 255
roadblocks 86–7
roads
  militarization of in Democratic Republic of the Congo 86–7
Rocard, Michel 236
Rodier, Claire 236, 237
Romaine the Prophetess 23
Romanticism 245
Rousseau, Jean-Jacques 219, 247–8
  Discourse on the Origin of Inequality 240
Russell, Bertrand 250–1

Sahara 89, 221–33
  desire to re-establish relations between both sides of the 231
  and drought 228, 229, 230
  economic potential of 228
  eliciting attraction and fascination 222–3
  European interest in 223
  expansion of due to climate change 230
  geophysical space of 228–33
  history 222–3
  and Islam 223, 225–7
  literary visions of African writers 224–30
  natural wealth of 231–3
  negative visions of in literature 226–8
  oasis cities 231–2
  as a region of employment 232, 233
  as a space of exchange 221–2, 222–4
  as a space of human and cultural transhumance 223–4
  transformation of by colonialism 223–4
Saint-Domingue 29–30, 36, 141
Saint-Élio, Rodney 263
Saint-Exupéry, Antoine de 223
Saint-Marc, Henriette 23
Salafism 7
Salih, Tayeb
  Season of Migration to the North 225–6
Sall, Macky 218
salvation 195
same-sex marriage 62, 63
Sankara, Thomas 129, 132, 216
Sanson, Henri 70–1
Sarkozy, Nicolas 201, 235–6
Sarr, Felwine 4, 117, 187
Sartre, Jean-Paul
  Black Orpheus 5
Sassine, Williams 229

savanna freedom 27
Sayad, Abdelmalek 103
Schouten, Peter 86–7
Schwarz-Bart, Simone
  Ton beau capitain 239
"scramble for Europe" 86
secularism 11, 67
  and Christianity 69
  and democracy 68, 69, 71
  and dictatorships 68
  and Islam 67–71
  and laicism (*laïcisme*) 70
sedentariness 94, 95, 113–14
Selasi, Taiye 105–6
self, re-founding of the 6–7
self-care
  Africa's subversion of compassion through 212–18
self-esteem 190
  and memory 179, 180, 190
self-management 122
self-sufficiency, compassionate 211–12
Senarclens, Pierre de 204
Senegal 62, 69, 159
Senghor, Léopold Sédar 12, 14–15, 110, 188, 191, 192
  "On the Appeal from the Race of Sheba" 215–16
Serres, Michel 197, 254, 258, 261
Sierra Leone 98
slave garden 23
slave women
  and manumission 22, 26, 30
  masculinization of Black women 33
  rape as demoralizing weapon 31
  use of poison to attain justice 32
  see also Maroon women
slavery/slaves 47
  and body double 27, 28
  and *Declaration and Programme of Action* 207–8
  dreaming of a return to Africa 98
  form of freedom under master's control 26
  and marronage 19–20
  and memory 189–90
  and mimicry 27
  plantocratic 21, 25–6, 32, 34
  and reparations 207, 208–10
  suffering of Africans during 206–7
  view of freedom from a legal standpoint 26–7
Sloterdijk, Peter 259
social wellbeing 119
sociologism 59
solidarities/solidarity
  distinction from identity 110–11
  and return to Africa 110–12
  "solidarities in time" 111
Solitude (Maroon leader) 31–2
song 269–71, 272
  and self-respect 271
  as a space for re-examining cultural heritages 270
South Africa 75–6
  Apartheid 76, 82, 92
  protests over education (2016) 134
South Korea 170
"sovereign currency" 164
sovereignty
  CFA franc and monetary 162–5
Sow, Cheikh C.
  Cycle de sécheresse 229
Soyinka, Wole 9
  Stockholm speech (1986) 9
spinning wheel 47
state, and education 133
subjectivation, compassionate 218–19
Sub-Saharan Africa 91
  divided from North Africa 230
Sudan 15–16
suffering
  distinction between pain and 248
  production of legitimate victimhood 205–11

Surgy, Albert de 260
surrogacy 62, 63
Sylla, Ndongo Samba 158

Tagore, Rabindranath 136–7
Tara ou la Légende d'El-Hadj Omar 226
teaching
  "lagging behind" 130
  rethinking of 129–44
  see also education
teleonomy 119
Tempels, Placide
  Bantu Philosophy 5–6
Tennessee legislation (1857) 29
Thévenot, Laurent 195
Thistlewood, Thomas 31
Thomas, Dominic 235
Thompson, Alvin O. 29
Thuan, Trinh Xuan 185
Tlatli, Soraya 145
Togo 62
tolerance, spirit of 10
Traïni, Christophe 196
transgender identity 62, 63
transhumanism 56
Trans-Saharan Highway 231
tree frogs 257, 260, 261
Tronto, Joan 195, 214
Trump, Donald 236, 255
Tunisia 121
Turkey 69

ubuntu 183–4
uchronia 124
UEMOA (West African Economic and Monetary Union) 161, 171
Ugandans 16
UNESCO 18
  report (2015) 130
United Kingdom 209–10
United States
  foreign policy and aid 203
  and migration 237
  withdrawal from Paris Accords 255
universities 18
  and the challenge of a multicultural world 18
un-learning (*dés-apprendre*) 132, 139
utopia 124, 140–3
  feminist 22
  and memory-making 189
  political 101, 102, 108
  utopian memory 189–91, 193

Vergès, Françoise 21–2, 28–9, 129
victimization/victimhood 205–11
voice
  relationship with music 271
volcanism 254

Wane, Ibrahima 268
weaving 41–51
welfare state 219
West 13
  body of the African subject in the 57–61
  current state of personal status in the 57–8
  and Eurocentrism 8
  legal system *see* legal system, Western
  presupposed acceptance of body in Africa 61
  territory of expression of the African body in the 58–61
West African Economic and Monetary Union *see* UEMOA
western Volta 159–60
Westphalia, Treaty of (1648) 122
white paranoia 29, 32
Wiredu, Kwasi 4
Wittig, Monique 20
Wolton, Dominique 66
women 13–14, 135, 142
  rights of African 23
  see also Maroon women; slave women

World Bank 202
World Conference Against Racism (2001) (Durban) 207–10
World Trade Organization 18
world-making (*faire mémoire*) 184–5, 186, 188–9, 192
world-memory 183, 184–5
writing 41–51

Yacine, Kateb 224
　L'œuvre en fragments 229
Yassine, Rachid Id 65
yela 269–70
youth, African 8–9

Zanahary, myth of 42–4
Zielinski, Agata 219